GERTRUDE NOAR

The Junior High School
—Today and Tomorrow

SECOND EDITION

Englewood Cliffs, N.J.
PRENTICE-HALL, INC.
1961

WHITWORTH COLLEGE LIBRARY
SPOKANE, WASHINGTON

To those teachers who know

and care about children

© 1953, 1961 by PRENTICE-HALL, INC.
Englewood Cliffs, N.J.

All rights reserved. No part of this
book may be reproduced in any form, by
mimeograph or any other means, without
permission in writing from the publishers.

Library of Congress
Catalog Card No.: 61-14283

PRINTED IN
THE UNITED STATES
OF AMERICA
51249–C

worth College Library

DISCARD

DATE DUE

DATE DUE		
JUL 1 7 1988		
JAN 2 9 1969		
FEB 1 1 1969		
MAR 1 8 1969		
JUN 2 1969		
AUG 8 1969		
SEP 5 1969		
FEB 2 1970		
MAR 2 6 1970		
JUL 2 0 1970 2007		
MAY 2 0 2007		

GAYLORD   PRINTED IN U.S.A.

The Junior High School
—Today and Tomorrow

PRENTICE-HALL EDUCATION SERIES

Harold Spears, Editor

47,902

5350

CITY

oxburg

Preface

The junior high schools, originally founded to meet the need for education on a level intermediate between elementary school and high school, have generally been accused of falling short of helping the children for whom they were designed. Many forces are being brought to bear on them in an effort to affect their ultimate destiny. Citizens and parents want children to come out of school with that variety of skills which is essential to preparation for modern life, rather than with the limited academic skills which were emphasized in the schools of yesterday. Other people campaign for economies in education, even at the expense of progress and growth. The children themselves demonstrate continually, by their attitudes and behavior, that they want a realistic education and that they are impatient with mere textbook learning about matters, places, and events that are too far removed from the reality of their own lives and needs.

Solutions for some of the schools' problems have been found but have not yet been widely implemented. The blocks of time in a core type curriculum, for example, seem to offer the best situation within which to work. However, those administrators who accept democratic principles and recognize the wide range of differences in children and in community needs leave many of the decisions about curriculum planning to the discretion of the local schools. In many school systems, the contributions which can be made by teacher-education institutions are recognized and their personnel and resources are being used to assist teachers in making practical applications of theories in the junior high schools throughout the country.

The purpose of this book is to provide some solutions to the problems that teachers and administrators face as they study the why and how of changing the traditional school patterns of today into the modern patterns of tomorrow. They are not the only answers that can be given; they are not final answers. However, they do describe practices that have been tested in junior high schools in many places. Although the details of execution differ from school to school, the broad patterns are similar.

This book is intended to serve _administrators_ who are seeking ways of beginning the long process of modernizing their schools. It should be of value to _teachers_ at various stages of development. The _beginner_ who knows little about classroom routines and management and who cannot "keep order" will find in it practical suggestions that work. Questions raised by the _academic teacher_ who wants to use modern methods in a traditional setting are answered. There are helps for those _experienced teachers_ who are seeking new ways of working with children.

The book is also intended for teachers of teachers on both the pre- and in-service levels. The suggestions for college classes are intended to provide actual experiences with the kinds of methods that teachers are expected to know how to use in their modern classrooms. Only as the teacher himself engages in these, does he understand how to use them with children, know how children feel about them, and sense the learning outcomes that occur. Many questions about these techniques are raised. Some answers are in the text of this book, and others are in the selected references that are included in each chapter. More answers will be found in the films that teachers and student teachers see and in the discussions that follow. Significant answers will come from observations in schools, experiments in actual teaching situations, and the exchange of past experiences.

This book would not have been possible without the years of hard and faithful service of many teachers in the Gillespie Junior High School in Philadelphia, Pennsylvania. _There_ was a demonstration of what teachers can accomplish in spite of the difficulties surrounding a school which must operate within the restrictions and limitation of a large city system, on a budget far below its needs.

The writer owes a debt of gratitude to a long list of educational leaders who, through their writings, speeches, and personal encouragement, have contributed to her knowledge and her belief in the destiny of the Junior High School of Today and Tomorrow.

G. N.

Table of Contents

PART TWO

Many Share
the Responsibility for
Creating the Program

PART THREE

Modern Curriculum
Content and Techniques

Unless a philosophy is to remain symbolic—or verbal—or a sentimental indulgence for a few, or else mere arbitrary dogma, its auditing of past experience and its program of values must take effect in conduct.

—*John Dewey*

PART
ONE

Basic Concepts
upon Which to Build
a Functioning Junior High School

CHAPTER ONE

The Functions
of the Junior High School

The best guarantee of collective efficiency and power is liberation and use of the diversity of individual capacities in initiative, planning, foresight, vigor and endurance. Personality must be educated, and personality cannot be educated by confining its operations to technical and specialized things, or to the less important relationships of life. Full education comes only when there is a responsible share on the part of each person, in proportion to capacity, in shaping the aims and policies of the social groups to which he belongs. This fact fixes the significance of democracy.

John Dewey, *Reconstruction in Philosophy.* New York: Henry Holt & Co., 1920, page 208f.

The junior high school came into existence about fifty years ago. There was hope then that it would solve many persistent educational problems. One such problem was the large number of pupils who dropped out at the end of the sixth and eighth years. Another problem was the difficulty in adjusting that children experienced when they went from the security of elementary schools, in which they were known and often loved, to the huge senior high schools in which, it seemed to them, no one knew anybody and no one cared. A third problem was created by the inability of the elementary school to make adequate provisions for the increased size of so many of the boys and girls and for the needs which grew out of the nature of developmental changes in the early teens. The new school, therefore, was planned with the emotional and social needs of the students in mind. In addition, some educators believed that the way to provide for the more gifted children was to get them into college as soon as possible. They planned a program of accel-

3

eration in the junior high school, believing that this could best be done after basic elementary education was over and before senior high school began. The idea that very able, mentally mature students should enter high school earlier than others, which had been largely given up by 1950 in favor of keeping pupils with their age-mates, returned when comparisons between American and European education, particularly Russian education, became popular in the latter part of that decade.

The functions and purposes of the junior high school that were set up at that time have not changed, except that vocational guidance, as such, has no real place in the modern junior high school program. Stated as briefly as possible, the basic principles on which the school was founded were: (1) *Articulation*—helping children to go from elementary school through junior high school and into senior high school with as little difficulty as possible. (2) *Exploration*—giving young teen-agers a chance to find out through brief experiences what some of the high school courses were like, with the expectation that this would help them to choose their senior high school courses more wisely. (3) *Educational guidance*—helping pupils to choose from among elective subjects offered in the junior, and later in the senior high school. (4) *Vocational guidance*—helping pupils to make decisions about jobs and careers. (5) *Activity*—providing social and athletic experiences and giving the students a chance to participate in administration and control of the school. These activities were organized into an "extracurricular program" of clubs. (6) *Time-saving*—permitting bright students to skip a semester and thus to specialize earlier and enter senior high school sooner.

In 1947, after an extensive study of the literature on the subject, Gruhn and Douglass constructed a list of functions for the junior high school which was evaluated and criticized by a group of recognized leaders in secondary education. Their final statement and an extensive discussion of each of the accepted functions are parts of their book.[1] According to those who participated in the survey, the junior high school of the middle 1940's was expected to provide for (1) integration, (2) exploration, (3) guidance, (4) differentiation, (5) socialization, (6) articulation.

---

[1] Gruhn and Douglass, *The Modern Junior High School*. New York: The Ronald Press, rev. ed., 1956.

While most of the same terms are now used to describe the functions of the junior high school, the concepts they symbolize have become both deeper and broader. Thus *integration* should be thought of as applying to three aspects of the program. It refers to the building of a unified program from the seventh through the ninth year which the modern school has substituted for the program which offered little more than an elementary school experience in the seventh and eighth grades and a senior high school curriculum in the ninth grade. A common philosophy now permits the faculty to build a three-year curriculum within which fundamental concepts can be established, habits of thought and action can be made secure, and developmental processes can be consolidated. In other words, the school becomes an integrated unit.

Integration of learnings is a second part of the concept. To accomplish this, the modern school is replacing the completely departmentalized program with one which permits a block of time within which units of work cut across subject matter lines. Here pupils have the chance to explore more fully the social and civic world and to get at the meanings of life in our democratic society. This remains, for the large majority of the schools, still to be achieved. Factual subject matter emphasis is still dominant even in those schools which have included a larger time block in the school day.

Integration of personality is a third aspect of the concept. It has become one of the most significant outcomes for which the modern school strives. Its accomplishment can be expected to a greater degree when the in-service education program for teachers and the learning experiences for pupils call attention to the factors which produce personality adjustment and mental health. These are fundamental in the modern junior high school.

Exploration was the objective that administrators hoped to achieve when they organized the so-called extracurricular club program which they added at the end of the day. It was supposed to give children the chance to experience new activities, to explore the community by taking trips, to try out new subject areas, to learn to do new things, and through all of this to know more about their own potential interests and abilities.

A second part of the exploratory program in the traditional school was the opportunity extended to boys, during the first three semesters, to go into the shops, and to girls to go to the home economics rooms. The former consisted of a carpentry, an electrical, and a metal shop; the latter was cooking and sewing. In the fourth semester, the pupils were permitted to choose from among alternative courses which were supposed to have exploratory values but which, in most cases, set the pupil into the curriculum groove he was expected to follow for the next three terms and even throughout the senior high school. This was, for the majority of the students, a narrowing rather than a broadening experience. The electives usually offered were elementary business training, more advanced courses in the practical arts, and, for those who anticipated preparing for college, a foreign language and algebra. There was a decade in which these "exploratory" courses carried credits, and children who failed in them had to repeat them or even the entire grade. It was out of such experiences that the pupils were to make an intelligent choice of senior high school curriculum and even of a life-long career.

The concept of exploration has been broadened and the practices accordingly modified. Much more time and many more direct experiences are being provided through which the children are getting to know far more about the working world, job opportunities, the social order, and themselves. Ways have been found in modern schools to give both boys and girls many significant experiences in practical arts, and to do this every term and in mixed classes. There the children have full opportunity to explore these fields, to find the connection between them and problems of human relations, to apply this new knowledge to the betterment of family life, and to discover many new leisure time activities. The experiences in the shops, kitchens, and living rooms also make a significant contribution to mental health and the development of balanced personalities. Organizational as well as instructional problems have to be solved in schools that take their exploratory function seriously.

The Southern Association of Colleges and Secondary Schools, in "The Junior High School Program," 1958, reports that some schools offer exploratory courses daily for nine or twelve weeks. Many southern schools provide two periods a day for such courses in seventh and eighth grades, and one daily period in ninth grade. *Guidance* has long been recognized as one of the critical needs of adolescent boys and girls. One of the reasons for creating the junior high school was the desire to meet that need, and so the *home room* was included in the plan. The concept was implemented by assigning a group of students to an adviser. His duty was to create warm, friendly relationships like those found in the home. The pupils were expected to bring their problems, both small and large, to the home room teacher. He was to counsel and advise them. His room was their *Home* room.

Little attention was paid to the fact that the guidance program was superimposed upon an already crowded day. The time allotted to it was a short fifteen or twenty minutes before the first period and one full length period at the end of one day during the week. A program had to be created to fill the time. In the morning period, attendance was the first order of business. Then the daily notices had to be read. In schools where Bible reading was required, that had to be done. By then the bell rang and no guidance had been attempted. The afternoon period was usually given over to reports from the student government officers. This plan, however, has such firm roots in tradition that it still exists in many schools where it is still called the "Home Room" or the "Advisory Period." There are schools in which it is merely the "Record Room," and guidance is not a part of the responsibilities of the teacher at that time.

From the very beginning of the junior high school, teachers knew that to do even a minimum amount of guidance they needed more time. Consequently, by the early 1940's, in many schools one or more full length periods were taken out of the club program for guidance purposes. Since this plan did not take time away from a subject field, it was an acceptable arrangement to teachers who did not yet feel that guidance was or ought to be an integral part of the school's legitimate program.

There are many schools today, however, in which the teachers know that the time element, per se, is not the most important factor. They realize that guidance cannot be accomplished unless they know their pupils. They also know that they are unable to establish guidance relationships with the large number of students for which they are responsible. They are frequently resentful because the home room group is added to a pupil-load already too heavy to carry. In some cases their frustration has caused them to exert sufficient pressure on schedule makers to secure the assignment of one of the classes regularly met each day as the advisory group. This lightens the pupil-load and enables the advisor to know that group somewhat better than the rest of his classes. When it becomes possible for the adviser to remain with his home room group for more than one year, guidance becomes more of a reality.

About 1940, curriculum makers began to construct courses of study and programs of guidance which teachers were expected to "cover" during the long home room periods. At that time, guidance was still something to be taught and something to be learned. Naturally enough the content took the form of character education —lessons about desirable traits, vices, and virtues, and on how to be a good school citizen. That was the era of "Direct Character Education."

It was not unusual in those days to see a teacher write on a board a logically developed outline, dealing with a virtue such as honesty, which he copied from his syllabus. The children in turn copied it into their notebooks, were required to learn it at home, and were expected to recite it the next week. Some conscientious teachers even gave tests on such material and recorded marks for Guidance on report cards.

In many places, teachers and administrators began to face the fact that children do not learn to be good by reading about it. They also realized that children do not usually learn to solve individual problems as the result of classroom guidance lessons. This led to the next step, namely, the attempt to do the job through projects and direct experiences. Units were written, and advisers tried to accomplish their function by having pupils make scrap books, write stories, and discuss books and plays. But still the idea failed to click.

And so, finally, the personnel in many junior high schools faced the hard fact that *guidance is not essentially something to be learned. It is a process by which one person, the adviser-teacher, helps the other, the pupil, to move in the direction of solving a problem, or of meeting a need, or of making an adjustment. The process can be accomplished only when the people involved know each other, care about each other, and have confidence in each other. It requires teacher-time as well as knowledge about children and the possession of good will on both sides.*

Those are the conditions which must be fulfilled if either group guidance or individual guidance is to be successful. Moreover, to be effective, the process must begin as soon as the need for help is discovered by either the child or the teacher. It cannot always be put off until the end of the day or until the next week because the period for guidance does not come until then.

Guidance is coming to full maturity in the modern junior high school. It is no longer regarded as an appendage to be "taught" to pupils in a "home room period" which students and teachers alike regard with disfavor. The best current practice is found where integration of the guidance function with teaching and living has been achieved. There, guidance characterizes the way of life in the school; the way teachers and children live and learn together; the way in which specialized services are marshalled around the needs of the individual child; the way groups meet and solve their common problems; the way in which everyone learns how to ease the difficulties that beset individuals in the course of life.

One of the major problems to be solved before this over-all guidance program can be accomplished is finding a way to provide teachers enough time with fewer pupils so that they can get to know their children well enough to guide them. This points up the need for reorganization of the structure of the school day and for major curriculum revision. A block of time must be provided within the day during which the teacher's first responsibility is to do whatever makes it possible for him to get to know his students.[2] In schools using this kind of organization plan, the time spent in the block varies from one-third to three-quarters of the day, depending upon the program, the grade level, and the maturity of the pupils. In order to fulfill his responsibilities as guide, the teacher must become familiar with each individual's learning rate and mental abilities, with his achievement levels and potentialities, with his interests and his emotional blocks. Many learning experiences and methods of measurement and evaluation have to be used to provide such facts.[3] The child's facility in handling the tools of learning, using the thought processes, and the social skills are all of importance.

---

[2] See Educational Policies Commission, *Education for All American Youth.* Washington, D. C.: NEA, 1944.

[3] See Gertrude Noar, *Freedom to Live and Learn.* Philadelphia: Franklin Publishing Co., 1948.

School proficiency is only one of the areas in which the help of a teacher guide is required. In early adolescence personality problems are plentiful. Boys and girls who at that time are normally in a state of conflict with parental authority need to have the teacher to confide in as a temporary substitute for the parent. The problems these childen present to their advisers include, among others, those dealing with family relations, with behavior, with leisure time activities, with personal health, with money, with interpersonal and inter-group relations, with moral judgments and ethical values, with religion, with choice of senior high school and elective courses, and with job opportunities and career possibilities.

In order to give effective guidance the teacher must know the child as a person and not only as a pupil inside the school building. This means he must have time to talk with each child, to observe him, and to meet his parents. When requirements of scheduling are such that time for this is not available, the school must move in the direction of adding trained counselors to the staff. When they are available they do the home visiting, making sure that the adviser hears about the visit and has the additional benefit of their interpretation of the relationships and problems that exist in the home. Whenever a particular child's problems are found to be so deep-seated or extensive that case study is required or outside agencies must be called in, the trained counselor takes over. If the counselor's work is to be effective, however, he must keep the teacher informed and work with all those who are responsible for teaching that child. Other specialists, including medical doctors, nurses, and psychiatrists, who work with the teacher, are being added to the staff in most modern schools.

It becomes obvious that much time and effort are needed by the adviser if he is to do all that is necessary to know even thirty pupils well enough to be their real guide. Certainly for him to pick up a new group each semester or each year is exceedingly wasteful. As the school continues its efforts to build an adequate guidance program, it therefore arranges for the adviser to remain with his group for an increasingly long time span. If this includes all three years, the teacher has the invaluable experience of seeing his charges change from children to young adults. He lives with them through the most critical period of physical change and development. He sees the breaking up of the last remnants of babyhood and dependency and the molding of the new adult personality. Few teachers can remain aloof and unmoved by such experiences.

The teacher assigned to be the adviser of a group of pupils in the reorganized school is usually responsible for carrying on what is coming to be accepted as the core of learning needs that are common to all the children. The methods of teaching that he uses give pupils many opportunities to practice critical thinking, to make wise judgments, to gather and appraise facts for their relative values, and to make wise choices and decisions. The traditional ways of learning have not given much emphasis to these skills, but they receive serious attention in the modern school where classroom life and work are not dominated by a syllabus of subject matter to be "covered." Whenever a problem of living or acting confronts a group, other matters can be put aside in order to deal with it promptly. The classroom begins to approximate the home, and becomes the center of confidence and belongingness out of which a really good school life can grow for every child; a place where needs are met and advice can be sought. The superimposed home room program, which in its traditional form causes teachers so much frustration and worry, ceases to exist. Guidance becomes the heart and soul of the total junior high school program.

Activity has come to mean much more than a traditional club program could possibly accomplish. Although the fairly recently agreed-upon list of objectives and functions quoted previously does not include the term "activity," this concept is still a vital one in the junior high school and it is still implemented, for the most part, in a club program. "Clubs" are the somewhat informal offerings which are usually scheduled for the last period in the day. They are designed to furnish activity as an offset to the passive sitting that is characteristic of the traditional classroom. They are also expected to implement the principles of exploration and socialization.

The development of the concept of activity stemmed from the realization that young adolescents need to relieve muscle tension. A generation ago, few teachers could see themselves conducting classrooms in which planned activity was a way of learning. Clubs were and are still expected to be different from classes because there are no courses of study for them, and marks do not have to be recorded. Unfortunately, however, in large schools, where a large number of pupils are involved, where many of the teachers do not have the required abilities and backgrounds, and where most of the rooms to be used do not lend themselves to activities of the kind that are envisioned, many of the so-called clubs differ little from other curricular offerings. In fact, during a club period it may be possible to see such extensions of classroom work as reading *The Reader's Digest* for an entire period, or drawing maps, or studying Latin.

In almost every school, however, there are exciting, meaningful programs for *some* of the children.[4] These range from recreational activities to school service projects. Among the most desirable are those in which pupils make things and have opportunities to express themselves creatively. In some of the more modern schools, the clubs have been replaced by "special interest" groups.[5] They are organized only when a number of students ask for them, and remain in operation only so long as the need for them exists. They may meet at times when other children are attending regular classes or after school, according to the flexibility of the program.

In large numbers of junior high schools, however, the clubs are still a source of dissatisfaction for both students and teachers. Therefore, when the school contemplates modernizing its program, some important questions should be raised about the club activities. First, the meanings of the terms used to describe these activities should be explored. For example, what constitutes an activity period? Does a group which just sits and reads magazines have the right to be called a club? Can it be placed in the same category as a ball club or a shop club or a dramatic club?

What is the meaning of the term "Club"? Can a very dull, boring experience be made more attractive by calling it a club? What activities should be required if the term is used? Should clubs be chartered by the students' organization? Are elected officers essential? Should officers be elected if they have no jobs to do? Is it meaningful to have a "president" or "chairman" when his only job is to call a group of children to order and then say, "Let us get to work at our reading"—this being the only thing the group has to do each time it meets?

---

[4] See Educational Policies Commission, *Learning the Ways of Democracy.* Washington, D. C.: NEA, 1940.

[5] R. E. Botts, "Lakewood's Special Interest Club Program," *California Journal of Secondary Education,* March, 1952.

There are schools in which "points" towards "honors" are given for membership in certain clubs. Why? Sometimes being an officer in a club is rewarded with points, whether or not the child in question ever functions. Are these trappings necessary to the activity program?

What are the purposes to be served by the clubs? Are some which have only recreational values to be permitted, while others meeting at the same time involve serious work? Can a large number of pupils be herded into auditoriums and "entertained" there with films of doubtful value, because there is a room shortage, and be led to believe that this is a club activity?

On what basis should students be permitted choice? Can they always get their choice? Is second or third choice still a choice and how does that affect the students' attitudes and actions? On what basis are teacher assignments made? There are prestige values involved with some activities. Clubs differ greatly in the kind of preparation and work required from teachers. Sometimes clubs have restricted membership on the basis of ability (writing or dramatics), social class (because of cost), or race (swimming, where pools are restricted). Can these inequalities of opportunities to learn be tolerated?

If a child likes to play checkers, is it reasonable to expect him to want to do so at the same time every week, and to continue it from the time he reaches the room until the bell rings? Singing, dancing, and other forms of self-expression are dependent upon mood, time of day, and physical well being. Can these be legislated into a regimented club program? All of these matters are elements in the complaints about the traditional extracurricular program which are heard in nearly every school.

Any club program which adds two or three groups of children to the already oversized pupil-load of the junior high school teacher, is in need of serious scrutiny and evaluation. The teachers often have no other contact with the pupils in their clubs, and do not even learn their names by the time the semester is over.

The method of assigning pupils to their clubs creates problems. Teachers say that the following factors affect the choices children make: Some want only to be with their friends. Some choose clubs sponsored by teachers who are "easy" and who allow them to have fun. A few pupils have no interests, do not care, and so "put down anything." Belonging to some clubs has prestige value. In others, "honors" can be won. Occasionally the title of the club does not really describe it and the pupils who get into it are disappointed and "take it out on the teacher." All of these conditions point to the need for guidance which is a time-consuming process.

There are schools in which choice and enrollment in a club is dependent upon who gets there first. When the bell rings, all doors fly open and the children run headlong to those rooms in which they want to be. When the room is full, the door is closed. An otherwise orderly school becomes bedlam during such a club period. Signs of misbehavior by frustrated pupils appear all over the building. Whistling, yelling, destruction of property, and cutting the last period are the inevitable outcomes. Teachers, already tired from the day's work, find themselves in conflict with their children and themselves.

In many schools, the student council and governmental committees are called clubs and meet only during the club periods. Making a club of it serves to destroy much of the meaning and value of the students' organization because that gets in the way of the function for which it is intended, namely, participation in administration and control of the school. This is not in any sense of the word a "club" activity. Moreover, since the pupils who are elected to offices *have* to attend the meetings every week, they are automatically barred from going to other activities. For that reason, many eligible candidates refuse to run for election or to serve on committees.

In the traditional program, usually the last period on Monday is set aside for class or section meetings. The student officers preside, report on their committee meetings, and conduct discussions of school affairs. When committee meetings have taken place nearly a week before, as must be the case if they are scheduled only in club periods, little can be expected, since the lapse of time results in forgetting, loss of interest, and lack of enthusiasm on the part of the student officers. Teachers pay little attention to these meetings and reports, in most cases, and if a student representative is absent, the group receives no report at all. The school government that is administered this way soon becomes a farce.

Another of the weaknesses in many club programs is the practice of forbidding clubs to those children who are failing in the current classroom work or who carry "conditions" because of failure at the end of the preceding term. They are sent to so-called remedial classes. Often the children work hard in these classes while others are having fun. Moreover, the teacher assigns drill work to be done at home and brought to the next "club" period. Pupils who really need activity are thus given more book work, more sitting, more listening.

Some junior high schools have abandoned the compulsory club program and replaced it with a voluntary program administered after school. While this may solve some of the problems, it creates others and does not meet the needs of all the children. Much dissatisfaction is engendered in those pupils who cannot attend after-school activities. Bus children, for example, must go home when the busses come, and that means at the close of the day. In urban communities many pupils cannot join because they hold after-school jobs, upon which they depend for expense money and for money to help feed the family. In rural areas there are tasks and chores to be done on the farms, and parents are unwilling to have the boys and girls remain after school for fun. There are also the isolates, rejectees, and children in the lower ability groups in every school, who go home because they believe they are not wanted, and who cannot therefore be reached with the kind of help that is needed to enable them to adjust and to gain acceptance in the peer group.

Teacher morale is not improved by inaugurating after-school programs. Some teachers are never able to take these assignments because they have other jobs, or are housekeepers, or do not have enough energy. A few people refuse to work after school hours. The willing ones are often imposed upon and may, in addition, earn the ill will of their colleagues. In some cities, the matter of after-school pay for club sponsorship has become a matter of bitter controversy.[6]

As the junior high school moves closer to the pattern which will enable it more nearly to fulfill its destiny, the artificial club program, tacked on to the end of the day, can be discarded. In schools where this step has been taken, the time allotted to clubs is absorbed into the regular schedule, thus providing for longer class periods and removing one of the barriers to the use of direct learn-

---

[6] Court action was necessary to settle the dispute in New York City (1951).

WHITWORTH COLLEGE LIBRARY
SPOKANE, WASHINGTON

ing activities which require more time than the forty-five minute period allows. The use of radio, films, television, recordings, speakers, and construction materials, which makes some clubs popular, becomes part of classroom work and *all* pupils participate in these activities. Exploratory experiences and opportunities for dramatics, trips, art work, practical arts, and music, are not lost when these experiences are made possible for all students because they have become part of the learning activities in many classrooms. Group and committee work which is needed and for which classroom time is provided requires elected officers, and so affords leadership experience and training for more students and in better ways than a club program can do. Moreover, no child suffers exclusion from any activity for a reason that he cannot understand or for which he is not responsible and therefore cannot change.

Elimination of clubs at once reduces the pupil load and the number of teachers to whom children must adjust. Both of these changes help to improve behavior. Discipline problems also decrease because the clubroom freedom is replaced by a democratic classroom in which pupils live and learn together and in which the climate and activities tend to relax tensions and dissolve hostilities. Moreover, all through the day there is less sitting still and much meaningful moving around. The children's growing muscles and bones do not have to suffer long periods of inactivity, and consequently there is less resentment and aggression generated in the minds of the children themselves. The only danger that may arise when the club program is dropped comes from the failure of teachers to change the character of the classroom work. If the longer time spent in the classroom is taken up with just more book work and more writing, the school will have moved back instead of forward, as far as implementing the activity concept is concerned.

Incorporation of activities into the classroom work raises the question as to when the elected officers of the students' organization are to meet and when they are to carry on the work of the groups they represent. It becomes essential for the entire faculty to recognize the immense importance of the students' association activities which afford real opportunities for students to learn the principles and processes of democracy. In those modern schools in which that attitude has been developed by the teachers, committee meetings are called whenever there is a job to be done or a problem to be discussed or a plan to be made. Then the students who are needed leave their classrooms and go to the meeting. On their return the teachers permit them to call class meetings as soon as possible in order to transmit their messages to their classmates without delay. Students' association work becomes vital and significant; there is no loss of vigor due to forgetting. Teachers play an important role in every discussion, realizing that they, too, have a stake in the decisions that are made and in the enterprises that are carried on.[7] In schools like this, teachers and children help the officers to make up classroom work that went on during their absence, and student representatives are not penalized by being required to make up time after school or by having marks lowered.

In many school districts, interest in the community centers around competitive sports. The development of teams and the big interscholastic game schedules overshadow all other activity programs. Some points of controversy deserve attention.[8] One of these is the question of centering too much time, energy, and money on a few children at the expense of the many. Too early specialization is another factor to be considered. One of the hidden costs of secondary education lies in this program which is undemocratic because many children cannot afford even to attend the games.[9] Pressures exerted on students to buy tickets often cause resentments and hostilities, to say nothing of unhappiness. Finally, there is every reason to suppose that adult spectators indulge in gambling at the games, and that children are subjected to the temptations of bribery.

Most medical authorities agree that during the hard growing years, the strenuous training programs and the gruelling experiences on the field are not good for the boys who make the teams. They say, "The general public would do well to accept the professional advice of physicians and educators and allow these youngsters to grow up without the unnecessary emotional and physical strain of playing gladiator in the public arena. . . . Interscholastic

[7] See Educational Policies Commission, *Learning the Ways of Democracy.* Washington, D. C.: NEA., 1940.

[8] E. D. Mitchell, "The Case Against Junior High School Athletics," *University of Michigan School of Education Bulletin,* 1951.

[9] R. Schultz, "Can Parents Afford to Send Their Children to High School?" *The School Review,* May, 1952.

leagues should be confined to senior high schools. . . . Junior high school boys should not compete in American football. An extensive program of intramural activities is strongly recommended for these students."[10] The Joint Committee on Athletic Competition for Children of Elementary and Junior High School Age, representing four national organizations, condemns highly organized competition for children of elementary and junior high school ages.[11]

Instead of great ballyhoo events, the modern school carries on a physical education program in which every child learns to play the major sports and games. All are involved in them, and every grade develops its champions. These grade teams have play-off matches after school hours in the gymnasiums, to which all can go without extra cost. Such events are valuable in the building of school spirit.

No matter how well integrated the activity and classroom work becomes, there are still opportunities for big after-school and evening social events. These include dramatics, song and dance programs, pageants, concerts, and programs which feature culminating activities of units of work done in the classrooms. Instead of training a few talented children, these large productions provide participation for hundreds. In most schools, large evening class parties and dances are special activities planned by the graduating class. In modern schools, parents, teachers, and pupils plan and carry these out together and get maximum results in attendance, good behavior, and fun.

Big social events present opportunities for teaching socially acceptable manners, speech, dress, dancing, and interpersonal attitudes. Students are eager to learn in situations so full of meaning to them. These occasions also afford unusual opportunity to iron out intercultural problems. During planning sessions, especially if parents are present, matters of smoking, drinking, late hours, and dating can be discussed with profit.

As the junior high school moves toward a more complete fulfillment of its destiny, activity ceases to belong to just one part of the day. It becomes respectable and welcomed as a process of learning. Active participation in many and varied direct-learning experi-

---

10 Dukelow and Hein, *Today's Health,* November, 1951.

11 J. B. Conant, "Some Problems of the Junior High School," *Bulletin of the National Association of Secondary School Principals,* April, 1960.

ences for all children, which is one of the purposes for which the school is organized, becomes a reality.

Differentiation has to do with meeting individual needs and providing for individual differences and abilities. For many years the practice has been to separate the "sheep from the goats" in so-called homogeneous classes. There are large numbers of junior high schools in which at least one group of the most retarded or the most emotionally disturbed children are offered different kinds of learning experiences. These vary from attempts to "water down" the regular courses to attempts to "entertain" the pupils, neither of which has produced satisfactory results. There are, on the other hand, schools in which the teachers of these special classes are freed from ordinary requirements, and are doing very significant experiments in the use of many varied direct-learning experiences.

Few, if any, school systems are now failing to consider the gifted child, how to identify him, and what to do for him. In some, the verbally superior pupils are segregated into advanced, or accelerated, or enriched, or honors groups—whatever they may be called. In other places they are given more work to do. In some they get the vicarious and direct-learning experiences from which all the other children would also profit. In most cases there seems to be no way to avoid increasing their competitiveness or developing their sense of apartness. Gifted children who have other kinds of talents are taken care of to some extent, in "special interest groups," in practical arts electives which are still looked down on as minor subjects, and in "clubs" which carry no credits or marks and are therefore considered to be of little curricular importance. Grouping by ability which, widespread in the 1930's, was judged to be invalid as the result of research in the 1940's, returned with renewed vigor in the 1950's. However, as the 1960's began, research was again casting doubt upon the wisdom of segregation by ability.

In the modern junior high school, differentiation is recognized as a function of the classroom. It is accomplished, in part, by group work in which assignment of appropriate tasks stretches the capacities and potentialities of the individual according to his needs. The many kinds of abilities that are needed in a democratic society are recognized, and children learn to utilize them and to value those who possess them. Everyone learns that if he contributes his best, the group will produce something that exceeds the possibilities of any one individual in it.

There are a number of aspects of the process of *socialization*. It means helping the child to accomplish personal adjustment to himself and to the peer group. It includes getting information about the dynamic processes of civilized society. It involves all the understandings, appreciations, and skills that are needed for effective participation in our democratic state.

The traditional social studies program, in which emphasis is placed most heavily upon factual learnings in the subject areas of history, geography, and civics, is being replaced by a program in which the pupils learn the principles and processes of democracy through direct contact with them in the community and by practicing them in the classroom. The objectives of the modern program include development of the ability to live and work democratically, to respect the worth and dignity and the contributions of everyone, to know the way of making life better for one's self and one's associates, and to create good human relations.

In the modern school the teachers are learning how to set up experiences that operate in some measure to counteract negativistic tendencies. By the time they reach junior high school, many children have begun to turn away from social life. That direction can be reversed if they are given sufficient opportunity to participate successfully. Many teen-agers lead very narrow lives and are already beginning to reduce their adventures in human relations. School experiences can help them to broaden the scope of their activities and to learn how to relate positively and warmly to others. Too large a number of young adolescents indulge in anti-social activities. They must learn to work and play constructively and in the interests of the group. Learning *how* to change behavior patterns and *how* to develop the characteristics which people need for effective, generous, and abundant living in a democratic society are major objectives in the modern junior high school. To accomplish them the teachers have to learn what to do to reduce the tragedy of failure and to capitalize on success. They must find out how to eliminate the practice of rejection and to increase the amount of acceptance in themselves and in the peer group. They have to discover ways of dispelling fear and of creating security, and must create methods of preventing frustration and of producing satisfaction.

How to change from traditional programs to new ones is of vital importance, for such change requires different organization, content, and methods. Principals need help with the planning of the new schedules. Teachers need help with the new teaching techniques and with classroom management.

Articulation, in the past, was concerned primarily with the adjustment of pupils as they moved into the junior high school and with getting them ready to move out into senior high school or work. In order to do this, the seventh and eighth grades were made to resemble the elementary program and the ninth grade electives were similar to and taught like senior high school subjects. Programmatic devices are of far less value in implementing the principle of articulation, however, than are the development of plans which enable the teachers of the several school levels to meet for the exchange of information about the children. These inter-school conferences have also helped elementary and secondary school teachers to develop a common philosophy. As this becomes a reality, many school districts begin to plan a continuous curriculum that reaches from kindergarten through the twelfth year.

Problems of articulation are not always due to changes in the school environment. They often stem from the rigidity of the child's personality which has not been corrected. The modern junior high school places importance upon the pupil's progress toward becoming a person who can make adjustments easily. To that end, the program and activities are planned so that the children get many experiences and much help in accepting themselves, each other, adults, authority, and the conditions of life in today's world. When they can do this, the pupils do not have serious trouble in adjusting to the new school, its size, the faculty, the changes they meet in ways of learning and living, and to the more rigid academic requirements. Nothing in modern life is more certain than change. Moreover, the rate of change is increasing rapidly. Those who cannot adjust are apt to suffer great damage.

There are many good schools across the land that are working hard to develop the kinds of programs required to accomplish their goals. However, a number of junior high schools are lagging behind, operating pretty much as they did in the beginning. This lag is due in part to the need for help with the difficult task of changing traditions, attitudes, school organization, teaching skills and content. It is also due to the slowness with which teacher-training institutions are equipping their graduates for the modern school—giving them both the philosophy and the experiences out of which they can develop facility with modern techniques. A third factor is the scarcity of consultants that are provided by school systems for the purpose of helping the teacher in his classroom.

In spite of all the difficulties that can be outlined, the junior high school must accept responsibility for deepening and strengthening the concept of democracy that the elementary school begins to develop in the pupils. Building a program to fulfill that objective requires realistic appraisal of the kind of school life which has produced too much bitterness for too many young people in the past. Out of their experiences in school, boys and girls carried into their adulthood resentments based on caste and class inequalities. Consequently, some of them now scoff and sneer at the word freedom. As children, they did not have an opportunity to clarify that basic concept by experiencing it in a meaningful situation.

In school, few students as yet have an opportunity to carry on a social action project. Therefore they do not know the way of social action in our democracy, and many do not believe that the "common man" can better the way of life for himself and his neighbors. In school, though they may have been told about it, pupils are not learning that it is essential to nominate only qualified candidates for civic offices. Too many boys and girls are not being confronted, in school, with the thought that executive and administrative authority should be coupled with responsibility rather than with privilege. In school too few pupils are receiving the guidance and leadership needed for them to develop a satisfying philosophy of life.

It is essential that the junior high school curriculum include both ethical and moral issues. Problems of deep significance to civilization must be introduced so that fundamental principles and concepts can begin to form in the minds of the students. Junior high school is not too soon for children to think about such things as conservation of resources for the use of all mankind; the evils of exploitation of people in our own and foreign lands; international interdependence and the inadequacy, in these days, of a narrow concept of nationalism; population trends, the population explosion and the increasing numbers of old people; crime; and mental health. This seems to many like a large order for the junior high school child. Yet, unless he has at least a beginning of these things in the school, he may not again have the opportunity to study them under instructors who are qualified to help him. Most certainly each of such problems has a direct bearing on the life of everyone and is, therefore, appropriate curriculum content. There is evidence of a dangerous trend backward to a more narrowly conceived curriculum with renewed emphasis on merely factual learning.

The junior high school teachers have always accepted without question the objectives of character education—the development of moral and spiritual values. However, too many of them still believe that this can be accomplished by lecturing, discussion, and reading. Yet in every classroom it is obvious that the result of such methods for many children is lip service. There are few pupils in any junior high school who do not "know the answers." They have read them in the books, memorized them, listened to the teacher, parent, and preacher expound them. But somehow they have not learned them in such a way that behavior change has resulted. Junior high schools are often described as places where children run riot and where no work is done. It is important, therefore, to consider what behavior modifications the junior high school can hope to achieve; out of what learning experiences they can be expected; how to look for them; and how to evaluate the results of the teaching that is done. The following rather typical incidents can be duplicated in every classroom. They will serve to illustrate the principles which are basic to modernizing content and techniques.

Jack Smith was a brilliant student. He had completed all the jobs assigned to him long before the other pupils in the class. The teacher asked him what he intended to do with his time. "Oh," he answered, "I'll just go on and get ahead of the rest." The teacher suggested that he might help some of his classmates who were having trouble. "No, no," said Jack, "I'm not interested in them. My job is to get the best marks I can so I can get to the top first."

Competitive educational methods, with its emphasis on marks as the way into college, has produced that kind of personality in many very able people who are destined to become leaders in our society. If the quality of their leadership is to be changed, children in the secondary school must taste the rewards which come from service to the less fortunate. They must learn from experience that a group, thinking, planning, and working together, will produce something larger and more significant than the ablest individual is likely to produce by himself. They must also learn the modern concept of democratic leadership.

A recording of school activities was just getting under way. The signal device needed to indicate when the accompanying film-strip was to be moved, had been forgotten. The teacher went to a nearby classroom and asked if anyone had a "cricket"—the metal noise maker well known to most children. No one had, and for a few moments no one offered a suggestion. Then Charles called out from the rear of the room, "I'll go to the metal shop and make one. It's easy."

Experience in attacking and solving problems, however simple they may be, produces the imaginative, creative personality ready to use his hands and brain to serve another's need.

"May I join the committee at the back of the room?" asked Tom. Mrs. Walters, pressed by other concerns at the moment, answered "No, Tom, they are busy with books. I'll give you something else to do in a minute." "But, Mrs. Walters, I want to work with them," Tom persisted. "I know I can't read very well, but I have ideas and I can talk."

Plenty of opportunity to produce at his own level, every chance to be recognized for what he can do, many ways of learning and of expressing himself other than through reading and writing, all combine to produce a person with respect for himself and for others. Such people are likely to know that every kind of human work is worthy and that there are other goals to be desired besides top ranking jobs and money.

A group of students, on their own request, were received in the principal's office. Bob, the school president, was the spokesman. "Dr. Miller, we feel bad about the condition of our school lawns and terraces." "Well, Bob," said the principal, "I've tried for years to get the janitor to clean up out there, but the job is just too big." "Dr. Miller," said Bob, "we've been talking this over and we have a plan for all the kids in the school to take part in a big project. Can we tell you about it now?"

A permissive atmosphere, encouragement to think and act, co-operative faculties who believe that the students should take part in administration and control, all work together to produce people with initiative, the ability to do creative thinking, and the courage both to speak up and to move forward.

"It says it in the book"; "but the book says"; "on page 9 I found"; "that's funny, the book we use in the history class says different things from the one I got in the library"; "my father doesn't think so but I know the book is right." Those statements, and more like them, can be heard in junior high school classrooms. They come, for the most part, out of the teacher's own almost complete dependence on a textbook which too often was written to follow a course of study which the teacher believes he must "cover" within the semester.

America needs people who know how important it is to challenge a statement, whether it is spoken or written, until its source is identified. The slavish use of a single book must be replaced by the free and intelligent use of many books. Covering subject matter, often by only the teacher, must give way to cooperative planning of what is to be learned, in which all who are to share in the learning experience participate. Fragmentary learning of facts must be supplanted by study of issues and problems which are of real concern to the learners even though they cross subject matter lines.

The junior high school is, in some respects, given a separate entity even when it is a part of a six-year school. Placement of the seventh, eighth and ninth grades in a junior-senior building is held to be necessary in suburban areas and localities in which population is small. The extent and nature of the junior high school when so incorporated was explored by a committee of the National Association of Secondary School Principals.[12]

Replies to an extensive questionnaire indicated a strong preference on the part of principals to administer the junior high school as a separate unit. They also prefer to assign teachers specifically to the junior high school grades, including the coaching staff for athletics and the guidance personnel. There is even a preference for separate faculty meetings.

Throughout the report there is evidence of a cleavage of opinion

---

[12] Gruhn, Tompkins and Roe, "The Junior High School Years in the Six-Year High School," *NASSP*, 1960.

and a gap between theory and practice. Conclusions drawn by the committee, as the result of their study, are that administrative personnel should be shared by the two schools, the instructional staffs should be separate, salary should be the same, there should be one bell schedule which would require similar organization patterns with variations in study periods and elective subjects. Separate programs of activities are suggested and it is recommended that equal consideration in the use of building facilities be given to both units.

Present practices operate largely to the disadvantage of the junior high school unit and its student population.

The junior high school of tomorrow exists in many schools today. It can be found wherever changes have been effected in the structure of the school day, in the content of the curriculum, in the kinds of learning experiences that are provided, and in the relations established among peers and with teachers. Teachers in the classrooms of the schools which are meeting the present needs of the children attest to the fact that the changes they have made have resulted in improved attendance, reduction of truancy to a minimum, and rapid decrease in discipline problems. Almost invariably the grounds and buildings of these schools show that the pupils have good attitudes toward public property and that they are not using the school building as an object upon which to release pent-up feelings of frustration and aggression. In communities in which intergroup tensions have been high, improvement in the school curriculum often results in reduction of overt conflicts and increases signs of friendliness and good will. This is especially true when the school emphasizes human relations education.

Teachers from those schools that have moved away from yesterday and toward tomorrow, tell of an increasing degree of pupil participation in learning activities. Achievement, according to standardized tests, remains as good or better than can be expected for the ability range of the students.[13] Accomplishments in art, music, athletics, and dramatics are usually above average. The effectiveness of student participation in administration and control (student councils) is evidenced in emerging group controls, in quiet corridors, clean, orderly lunch rooms, purposeful activity in

---

[13] "How Much Did They Grow?: An Evaluation Study of the Junior High School's Unified Study Program," *Bulletin #164*. Kalamazoo Public Schools, 1952.

the absence of a teacher, and a fine spirit in assemblies. Visitors find in these schools an atmosphere of happiness, satisfaction, and industry and an absence of tension.

Learning Activities for Members of Pre- and In-Service Teacher Education Classes

In addition to reading, set up such learning experiences as:

1. Exchanging of experiences in respect to the kinds of guidance teacher-members of the class perform.
2. Writing case histories.
3. Talking with some junior high school pupils.
4. Securing speakers and consultants.
5. Showing films.
6. Interviewing junior high school principals.

References

GENERAL

BOOKS

Caswell, Hollis, et al., *Curriculum Improvement in Public School Systems*. New York: Bureau of Publications, Teachers College, Columbia University, 1950.

Gruhn and Douglass, *The Modern Junior High School*, Rev. Ed. New York: The Ronald Press, 1956.

Koos, Leonard, *Junior High School Trends*. New York: Harper and Brothers, 1955.

PERIODICALS AND PAMPHLETS

Benjamin, Harold, "Whose Fundamentals?" *The Phi Delta Kappan*, October, 1951.

Bossing, Nelson L., "Junior High School Designed for Tomorrow," *Clearing House*, September, 1954.

Briggs, Thomas, "The Secondary School Curriculum: Yesterday, Today and Tomorrow," *Teachers College Record*, April, 1951.

Burnett, L. W., "Core Programs in Washington State Junior High Schools," *School Review*, 1951.
Lewis, G. M., "Educating Children in Grades 7 and 8," *Office of Education*, Washington, D. C., 1954.
McNassor, D. J., "Future of the Junior High School," *California Journal of Secondary Education*, February, 1958.
State Department, *Wisconsin Cooperative Planning Program Bulletins*, Madison, Wisconsin, 1948-49.
"The School of the Future," *Educational Leadership*, May, 1960.
Wright, Grace, "State Policies and Regulations Affecting the Junior High School," *Office of Education*, Washington, D. C., 1955.

GUIDANCE

BOOKS

Association of Supervision and Curriculum Development, *Fostering Mental Health*. Washington, D. C.: The Association, 1950.
Jennings, Helen, *Sociometry in Group Relations*. Washington, D. C.: American Council on Education, Rev. Ed., 1959.
Johnson, Grant, et al., *The Role of the Teacher in Guidance*. Englewood Cliffs, New Jersey: Prentice-Hall, 1959.
Nelson, H. B., ed. *Personnel Services in Education*. National Society for the Study of Education. 58th Year Book, Part II, 1959.
Redl and Wattenberg, *Mental Hygiene in Teaching*. New York: Harcourt, Brace & Co., Inc., 1951.

PERIODICALS AND PAMPHLETS

Burrell and Raths, "Do's and Don'ts of the Needs Theory," *Modern Education Service*, Bronxville, N. Y., Rev. ed., 1951.
Hanson, J., "Guidance in an Atmosphere of Crisis," *Educational Leadership*, November, 1951.
Lloyd-Jones, Esther, "Goals and Roles in the Guidance Program," *Teachers College Record*, October, 1951.

CLUBS

BOOKS

Commission on Secondary Schools, *The Junior High School Program*. Southern Association of Secondary Schools and Colleges. Atlanta, Georgia, 1958.

Frederick, R. W., *The Third Curriculum: Student Activities in American Education*. New York: Appleton-Century-Crofts, 1960.
Means, Lois E., *The Organization and Administration of Intra-Mural Sports*. St. Louis: C. V. Mosby Co., 1949.

PERIODICALS AND PAMPHLETS

Johnston, E. G., "Criticism Problems in the Administration of Student Activities," *Bulletin of the National Association of Secondary School Principals*, February, 1952.
Mitchell, E. D., "The Case Against Inter-Scholastic Activities in the Junior High School," *Education Digest*, March, 1952.
National Association of Secondary School Principals, *The Student Council in the Secondary School*. The Association, 1950.
Rowe, F. A., "Should the Junior High School Have Organized Competitive Athletics?" *School Activities*, November and December, 1950.

CHAPTER TWO

Meeting the Needs of Youth

Few schools have yet recognized that their central function is that of helping young life to grow into mental, emotional, and social maturity. This recognition must come as our next great educational adventure. Everywhere there are signs that the new imperative is being heeded . . . the curriculum becomes the very stream of dynamic activities that constitute the life of the young people and their elders.

> H. A. Overstreet, *The Mature Mind.* New York: W. W. Norton and Co., Inc., 1949, page 259.

The facts of human growth and development provide the base upon which tomorrow's junior high school is being constructed. A firm foundation for the new school is possible only when those concerned with developing its curriculum are guided by sufficient information about the basic needs and drives that motivate their pupils. Unless the work and activities of the school are planned to meet those needs and to satisfy those drives, the junior high school's ultimate survival remains doubtful.

Satisfaction of life's emotional, social, mental, and physical needs cannot rest solely with the school; nor does the school take over all the functions of the home, the church, and the community. All the social institutions must share in society's responsibility to its youth. The conditions of modern life, however, often make it necessary for the school to accept a major role in meeting the emotional and social as well as the mental needs of a large number of children. Moreover, the child is an entity and cannot be separated into parts. He brings his whole self, his background, and his community into the school, and, in the modern school, the needs of that totality become the concerns of the teachers. Meeting those needs is the goal for which they strive.

Those who are engaged in curriculum change become aware of the problems confronting them when they examine the reality of today's junior high school, and envision its potentiality. Then they design action programs to close the gap which exists between what *is* and what *can be.* As defects and deficiencies are sighted, they become the targets at which action is aimed. Many of the weaknesses are discovered when a study of the fundamental needs of early adolescence is undertaken.

Insofar as the school fails to meet the basic needs of youth, it becomes a contributing factor to the physical and emotional breakdown that so many people in our society are destined to suffer at some time in their lives. In fact, we are told that more than half of the illnesses an ordinary medical doctor treats in his office are emotionally caused, and that about one in every seven people will suffer from some degree of mental illness at some time in his life. Educators cannot ignore the large amount of maladjustment which, beginning in childhood, is often the forerunner of neurotic personality, neuroses, psychotic tendencies, severe mental illness, marital conflict, divorce, juvenile delinquency, or crime. The school has not been absolved from blame by those who have studied the causes of personality disorders. In a recent study of the causes of delinquency, there is, for example, the statement ". . . intelligent intervention is the responsibility of the schools." To meet this responsibility, the authors suggest that ". . . fundamental changes in the school curricula and teacher training are necessary." They further state ". . . The problem calls for greater flexibility in supplying a rich variety of satisfying school regimes."[1] Psychiatrists, too, have urged teachers to study mental hygiene and to apply its findings to create a better climate in the classroom and to use it to make changes in methods of teaching and guiding children.

It is essential, of course, to recognize other factors which contribute to the maladjustment of so many people. There is the impact of war which results in disruption of life plans, in the breakdown of home life, and in social upheaval. There are the enormous stress and strain which result from modern technological developments—those which have filled our days and nights with noise; those which have taken mothers out of the home to work

---

[1] Glueck, Sheldon and Eleanor, *Unraveling Juvenile Delinquency.* Cambridge: Harvard University Press, 1950.

in factories; those which have changed our conceptions of time and space; and those which have increased the possibility of violent death. Such factors cause anxiety and tension, and make it essential for the school to find the way to become a stabilizing force in the child's life, and to provide those experiences which are critical for his adjustment in early adolescence.

A large amount of research has brought to light much knowledge about the nature of learning, the needs of adolescents, and the tasks that children must accomplish as they grow up. Nevertheless, many teachers are still unfamiliar with the facts of human growth and development. Consequently, they continue to teach subject matter that is far removed from the basic needs of their pupils, and to use methods that fail to take into account much that is known about the nature of the learning processes.

The needs which all children experience as they strive to lead emotionally comfortable lives, in which they can make normal progress toward maturity, fall into the following categories:

1. The need for affection and security, which create feelings of being wanted and a sense of belongingness.
2. The need for recognition and reward.
3. The need for achievement and success, which help to create feelings of adequacy.
4. The need for fun and adventure: new experience.

In the following pages, what the school does with respect to these needs is explored. Suggestions are made for changes in programming which, if carried out, will give students more of the kinds of experiences they require.

The category of needs called *affectional security* includes the need to be liked, wanted, understood, and accepted for oneself alone. There is too little evidence of teachers' affection for pupils in the ordinary classroom. Instead, it is there that many pupils suffer rejection. One reason for this can be found in the still widely used practice of appointing teachers on the basis of courses they took in college and written examinations they passed. Neither of these criteria has any relation to a person's feeling for human beings. Another reason lies in the kind of background experiences which most teachers now in service have had. They themselves were taught by mass instruction techniques. In fact, in many schools mass instruction, the suppression of the individual, and rejection of the ones who do not conform or succeed are behaviors expected of the teachers. Moreover, no teacher can show real affection for a mass of children whom he does not know as individuals. This, a teacher who has a daily load of 150 to 200 pupils cannot do. In the traditional school, individuals are lost in the drive to teach subject matter and to cover courses of study. Most teachers believe that their superior officers and the community expect them to devote their time and energies to that end. It is still possible to hear people say that teachers are employed to teach children, not to love them. Nevertheless, all must face the fact that the child learns to love by being loved. Only then can he see himself to be a lovable person. Unless he does so, he cannot move positively towards others; he cannot create or participate in warm human relationships.

Teachers whose efforts are given to the teaching of subject matter rather than to children are not likely to be sensitive to the meaning of behaviorisms. They do not know, for example, that the show-off and the class clown may very likely be signalling for affection, for success, and recognition. As a result, such teachers are apt to use punishments that are calculated to shame the offender, when what he needs is treatment that will build up his self-confidence and self-respect. Sarcasm, mimicking, ridicule, scolding before the class, and banishment from the room are not effective methods for changing the behavior of children who need love, attention, self-respect, and a sense of belonging.

There are other signals that pass without notice in many classrooms. The pupil who is overly quiet, who never talks, who is withdrawn, is often neglected by the teacher who fails to realize that the child's behavior may be the result of unmet emotional needs. Instead of drawing such children into the midst of activities, instead of giving them full opportunity to unload their fears or their feelings of being unwanted and of disappointment in human beings, teachers tend to leave them strictly alone. That is especially harmful to lower class children and to minority racial and religious groups who suffer so much rejection in their lives.

If the school is to make a real attempt to satisfy youth's personal emotional needs, examining boards will have to require candidates for teaching positions to have much knowledge of human growth and development. They will also have to use both written examinations and oral interviews to explore the candidate's understanding of adolescence and of human behavior. Not only will supervisors and principals have to insist that methods of mass instruction be abandoned, but they will need to help teachers to learn how to use modern techniques and new ways of handling atypical behavior. Every effort will have to be made to implement the principle of the worth and integrity of the individual, for lip service is not enough.

These changes cannot be accomplished until new agreements are made between local school authorities, state departments of education, and officials of teacher-training institutions. Requirements must be set up and curricula constructed so that teachers will be more adequately prepared for their work. Principals will have to create in-service education programs in their respective schools so that all teachers can be reached for retraining. All who are concerned should encourage, praise, and reward teachers who are willing to undertake serious study and to move forward into experimental programs which are directed toward meeting the needs of the children in the school.

The need for accomplishment and achievement includes the need for success, for freedom from fear and guilt, for reduction of frustration in the learning processes. In every classroom there are children who experience little other than failure. This creates anxiety and fear, and develops feelings of inadequacy. Authoritarian methods and autocratic atmospheres prevail and children are frustrated because what they have to learn bears so little relationship to the problems that worry them. Many are unable to read the textbooks out of which the learning is to be done. Failure creates in the child a concept of self as a person who "can't." This blocks effort and learning. Once again, the individual behaves as he sees himself to be, and he does not learn.

One of the greatest blocks to learning is anxiety. Children who are rejected and those who fail are beset with anxiety. They do not know how to channel their anxieties or how to change the situations which created them. Some children try to escape from anxiety by daydreaming, truancy or running away from home. Others get sick. The teacher who wants more children to learn more, must find out what occurs in his own classroom that causes anxiety. The whip of failure and the experience of rejection stand out as primary causes.

All children need to experience success of some kind every day, and teachers must find the way for them to do so. There is no justification for the belief, commonly expressed by teachers, that children must "learn to fail" in order to be ready to experience failure in life. Life itself, as children live it, gives them plenty of experience in making mistakes, but in the good life in and out of school, mistakes are legitimate and regarded as learning experiences. The person who comes to regard himself as a failure is apt to commit suicide or become mentally ill. The school has no moral right to teach failure. Its task is to teach success.

In the school the child needs to develop a self concept full of "I can's." We behave as we see ourselves to be. They must make freer use of praise and rewards. Studies show that it is easier for most teachers to reward children who are like themselves—the middle and upper class children.[2] The lower class pupils are more frequently punished for their differences, many of which are not within their control, being a part of the culture into which they were born. This practice can be changed by the teacher if he will examine what he does, with care and insight. There are ways to praise even the naughty and dirty pupils, the retarded and the slow ones as well as those who are clean, comforting, and bright.

If the principle of the worth and integrity of the individual human being is to be implemented, segregation of every kind must be questioned. In the light of that principle it is necessary to reexamine the practice of grouping—of so-called homogeneous grouping, of grouping by ability.[3] Whenever children are separated on the basis of partial measurements of one or another mental characteristic, the pupils who are placed in the lower group feel guilty, fearful, inadequate, and may even hate themselves. These emotions engender others—hatreds for people, or feelings of aggression and hostility, or the desire to withdraw. When social or racial or religious or ethnic factors are also present, the children are apt to become confused, bewildered, and embittered.

One of the reasons for segregated classes is preoccupation with academic preparation for senior high school and for college which persists in many traditional junior high schools. As soon as more

---

[2] Stephen Abrahamson, "School Rewards and Social Class Status," *Educational Research Bulletin*, Ohio State Univ., January 16, 1952.

[3] Bruno Bettelheim, "Sputnik and Segregation," *Commentary*, October, 1958.

basic goals of personality development and preparation for effective citizenship are accepted by a school, other methods are found to classify pupils, other criteria are used for determination of the content to be taught, and many differentiated learning experiences and assignments are devised to stretch and challenge each one and to insure his growth.

In place of predetermined subject matter courses, the modern junior high school teacher uses pupil-teacher planning techniques to explore the areas of their interests and the learning needs that are common to the pupils in the groups. This does not relieve the teacher from his responsibility for also finding out and meeting the specific learning needs of individuals. Modern techniques promote the development of a permissive atmosphere in which creativity, originality, and initiative are encouraged.

Problems of grouping within a class, of classification in a school, and of reclassification from grade to grade are complex. It is important to review them in the light of children's need for reward, success, growth, freedom from fear, and freedom from guilt. Eventually, placement on the basis of these needs will replace the current practice of placing pupils on the basis of their ability to pass certain tests, read books of a certain difficulty, or make certain scores on verbal ability tests, or according to the letter with which their · last names begin. Moreover, the time of reclassification will be more flexible. All children should not have to wait until the end of the semester or year to be placed in groups where they would be more successful or happier. At the time when a teacher discovers that a child would be better off in another grade or class, the change should be made. Changes of this kind may be the means of overcoming social disadvantages or of dissipating personal antagonisms that may block a particular child's progress.

Sociometric instruments are often useful in discovering the needs which can be met by changes in classification. These include the *Wishing Well,*[4] social distance scales, and social status inventories. The use of group processes is a way to provide for all kinds of abilities and interests, and to give equality of status to all the children. In such groups, all children have greater chance to experience group membership, to feel wanted and of value. Junior high

---

[4] Bureau of Educational Research, Ohio State University, *The Wishing Well.* Columbus, Ohio: State University Press, 1945.

school boys and girls need many opportunities to build up their feelings of personal pride and status. They gain these when their contributions to group work are accepted and when they see themselves in the group product.

The demand for *recognition and reward* involves the need for praise and success and is necessary for growth. Many teachers use praise sparingly in the belief that when children fail and are scolded they try harder. Yet it is true that nothing succeeds like success and that failure is a destructive experience. When teachers themselves have the kinds of new experiences that they so often get in workshops and in arts and crafts classes, they develop new insight into the crushing effects of the frustration which comes from being given a task that is too hard. On the other hand they experience the release of creativity that comes from receiving praise, from being successful.

Large numbers of gifted students are never recognized in the public schools of America.[5] The potentialities of many are underdeveloped because of lack of experience and the emotional blocks they suffer both in and outside of school. Many of them may have had very few success experiences in their lives, and hardly know how it feels to be praised. It is important for teachers to look for these pupils, and to meet their needs.

Much failure centers around reading. Before they get very far along in elementary school, children who cannot read are convinced that they are not much good. This feeling of inadequacy is intensified when they find themselves rejected for the very same reason by many of their new junior high school teachers. Although the children themselves know that they did and do continue to learn without the help of books, it is hard for teachers to accept that fact. When, in the modern program, direct learning experiences are added and the needs for recognition, success, and growth are met for even the non-readers, some of the blocks to reading are removed, and reading levels go up.

Completing the change-over from the traditional to the modern is a slow process, but it has to begin. A good start is made when teachers re-study the nature of the learning process and take steps to implement the theories. A second step is taken when a faculty

---

[5] See Warner, Havighurst and Loeb, *Who Shall Be Educated?* Chap. XI. New York: Harper and Brothers, 1944.

accepts responsibility for the kind of human relations that exist
in the school, and becomes sensitive to the emotional needs of the
students. A third phase of the task is to find and use all the kinds
of abilities the pupils possess. Research indicates that there are forty
known attributes in intelligence and forecasts many more. The best
analysis of the Benet-Stanford Revision Test reveals ten of them.
The Wechsler-Bellevue tests only six. On the basis of rather slim
evidence, then, children are being grouped and separated for learning.[6] Teachers need much more information than they ordinarily
have about individual levels of achievement and rates of learning,
about pupil potentialities and aspirations. When these facts are at
hand, teachers cannot help but encourage children to express their
thoughts, their learnings, and their feelings in many ways besides
writing and talking. The classroom begins to blossom with art work,
creative handwork, dancing, singing, dramatics, collections, and
constructions.

Many kinds of measuring instruments are needed in modern
schools. Tests of mentality that do not place a premium on social
class are being sought to replace the older, less valid standard tests
of verbal ability.[7] Experiments are being made with new systems
of rating and reporting to parents, which aim to show more clearly
the relation between level of achievement and ability, and which
place emphasis on growth. In these, letter and percentage grades
are usually replaced with more meaningful words and phrases, and
the report form is supplemented by interviews with the child and
his parents.

One of the most serious barriers to development of more meaningful forms is parental opposition. They have had experiences only
with marks. They do not yet know that marks are not facts but merely
teachers' opinions, which can be wrong.

When reporting practices are improved and children remain with
their age-mates, progressing normally through the grades, success,
praise, rewards will be experienced more frequently by all children.

The demand for new experience, for fun, and adventure includes
the need for recreation, for contact with things and ideas that are

[6] J. P. Guilford, "The Structure of Intellect," *Psychological Bulletin 53*, July,
1956.

[7] Unpublished studies of Allison Davis, Robert J. Havighurst, and their
collaborators.

beautiful, for the use of new powers of mind and body, and for employment of the developing ability to use ethical and moral judgments and values. Many teachers think that unless work is hard and unpleasant it is ineffective. To them, fun means that children are playing. Consequently, they plan classroom work in such a way that children are bored. They do not question whether or not the lessons they teach make sense to the pupils. They drive for perfection that is beyond the ability of their students, and this serves to destroy creativity. For example, the creative writing papers must be rewritten until they are perfect. Moreover the subjects and topics that are assigned for the themes and composition too often are far removed from the ordinary experiences of most of the children. Since the papers that are written are judged largely on the basis of grammatical perfection, fun and humor cannot be expected in them.

If the need for fun and adventure is to be met, teachers will have to plan learning experiences for their children that will give pleasure. That means plenty of time for pupils to exchange experiences with each other, for them to get to know many of their classmates, for real friendships to begin. Time will have to be devoted to art, music, the dance, dramatics, the theatre, and nature so that appreciations will flower. Just reading about such things is not effective for most children. They need direct experience, which will mean trips to the theatre, to art exhibits, to art and science museums, to parks and forests, to new kinds of eating places, to the lakes, the shore, and the mountains, on hikes and picnics, by bus and by train —all, of course, depending on the resources of the community.

Modern schools are already providing the equipment and supplies that are required for creative handwork: oil paint as well as water color, metal, wood, clay and plastics, textiles and foods. Few schools, as yet, permit students to borrow tools and materials to use at home. In the school of tomorrow, all forms of expression will be deemed worthy of home assignment, and the responsibility for providing the wherewithal to promote these creative abilities will be assumed by the public. Until this is so, assignments of enrichment projects to be done at home are not fair, since some children have not space there, or equipment or encouragement from parents. Unless the school provides these to all alike, some suffer inequality of opportunity to develop, to the full, their potentialities. Films and radio are being used more often and more effectively, but there is a long way to go to overcome the frustrations of poor equipment, out-of-date pictures, and the inability of teachers to get what they need when they want it. As these media are used, attention can be given to the development of discrimination in selection, of appreciation of what is good, true, and beautiful, and on development of the ability to hold intelligent conversation about the programs. Schools have long accepted these as part of the literature work, but are slow to recognize the need for the same kind of teaching in connection with these new media of communication and learning.

Of course, reading is not to be neglected in either the traditional or the modern school. If however, pupils are to learn that reading is fun, they must be provided with books that deal with people and events that are closer to real life and are suited to the reading level of the individual. This means that rarely will an entire group be reading the same title. In addition to the classics, for those who can digest such fare, modern reading lists for junior high schools include romance, detective and mystery stories, and travelogues. Biographies fascinate older adolescents when they are within their comprehension.

In large numbers of school districts, the walls between school and community are coming down. There teachers take their classes out of the building and use the community as the laboratory in which firsthand study of society can best be done. In these experiences the pupils learn that people are fun. They meet with adults in new relationships and get from them the excitement of living. Children can also have adventures with people called in to be speakers or consultants at various times and in appropriate settings.

In the modern classrooms, students are having vicarious experiences with people through seeing and discussing films and stories of human relations. These, as well as the many opportunities in which they get to talk about their own immediate problems of life, help them to envision and prepare for the adventures that lie ahead in the realms of courtship, marriage, and family life.

Those schools which already are opening their doors for after-school and evening activities are meeting needs for fun and adventure. One of the greatest joys in life for junior high school boys and girls is being with their peers. In the eighth grade for many, and in the ninth grade for nearly all, the youngsters want very much to learn how to dance. Both square and social dancing open doors for them. Not knowing how to dance is a great handicap. Almost every school caters to this need to some extent. Just providing the time and the music is not enough, however, for most of the boys need instruction in dancing from sympathetic and understanding teachers or from more mature classmates. There is controversy between teachers and parents in some places over the question of evening dances for seventh and eighth graders. Twelve-year-olds are increasingly sophisticated, even to the point of dating and going steady. Some parents who do not object urge the school to have evening affairs for them.

In addition to needs which are basic and common to all people throughout their lives, there are also those which are peculiar to adolescence. These have a special bearing on the development of curriculum in the junior high school.

At every stage of his development, the human being is capable of achieving certain physical and mental competencies. These are called *developmental tasks*,[8] and they come along at chronological periods that have been identified. If the individual fails to accomplish them within a more or less limited span of years, he may be seriously retarded in his quest for maturity.

In early adolescence, new spurts of physical growth, curiosities about the world and society, interests in developing new social and manual skills, needs for relating self to other human beings, urges toward independence of thought and action, and a quickening wonder about the meaning of life are manifested. With few exceptions, children are in this period for some part of the time they spend in the junior high school. If growth toward physical, social, and emotional maturity is to be accomplished then, they must get certain jobs done. These are the developmental tasks of adolescence. They can be divided most simply into the following categories:

1. Making heterosexual adjustments.
2. Gaining emancipation from adults.
3. Finding a role in and making adjustments to the social order.
4. Adjusting to the vocational order.

Traditional junior high school curricula and practices have to be

---

[8] See Havighurst, *Developmental Tasks and Education.* Chicago Univ. Press, 1948; Havighurst, *Human Development and Education.* New York: Longmans, Green and Co., Inc., 1953.

42   *Meeting the Needs of Youth*

examined in the light of the needs of the pupils which grow out of the developmental tasks that confront them.

Adjustment to sex involves three areas: (1) acceptance of one's own sex role and of self; (2) understanding of the opposite sex role; (3) ability to meet and talk to, to work and play with members of the opposite sex. As the reality of the present situation is scrutinized, the following common practices stand out. In most schools, the study of sex hygiene is either forbidden or so superficially done that pupils are bewildered and frustrated. Little attention is given to evidence of neurotic habits and attitudes that attend the menstrual cycle. Girls are excused for regular absences, and are even encouraged to stay at home. On the other hand, especially with boys, no attention is paid to evidence of glandular disturbance. The possibility of physical disabilities, such as undescended testicles, is ignored. Many teachers are not even aware of sex play that goes on under their eyes. All of these weaknesses in the curriculum could easily be corrected.

Instituting a course in sex hygiene calls for education of the faculty and the community. Responsible teachers whose backgrounds of experience are adequate and whose personalities are stable have to be selected and given additional training. The medical division should be enlarged and provision made for strip examination of all pupils at regular intervals. Counseling services have to be secured, either within the school or from outside agencies. Although some changes must wait upon additional appropriations, nothing stands in the way of beginning the education of teachers and parents. In all probability in every school at least one teacher can be found who is willing to help children with the problem of sex education. The cooperation of parents is critical in many individual cases. It can be sought in interviews in the school building or by sending nurse or counselor to visit the home. Where there is neither nurse nor counselor the job must be done by principal and teacher.

A large part of the instruction needed to help children to adjust to the opposite sex can be done incidentally in connection with science, physical education, family living, home arts, and social activities. Reading and hearing about the ways in which men and women relate themselves to each other in social situations may not be sufficient to enable students to act in socially acceptable adult ways. Social grace can be developed through practice. Home arts classes, industrial arts shops, and hygiene classes can function as places in which boys and girls together have freedom to talk about common problems of work, to experience the good will that comes when people share their tools and help each other, and to learn about their respective roles in society and in the working world. Classes that are devoted to specific sex instruction, however, should be segregated because in the junior high school the pupils are not ready to discuss, in mixed groups, the sexual side of life. Some excellent films have been developed to teach about sex and reproduction. "About Your Life," a color strip of thirty frames with a recording, is good. It can be obtained from the Denver, Colorado, school system.

In some large schools, where two rooms are used for cafeterias, it is still not unusual to find that girls are sent to one, boys to the other. In schools where it is customary to assign seats in the lunch room, girls are often seated on one side, boys on the other. Such arrangements used to be suitable for seventh graders who normally prefer their own sex, but for the others, separation of the sexes during their free time increases frustration and tension and may lead to behavior problems. Seventh grade girls, especially, are not now so shy.

Much help in making heterosexual adjustments could be given in the gymnasium by making arrangements to mix boys and girls for periods of instruction in dancing, square dancing, cooperative games, as spectators, and even in competitive games played for fun.[9] This gives every child a chance to do those things that many of them are not able to do when such activities are limited to clubs. Clubs of this type are very popular and the enrollment in them has to be limited. Moreover, children of the lower classes and of minority groups often feel so unwanted in social activities that they select other clubs.

In all regular classrooms, free choice of seating should be allowed at least part of the time. This gives children a chance to sit with their friends as well as to make new friends. Group work, in which many lines of communication open up, is another means of helping children to make the social heterosexual adjustments that are so important to them.

---

[9] See Kozman, Cassidy and Jackson, *Methods in Physical Education.* Philadelphia, Pa.: W. B. Saunders Company, 1952.

Some of the changes that are needed can be facilitated by so organizing student associations for participation in administration and control that large numbers of children hold offices. If every classroom group in the school has representation on the major committees, free discussion of all student affairs seeps through the entire school without delay. Teacher education regarding the importance of these activities is essential in order to get them to permit class time for student reports and class discussions. Participation in policy making and in projects designed to improve the quality of living in the school has to become part of the school day and respectable enough to devote time and effort to it. In most schools it is still relegated to the extra-curricular club program, few students hold offices in it, and they rarely undertake activities that are important to themselves or to the student body.

The establishment of an independent personality requires emancipation from parental control and aims at securing equality of status in the adult world. This need causes much misunderstanding and conflict in the home and in the school. If rebellion against grown-ups could be seen to be evidence of maturity, adults would look upon it with favor as they do upon the evidence in little tots of growth in the accomplishments of their tasks—walking, talking and toilet control. Teachers who do not fully understand the need for independence are prone to bemoan the seeming loss of respect for their authority. They resent the desire of students to express their own opinions and to make their own decisions. Instead of encouraging growth in these directions, the school too often makes rules and regulations that deprive pupils of independence of thought and action. Adolescents are further confused by the way adults vacillate in their attitudes and demands. Whereas in one situation parents and teachers expect teen-agers to have adult control over their behavior, in the next one the same adults treat them with disrespect when they try to express their ideas and opinions.

It requires more insight than many teachers have, to connect the surliness and disobedience some students exhibit with the conflicts they are having in the home. Classroom behavior is often a projection of the hostility generated by unreasonable demands made by authoritarian parents. When teachers align themselves with parents and against the child, his confusion becomes more confounded. To combat these difficulties and to meet the emotional needs of students requires patient and understanding teachers.

Teachers who are meeting the need for emancipation are sensitive to the signals and symptoms that signify growth in that direction. They are able to remove themselves from conflict situations and to look objectively at the evidence of tension and anxiety that so often become effective blocks to learning. One teacher described this condition students get into as "lost days." On such a day, punishment for inattention adds fuel to the fire. In fact, the entire problem of punishment for adolescents has to be reconsidered in the light of their need for grown-upness.

Classroom administration, control, and teaching techniques are all affected when schools change from authoritarianism to democracy. Teachers seek ways of allowing the students to have their rights respected. They admit them to the process of planning for the work to be done, and give them many opportunities to make decisions that are of importance to them. Students take part in setting up their goals and in evaluating the outcome of their activities in terms of their objectives. In these experiences, children clarify their thoughts, identify their problems, and learn to take action. Practice in doing adult things of this nature contributes to maturity.

Adolescents need help in understanding themselves during these difficult years of physical and emotional growth. They need to understand their worries, where their tensions come from, what to do about their feelings, and how to fit into the adult patterns of behavior. In many schools, batteries of self appraisal tests, followed by conferences with the students and their parents, help to achieve these ends.

Part of the work of emancipation must be done in the peer group. As ties to parents loosen, those which bind the individual to his age-mates become stronger. The time and place for interpersonal relations are too small in schools that send the students scurrying over the building every forty-five minutes. Those schools which recognize the importance of peer relationships arrange schedules which permit children to be together for a longer block of time at least once every day. Moreover, in these schools children are permitted to talk to each other, to help each other, to work in groups. They do not remain in formal rows of seats, looking at the back of each others' heads all day.

The kind of school that is emerging makes it necessary for teachers to learn how the adolescent society is formed and operates.

WHITWORTH COLLEGE LIBRARY
SPOKANE WASHINGTON

Teachers study the connection between group dynamics and successful classroom performance. They make use of the instruments that have been developed which reveal the forces that are at work in the peer group—social distance inventories, the open end question, and role playing.[10] At times, teachers sit by for the purpose of observing the students, and they record what the individuals say and do so that they can learn to interpret behavior and discover needs.

Economic competency, another aspect of social need, involves earning and managing money. A large proportion of teen-agers experience acute needs in this area, yet many of them find it is impossible to experience earning and managing an income. One reason for the denial of satisfaction is the habit teachers and parents have of filling up the after-school hours with homework and chores. Even those students who have jobs are often frustrated because teachers believe that it is their right to punish them when they do not prepare their lessons, by making them give up their jobs. In many schools the need is for an extension of the use of work-study plans in which the student works part time, attends school the rest of the time, and gets guidance and instruction in school that are related to his work and the problems that arise on the job. Work for teen-agers is hard to find. Community understanding and cooperation must be secured.

Arithmetic courses are natural media for instruction about money.[11] In most schools, however, these are still largely devoted to repetitive drills in fundamentals for the seventh and eighth graders, while many are taught algebra in the ninth grade. The skills are apt to be better established in meaningful situations. Units about money would also provide opportunities for understanding and appreciating the economic elements in democratic life. Many modern schools are developing mathematics courses that are tuned to the stream of daily living.[12] The trend toward delaying algebra

[10] Taba, et al., *Diagnosing Human Relations Needs.* Chapter VI. Washington, D. C.: American Council on Education, 1951.

[11] Wm. Betts, "The Place of Mathematics in Human Affairs," *Mathematics Teacher,* January, 1952.

[12] Courses of this kind are being used in both Philadelphia and New York City schools. See also, "General Mathematics in Human Affairs," *Bulletin No. 17,* Wisconsin Cooperative Education Planning Program, Madison, Wisc., June, 1950.

until the senior high school has been reversed under pressure from critics.

A second phase of the task of making vocational adjustment is concerned with moving in the direction of making a living. There are many schools in which this is begun by requiring pupils in the ninth year to take at least one elective which has vocational implications—business training for commercial work, home economics for family life, shop work for industry. Usually this "major" interest has to be continued in the senior high school. Modern educators know that the junior high school pupils are far too young to make such selections. They know too little about themselves and the world of work. Their experiences need to be broadened rather than narrowed into specializations.

One change that is being made, so that the needs of the adolescents can more nearly be met, is the use of exploratory courses rather than electives. Failure in them is not penalized but is used for guidance purposes. The student is not required to repeat such courses if he is not successful; instead, he merely changes his direction and tries another field. The content of exploratory courses is designed to introduce the student to the working world, to give him occupational information, to show him job outlets, to help him to find his strengths and weaknesses and do something about them, and to develop in him the skills of human relationships that are necessary for vocational success. To accomplish these purposes, the classes go out into the factories and stores to see and hear what goes on there. They interview and consult with experts in business, management, labor, and personnel work.

Schools which are concerned about giving their pupils full opportunity to move towards vocational competency make it possible for both boys and girls to have experience in the fields of home arts and industrial arts all three years. There are equally important job opportunities and emotional satisfactions for both sexes in both areas. The objectives of the courses, however, are not skills which are bound to be lost in the years intervening between school and work, but rather the cultivation of creative individuality, the production of artistic handwork, and the development of skill in getting along with fellow workers, supervisors, and those in authority.

Adjustment to the social order includes four areas, in each of which there are needs to be met: (1) marriage and family life, (2) citizenship, (3) religion, and (4) developing a philosophy of life and socially acceptable values. When the conventional program is examined in terms of opportunities to satisfy these needs, a large discrepancy is uncovered. For example, instead of teaching values, facts, and a philosophy about the sex side of life, the program makes these matters taboo. Problems connected with them are apt to be ignored, treated superficially, or regarded with horror. Although the need for human relations education is acute, the necessity for covering courses of study precludes the possibility of giving time to it in most classrooms. Home arts courses in many schools do include some of these problems, but, for the most part, they are still "minor subjects" for girls only. Considerable progress in home arts is to be expected when administrators take advantage of the preparation which teachers are getting in this field.

The needs in the area of social adjustment cannot be met in any one subject field. Instruction in many classes must be broadened to include the requisite experiences. Teachers in social living, social studies, English or language arts, and science are meeting some of the needs when they plan with their students for the study of such units as mental health, family problems, teen-age problems, intercultural differences and tensions, consumer education, occupational information, other lands and people, conflicting ideologies, and labor-management relations. Learning activities in such units include the use of socio- and psycho-dramatics, and role playing, which help students to gain insight into human nature and social relationships. Creative writing that deals with personal and group problems, stimulated by open end questions, helps teachers to identify individual needs. Excellent films and recordings are also available to teachers. Experts in the community are usually willing to come into the school as speakers and consultants.

Adjustment to the demands for democratic citizenship is an important area in which there are many unmet needs. To satisfy them, pupils must be given many opportunities to practice the skills of democracy. This requires the school to set up situations in which their use is meaningful. In the schools in which this is done, the outcomes are more favorable than in those schools in which all available time is concentrated on historical facts. The modern teacher who is released from pressure to cover a course of study, using a book that many of his students cannot read, finds it possible to teach the appreciation of democratic principles and the skills of effective citizenship to his slow as well as to his bright pupils. In these and other schools, questions are being raised as to the advisability of devoting a year or even a semester to the study of state history in a world that is moving toward internationalism. Teachers are also realizing that reliance on competition is not the way to prepare pupils for living in an interdependent world, which is taxing all the cooperative effort that can be mustered to secure and maintain peace.

Students do not get an appreciation of democracy in action while they live and work in an authoritarian classroom in which a dictatorial teacher relies heavily on one book. Controversial issues and real life problems must be included in social studies content in order that both teachers and pupils may learn the way of democratic discussion, of dissent without anger, of collective thinking, of cooperative planning, and of social action. There are enough classrooms in the junior high schools across the country in which these elements are functioning, to point out their values and the changes that should be made in the others.[13] The junior high school is the place for the study of government, politics, democracy, communism, war and peace, internationalism, the air age, housing, delinquency, propaganda, superstitions, other lands and peoples, modern inventions and their effects on society, and a host of other units that are full of facts, yet may also produce attitudes, skills, and appreciations which society demands of the school's graduates.

The third aspect of the adolescent's progress toward achieving social adjustment, is the broadening and deepening of spiritual and ethical concepts. This has always been one of the accepted objectives of public education, but, for the most part, the school is expected to accomplish it incidentally.[14] Recent heated controversies over church-state relationships have occurred. Some schools rule out all references to religion. Others authorize released time for religious instruction outside the school. Some states require Bible reading; others require prayers. These matters are being decided in the courts in many states.[15] Many schools take advantage of December

---

[13] Grace Wright, "Block-Time Classes and the Core Program in the Junior High Schools." *Bulletin #6,* Office of Education, Washington, D. C., 1958.

[14] Hunt and Stanek, "Are the Public Schools Godless?" *The School Executive,* May, 1952.

[15] "The State and Sectarian Education," *NEA Research Bulletin,* December, 1956.

festivals to teach about the major faiths of the world. The practice of developing intercultural programs and projects around the December festivals is growing throughout the nation.

The Federal Constitution, American tradition, and the wishes of the people point to the necessity of teaching *about* religion. They rule out the use of creed, dogma, ceremonies, and rites that involve the act of worship. The spiritual values that are outcomes of understanding of people can be deepened by engaging pupils in units of study that include learning about cultural backgrounds and religious customs; that require sharing experiences, seeing films and dramatizations, the use of literature, and the study of history. When pageantry and demonstrations are involved, many schools are seeking parents and members of the clergy who are willing to participate in the development of policies and plans. Teachers and parents should expect, as outcomes of these learning experiences, destruction of prejudices and elimination of rejection and discrimination on the basis of religious and racial differences.

Finally, adolescents must get on with the job of *developing appropriate value systems and beginning a philosophy of life.*[16] It is true that these are also the outcomes of the kind of work described above. That goal is not likely to be reached, however, unless the child in school has much opportunity to study relationships among people, things, and ideas; to experience interrelationships; to solve social and personal problems in the light of all the facts that can be gathered; and to experience the unity which exists in life. Division of curriculum into water-tight subject matter compartments is a block to the development of such insight. More progress will be made toward reaching these goals when unit teaching replaces departmentalization in at least part of the curriculum.[17]

Of equal importance in developing values is providing for continuous experience in weighing relative values and in making value judgments. This is impossible in classrooms where teachers make all the important choices and decisions. Pre-determination of content and activities and allocation of responsibilities must give way

---

[16] Judah Goldin, "Spiritual Values in Public Education," *NEA Journal,* December, 1952.

[17] See Alberty et al., *Utilizing Subject Fields in High School Core Program Development.* Columbus, Ohio: Ohio State University, 1950.

to granting pupils a voice in the making of decisions that matter to them.

Attention needs to be directed to the many ways in which the school sets up false values and perpetuates values that have little validity in terms of today's world. Some of these can be found in practices connected with testing and marking. Others have to do with segregation and ability grouping. Still more are concerned with failure to recognize and appreciate cultural differences that are inherent in the various social classes, religious groups, races, and in the ethnic origins of the people who comprise our society.

Efforts must be made to' eliminate the gap between philosophy and practice if the confusions and bewilderments attendant upon adolescence are to be resolved. What is honesty? integrity? courage? loyalty? These are questions of more than academic import, and they must be faced frankly and with reference to the realities of these times. The teacher in the classroom must himself implement the great principles of the worth of the person and of his right to share in policy making. Teacher education on both the pre- and in-service levels must deal with such problems if teachers are to get the help they need in making the necessary changes.

In this chapter, the reality of the school has been examined in the light of the demands of youth which grow out of their common and individual needs. When those which are basic to life are not met, the individual has little chance to develop into an adjusted mature person. Of equal importance are the needs that grow out of the developmental changes of early adolescence. When these are not met, unrelieved tensions and anxieties block learning and may result in the development of anti-social tendencies. It has become clear that the program of the traditional junior high school falls short of meeting these crucial needs.

As today's school reorganizes and re-vitalizes its program, its development must be based upon critical self-evaluation. The tasks to be done by the principal and the teachers have to be reconstructed. As the staff work at the job, using the needs of youth and the nature of the learning processes as their guide lines, they will pull their school closer to the stream of life. Democracy will take on reality in the classroom. The structure of the day will make it possible for the faculty to create the kind of climate and the learning situations in which children will find that freedom and responsibility go hand in hand and characterize the good life.

It is not enough for school personnel to know what to do to create the school of tomorrow, today. They must also know *how*. In the following chapters the know-how is emphasized.

Learning Activities for Members of Pre- and In-Service Teacher Education Classes

In addition to reading do such things as:

1. See a film on emotional needs such as *The Feeling of Rejection, The Feeling of Hostility, The Quiet One, Angry Boy*. These and others are in most university film libraries and can be obtained from McGraw-Hill.

2. Visit two schools, one in which there is freedom in the cafeteria and one which is under authoritarian control.

3. Secure a psychiatrist as consultant.

4. Arrange a panel discussion which includes teachers, parents, and students, to discuss the question "What we want (our children) to get in school."

References

BOOKS

Anxiety in Elementary School Children: A Report of Research. New York: John Wiley and Sons, 1960.

Association for Supervision and Curriculum Development, *Fostering Mental Health in Our Schools*. Washington, D. C.: National Education Association, 1949.

Cunningham, Ruth, and associates, *Understanding Group Behavior of Boys and Girls*. New York: Teachers College, Columbia University, 1951.

Gesell, Ilg and Ames, *Youth: the Years From Ten to Sixteen*. New York: Harper and Brothers, 1956.

Gillman, H. L., *Helping Children Accept Themselves and Others*. Teachers College, Columbia Univ., 1959.

Havighurst, R. J., *Development Tasks and Education*. Sec. Ed. New York: Longmans, Green and Co., 1952.

Miner, J. B., *Intelligence in the United States*. New York: Springer Pub. Co., 1957.

Nelson, H. B., (ed.), *Mental Health in Modern Education*, National Society for the Study of Education. 54th Year Book, Part II, 1955.

Rasey and Menge, *What We Learn From Children.* New York: Harper and Brothers, 1958.
Taba, Brady, Robinson, Vickery, *Diagnosing Human Relations Needs.* Washington, D. C.: American Council on Education, 1952.

PERIODICALS AND PAMPHLETS

Havighurst, R. J., "Poised at the Crossroads of Life," *The School Review,* 1953.
Klausner, S. J., "Social Class and Self Concept," *Journal of Social Psychology,* November, 1953.
"Recommended Grade Organization for Junior High School Education," *National Association of Secondary School Principals,* September, 1959.
Stavsky, W. H., "Using the Insights of Psychotherapy in Teaching," *Elementary School Journal,* October, 1959.

CHAPTER THREE

The Role of Human Relations

Education . . . is a world and race building function. It means the creation of circumstances that call forth initiative, responsibility, conscientiousness, sensitivity, that cultivate judgment and refine sensibilities, that awaken and create identifications of self with others, that build insight regarding the forces that impinge upon society and the individual and competence in their manipulation.

> George Axtelle, "Significance of the Inquiry Into the Nature and Constancy of the I.Q.," *Educational Method*, November, 1939.

Life's most important experiences stem from the relationships one establishes with people. The way in which the members of a family relate themselves to a new infant affects his personality pattern. The treatment he receives from people during the periods of weaning and toilet-training and in the growing periods of walking and talking plays an important role in his life.[1] The degree of affectional security he experiences with people and the amount of praise and reward he gets from people affect his adjustment and growth.

The need for warm human relations persists throughout life. When the child goes to school, his teacher becomes the parent substitute to whom he looks for a continuation of the affectional bonds he has with his parents. If the parents have failed him, the need for satisfying relationships with teachers is even more acute. At the same time, the growing child has the need to relate himself to his age-mates. Their responses to him are often conditioned by the ex-

---

[1] Davis and Havighurst, *Father of the Man*. Boston: Houghton Mifflin Company, 1947. See especially Chapters 1-4.

ample set by the teacher, who can do much to help the child to become happily adjusted in the group.

As adolescence approaches and the child begins his life in the junior high school, he has increasing need for recognition from his teachers, for success as a human being, and for being wanted in the peer group. Problems of interpersonal relationships loom large in both the home and the school. The boys and girls struggle with the need for emancipation from adults. Conflicts arising from this normal growing-up process bewilder and frustrate them. Life is made difficult by adults who alternately treat them as children, when they want submission and conformity, and as adults, when they want to be released from responsibility. Adolescents often vent their pent-up hostilities upon the teacher in confused projection of what they would prefer doing to parents.

When junior high school teachers know how real those needs are, they dedicate themselves to the philosophy of human relations education. Then they face the problem of implementing it in a program which requires content, learning activities materials, methods, and evaluation of outcomes.

There are many people, in and out of schools, who believe that the primary responsibility of the school is to give children information. They view the teachers, especially of secondary schools, as purveyors of information. Many of them think that the solution to interpersonal and intergroup tensions lies in giving people—both young and old—information about race, about religions, about the social class and caste structure of American society, and about distant lands and cultures.

There is no doubt that information about all these things is important. Any school in which pupils fail to get facts, and fail to learn how to get facts, is not as good a school as the American public demands. Nevertheless, there is evidence that information is not enough—*not enough* to create people with generous outgoing personalities able to lead rich and abundant lives; *not enough* to help people develop and utilize to the fullest extent their own and other individuals' potentialities; *not enough* to give people the courage needed to stand up and be counted in the fight against prejudice, discrimination and bigotry; *not enough* to enable adults of this generation to cure the human relations illnesses which beset our times:

delinquency, crime and moral breakdown, divorce and the deterioration of family life, mental illness and emotionally caused illnesses, interracial and international strife.[2] ⋋

In traditional schools there is not much evidence of progress in developing a human relations program. Teachers say, "Does there have to be another course? Where will the time for it come from? I can't get it in and cover the course of study, too." At the same time, the teachers express deep concern over the limited success they have in teaching so many of their pupils. They search for the causes, and eventually come upon the connection between their failures and human relations.

Some teachers place the blame for unsatisfactory classroom work on the difficulty of content. Others place it on the children who, they say, "aren't interested," or "won't work," or "are defiant," or "have no ambition." A few believe that the fault lies with the parents who, they claim, "don't care" or "can't or won't help their kids," or "are too dumb to understand," or "don't speak English." Many are convinced that the elementary teachers are to blame because "they promote everybody" or "don't teach reading any more." All are convinced that pupil-load has much to do with it. The really significant thing they say is, "We have too many pupils each day. We cannot learn even the names of our students. What can we do when we meet two hundred a day, but give them books to read and writing to do; there is no other way to control them. All they seem to do is troop in and out every forty-five minutes and wait for the bell to ring so they can get to their friends again. They don't care about us at all."

✗ *The deepest source of the trouble teachers have in carrying out their purposes lies in the conditions which prevent them from relating themselves to their pupils with any degree of human warmth, and which prevent the children from interacting with each other inside the classroom.* ✗ The constant frustrations which result condition the attitudes of teachers to their colleagues, to the children, and to the parents. When there is no time for people to get to know each other, group and personal antagonisms, class biases, stereotyped ideas, hostilities, and conflicts grow apace, and create bad

---

[2] This material first appeared in Gertrude Noar, *Information Is Not Enough.* New York: Anti-Defamation League, B'nai B'rith., 1958.

human relations which inevitably get in the way of learning.[3]

Teachers must become aware of the role that human relations plays in their classroom work. When human relations are bad in either the school or the home, instruction is interrupted, discussions deteriorate, and individuals are prevented from following directions. They make it impossible for a child to listen and to hear what is being said. They interfere with the carrying out of home assignments. When they become intolerable, pupils escape into truancy, or leave school at the earliest opportunity.

On the other hand, good human relations facilitate learning.[4] They motivate school work as pupils plan together and evaluate their processes and products. They make it possible for a child to become absorbed in his activity. They inspire some to set their sights on college in spite of severe handicaps.

The interpersonal forces that play upon individuals in the adolescent society often absorb all their attention. If the teacher knows and understands what to do with human relations, he can utilize them to improve the quantity and quality of classroom work. The strategy with which he uses them can either increase or resolve tensions, kill or generate energy, bottle up or release creativity.

The junior high school years are particularly fraught with problems of relationships in the peer group. The peer group claims the individual's attention, loyalty, respect, and love from this time on through life. No place is more attractive to the teen-ager than the one in which he will find his gang. No fashion experts can lure a girl away from the fads and fancies of dress that have been adopted by the gang. Any pranks they play at the expense of adults are fun. Pressures from age-mates often are great enough to cause individuals to become defiant, disobedient, and even delinquent. The "group code" governs, and adults are rarely given insight into it.

In early adolescence both boys and girls are deeply concerned about popularity. Many of them experience real or imagined rejection. Members of minority groups know, or think, that they are

---

[3] See Anna P. Burrell, "Facilitating Learning through Emphasis on Meeting Children's Basic Emotional Needs," *The Journal of Educational Sociology,* March, 1951.

[4] See Stuart Chase, *Roads to Agreement.* New York: Harper & Bros., 1951.

not wanted. Even when in-school relations are good, groups divide at the school door. Large numbers of pupils know what it feels like to be left out when invitations to parties are distributed. These hurts are softened when the school curriculum includes the study of why people live as they do, act as they do, believe as they do, and when the teacher helps children to learn that "people are like that," but that difference is not a reason for rejection.

There are rejectees in every group. Teachers and pupils need to know what causes this rejection, what kinds of actions are disliked, what personal characteristics are objectionable. For example, middle class children react vigorously against those who swear and use sex words. All adolescents hate bossing and teasing and gang up on those who are guilty of these offenses. They also dislike children who call upon adults for help. This is evidence of immaturity, and children will exclude those who attempt this solution from participation in group activities. Teachers must help children to learn these things.

Very few junior high school pupils do not have arguments and quarrels at home with siblings, both older and younger, and with parents. These are the result of "growing pains" and the constant drive for emancipation. Adolescents like to tease service people, store-keepers, and policemen just because they are adults and in positions of some authority. Defiance of teachers and disobedience of student officers is another facet of the urge to be grown-up and on one's own. Teachers must help children to understand these actions and how adults feel about what they do to them. The school can help them to substitute constructive activities for those which create bad human relations.

"If information is not enough, then what else is required in the classrooms of America? What else must the teacher do besides tell? What kinds of learning experiences do children need besides reading, writing, figuring and reciting?

"First, schools must help the pupil to create a self-concept that permits him to like himself and, therefore, to like others; one that enables him to move positively toward others who, in one way or another, are different from himself.

"Second, pupils can and, indeed, must learn certain human relations skills. These are as essential for effective living as are the fundamental skills of reading, writing and arithmetic.

"Third, education for good human relations requires the inculcation of positive attitudes towards others, towards differences, towards democracy, towards life itself.

"Fourth, the school teacher has the primary responsibility for providing minority group children with status-building experiences. This kind of education requires resources and materials which are already available."[5]

Teachers are responsible for helping pupils to learn the social skills and techniques, even though people in some circles feel that this is a function of the home. In addition to the familiar skills that are usually included in this category, children must learn how to make people like them, how to share, how to help, how to avoid conflicts, what to do when they see others fighting, how to treat name calling, and the dangers of spreading rumors and carrying tales. While it is true that teachers are busy with these from kindergarten on, many teen-agers have not yet acquired the necessary facility in handling their relationships with other people.

Then there are the skills of democratic practices and processes. One of these is the skill of planning which can be developed through many experiences in pupil-teacher planning for classroom work and when children work together in small groups. Another is the skill of participation. This is acquired as pupils play various roles in discussion groups and take part in work and play activities. The skills of sharing are built up by practice in telling about cultural traditions and holidays, by entertaining the group with one's musical, artistic, and dancing talents, and by lending one's toys, utensils, and equipment.

"Leadership requires a constellation of skills learned by practice in group work in the classroom, gymnasium, and play areas. The skill of critical thinking——gathering facts, weighing them for relative values, using good judgment, making wise decisions——is of tremendous importance and this, too, cannot be acquired through reading alone, but only through frequent use in situations that are meaningful to the child. Evaluation of self and others, of process and product, requires skills which can be learned only through constant repetition, but which will be of inestimable value throughout life. Basic to human relations are the skills of communicating,

---

[5] Gertrude Noar, *Information Is Not Enough.* New York: Anti-Defamation League of B'nai B'rith, 1958.

expressing self in words, looks, gestures. Reading, writing, and listening are included. The skills involved in interpretation and evaluation of such mass media as radio, TV, advertising, and the comics, though of increasing importance, have not as yet found wide recognition in the school.

"Social skills need to be learned but the approach and planning should be somewhat different from what is ordinarily done under the heading of etiquette. The skills of interpersonal relationships in family life are equally important and yet are rarely included in courses which are largely informational. If these essential skills could be emphasized and practiced in secondary school home arts courses for mixed classes of boys and girls, the students would be far better prepared to stem the tide of deterioration in home living. Children, for example, can learn such simple skills as when to say, "I'm sorry," how to say it in many ways and how to time it. They need also to learn to say, "Thanks" in many different ways, to ask for and give opinions, and to differ and to accept difference without anger."[6]

The teaching techniques which can be used to help adolescents to develop these skills include discussions of all types, showing films and filmstrips, playing appropriate recordings of human relations plays that have been broadcast, dramatizing social situations, and role playing. Writing about personal experiences is useful for those pupils who can write without too much frustration. When acute problems arise or are discovered, personal interviews and sympathetic counseling are essential. Home visits and in-school conferences with parents are usually needed. Skill of every kind is developed best by practice in situations meaningful to the learner.

The teacher will find it useful to know what cluster of personality traits have most prestige value in the group with which he deals.[7] For example, in most seventh grades a child can be popular if he is clean, well-mannered, and conforming. In the eighth grade, however, prestige is more likely to be attached to untidyness, a show of independence, and defiance of authority. Another shift, in the ninth grade, brings social maturity and knowledge of the facts of

---

[6] Gertrude Noar, *Information Is Not Enough.* New York: Anti-Defamation League of B'nai B'rith, 1958.

[7] Caroline Tryon, "The Adolescent Peer Culture," *National Society for the Study of Education,* Chicago: University of Chicago Press, 1944.

life into first place. The popular tomboy of the eighth grade gives way to the young lady who is using cosmetics and more adult modes of dress. The teacher who is informed about these changes in values, who is sensitive and observant, will tune his own actions to suit the needs of the students. For example, he will not persist in praising things which the group does not admire, nor will he nag children in a vain effort to make them to conform to his standards. He will, on the contrary, help them to adjust to their growing pains.

There are many cultural attitudes that influence human relations in the school.[8] Socio-economic values, the location of homes of individual pupils, social class mores, intercultural biases and stereotypes enter into the configurations of the peer society, and cause the formation of in-groups and out-groups. Children who are outside the prestige circle want desperately to be in. That desire may consume a large part of their thoughts and dictate actions that give the teacher great concern if he does not know the cause. On the other hand, if he does know about the tensions and relations that exist, he can plan work and play groups so that hostilities are cured and conflicts averted. For example, a child who is in the out-group can be asked to help one of the in-group members with his spelling, reading, or art work. When committees are formed, members of both groups can be included. As they work together, they will get to know and like each other, to value each other's contributions. The walls between them will go down. New friendships will be formed.[9]

There are times when children should be permitted to work with the classmates they know and like best. Groups of that kind can be highly productive. As he arranges for this, the teacher will have to create the climate and motivation for work so that the time wasting that can happen when friends get together does not occur. He must also take the isolates into consideration and plan so that they will not be left out.

A sociometric instrument that has been used for finding friend-

---

[8] Taba, et al., *Diagnosing Human Relations Needs,* Washington, D. C.: American Council on Education, 1951.

[9] See Helen Hall Jennings and associates, *Sociometry in Group Relations.* Washington, D. C.: American Council on Education, rev. ed., 1959.

ship patterns and needs is the "Wishing Well."[10] In the answers children give to the questions in it, they reveal the classmates they like best and those with whom they prefer to work and to play. The wise teacher makes use of the information he gets in arranging seating, work groups, and play teams. There are other instruments that can be used to find the attitudes that children have toward minority groups. Among them are the Human Relations Inventory, the Scale of Social Distance, and the Ohio Social Acceptance Scale.

Human Relations Education is of necessity concerned with acquainting teachers and students with the differences that characterize the various groups that make up our society. There are customs, language patterns, moral values, and attitudes that cluster around social class, race, religion, and ethnic origins. An interdisciplinary approach is essential, and this involves knowledge of anthropology, study of religions, and of the psychological nature of prejudice, as well as sociology and education. Classroom work for the students must include some basic concepts of religion that are common to all faiths: the meaning of such terms as prejudice, stereotype, discrimination, minority group, and cultural heritage.[11] Learning activities should provide opportunity for pupils to share their customs and celebrations. For example, beautiful projects can be developed around the December festivals of Hanukkah and Christmas, if the understanding of parents and religious leaders in the community is established and their help is solicited.

Many teachers resist the facts about the nature of American society. They prefer to believe that it is classless and that prejudice does not exist in their schools. They say, "We don't have any conflict over race or religion." Some say, "We have only a few colored (or Jewish) pupils, and every one treats them all the same. They are all alike to us." Some ask, "Why should we even mention class (or race or religion), when we have no minority problems? Why not 'let sleeping dogs lie'?"

This is the attitude of people who hide their heads in the sand, refusing to look at the nature of the colossal conflicts that continue to tear the world apart. The worst of them was marked by doctrines

---

[10] Bureau of Educational Research, Ohio State Univ., *The Wishing Well*. Columbus, Ohio: Ohio State University Press, 1945.

[11] Resource unit on "Prejudice and Discrimination" is available from the Anti-Defamation League of B'nai B'rith, 517 Madison Ave., New York 22, N. Y.

of racial superiority, the spread of second class citizenship, and the practice of genocide. None of these has been eradicated; some of them persist in our own land.[12] Teachers cannot ignore their responsibilities for doing their utmost to destroy the myths that surround human differences. They cannot pay mere lip service to the ideals of democracy if they wish to implant them in the minds and hearts of their students. They must stand up and be counted in the struggle to show the world that the democratic way is the good life for all people.

The school that is building a curriculum in which human relations play a vital role must gather many facts about its students. The teachers must know what constitutes the family group; what are the family attitudes to race, religion, social class, and ethnic backgrounds; and where the home is located. They need to be realistic about the conditions of life that society imposes upon the members of various groups. These often determine where people have to live, the kinds of jobs to which they can aspire, how and by whom they are accepted and rejected socially, and the amount of education they may reasonably expect to acquire. Teachers cannot talk to pupils as if there were no restrictions or limitations on the individual. Children already know the facts from experiences of friends and family members. They see and hear the realities on the screen and radio. When the teacher is not truthful, or when he retreats from the task of helping students to understand these conditions, he creates distrust and hostility. On the other hand it would be equally wrong for the teacher to omit discussion of the forces that are at work slowly correcting inequalities. Students must be counseled to prepare themselves for the realization of their utmost potentialities. Avenues that are closed today may be open tomorrow.

Socio-economic conditions, social class backgrounds, culture patterns, and the powerful force of social mobility are reflected in value systems. When they differ among people, they give rise to conflicts. This can happen when the values of the teacher are different from those of a child. Then the teacher can help the pupil to learn that actions, language habits, forms of speech, modes of dress, and etiquette are connected with social class, and that the

---

[12] See N. Belth, "Barriers," New York: Anti-Defamation League of B'nai B'rith.

person who wishes to move from one class to another must learn the ways of the class to which he wants to belong. Such learning is not accomplished by punishing the child who does not conform to the teacher's standards. It is forwarded by the teacher who distributes his favors and rewards and his affection without discrimination, while he provides children with many experiences to practice the desired behaviors.

There are many other confusing differences in value systems. School requirements are based on one set of values that may be quite different from those of the neighborhood. The school's emphasis on promptness is in this category. In the school, rights of private property are sacred, while in the homes, siblings may own, in common, all the clothing there is, each taking what he needs. Age levels have different sets of values. This separates insensitive teachers from their adolescent pupils. Standards of personal cleanliness and what constitutes fun are examples of age differences. Children are bewildered by teachers who stress the evils of alcohol when their own good parents own taverns, and when all the advertisements they see show that people who drink live on a high standard and seem to be lovely and desirable.

Value conflicts create some of the fears, worries, anxieties, guilt feelings, and hatreds that beset junior high school boys and girls. The school must provide many opportunities for them to externalize these feelings by writing and talking about them. The teachers who are responsible for literature can do this through discussion of the people and their lives in the books that are read, the films they show, the radio plays and recordings they use. Intimate writings and role-playing are also effective devices. The most important learnings come from units of work that develop from the concerns of the students. Some of them make the approach through race, others through religion. Some are planned around the problems of delinquency, of labor and management, and some grow out of discussion of the conflicting major ideologies: democracy and communism. None of them stops with information alone. In all of them, direct experience plays a major role and out of it comes new light on human relations.

Relationships between individuals and groups and the behaviors through which relationships are expressed depend upon attitudes. The teacher, therefore, is confronted with the question, "What attitudes need to be developed and how can they be changed?" In a democracy, children need to develop positive attitudes towards intergroup differences so that they cease to be reasons for rejection. They must also develop positive attitudes towards freedom, towards responsibility, towards self and others, and towards life itself. To do an adequate job, teachers may need to consider how they can create in children a devotion and a commitment to freedom. Among the questions this raises is: what can teachers do about the confusion created in the minds of minority-group children when adults say one thing but do another, when these adults pay but lip service to the principle of the worth and integrity of every human being? Perhaps teachers need to examine the prestige which our society places upon being white, Anglo-Saxon, and Protestant.

When teachers ask: how are attitudes created and how can they be changed; psychologists, psychiatrists, and sociologists respond that part of the answer lies in creating a self-concept. A second part lies in the use of rewards and punishments—psychological as well as tangible rewards for conformance, and punishment for non-conformance, meted out by both the teacher and the group.

Success in changing attitudes is difficult to achieve when the community supports prejudice and discrimination. In such situations, the teacher finds it necessary to help the child develop the ability to think critically and the strength to stand by those judgments and decisions which are best in terms of democratic life.

Strength of mind and character grow in an atmosphere of free discussion, during which the individual can test his judgments against the group. An illustration of this principle occurred in an eighth grade class which had just seen the film, "The Toymaker." After a discussion of the kinds of people who are in conflict (represented in the film by two puppets, one of which has stripes and the other spots), the reasons for such conflict and what can be done about it—one student pinpointed the issue with the question, "But what can we do when our parents say that what we learn in school about liking and associating with people who are different is wrong?" After a few minutes of silence another student said, "Well, parents are like that, but we don't have to agree with them. That doesn't mean we have to stop liking them." Again there was a thoughtful silence which was broken by a third student who said,

"But the important thing is that when we grow up and have our children, we don't have to teach them to hate." ×

A powerful factor in developing and changing intergroup attitudes is contact-acquaintance with people who are different. The success of such contact-acquaintance is more likely if those who are brought together are fairly similar in educational backgrounds and socio-economic status. Moreover, it is most effective when the mixed group is assembled for the purpose of working together on common problems and to achieve commonly desired goals.

Teachers raise the questions: how does one find out what attitudes children have? which ones need changing? Some of the tools which the teacher can use are described in "Diagnosing Human Relations Needs," by Taba and others. These include the open-end question, the personal interview, role-playing, and the use of social distance instruments. In Trager and Yarrow's report of the study of prejudice in young children, "They Learn What They Live," the use of social episodes tests, social roles tests, and such experiences as intergroup visits and parties are described. As children play with dolls of different races or make known their preferences in answer to such questions as, "With whom do you want to work and/or to play?", some reveal prejudices, others reveal their hurts and their feelings of inferiority. Through the use of dolls and pictures, teachers are able to explore the young child's awareness and feelings about the adult social world, about the economic roles which minority and majority groups play, about occupational patterns—and thus to light the child's prejudicial stereotypes.

In their case studies of both little children and older ones, counselors have much opportunity to explore the existence of prejudice and bias. When they visit the homes of children in trouble, and of minority group children, they can there discover how parents transmit their own values, prejudices, and bigotry to their children. A study of parents' attitudes and how they transfer them to children is also reported in "They Learn What They Live."

Another principle is that to change attitudes, the influences acting on the individual must be consistently in the same direction, reinforcing each other. This will require the teacher to take stock of his own actions towards children whose religious beliefs are different. He will have to be sure to challenge those who trespass on the rights of others and, at the same time, make sure that he grants to all children their own democratic rights. The use of physical punishment, of sarcasm, of shaming and "breaking children down" will have to be stopped. Children who are in the presence of teachers after school hours will have to see them practicing what they preach with respect to free and voluntary association with all kinds of people.

Another area in which information is not enough is that of status-building. The minority group child must be given equality of status in a mixed peer group. Only then is he able to express openly his pride in his family, in the ethnic group to which he belongs, and in the religion to which he adheres. Given status, he need no longer hide, shrink away from, or deny his origins. He finds good answers more readily to his constant question, "Who am I?"

How can a child acquire equality of status in school? The teacher lets him share with the peer group his work, as well as his possessions, his personal assets of talent and ability, and his culture (songs, dances, holiday celebrations, food, language, traditions, beliefs). In order to share these things, the child tells, he shows, he teaches, and he participates with others. Second, teachers must acquaint themselves with the contributions of every culture group represented in the classroom and, as occasion permits, of groups who are not there. When freedom of religion is being discussed, for example, the story of the Maccabees might be used as an illustration. When the advancement of science is studied, the teacher doesn't forget the contributions of George Washington Carver, a Negro, and Einstein, a Jew. When the settlement of world problems is being studied, Ralph Bunche's name should be introduced.

In some schools, establishing equality of status must begin with an examination of the activity program to discover practices of discrimination and exclusion. All clubs, whether in or out of the building, need to be accessible to all children. For example, swimming, bowling, horseback riding, service clubs, and Greek-letter fraternities frequently exclude minority group children and lower-class children who do not have enough money to pay the required dues.

When the teacher shows respect for a minority group, he thereby gives status to the children who belong to that group. He helps them to consolidate their places in the class when he makes sure they have as many opportunities as others have to perform and be successful. He assures them of equality of status by rewarding and praising them in equal measure, and by giving them equal opportunity to get such status jobs as leader, recorder, and reporter for committees. It is important, however, that leadership jobs should not be given to children just because they belong to a minority group. Moreover, no child should be asked to assume leadership responsibilities when the teacher knows he is incapable of carrying them out successfully.

The teacher demonstrates that he likes a child and that he accepts the group to which the child belongs when he recognizes that child in any way. For example, when all the children alike receive birthday and "get well" letters and cards from the teachers, the minority group child realizes that he too is recognized and deemed to be of importance. If the teacher never forgets or omits minority group children, the peer group will not do so either.

In one-class, one-religion, one-race schools, another method by which the status of minority groups can be established is to develop a program of interschool visits. These visits are especially important because they afford children an opportunity to plan and engage in activities across group lines, whether these lines be of age or race, religion or social class.

A familiar intergroup activity, one which has been produced with magnificent and dramatic effect in some cities, is the folk festival. Here parents, teachers, children, city officials, and representatives from the organized ethnic groups in the community join in collecting, displaying, and appreciating folk ceremonies, dances, costumes, songs, and characteristic foods.

When children and teachers go on trips together, the teacher has an excellent opportunity to provide status-building experiences for minority group children by walking with them, helping them, talking with them, and learning how they play and think and how they live at home. Such a trip might be a simple walk around the neighborhood, or attending a nearby theatre to see a film—especially one that is relevant to intergroup problems existing in the school. Sometimes a teacher can arrange brand-new experiences, for example, attending the legitimate theatre or a concert, going on a hike or a picnic in the country, on a visit to a farm, or even on a camping trip.

Representatives of all the groups present in the community and in our democratic civilization should be among the important speakers invited to address school assemblies during the course of the year. As children arrange for these speakers by sending them letters of invitation, preparing speeches of greetings, learning how to express their thanks after the speech or to write appreciative "fan" letters, they acquire experiences which involve recognizing and accepting people of groups different from their own. The children who are members of the speaker's ethnic, racial, or religious group feel especially important at such times.

When children plan to get information they need by interviewing people in the community, the inclusion of minority group persons among those to be interviewed gives status to the children who belong to the same groups.

Discussion of people, their behavior, and the problems they face as related in films, radio plays, TV productions, literature, and newspapers helps all students to recognize that minority group people live and think and act in the same way that people of the majority group do. The documentary film, *To Live Together,* a study of children at an interracial camp, is one such discussion resource available to teachers. *Books Are Bridges,* published by the American Friends Service Committee and the Anti-Defamation League, is a bibliography of stories that can also be used for this purpose. Another excellent list of books is *Reading Ladders* by Helen Trager, published by American Council on Education, Washington, D. C.

When creative work in art and composition has been done, it is extremely important that the products of all the children receive recognition. Every story and every picture should be mounted with equal care and should be displayed at some time. Too often, only the papers of those children who are at the top of the ladder of achievement and accomplishment are displayed. Too often, the children who receive this kind of recognition are children of the preferred social class, race, and religion.

At many grade levels in both elementary and secondary schools, specific units of learning deal with the immediate community. In the course of these, pupils gain insight into the nature of the population. This gives them an opportunity to study minority groups and is, therefore, one of the most fruitful ways of establishing the status of minority group children. If the local neighborhood is a homogeneous one, the next learning unit can deal with the study of a nearby neighborhood that is mixed or changing in character.

Learning activities should include: making a map, walking around the neighborhood; interviewing people in the neighborhood; role-playing or play-acting neighborhood relationships; writing stories (those who cannot write alone can participate in group writing); using a "guess who" game; painting pictures of the neighborhood; visiting shops, factories, industries to see people at work and to interview them on the job; visiting the various kinds of churches; planning and having parties in school and in the homes, and evaluating and role-playing after the party is over; inviting guests, particularly of minority groups, for parties, for lunches or teas, arranged by the children through the Home Economics department; using a cartoon book such as *The Rabbit Brothers*[13] to study the values of people; singing songs such as *Little Songs on Big Subjects* and "Songs of Friendship," as well as the folk songs of the many groups represented in the neighborhood. A culminating activity to consolidate gains might be holiday celebrations— those of all the groups represented in the class or the school or the neighborhood. Some could take place in the school, others in the homes and in the churches.

Audio-visual aids provide an excellent means by which minority group children can be recognized and have their status established, when these aids are properly used in the classroom—which means that they are never used for entertainment purposes but are always introduced, always connected with what is going on in the classroom and always followed up with appropriate discussion. Excellent films for such purposes are, *The Toymaker, An American Girl,* and *The High Wall.*

Role-playing is an especially effective follow-up technique. Here, students imagine and role-play the episodes which might occur next or replay some of the episodes to try out different ways of behaving. Another device to secure good follow-up discussion is to assign sub-groups to watch specific characters as the film proceeds, in order to gain greater insight into individual behavior. After a film, children who are able to do so can rewrite some of the episodes or write new ones. Creative art work can also be based on such films.

Events in the community and on the national and international fronts, when discussed in the classroom, give status to children belonging to those racial, national, and ethnic groups which are the focus of attention in the newspapers, on television, and on the radio.

In all classroom discussions, teachers must be constantly alert to

---

[13] Pamphlets of this nature are published by the Anti-Defamation League of B'nai B'rith, 515 Madison Ave., New York 22, N. Y.

the use of derogatory stories, supposedly factual statements, and stereotypes. They must never fail to challenge and examine such stories and statements for truth, and must always subject prejudicial stereotypes to reality testing.

The achievement of equality of status is strengthened when the contributions of minority groups to American history are not omitted.

Perhaps the area of establishing equality of status can best be summarized by saying that teachers must act positively toward minority group children. They must no longer attempt to ignore them, hide them, or send them undercover. A child cannot endure rejection—hearing people say he is "not one of us" or "he doesn't do things our way." Teachers must stop pretending that minority groups do not exist, or that they are quaint and interesting, or that all people are alike under the skin. Difference must be recognized, it must be made acceptable, and it must be appreciated for its contributions to our culture. Understanding the potentiality and significance of difference in our culture is of primary importance. This is the heart of the philosophy of cultural pluralism.

In traditional schools, human relations function in the extra-curricular and home room activities: student elections, pep rallies, ticket sales, planning for programs and parties, and guidance lessons. Home room advisers do their best to know and help the members of their groups. Counselors, where they are employed, make contacts with many children. Disciplinary cases become well known to the principal. However, the kind of program which has been described here cannot come into being until the basic organizational structure of the school day has been changed so that teachers are responsible for knowing and working with much smaller numbers of children. The new organization must also provide class periods that are long enough for people to *live* together as they work and learn.

When departmentalization gives way to organization of the day so that it includes periods longer than forty-five minutes, pupils are at once less confused. Where before they were rootless and sure that no one cared, they become more secure and feel wanted.[14] Where before they paid little attention to guidance lessons, did a

---

[14] This has been the experience in many schools where teachers who do not use unit teaching, but who have pupils for more than one period a day, are willing to admit the benefits of the plan.

little reading *about* human relations, and paid lip service to character and citizenship ideals, they soon find themselves in situations
that require the practice of good human relations as they react and
interact with each other. Changes in attitudes and behavior occur
when teachers and children have the chance to work and play with
many different kinds of people whom they like because they are
good and whom they respect because they are worthy.[15]

[15] Trager and Yarrow, *They Learn What They Live*. New York: Harper &
Bros., 1952.

Education in human relations does not mean that a new course
is to be added in the junior high school. Human relations must
seep into every part of the program and be manifest in every classroom and activity. The basis for it is knowledge of self, of the
emotional side of adolescent life, of the relations with other people
that concern the students, of the community, of the kind of society
that exists in America, and of the great human issues that face the
civilized world. Among the outcomes to be expected from it are
deeper and broader concepts of democracy. Through the learning
activities that it requires, junior high school students will go out
into life better equipped to handle their family relationships and
to avoid family strife and breakdown. They will be better citizens
more capable of thinking clearly about such matters as civil rights
and civil liberties, and able to participate in programs for the
betterment of living conditions for all people. They will have
something of a philosophy of life which will include more satisfactory answers to the questions: What human differences really matter
and what ones do not? What does equality mean? What constitutes
freedom? What is the meaning of "the worth and integrity of the
human being"? How does one live who believes in the fatherhood
of God and the brotherhood of man?

Learning Activities for Members of Pre- and In-Service Teacher Education Classes

In addition to reading, use other kinds of learning experiences such as:

1. Writing about racial differences.
2. Surveying the ethnic elements in your class.
3. Planning a classroom experience designed to give equality of status
to members of a minority group.

4. Showing a film dealing with human relations. Many are available from the Office of War Information, the National Conference of Christians and Jews, The March of Time, the Anti-Defamation League of B'nai B'rith, Brandon Films, and other agencies. Follow the screening with a discussion of the use of such films in the junior high school.

5. Holding a panel discussion on the issue of segregation in public schools, or on discrimination in institutions of higher education.

References

BOOKS

American Association for Health, Physical Education and Recreation, *Developing Human Relations through Health Education, Physical Education and Recreation*. The Association, Washington, D. C., 1951.
Bigelow, Karl W. (ed.), *Cultural Groups and Human Relations*. New York: Teachers College, Columbia University, 1951.
Goodman, Mary Ellen, *Race Awareness in Young Children*. Cambridge, Mass.: Addison-Wesley Press, Inc., 1952.
Kaplan, Louis, *Mental Health and Human Relations in Education*. New York: Harpers, 1959.
Packard, Vance, *The Status Seekers*. Philadelphia: David McKay, 1957.

PERIODICALS AND PAMPHLETS

Alpenfels, Ethel, *Sense and Nonsense About Race*. New York: Friendship Press, Inc., rev. ed., 1959.
Anti-Defamation League, *Freedom Pamphlets*. B'nai B'rith, New York.
Cummings, Howard H., *Improving Human Relations*. Washington, D. C.: National Council for the Social Studies, 1949.
"Dealing with Fear and Tension," *Service Bulletin No. 24*, Washington, D. C.: Association for Childhood Education International, 1952.
Noar, Gertrude, *Information Is Not Enough*. Anti-Defamation League, B'nai B'rith, 1958.
One Nation Library Series with Supplements for Teachers, Anti-Defamation League, B'nai B'rith:
    Prejudiced—How Do People Get That Way?, William Van Til
    What We Know About "Race," Ashley Montagu
    Civil Rights, Justice William O. Douglas
Resource Units for Teachers, Gertrude Noar. New York: Anti-Defamation League, B'nai B'rith:
    Prejudice and Discrimination
    Desegregation in the Public Schools
    Human Rights

CHAPTER FOUR

Some Applications of
the Nature of the Learning Process

Instruction is . . . the process of guiding and directing the experiences of children to the end that they learn. . . . Instruction in the school should consist of the guidance and direction of the experiences which children have there so that behavior patterns in harmony with the objectives of education will emerge.

Schools should be learning laboratories. . . . Classrooms . . . should cease to be lesson-hearing rooms. Rather they should be centers where children engage in the activities that will lead to the learning that is socially desirable.

> Anderson, Whipple and Gilchrist, "The School As a Learning Laboratory," *Learning and Instruction*, 49th Year Book, Part I, Chapter XIII, page 337. Chicago: The National Society for the Study of Education, 1950. Quoted by permission of the Society.

In the junior high school, as in all other educational institutions, the objective of instruction is learning. Teachers commonly show dissatisfaction with the children because they do not accomplish the desired goals. The obvious answer, it would seem, would be for the instructional personnel to examine their techniques in the light of the best that is known about the nature of the learning process. Such study, however, is not commonly found in large numbers of schools. In fact, there are many teachers who are unable to put into words any of the principles of learning upon which their teaching methods presumably are based.

It is necessary for teachers to recognize the fact that "learning is not a simple, isolated, discrete process, and (that) desirable learning cannot be achieved by the A-B-C procedures, rules, regulations that masquerade in its name."[1] Hopkins says the conditions which contribute to a conception of learning are six: (1) The philosophy of life of the group in which it takes place; (2) the available information concerning child growth and development in the specific culture; (3) the traditions or the existing theories back of the traditions; (4) the experimentation of the psychologists; (5) a theory of knowledge and experience; (6) the results of practices in the American schools.

G. Lester Anderson and Arthur I. Gates state the elements which are essential in a learning situation to be "environmental stimulation of a living, motivated organism; incentives which when attained will lead to satisfaction of the motives; and at least a temporary blocking or inability of the learner to respond in ways that will enable him to gain the incentive. . . . Need, wants, interests, and sets are terms which are used to refer to motivating conditions . . . When satisfactions of a motive are blocked, the learner under appropriate stimulation, makes a series of responses. . . . These successful responses are ultimately stabilized as variability is reduced. . . . The attainment of the incentives . . . with consequent satisfaction of the motive is the condition that determines which responses will be retained (learned)."[2]

They further illustrate this statement in diagrammatic form, as shown on the following page.

If modernization of instruction is to be accomplished in the junior high school classroom, the teachers must be able to translate the foregoing analysis of the processes into actual teaching-learning situations. They must see it as a base on which to build their plans for the daily work they do with both individuals and groups of pupils. Furthermore, they must realize that the same principles are to be implemented in all of the aspects of life in which they are responsible for helping to bring about behavior change (learning).

The following illustrations are designed to help teachers and prospective teachers to put into practice this theory of learning in

---

[1] L. Thomas Hopkins, *Interaction: The Democratic Process.* Boston: D. C. Heath & Company, 1941.

[2] Anderson and Gates, *The General Nature of Learning,* 49th Yr. Bk. Part I. *Learning and Instruction.* Chapter I, page 16. Chicago, Ill.: The National Society for the Study of Education, 1950, quoted by permission of the Society.

connection with the teaching of a tool subject (how to read), teaching a thought process (how to make a wise decision), and teaching a social skill (how to introduce people to each other).

Stated very simply, learning begins when a person moves in the direction of getting something that he wants. It continues as he

ESSENTIAL ELEMENTS IN A LEARNING SITUATION

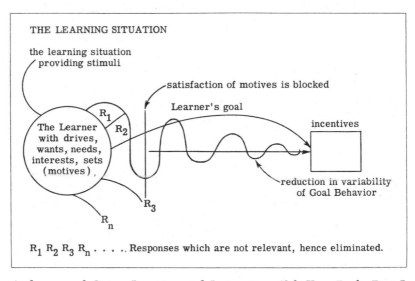

Anderson and Gates, *Learning and Instruction,* 49th Year Book, Part I, Chapter II, Chicago: The National Society for the Study of Education, 1950. Reproduced by permission of the Society.

meets with some degree of success and modifies his behavior accordingly. In terms of the junior high school pupil, *learning is dependent on his recognition of a feeling tone as one of desire or need.* Suppose that Jack is uncomfortable in the classroom whenever reading is being done. He wriggles and squirms, hides behind his book, or even begins to misbehave more seriously. The teacher must help him to know that his discomfort has to do with his feeling of being different from the other children, or with his fear of being asked to read aloud, or because he thinks he is guilty of sin when he cannot read. Above all he must believe that *when he feels uncomfortable it may mean that he wants to or needs to learn to read.*

Next, Jack must identify the goal or end in view which he hopes will satisfy his need. In other words, he must say, "Yes, I want to learn to read so I will be up to the other kids," or "So Ma doesn't scold me anymore."

Once he has recognized the need and the goal, Jack must now accept the fact that *he* and he alone, must *do* something about it. *He therefore moves toward the end in view.* He picks up his book, opens it to the required place, tries to recognize the words, says them aloud or to himself, does what his teacher tells him to do about sounding the parts of the words he is not sure of, looks at the pictures to get the idea, and asks for help when he needs it. His teacher praises him and he feels successful. A weight seems to be lifted from his chest.

In general, *learning is a continuous process*—not accomplished at one time, or through one experience or in one situation. *Successive experiences in varying situations are required, each one of which has been modified in accordance with the learner's previous accomplishments.* In each one, the individual remembers his previous success, practices moving in the direction of his goal, uses what he learned before, avoids doing what did not work, again meets with success, and has a good feeling with which to counter the feeling of discomfort. This means that the next time books are distributed Jack will not feel afraid. The teacher will not have to tell him what to do. Instead he will use his learning and pick up the book before he is told to do so. He will find the place and, remembering the words he learned before, he will try new ones the way he did before. He will ask for help with more confidence, knowing that it will be given freely. Again Jack feels happy and successful. Obviously, this process takes much longer to accomplish than the simplified illustration may imply.

Learning is evidenced by behavior change. If Jack feels just as badly on the second day, if his teacher must again talk things over with him, if he makes no move to use his book until he is told to do so, the teacher knows that no learning has yet taken place. In that event, he considers what factor in the learning situation requires change. Were there too many unknown words in the book? If so, an easier one must be provided. Did Jack not know the sounds of any letters or syllables at all? If so, then he must be taught these today before he is given a book. Are eye defects present? The medical record must be consulted and, if necessary, glasses provided. Did anyone laugh at the boy? That must be stopped so that no feeling of shame or self-consciousness will slow up the forward motion. Did the teacher push the boy aside, reject him by word, look, or gesture, or show impatience at his questions? Rejection must not be allowed to block the learning process.

As behavior changes, learning is accelerated and consolidated. With every gain, the experience situation which is set up needs to be changed so that progress continues. Jack's easy book will be replaced by a harder one. A few minutes' help alone before class begins will be discarded in favor of a place in the small group receiving special attention. A pal will be assigned to assist in a practice period. As soon as possible, Jack will be given a chance to tell his committee something he has found for them in the newspaper. Then he will help the committee when it reports to the class by reading the list of words they want the whole group to learn.

It will be helpful to spell the learning process out in terms of a social skill. Teen-agers are very much embarrassed over the problem of making introductions. They do not know what to say or how to act. In elementary school they were probably told, but somehow they just can't seem to remember. Maybe they know the words, but cannot connect them with action in a specific situation. As yet there is no evidence in behavior that the skill has been learned.

The seventh graders are reaching the end of the orientation unit. They have decided that parents ought to know something about the school of which they are so proud and in which they already feel at home. A parents' reception has been suggested, and plans are under way.

Mary says, "Shall we introduce our parents to you (the teacher)?" "How about to the other parents?" asks Harry. "And what about to other kids?" sings out Joan. "Suppose the principal, Mr. Big, comes in. What'll we do about that?" sighs Sheila. So *the need* they have in common *is out* in front of the children and the *desire to learn is being felt and recognized* by all of them. The students and the teacher move forward into the second learning situation.

Maybe some of the pupils can remember what their parents say when company arrives at home and the guests are being introduced to each other. The teacher suggests that they tell each other about these occasions. *Facts are gathered from people.* Lila says, "Well, when it is a formal kind of party my father says, 'May I present Mrs. Smith to you,' but other times we say, 'Mrs. Jones, I should like to have you meet Miss Black.' " Some of the children look askance at this. In their two room apartments visitors are seldom seen. Everyone in their streets knows everybody else; so the teacher speaks to one of them: "Jim, tell us how you introduce a new boy who comes to live next door to you." "Gosh, Mr. Better, we just say 'Hello, what's your name?' " Many pupils are now seeking the chance to tell of their experiences. Ben moves in with, "When we have a substitute teacher Mr. Big always says to us, 'Boys and girls this is Miss Miller, your teacher for today. Miss Miller, this is 7A4.' " Others are heard from, and each illustration seems to be different from the rest.

The children are quick to see that circumstances, the ages of the people involved, and the customs of the family and neighborhood are among the factors to be considered. They decide that *books might help them to gather facts.* One girl remembers some literature books she read in which such social customs are used. A committee of good readers volunteers to hunt up the places in several books they know are in the library closet in the room, and have them ready to read to the class next day. A boy suggests using etiquette books written by Emily Post and other authorities which he saw in the school library. A committee is sent for them, and will have its report ready the following day. Some one says that they could all ask their parents and older brothers and sisters that night. They agree to do this for homework.

Recognition of need in relation to a goal came first. Gathering of information moved the learners forward. The third situation involves the determining of forms to be used at the reception, and practicing the skill. Committee reports are called for and discussed. Then a variety of demonstrations are given. These provide practice for the children taking the roles and vicarious experience for the others. The facts are out; decisions are made. The pupils accept this as a semi-formal occasion. They agree to present their parents to the teachers and to the other parents by saying, "Mr. Better, I want you to know my mother, Mrs. Blank." They also decide that it would be best to use the same form for all, so as not to get confused. Many children say they feel better about the whole thing, but are not yet ready and suggest a fourth learning experience. Again the *situation has to be changed. Practice of the skill is now required.*

Next day, therefore, a plan is devised in which everyone will have the chance to practice. Groups are organized. Observers are selected. Individual pupils think up as many different kinds of roles as they can. Observers criticise and correct until it seems as if everyone shows by his behavior that the skill has been learned. Now all are *experiencing success* in a play situation.

The test of learning lies in behavior in a real situation. The teacher looks for this during the reception that takes place at the end of the week. He finds it in varying degrees in most of the children, but realizes that some are still uncomfortable, that a few revert to very familiar introduction forms, and that one or two permit their parents to introduce themselves. He makes a mental note to let those pupils who still have not learned the skill practice it through role-playing during the evaluation discussion which he has scheduled for the following day.

It is important to have one more illustration of how learning takes place. This will be in the area of learning such thought skills as those involved in making wise choice, which requires both critical thought and the use of good judgment.

The class is approaching the point of deciding what the center of interest shall be for the unit of work to be done during the next six weeks. There has been trouble in the neighborhood and even in the school building. Several youngsters have been sent to the House of Detention. The newspapers have been playing up cases of juvenile delinquency. Children are saying to each other more or less in fun (but anxiety is also detected by the sensitive observer), "I don't want to be a J.D., do you?" A large group in the class wants to move into a unit dealing with the causes and prevention of juvenile delinquency.

Mr. Brown says, "But wait a minute. We will have to find out something about what is going on in other classes before making a decision." "No, we don't," says Sam. "We've just as much right to study delinquency as they do." "But what about materials?" counters Mr. Brown. "Oh there are slews of it. I saw the files in the library the other day," offers Mary. "How about trips?" asks Sue. "Yes, if too many people want to go to the same place then none of us will get to go anywhere," answers Jim. "Don't worry about that. There are enough places to go to take care of us," returns Tom.

With the obvious *enthusiasm and need acting as intense motivating forces,* the teacher gives in. The next day, content is planned and the group moves into the fact finding stage. Books are hauled down from the shelves. A committee goes for the newspapers. They return empty handed. Miss Smith's class is working on delinquency, and yesterday they arranged to get the papers this period every day for the next three weeks. A second committee flies to the library. The children return empty handed. All fugitive materials are out in other classrooms. Other groups had got there first. A third committee goes across the street to the public library. They return empty handed. The librarian said, "All books are out. Pupils have been coming for them all during the past week. It seems to me that too many classes are working on delinquency right now."

Meanwhile, planning for learning activities that do not involve the use of books is also under way. A requisition is prepared and sent to the office for bus service for a trip to the City Hall. "Sorry," says the secretary, "all buses are booked up, and two classes have already arranged to go there. You know that no more than two are permitted to go to City Hall in any one month, don't you?" When this has been added to the reports on the reading materials situation, the class recognize that they must stop and consider what is to be done.

The teacher says, "Let us look at the situations as they were set up, and the learning experiences that were involved." As they do so the children find that there was the period of discussion in which questions were raised—a first step in learning how to think critically. Objections were overruled too easily. The second learning experience was one of failing to gather all the facts, but everything the teacher said was ineffective. The pupils had moved in the direction of attaining their goals and felt successful as they carried out their plans. This feeling made them believe that their choice had been a wise one.

The third learning situation was one in which they planned to gather facts from books, papers, and the officials at the City Hall. Here the wisdom of their choice was to be tested. Now the experience did not bring success. The pupils could not move forward toward their goals.

The fourth situation was the evaluation discussion in which mistakes in thinking and errors in judgment were recognized. The original conversation will be retraced in that discussion. The children will find different things to say which will reveal more critical thought. In other words, this situation will afford a period for practice of the thought skills which are to be learned. The teacher will change it in accordance with the progress the children have made to date. The resulting conversation will probably run like this:

MR. BROWN. Wait a minute. We will have to find out something about what is going on in the other classes before we make a decision.

SAM. No, we don't. We have as much right as they do to study juvenile delinquency.

MR. BROWN. But what about materials?

MARY. There was lots of it when I was in the library the other day.

JAMES. We better go see, though. I know that 9A-6 chose juvenile delinquency only yesterday. They may have taken the folders and books out by now.

SUE. How about trips?

JIM. Yes, if too many classes want to go to the same places, none of us will get to go anywhere.

TOM. I guess we ought to put down some of the places we could go, like City Hall and the police station, and go find out in the office.

ALBERT. Well, let's go get the facts about books, papers, and trips at once and reserve our decision until we have them.

MR. BROWN. This is good thinking and good judgment. I'm sure that when you come to the point of making a decision it will be a wise one.

As this situation unfolds, the pupils experience praise and reward from the teacher who shows in gesture and facial expression that he is pleased. Nods of approval come from classmates, too. In addition to finding out how their faulty thinking led to failure and disappointment, they now feel successful because they are able to correct the situation and move forward into a wiser choice, using the skills they have just been practicing.

Each of the three illustrations above has been developed to show that learning takes place in real life situations and experiences in which the learner identifies his need; wants to satisfy it; sets up his goal; moves toward the acquisition of knowledge, be it information or skill; modifies his behavior in accordance with success because that makes him feel good; and with each successive practice comes nearer to the goal until the learning becomes evident in his changed behavior.

Dr. Kilpatrick has said, "Since growing is learning and learning is strictly personal, the child must himself practice all the directions in which he should grow including exercise in judging and choosing . . . increasing self-direction, decreasing control by us, but all during childhood our part is positive, to help forward the process."[3]

Learning Activities for Members of Pre- and In-Service Teacher Education Classes

In addition to reading try some of the following:

1. Plan a lesson in two ways: (1) when teaching is based on the mind storage theory of learning; (2) when teaching is based on the experience theory of learning.

2. Outline the steps you would take to teach a specific skill in a tool subject; to teach an attitude; to teach appreciation of something beautiful.

3. Arrange a panel discussion on the value of direct experience.

4. Using your group as a class, try out various techniques to motivate interest and the desire to learn.

References

BOOKS

Association for Supervision and Curriculum Development, *Learning and the Teacher*. Washington, D. C.: 1958 Yr. Bk.

Fleming, Charlotte M., *Teaching: A Psychological Analysis*. New York: John Wiley and Sons, 1958.

National Society for the Study of Education, *Learning and Instruction*. Chicago: University of Chicago Press, 1950.

Ibid. "Integration of Educational Experiences," 57th Yr. Bk. Part III, 1958.

Smith, B. O. et al., *A Study of the Logic of Teaching*. Urbana, Ill.: Bureau of Educational Research, 1960.

---

[3] William H. Kilpatrick, "Behavior Problems." *Childhood Education*, 1928.

PERIODICALS

Baldwin, A. L., "How Children Learn," *Educational Leadership,* September, 1958.
Eberman, P. W., "The Common Tasks of Teaching and Learning," *The Elementary School Journal,* March, 1959.
Freehill, M. F., "How We Learn," *N.E.A. Journal,* May, 1958.
Kowitz, G. T., "The Motive to Learn," *Elementary School Journal,* April, 1959.
"Learning and the Teaching Process," *Educational Leadership,* December, 1955.
Tyler, Ralph W., "Conditions for Effective Learning," *N.E.A. Journal,* September, 1959.
Waetjen, Walter B., "Myth and Fact about Learning," *Educational Leadership,* Oct. 1960.

PART
TWO

*Many Share
the Responsibility for
Creating the Program*

CHAPTER FIVE

Teacher Education

The work of the teachers in educating citizens of the world is not spectacular, yet it may prove, if time be given, the most effective answer to the threat of life on our planet and the surest hope in using man's great powers for man's benefit.

> Report of Citizenship in the Training of Teachers, Report of the Association of Education in Citizenship, New York, Oxford U. Press.

At the same time that the principals of junior high schools are struggling with problems of curriculum development in their in-service education programs, and teachers are experimenting in their classrooms, teacher training institutions are conducting courses for teachers in service, and are preparing undergraduates to hold teaching positions. If the junior high school of tomorrow is to become a reality today, the college departments of education will have to do more to provide the kinds of courses that are needed.[1] This means that in addition to such courses as Educational History, Theory, Philosophy and Psychology, Human Growth and Development, and Social Science, they must offer courses in Classroom Techniques and in the Nature of Unit Construction and Teaching.

In addition to emphasizing modern curriculum content and methods, the courses themselves will have to be conducted in such fashion that the members of the classes will experience the kinds of learning experiences that they in turn will be required to use with children. In time, it is to be hoped, some of these same techniques

---

[1] See *We Look At Curriculum Growth*, New Jersey Secondary School Teachers Association, 1952 Year Book.

will find their way into other courses in which their use is appropriate.

This chapter discusses the use of modern techniques in the college class for teachers. Many instructors will find in it the methods they now use. Others may think that these suggestions are too pat because they themselves have better ways of teaching teachers how to teach. Others, wishing to take the first steps away from traditional practices, will find the following pages helpful.

In courses for teachers on both the pre- and in-service levels that are designed to give insight into the arts and science of teaching, *process* becomes *content*. The instructor faces the necessity of setting up experiences out of which the members of his class will learn not only *what the processes are* but also *how to use them*. It is not only justifiable, but essential for him to devote time and effort to these direct experiences in method, if he sincerely wishes to prepare his students for the job of teaching today's as well as tomorrow's children in their modern schools.

The *how* is rarely learned by reading about it. This is as true with adults as it is with the young. "We learn what we live." Inexperienced graduates and teachers in the schools voice the same reasons for not changing their classroom techniques. They say "We were taught by the lecture-reading-memorization-recitation-test techniques. If they want us to teach differently, why don't the college professors show us how? Unless we observe them and unless we have a chance to learn by these modern methods, we cannot use them in our schoolrooms."

The call for modern techniques in the college classrooms has not gone unheard.[2] Wherever serious attention is being given to the preparation of teachers for core curriculum in the public schools, the use of modern content and methods is required. The changes that have been made were reported at a National Conference in Cleveland, Ohio by Dr. Harold Alberty, the chairman of a committee of the Association of Supervision and Curriculum Development, whose purpose it is to study the preparation of core teachers. He spoke of three trends: (1) assignment of undergraduates to do student teaching in schools having core curriculums; (2) readjustment of major and minor courses, use of broad fields courses, and

---

[2] For a list of colleges, see Grace Wright, *Core Curriculum*, Bulletin No. 5, 1952. Federal Security Agency, Office of Education, Washington, D. C.

use of large problems of living as centers around which courses are developed; (3) introduction of professional courses and seminars on core teaching.

Large numbers of college teachers, on the other hand, who have had no background experiences with other than traditional methods express doubt about the possibility of departing from them. Moreover, they, like the public school teachers, face the limitations of fixed furniture, crowded lecture halls, traditional course content, textbooks that are not suited to modern procedures, and inter-departmental or personal hostilities. The following suggestions have been developed to help them. The procedures outlined in this chapter are typical of those in use in many schools. It is important that the instructor who is interested in trying them out realize that they are not set patterns to be rigidly followed, but, rather, that he must adapt them to the specific conditions under which he teaches.

As the instructor begins to use these techniques he must give thought to the physical aspects of the classroom. Since the immediate objectives of the first meetings of his group include the establishing of rapport among the students and with the teacher, a room with movable furniture is highly desirable. If it cannot be secured, decisions concerning the use of the existing furniture have to be made. Problems such as these can become obstacles, but should not be used as reasons for not going on.

The first experience with a class should be devoted to *getting acquainted.* The teacher himself needs to know certain things about the composition of the group, and the members of the class want to know about each other. As the instructor gets the information from the students, he, or one of them, can record the findings on the board. The statistics accumulated in this way may include the states from which the students come; the sizes of the cities or towns; the kinds of schools in which they teach; and if this is an in-service group, the kinds of schools in which they had their past experiences, any kinds of work experiences they may have had, the kinds of teaching or administrative positions they now hold, and the kinds of schools in which they now work. The group will most certainly want to know these same facts about the background and experience of their teacher.

Exploration of the composition of the group, however, does not mean that the students now know each other. A face to face experience is needed. The class can discuss the manner of accomplishing this, and the instructor ought to be ready to make some suggestions to them. A good plan is to form small conversation circles or buzz groups. If furniture is fixed, students may have to stand, or sit on table tops or desks. The decision about how to form the groups should be made by the group before the circles are formed; a signal should be identified which will call the group together again.

At the close of the period, a brief discussion will be necessary in order to determine whether or not the time was sufficient to accomplish the purposes and in what manner the members of the small groups are to be presented to the rest of the class. In all probability, part of the next meeting of the group will have to be devoted to completion of this experience. Then discussion should be turned to the meaning of the experience in terms of teaching children. Attention must be called to the need for preparing pupils to move furniture quietly; for having one person in each group responsible for leadership; for observing the rights of all to be heard and to speak.

When adult teachers have engaged in a direct experience they are in position to notice the effect of it upon themselves and to transfer this to their pupils. For example, they will understand the emotional release, the relaxation of tension, the importance of the peer group, and the reasons why time devoted to such an experience is time well spent.

There are many things that the teacher can learn about the members of the group from this initial experience. This is true for the teacher in the junior high school as well. Among them are the relative amount of poise possessed by the students, their individual honesty in their relationships with people, the distribution of leadership ability, the range of language usage and indications of differences in social class.

When the business of getting acquainted and its implications are out of the way, the teacher needs to clarify for his class the amount of reading that he expects them to do. This requires discussion of bibliography lists which are included with each chapter in this book. Instead of assigning readings, however, it is well for the teacher to find out first with which publications members of the class are familiar, whether or not they want to make additions to the lists, and to tell them about some of his own favorites and why they are important. Discussion should include the various ways in which readings can be shared, notes about them recorded, reports on them given. Early clarification of reading requirements gives the group security and assures the teacher that outside work will begin. If the group is new to the college, a class period should be spent in the library as soon as it can be arranged. There the librarian can help the students to find materials and they, in turn, can make their needs known to her.

Up to this point there has been no exploration of the general content of the course and that is now of first importance. It will be a new experience for members of a class to participate in the planning of content, and it can best be done by introducing the fact that learning experiences of all kinds should be tuned to the needs, interests, abilities, and objectives of the learners. This makes it necessary to discover what problems are common to all, those in which small parts of the groups wish to be involved, and which ones individuals may wish to work on as their specific responsibilities. The second kind of direct experience, then, is *teacher-pupil* planning of content.

Since the members of the group have already participated in planning the previous experiences, they are better prepared at this point to discuss ways in which the clarification of problems can be done. Among those for which the instructor should be ready are the following possibilities: Each member of the group can state his interests while someone writes them on the board. Everyone can write a paragraph or a list on paper, and these can be given to a committee to organize with the help of the teacher. Small cross-section groups, or groups formed specifically around common needs or similarities in background, can be formed for discussion. Such groups would need to be directed to explore the field, clarify thought, develop the main issues and formulate questions. If the sub-group method is chosen by the class, they should also decide how the groups are to be formed. Their attention will again have to be called to signals to stop noise, signals to reassemble as a class, to the need for selection of leader, recorder, and reporter for each circle, and to the necessity for conserving time.

While groups are engaged in discussion, the instructor will want to circulate among them. In some cases he may be needed to start things going; in others he will have to clarify procedure. Some groups will want to spend their time discussing problems instead of formulating questions, and he may need to point out the distinction. Occasionally, no one in a group is willing to take leadership, and time is wasted unless the instructor is at hand to settle the issue.

When sufficient time has been allowed, the groups should reassemble to hear reports, to list the questions, to organize the problems into a framework. The teacher should be ready to add any that have been forgotten and that he regards as essential. It may be that the organization of the questions presented will be such that it can best be handled by a committee which can be made up of volunteers, or selected by the class. The instructor will need to direct attention to those chapters in the book that deal with the several problems that have been presented. Time should also be given to evaluation of the experience of cooperative planning, the process used, the strengths and weaknesses of the groups, and plans for improving group work. It may be possible at this point to discuss and plan for the use of the "process observer."

Although, during these experiences, attention will surely have been given to goals and objectives, it is important to have them identified and consolidated. *Setting up of individual and group goals* is a third kind of experience, the implications of which for evaluation and motivation purposes must be brought to the attention of teachers. When the members of a group know what they want to get out of group experiences, they are in position to discuss the ways and means of achieving their objectives. This will be facilitated by use of the lists of learning experiences that follow each chapter in this book. Among them are: reading; exchanging and pooling information and experiences; consulting experts and authorities in and out of the class; arranging for and listening to speakers; seeing films and film strips; listening to recordings; conducting and participating in all kinds of discussion experiences; committee work; planning and presenting all kinds of reports—individual, progress, and final group reports; role playing; observing; creative writing. It will also be necessary to discuss the ways and means of audio-visual work. The members of the class should be given the responsibility for deciding what kinds of experiences they want to have as individuals, what kinds the entire group should have, and how responsibilities should be allocated.

This part of the class work has important implications for the junior high school teacher. In the light of their immediate experiences, the teachers and prospective teachers in the group will be able to see the reasons for, as well as the problems involved in, the use of pupil-teacher planning in the modern school.

Although there has been a considerable amount of sub-group work, the class has not yet been organized into *working committees*. They are now ready for this fourth type of experience. The group must discuss and settle which of the content questions can best be handled this way; how the committees should be formed; what leadership the committee shall have and what records shall be kept; where and when meetings are to take place; what individual responsibility within the committee shall be; how frequently progress reports shall be made, and of what they shall consist; and what kind of final reports are to be made.

When all of these matters are understood, committees can be formed and the first committee meetings held in the classroom. At the end of these meetings, time must be devoted to hearing reports. They will include the names of the officers chosen in each group, the plans that have been developed thus far, the problems of process that have arisen, and any question on which the committee is not clear. The class then should be given the opportunity to comment upon these, criticise, call for additional information, ask the committee to include forgotten points, and assist the committee to solve their problems of process.

Once again it is essential to take time out for evaluation, for learning the meaning of the experience to the participants, for directing attention to ways of improving, and for discussing the implications in terms of working with children in the junior high school.

The fifth kind of experience now gets under way. It is the job of *committee planning*. This may need to be interspersed with class discussion of how to go about planning, and what this would include. With children it is usually necessary to develop some guide lines which may be merely a set of the key words—what and what for, why and why not, how, when, where, who is to be responsible for what. Even with adults it is necessary to make sure that they know that all the committee meetings cannot occur in class time, and necessary to clarify the mechanics of scheduling meetings outside of and within the class period.

As experiences accumulate, they must be related to the junior high school classroom. The group needs to explore just what additional help pupils need to have so that they do not waste time; are secure in the feeling of accomplishment; know how to check on achievement and participation; understand what is required in the way of daily preparation; get sufficient help in dealing with behavior problems of committee members; and give time to evaluation of individual and group work.

A sixth type of experience has already been suggested and used, but needs further explanation at the time that it becomes important in the course. This has to do with the *making of reports.* Attention should be directed to the necessity for making frequent progress reports. These can take several different forms, and should be developed according to the needs of the individual or committee that is concerned, or to the necessity for keeping the entire group informed. It may be of value to organize a steering committee whose responsibility will be to keep the class moving, to check on the contributions of the several committees, and to schedule reports, meetings, speakers, consultants, screenings, trips, and other activities at the request of committee leaders and individuals. The instructor will need to work closely with such a committee.

Consideration has to be given to the timing and nature of final reports. If a series of factual reports, read from papers, is left for the last few days of the course, the class will find the experience boring and frustrating. Final reports should be concerned with meanings and implications for the classroom teachers, since the factual parts of the assignments have already been reported to the class in progress reports. There are many ways of expressing meanings besides the use of written reports. Some committees should use dramatization; others, role-playing. Some can make murals, posters, and other graphic representations. Panel discussions, forums in which two sides are presented, and quizzes are appropriate. Simulated radio and television broadcasts may be attempted. Creative people will find still other ways, if they are encouraged to do so.

It is apparent that the experiences suggested in this chapter do not correspond to classroom periods. It is impossible to predict how much time will be required to explore the implications, to make comparisons with traditional methods, to evaluate, to see films, to hear speakers, and to take care of the mechanics of classroom work.

When committees begin to present speakers, films, recordings and other teaching techniques, time should be given for discussion of children's language arts experiences in connection with preparation for and follow-up of similar experiences in the classroom. These are real experiences, in which pupils can learn to write letters of invitation and thanks, make telephone calls, introduce and thank speakers, formulate questions for discussion, present a film, and conduct discussions. Prospective teachers, as well as teachers in service, will benefit from actually using these techniques themselves, and from the constructive criticism they get from the class and the instructor.

It is important to consider the use of a formal instrument for *evaluation* purposes. A committee can be given the responsibility for the formulation of a mid-term questionnaire. If one is used, students must be made comfortable enough about it to be able to express their feelings about the course, and to tell in what ways it is not meeting their needs. On the basis of such replies, after careful consideration by the class and the instructor, changes should be made. Before the final week of the term, it would be well to have a committee set up to plan a more elaborate, final evaluation experience. Whatever the group and the teacher have decided should be the basis for the marks that have to be recorded should be taken into account here.

It has been suggested from time to time, that the implications of the experiences the class members are having are of great significance. The following suggestions, for points to be covered in these discussions, are presented with realization of the fact that complete coverage of them will depend upon the time at the disposal of the group, the maturity level of the group members, and their backgrounds of experiences and needs.

When a committee presents a film and conducts a follow-up discussion, the techniques of audio-visual education should be explored. These will involve the group in such questions as: who should be given the responsibility for reserving the projection room, the projector, and other equipment that may be needed?

Who should pre-view the film and who should prepare the presentation talk? What should be the nature of this presentation? What guide lines are needed for discussion of a film? Can buzz sessions be used effectively in the junior high school? What other methods of stimulating discussion can be tried? Should a film be shown if the class is not ready for it, merely because it is available in the building? What are the values of showing a film the second time? How can the results of seeing a film be determined?

The same kinds of questions need to be discussed in reference to the use of recordings.

When a speaker is invited, the following questions can be raised: Who should contact the speaker and how—by letter, telephone, or personal interview? What preparation is required in connection with each of those methods? Who should write letters of invitation and thanks? What should be done to prepare a speaker, and who should do it? Should questions be formulated for the discussion period? Should they be censored? Should other classes be invited to hear a speaker; if so, which ones and how should the invitations be extended? What behavior problems need to be discussed before a speaker comes? Who should set up the behavior code? Who should present the speaker, and thank him at the end of the session? What records should be made of the experience, and by whom? How should the experience be evaluated, and by whom?

Taking a trip raises still different questions: What kind of clothing should be required? Should smoking on the street be permitted? What kind of behavior should be required and who should set up those standards? What methods of accounting for the children are needed? What dangers should be anticipated? Can private automobiles be used to transport pupils? Can parents be invited, as drivers, to go with children without the teacher? Must parental consent be obtained, and how should this be arranged? Who should be entrusted with making arrangements for the trip? What are the differences between a "look-see" trip and one taken for a specific purpose? What in-school adjustments are needed and how can they be done? What are the multiple learnings to be expected from a trip and how can these be brought to the attention of other members of the faculty? How can faculty cooperation be obtained? What records of trips should pupils keep? How can the experience be re-lived for clarification purposes? Should trips be regarded as rewards for good behavior? Should troublesome children be left at home? What safeguards must be taken in respect to expenditures? How should absence on the day of the trip be handled? What are the implications when a child stays at home on such a day?

When writing of any kind is required, the following questions can be explored: Must all writings be done on uniform size paper, with a uniform arrangement, in ink? If penalties (reduced marks) are to be imposed for any reasons, should children know about them and when should they be discussed? What kind of penalties, if any, should be imposed for failure to hand in a paper on time? for illegibility? If the paper shows that the assignment was not understood, who is to blame? What should be done about it? Should the teacher require the writing of any kind of skit, story, poem, essay, and the like, which he himself could not do? What value is there in the terms "composition" and "theme"? Should perfect English be given high reward when there is faulty thought, or absence of thought? How much "red pencil" can a child be expected to take on any one paper? Should papers be re-written until they are perfect? Should the writing of papers be assigned as punishment? Should written work for a semester, or longer, be kept in the classroom? How can such a folder for a child be effectively used? How much talking is needed before writing can be done? If this differs according to individual ability, how can varying opportunities be arranged?

Every time a different type of discussion is used in the class, some aspect of the use of discussion in the classroom can be explored. The questions to be raised include: Why do children not participate in class discussions? How can smaller discussion groups be arranged and made varied? How can the tendency for all to talk at once be controlled? How and when can the teacher train the leaders? Can he gradually ease out of the leadership position? What kinds of children should be given the various roles—leadership, recorder, reporter? What records of generalizations, conclusions, or of facts revealed should be placed on the board and by whom? Should records be kept by all the pupils in their notebooks, and when should these be made? How much preparation time should be set up before a discussion begins? Should discussion be interrupted for correction of mistakes in English? If not, who should keep records of them, and when should instruction in correct usage be given? What kinds of records should be kept by the teacher? When should the experience be evaluated, by whom, and how?

As the class lives through the experience connected with committee work, it is important to watch for those occasions on which the discussion of specific techniques is appropriate. For example, absence of a committee leader on the day a report is to be given calls for discussion of the ways of developing group pressures that induce children to be more responsible for carrying out their promises and commitments. All the other manifestations of behavior and work problems that occur with pupils will show up in the adult classes. There will be instances of failure to accept responsibility or to live up to accepted responsibilities, sliding by on a minimum amount of work, inability of a group to get under way, individuals who want to do all the talking, closed-mindedness, unwillingness to accept a majority decision, inability to get a consensus, refusal to use time out of class for committee meetings, noise and its control, space for materials and work, inability to get resource materials, and many others.

Another problem that can best be understood when occasion for it arises is the timing and number of progress reports to be made by committees. Every effort should be made to get members of the group to try out all the different kinds of reporting processes and forms that are of value in the junior high school classroom. There should be times when dramatics are used. These can include the writing and production of skits, as well as the spontaneous use of psycho- and socio-dramatics. The use of posters, illustrations, and even murals can be encouraged. The very fact that of necessity they will be crude and unfinished will show that perfection of art and technique is not the desired outcome, and that the core class teacher is expected to provide only time, place, and materials, and not instruction in art.

The effect which these kinds of learning experiences can have upon teachers is expressed in the following excerpts from one of the papers written by mature and experienced teachers at the close of a summer session during which they tried them out.[3]

---

[3] University of Minnesota, 1952.

"We brought our whole selves to the class and got whole experiences. We did not 'chant back' what the teacher said. . . . Now I believe that I can do pupil-teacher planning in my classroom. I think I can listen to kids now, too, and I know more about myself. . . . It isn't the course of study that counts, it's the pattern of living. We've learned to honor each other as persons, and will carry this way of looking at people back to our faculties and schools."

The problems confronting teacher education are well stated by Theodore C. Blegen, who said,[4]

> Scholarship is fundamental, but we know all too well that it is not enough. . . . We need a glowing enthusiasm for teaching itself, an understanding of those human beings called students and of the nature of the learning process, and some clear ideas of what we are trying to do in our teaching. . . .
> We want the college teacher to know his subject and its interrelations with the world of knowledge, but we also want him to take advantage in his classroom of what man has learned about the learning process, about the art of teaching, about the art of dealing with people.

An outstandingly successful experiment on unit teaching and the use of direct learning experiences and group processes was carried on at Fredonia State Teachers College in New York State, under the direction of Daniel Roselle. It was an action research project sponsored by The Center for Community Studies of the State University. Its purpose was to demonstrate that through such an activity would come changes in the participants and in the existing situation. The center around which the project developed was the need for an experience in Nursery School Education in the community of Fredonia.

The planning was done cooperatively by the students and their teachers. In the meetings of the group they rotated leadership functions and used consensus rather than voting to arrive at decisions. Their first step was to mobilize information. For this purpose they organized their first committee so as to enlarge the scope of their reading and study by sharing the work. As other learning experiences were planned, other committees were set up and commissioned. Committees met to plan, to pool their findings, to organize

---

[4] Theodore C. Blegen, "A Movement Gains Momentum," *School and Society,* January 12, 1952.

both progress and final reports. These were given to the class, to administration, and to outside groups.

The committees prepared the way for the class to have many learning experiences: They saw films and listened to recordings and broadcasts. They observed in local nursery schools and elementary grades. They took a trip to Toronto, Canada, to interview experts and observe nursery education and broadcasting. They visited local broadcasting studios, and consulted with experts about writing and producing programs. They interviewed and studied with teachers in the college and local school system.

There was much writing to be done. Letters were sent to some thirty studios. Requests for materials went out. Letters about the programs were sent to parents. Articles and advertisements had to be prepared for the local press. Class logs, minutes of meetings, and individual diaries required different kinds of writing. The interview forms and preliminary and follow-up questionnaires had to be constructed. Trips, interviews, and speakers necessitated the writing of invitations, questions to be used, and thank-you letters. The largest job was the writing of the stories and adult programs for the two series of broadcasts they produced.

The programs could not be constructed without knowledge about the community. The students made a house-to-house survey to determine the needs and desires of the parents and the children. They also spoke to local groups of citizens—Kiwanis Clubs, Women's Clubs and PTA's. They analyzed their findings in terms of social structure of society and the existence of tensions.

Evaluation was an integral part of the total project. Fan mail was read for hints on which to base improvements of the programs. Many hours were spent discussing the weakness and strength of the project, individuals, group work, and outcomes. Logs and diaries were analyzed for evidence of growth. The basis for final grading was arrived at cooperatively. The constant need to interpret their experiences to others in the college was one of the reasons for critical review and discussion of all parts of the enterprise.

One of the questions the students were called upon to answer was, "Did you study any subject matter?" This was their answer: "We studied English—writing, speaking, dramatics; Radio—construction, programming, producing; Economics and Business—household, mass-communication; Recreation; Art—creation, appreciation, and interpretation; Child and Adult Psychology—emotional needs and how to meet them, the nature of learning, and problems of parenthood; Administration—of the college, of a project, of transportation; Social Science—the structure of society, and the nature of intergroup hostilities."

These prospective teachers said the following things about their experience: "It's a wonderful way to learn!" "It's a wonderful way to study!" "I want to teach that way!" "We learned so much more than in any other course." "We got a lot out of working together. We got to know the faculty and they got to know us as people as well as students." "We were glad to give up our leisure time—after all it was fun!" "We were willing to sit up nights to produce the best possible program." "Other students felt left out. In fact, I was sorry for them." "We gained poise, self-confidence, self-respect, and respect for each other." "We gained so much respect for the people in the town." "We built up intellectual integrity. We had to tell people what was poor about our work as well as what was good." "If all our courses used these methods, we would be a lot better prepared for teaching."

That story speaks for itself.

Teacher education institutions have given little attention to preparation of teachers specifically for teaching in the junior high school. Many educators are committed to the learning of subject matter and often are Liberal Arts enthusiasts who regard specialization in a subject to be of the greatest importance in secondary education and all that is necessary to prepare a teacher, regardless of the age level of the pupils. Liberal arts graduates who find themselves in junior high school positions are, therefore, at a distinct disadvantage because of their lack of understanding of the problems of growth and development that confront young adolescents and of the teaching methods best suited to their needs.

During the last five years, however, many colleges and universities, responding to the appeal of junior high school administrators, have offered courses and workshops on the junior high school and on core curriculum. These have been available at both pre- and in-service levels. In the summer of 1960, about one-third of the 300 leading colleges and universities surveyed offered one or more such courses. Another 15 per cent indicated that comprehensive courses in secondary education included the junior high school.[5]

Courses offered included general surveys, methods in reading, science, art, language arts, mathematics in general, the psychology of adolescence; curriculum in general and core curriculum, administration and supervision, activities and guidance. Only 11 per cent of the courses were workshops.

The institutions offering specific junior high courses are spread across the country. The number of them in some states, as compared with others, is probably an indication of the increased number of junior high schools in those states. From the character of the courses offered, the conclusion may be drawn that emphasis is being placed on core curriculum in Washington, Oregon, Kentucky, California, Colorado, Georgia, Maryland, Michigan, New York, Ohio, and Wisconsin.

References

BOOKS

Adkins, E. P., ed., *Television in Teacher Education*. Washington, D. C.: American Association of Colleges for Teacher Education, 1960.

Cantor, Nathaniel, *Dynamics of Learning*. Buffalo, N. Y.: Foster and Stewart Publishing Co., 1946.

Johnson, E., and R. E. Michael, *Principles of Teaching*. Boston: Allyn and Bacon, 1960.

Moldoon, Mary, *Learning to Teach*. New York: Harper and Brothers, 1958.

Spears, Harold, *Principles of Teaching*. Englewood Cliffs, N. J.: Prentice-Hall, Inc., 1951.

Wood, Jean Marie, *A Survey of Objectives for Teacher Education*. Washington, D. C.: Commission on Teacher Education, Association for Supervision and Curriculum Development, 1960.

PERIODICALS AND PAMPHLETS

Coleman, Mothen, and Skubic, "Liberalizing the Professional Curriculum," *Journal of Teacher Education*, March, 1960.

Hansen, R. K., "Action Research in Teacher Education," *Journal of Teacher Education*, December, 1959.

[5] Trump and Trumbo, "1960 Summer Session Courses on Junior High School Education in Colleges and Universities," National Association of Secondary School Principals.

"In-Service Education," *Educational Leadership*, Association for Supervision and Curriculum Development, March, 1960.

McConnell, G., "They Helped Us, But —," *Journal of Teacher Education*, March, 1960.

National Commission on Teacher Education and Professional Standards, *The Education of Teachers*. N. E. A., 1958.

Steffens, D. R., "Learning About Teaching," *Adult Leadership*, December, 1958.

Waskin, L. S., "Organizing for Curriculum Study," *The Bulletin of the National Association of Secondary School Principals*, February, 1959.

CHAPTER SIX

The Principal's Role

The principal is the responsible leader for the school in all of its internal and external relationships and activities. He affects [the management of learning] by the aid he gives teachers in improving their leadership practices, the relationships he has with the school community, the kind of contacts he has with the central office, and the general climate of opinion which he helps to create in his school.

L. Thomas Hopkins, *Interaction: The Democratic Process,* Boston: Heath and Co., 1941, page 338.

The principal of a junior high school has an unusual opportunity to make a significant contribution to American education in the creation of a modern school which will serve all the children of all the people. He must think in terms of meeting the needs of all the children, because the policy of keeping them with their age mates, a policy which is gaining momentum throughout the nation, will bring them all up to the seventh year. The rising compulsory age limits will serve to keep them in school through at least the ninth-year level. In the foreseeable future, however, it still seems likely that graduation from junior high school will be the only such experience for many boys and girls, for they will not remain in school for twelve years. Because the junior high school will offer these children their last opportunity for formal education, the responsibility of the principal is to create a school in which the students will continue to develop their mental and manual skills, to learn what it is that society requires of them, to learn more of the know-how needed to become contributing members of productive groups, to discover a wide range of interests which will direct their leisure activities, and to become emotionally and socially adjusted enough to escape the pitfalls of mental illness, family breakdown, and crime. This school will differ in many respects from most of the junior high schools of today.

In-Service Education

A principal takes the first step toward reaching such a goal when he accepts responsibility for directing faculty discussion, study, and action to the end that common understandings and a philosophy emerge that all accept and know how to implement.

According to a study of junior high schools in America,[1] some seventy-one of them in twenty-four states were engaged in creating modern programs. The most significant thing happening in them was the scheduling of pupils to a single teacher for a long block of time. Hundreds of the teachers in those and other junior high schools were working seriously at the job of meeting pupil needs by organizing content in new ways and by using new methods. Some called their classes "common learnings," others "core curriculum," still others referred simply to unit teaching. The important common promise in them was the breaking down of subject-matter barriers.

Spread across the nation are outstanding schools in which teachers, under the leadership of their principals and others, have accepted the challenge to create the school of tomorrow, today, and have studied, planned, experimented, and evaluated to that end. Some of the programs have been inspired by state departments.[2] Others have been led by curriculum officials in urban localities.[3] In some places single schools have plowed ahead in spite of conservative and even reactionary forces. County supervisors have played a major role in some states.[4] In other places, progressive teachers colleges and well known educators in universities have furnished leadership, consultant service to faculty

---

[1] A. H. Lauchner, "Trends in Junior High School Practices," *Bulletin of the National Association of Secondary School Principals*, December, 1951.

[2] Pennsylvania, Utah, California, and Michigan, for example.

[3] Denver, St. Paul, Minneapolis, and Arlington, Va., are good examples.

[4] In Maryland, West Virginia, and California this has been true.

groups, and follow-up service to young teachers in the field.[5]

In all in-service education programs which are concerned with curriculum change, the goals which have to be set up cannot be reached unless changes are effected in teacher attitudes. *The principal is confronted with the task of helping teachers, and all others who may be concerned, to make these attitude changes.* Teachers' attitudes toward teaching have to change. They have to see that teaching is a science, is an art, is a medium for accomplishing behavior change. Their attitudes toward children need scrutiny and, in many cases, alteration. Teachers and others have to accept children as human beings worthy of respect—all of them. They must recognize that children are our most precious resource and our instrument for preserving democracy. People need to see children, to hear them, to love them.

Attitudes toward content and its scope and sequence need modification. Teachers will not accept changes in these until they have faced the facts in some of the controversial areas. They and the principal must come to agreements about such questions as: shall content emphasis be placed primarily on facts, or on process, or equally on both? Shall major attention be given to tool subjects, or to the skills of democratic living, or are they of equal importance?

An area in which it is difficult to make attitude changes is that of evaluation. The problems to be considered are those of measurement of accomplishment, of marking, and of ways of reporting to parents. Some of the hardest issues to settle are questions such as: shall a child be judged on the basis of his ability to recite facts, or on his level of accomplishment or development, or on the rate and degree of his growth? For which of these has the school been responsible? If all of them are to be considered in making a judgment, can they be measured and equated? What kinds of marks should be recorded—letters, numbers, percentages, words, or descriptions?

Changes in attitudes are not enough to bring about changes in curriculum. A school's personnel may agree on basic philosophy but differ on their ideas about how it should be implemented. If the philosophy places emphasis on the development of good human relations in the classroom and on the use of experiences in addition

---

[5] For example, New York University, Columbia University, and the University of Minnesota.

to the use of word symbols in teaching-learning situations, then *the principal, recognizing the gap which exists between knowing what to do and how to do it, has the further responsibity for helping his staff to acquire the necessary teaching skills.* The new methods to be learned include pupil-teacher planning; the use of community resources—people, places, and things; the use of a wide variety of reading materials on a wide range of difficulty; and the operation of, as well as methods of teaching with, audio-visual equipment. In addition to these new ways of working, teachers must know how to set up experiences and situations in which pupils are encouraged to use initiative and creativity as they express their thoughts and information through art, music, the dance, construction, writing, and dramatics.

Many of the desirable changes involve deeply rooted traditions. For example, the customary regimented, repetitive drills and the demands for recitation of memorized facts have to be discarded in favor of individualized, thoughtful practice and carefully prepared and well conducted group discussions. The reliance on one text book, that is comforting to many teachers and pupils, has to be weighed against the use of many sources of information, from which readers and non-readers alike can gather the facts they need to answer their own questions and solve their own problems.

One of the most important teaching processes with which the principal and his teachers need to have facility is the group process. This requires clarification of the relative values of cooperation and competition, the conditions which call for the use of each, and the emphasis to be placed on each of them in the light of their relationship to the democratic order. The distinction between recitation and discussion, the relative values of paying attention and of participation that is evidenced in activity, and the need most children have for direct experience in addition to reading, are among the pertinent matters that require study by the faculty.

Good teachers and good principals have little trouble in reaching agreement about what they want to do for children. Strong leadership from the principal will help the teachers to accomplish their joint purposes. He must lead the way. When he places value on removal of blocks to learning, on creation of a permissive climate in the classroom, on the use of many kinds of resources—materials, people, places, and things—on recognition of the worth and integrity

of every child, on initiative, creativity, and freedom, his teachers
will make them come true in their classrooms. The speed with
which changes are brought about will depend upon whether or not
the principal makes them the substance of his in-service education
program.

A study of schools in New York State, revealed that 96.6 per cent
of 81 schools had in-service education programs. In only 48.3 per
cent, however, was leadership furnished by the principal. 77.6
per cent of the schools did not require teachers to attend or participate. Only 46.6 per cent of the programs were planned specifically for the junior high schools.[6]

Many principals in New York State and elsewhere ask, "How and
with what can we begin an in-service education program for our
own faculties?"

Some administrators use the device of a faculty committee which
has responsibility for creating a program of professional study.
Others have organized curriculum committees who do the research
and planning and report their work to the faculty. Both of these
methods work well when every one in the school accepts his own
responsibility for keeping up with new developments. The danger
lies in the unwillingness of teachers to regard service on such
committees as a privilege and an opportunity and in the gap that
is created between an "in-group" with prestige and a resentful
"out-group."

In contrast to the plans which involve only a portion of a faculty
are those which include everyone. This raises the question, do all
teachers need in-service education? Isn't it better to make this a
completely voluntary enterprise? There is little doubt that many
newly appointed teachers have idealism, enthusiasm, and theory.
On the other hand, most of them lack facility in the commonest
classroom routines. All of them have to learn how to implement
their theories. Many of them know only how they were taught,
and want to see themselves in the role of professor, sitting behind
the desk, lecturing to eager listeners. *The new teachers are in great
need of in-service education.*

Among the experienced teachers are those who recognize their

---

[6] Ross J. Willink, "In-Service Training of Junior High School Teachers,"
The Bulletin of the National Association of Secondary School Principals,
December, 1959.

need for new knowledge and skill and for increased insight and understanding of today's children in today's world. Often they readily become leaders in the program. There are apt to be just as many of them, however, who fight hard against the intrusion of anything that is modern, who refuse to read educational books and periodicals, who pride themselves on what they call their specialization and high standards, who resent and resist efforts to bring about change. Some teachers who have been in service for many years, need to find new reason for continuing to teach. Others are in danger of losing the vision of education as a service to children and to society. All of them want inspiration. *Experienced teachers are in great need of in-service education.*

Preliminary to setting up the professional study program, *the principal must study his personnel.* His strategy must be worked out in terms of the teachers' personal and professional relationships to him and to each other, in the light of whatever hierarchy exists among them, and with respect to individual and common concerns, needs, interests, and abilities. Unless it is, the plans may be ineffectual.

The first step to be taken is for *the principal to seek enterprises which will enlist teachers in study and activity.* One approach that is usually successful begins with the "gripes" that they have, but which are rarely expressed at times and in places that will facilitate action and cure. Their complaints deal with dissatisfactions over facilities, equipment, pupils' failures, the general lack of ability to read, inadequacy of materials, the promotion policies of the elementary school, the unreasonableness of the senior high school, and the indignity they suffer when they are required to give children passing marks even though their work is not up to grade standards.

Complaints about materials, equipment, and furniture can well be used to stimulate the first faculty study and activity. The principal can turn over to his teachers the regular requisition channels. He can also make any existing school funds available so that both a long and short term plan for securing what they need can be made by the teachers instead of by himself. The total resources and facilities that already exist in the building and the community can be opened for the use of the entire faculty. For example, plans can be made by the teachers, instead of by the principal, for all to share in the best of what is available. This will involve rotation of choice rooms, cooperative use of and responsibility for pieces of fine equipment, circulation of the new and most interesting books as well as the old ones. So often these things become the "property" of the senior teachers, the favorites, and the department heads. This very practical group enterprise will be an experience in identifying problems of common concern and developing plans for group action. It can be a first step toward making an effective, functioning group out of the faculty. To do that is essential if plans for modernizing the school's curriculum are to mature.

Professional study will get under way much faster if teachers have at hand the books that they need. The lack of a professional library in the school building can become the second common problem upon which to base a project. The first step will be for the teachers to identify areas in which they want to do some reading and study. The principal's leadership of such discussions is important. He will want to make sure that new and old books on educational philosophy and the nature of learning are included. Anthropology is an area in which many have done no reading, yet teachers have need for information about the races of mankind. Modern books on sociology will provide facts about the structure of American society which has deep implication for the classroom. Problems of rural and urban life need clarification. The critical controversial issues of our times have a relationship to the problems of modern education and must, therefore, be freely studied and discussed. Among these is the problem of war and peace, and what has to be done for youth to prepare them for war yet keep them tuned to the ideals of universal peace. Teachers need much information about internationalism, the United Nations, and UNESCO.

Although this proposed inter-disciplinary approach is essential in re-orienting teachers, a large part of the library must, of necessity, be devoted to books on human growth and development, adolescent problems, emotional needs, mental health, human relations, teaching techniques, and evaluation.

The importance of a professional library in the school building is so great that the principal should leave no stone unturned in his efforts to procure it. The job can become a faculty adventure in cooperative thinking and planning. Problems of many kinds have to be solved—getting the money; the room to be used; the book cases, tables, and chairs to buy; the titles to be ordered; methods to be used for circulation of the books; the organization of committees; finding the time and place to share readings and discuss plans.

Requisitioning supplies and creating a professional library are two of the many projects that can be used by a principal who wishes to give his faculty opportunities to learn how to do cooperative planning, how to set up and commission committees, and how to arrange for the giving and hearing of reports. These are experiences teachers need to have if they, in turn, are to use them effectively in their classrooms. As they work at such enterprises, *the principal must continuously interpret the process they are using in terms of classroom work with children.* This will lead into the subject of social dynamics, which teachers need to study. The faculty meetings, in themselves, will provide opportunities for the practice of processes of group dynamics and for the playing of the various roles individuals use as they carry on discussions and move into action.

The concept of leadership will be enlarged and deepened for both the principal and the teachers as the opportunity to practice it is extended to many of them. The necessity for and the know-how of creating a permissive, democratic climate characterized by friendliness, seriousness of purpose, sincerity, and industry will be demonstrated and learned during these experiences. The teachers will find it easier to use group processes in their classrooms as they come to understand the roles of discussion leader, chairman, reporter, recorder, and their own responsibilities when such roles are taken by pupils. Interest will grow as they receive new assignments, play new roles, and have new responsibilities delegated to them.

Inevitably, as the principal and faculty discuss important problems, the need for extended study in many areas will emerge. Some will want to devote themselves more specifically to problems of adolescence, others to the nature of society and its implications, still others to classroom methods. Study will not be enough, and it may become frustrating unless along with it goes cooperative planning of ways in which to put the new ideas to work in the school. Things must get done, and for this purpose it will be necessary to organize sub-groups and committees. Once again the teachers will be experiencing the methods of learning that they are to use in teaching their pupils.

The actual attack on the problem of curriculum change has to be done in the classroom and will be done there according to the individual interests of the individual teachers. Definite trends are not likely to emerge until many months have gone by. In the meantime, the principal will have to make sure that the entire faculty is kept informed of the research projects and classroom experiments that get under way in the several parts of the school. Unless he does that, suspicions and rumors may arise that will get in the way of good human relations.

Students and parents will also have to be informed of these plans, so that they, too, can understand the changing procedures they experience. If they are not admitted to the planning sessions, given the right to help to determine the goals, and permitted to engage in cooperative evaluation, anxieties and insecurities will disturb them and react badly upon the teachers. *The principal faces the task of creating and administering a series of parent-pupil-teacher meetings at which these sharing, clarifying, planning, and evaluating activities can be accomplished.*

The question of time for professional meetings is important. Many junior high schools have been accustomed to the use of a part of an afternoon session once a week for this purpose. This is not enough for a school that is engaged in a program of curriculum revision. Superintendents will not fail to see the necessity for the program. However, many of them may not be willing to allow the use of school time to accomplish it. In that case, the main argument to be used is that every bit of time spent in purposeful study results in manifold returns to the community because of the consequent improvement in the education of the children. The principal who is sure of his ground will not lack the courage to present his case.

It is entirely possible that an uninformed group of parents may stand in the way of using school time for professional meetings. They are apt to feel that children belong in school during the day. This will be less likely to happen when parents are kept fully informed about the purposes, methods, and progress of all the developments that take place in the school.

A valuable device that will help parents to accept the idea of released time is the creation of a series of jobs to be done at home, for school credit, during the hours the students are not in the building. They can best be set up cooperatively by the parents, teachers, and pupils. This will ensure variation of assignments in accordance with the objectives and environment of individual pupils. The tasks can be academic in nature, for some. For others, they might be construction of articles that are needed at home. The school may have to lend tools and materials for them, but why not permit these, as well as books, to be taken home? Some students will want to be assigned to housekeeping responsibilities—marketing, cooking, baby-sitting. There will be some who should have outside jobs at which they can earn money—running errands, delivering packages, child care, light housework, assisting storekeepers with accounts, decorating store windows, printing signs.

The time of day and the day of the week to be used for meetings have to be settled. The last hour on Friday is the wrong time for most teachers. They are too weary then, and week-end trips are delayed; this is not fair. If the last part of the day seems to be the best hour, a schedule can be devised that will alternate the days so that no one subject which may be assigned to pupils at the end of the day will suffer from too much loss. It is necessary to publish such a schedule early in the year so that parents and pupils, as well as teachers, can make their plans.

Early morning meetings are good. In a similar amount of time, more can be accomplished. If meetings are planned, parents also need to have advance information because it means that the pupils report to school later on those days. If it is customary for half of the time used for meetings to be taken from the school day, while the other half comes out of teacher time, in the morning the teachers would begin their meetings at eight o'clock, continuing until nine-thirty when the pupils would arrive.

There comes a time in the development of teachers and plans when outside expert help is needed. *The principal then has the job of providing for consultant service.* Money has to be found for this. In some places, teachers pay small registration fees for conferences. Some schools take the money out of school funds. In many districts, the cost of such service is a recognized part of the budget.

Teachers should have a share in the planning for consultant service. They should help the principal to make decisions about which areas are to be covered, whom to call in, how to set up the conference schedules. Considerable thought and preparation is needed in order to get the most return from these experiences. In

some communities, school is closed for an entire day several times
a year. Sometimes a holiday period is used. For example, if pupils
are excused for a week at Thanksgiving, teachers report for three
days of that week for professional meetings. If the regular school
day is to be used, it can be one of those that are on the schedule
for faculty meetings. The consultant will address the faculty and,
in so doing, prevent some teachers who might otherwise not have
been included, from feeling discrimination. Unassigned periods
throughout the day can be used for individual and small group
conferences. Large groups of students can be sent to the auditorium
for specially prepared programs. A few teachers can remain there
for proctoring duty while the rest can meet with the consultant.
Teachers are willing to substitute for each other in their unassigned
time when they know that the courtesy will be returned another
day.

The professional study program springs from appraisal of the
schools' program and must include constant evaluation of changes
that are made as it progresses. In the course of time, the staff will
have to make decisions about the continuation of departmentalization, modification of bell schedules, courses of study that are out
of date, and arrangements for periods that are long enough to
accomplish the purposes of guidance and direct experience methods.
This means that *the principal faces a major task—planning a
modern organization of the school.* How to schedule the core or
common learnings classes, what to do with the club program, how
to incorporate guidance in the core and eliminate the super-im-
posed home room program are some of the more difficult problems
to be settled. Along with them go questions about content—scope
and sequence, subjects to be included in the core and those to
remain in the specialized areas, methods to be used in classroom
work.

Hunting for the answers to some of the questions about content
will take teachers into the study of the issues which face the
civilized world today. They will have to give thought to the areas
and the processes of civilized life into which their students must
be inducted. The elementary school curriculum will have to be
studied in order that the teachers may know with what skills, information, and concepts their pupils are equipped when they
arrive. The philosophy and practices of the higher schools must be

investigated in order to know with what skills the students must be equipped before they leave the junior high school. Business and industrial leaders will have to be interviewed to understand their complaints about their employees and to understand how the school can help children to know and adjust to their demands.

When unit teaching begins to take place in classrooms, *the principal faces the necessity for arranging for coordination of the program.* In large schools there may be a director of instruction or a curriculum coordinator to whom the task can be delegated. Occasionally an assistant or vice-principal takes it over. Ways of recording the units that are selected in the various classes have to be devised. A chart showing them ought to be available to teachers and the administration at all times. It can be placed in the library, the faculty room, or the main office. Teachers have to learn to consult it frequently so that they know what their classes studied in previous semesters. Whenever a new unit is to be chosen by a class, the teacher has to know whether or not other classes are working in the proposed area and, if so, whether or not there is sufficient material for another class to use. When the program is being evaluated by the staff and by people interested in curriculum research, it must be possible for them to find out what units every class has studied during the years it has been in the school. Examples of such charts are given in Chapter 9.

The principal can make use of the record of the units selected in a class, to assist a teacher in his guidance and direction of classroom planning. *Improvement of teachers is another of the tasks a principal must do, as the school moves forward.* In order to be specific in teacher-principal conferences about the units that are undertaken, the teacher must have a record of what was done in the course of the unit. Records of this kind should be filed as soon as a unit is complete. The files provide much help to new teachers as well as to supervisors and curriculum coordinators. Examples of unit records are the content of Chapter 17.

Organization

Underlying all of these changes, is the change that must be made in the organizational pattern of the school day. Creating it may

WHITWORTH COLLEGE LIBRARY
SPOKANE, WASHINGTON

become the obstacle to progress. This task is usually the principal's responsibility. In large schools he may delegate it to an assistant or to a teacher who is released from some teaching periods for the purpose. Sometimes a committee of teachers does the work. In every event, however, the principal remains the one who is responsible for seeing to it that the philosophy of the school finds expression in the schedule. He cannot administer the school unless he is intimately acquainted with that schedule. His staff will be most secure when they know that he is the one who decides questions of distribution of extra assignments and classification of pupils. The teachers themselves should be consulted in regard to what grades they want to teach, what class groups they want to retain, what changes should be made in the make-up of the classes they know best.

The organizational structures of junior high schools vary in accordance with all the variable factors that have to be taken into consideration—size of building, number of teachers in relation to number of rooms, the amount of time to be given to each learning area, the subject areas to be included in the core of common learnings and the time to be devoted to it, the grades to be included in the reorganized program, the number of practical and fine arts rooms, and the capacity of the gymnasium. The plan used may be as simple as blocking time, subjects, and pupils on a departmentalized basis. This is traditional but may still be the schedule which remains in operation for some schools. It looks like this:

	1	2	3	4	5	6	7
MON.	ENG.	ARITH.	SOC. ST.	L	PHYS. ED.		HOME ROOM
TUE.	ENG.	ARITH.	SOC. ST.	U	FINE ARTS		HOME ROOM
WED.	ENG.	ARITH.	SOC. ST.	N	PRACTICAL ARTS		CLUB
THU.	ENG.	ARITH.	SOC. ST.	C	MUSIC	HYG.	CLUB
FRI.	ENG.	ARITH.	SOC. ST.	H	PRACTICAL ARTS		FACULTY MEETING

✗A similar set of required subjects is often arranged in a mosaic pattern, in the belief that the time of day affects the learning possibilities and that no one subject should have a favored place. See the schedule below. ✗

In neither of the above plans is attention given to the implementation of the philosophy of modern education. There is no long block of time. There is no provision for unification of subject areas. Activity and guidance are still apart and relegated to the last period. Translation of this into teacher schedules would mean that teachers would still be responsible for large numbers of pupils, except for the few who would be required to teach the same group of children two or more subjects. For example, 7A-1 could be sent to Miss Smith, the English teacher, for both English and Social Studies. This would reduce her pupil-load by the number in the class.

	1	2	3	4	5	6	7
MON.	ENG.	ARITH.	SOC. ST.	L	PHYS. ED.		HOME ROOM
TUE.	SOC. ST.	FINE ARTS		ENG.	L	ARITH.	CLUB
WED.	PRACTICAL ARTS		ENG.	ARITH.	SOC. ST.	L	HOME ROOM
THU.	MUSIC	SOC. ST.	ARITH.	L	ENG.	HYG.	CLUB
FRI.	ARITH.	ENG.	PRACTICAL ARTS		L	SOC. ST.	EARLY DISMISSAL

A modern school departs from the traditional pattern in the names given to subject areas as well as in the time distribution. One pattern that has had profound effect on the modernization of the junior high schools is that which is described in *Planning for American Youth,* which is the Secondary School Principals Association's implementation of *Education for All American Youth,* published in 1944 by the National Policies Commission of the National Education Association. The following diagram shows their division of the day into three parts.

HOURS → 1	2	3	4	5	6
	PERSONAL INTERESTS	COMMON LEARNINGS			HEALTH & PHYSICAL FITNESS
7	Exploration of personal abilities and individual interests; discovery of interests in art, music, science, languages, sports, crafts, home and family problems, leisure time activities.	A continuous course in social living to foster growth in personal living and in civic competence. Guidance			Includes games, sports and other activities to promote physical fitness, together with the study of individual and community health.
8					
9					

(GRADES 7, 8, 9)

In *The Junior High School Program*, published by the Southern Association of Colleges and Secondary Schools, this kind of program is implemented in the following simplified schedule:

Grades	60 Min.	60 Min.	60 Min.	40 Min.	60 Min.	60 Min.	60 Min.
7	CORE			L U N C H	EXPL.	MATH.	PHYSICAL EDUCA- TION
8	CORE		EXPL. [a]		EXPL.	MATH.	PHYSICAL EDUCA- TION
9	CORE		EXPL.		ELEC- TIVE [b]	MATH. ELECTIVE	PHYSICAL EDUCA- TION

In the above plan, mathematics is absorbed in units of work that cut across subject matter fields. Specialization is deferred to later years. Implementation of the broad field indicated in the first block would call for individual scheduling in accordance with needs, abilities, and interests. This, however, is not thought of as specialization.

A commonly used form of the general plan proposed by the National Association of Secondary School Principals unifies the areas of the language arts, social studies, science, and guidance for the seventh and eight years. It provides a block of time for the same multiple learnings, with the exception of science, in the ninth year. Foreign language, algebra, and science are offered as specialized subjects in the ninth year because of senior high school requirements and of the requirement of certain units for certification purposes, which still exists in some states. Many schools keep mathematics out of the core because of pressures from teachers and community to continue it as a separate subject. This does not usually prevent the core teacher from including it in the units when it becomes necessary to do so. In this type of program, as in the one above, guidance is an integral part of the common learnings area. The nature of the learning activities throughout the day makes a separate club program unnecessary.

TIME DISTRIBUTION IN PER CENT

Subject	7th grade	8th grade	9th grade
Social living (Social Studies, Language Arts and Guidance)	38	42	35
Practical and fine arts	31	27	23
Health and physical education	12	12	12
Mathematics	15	15	13
Science of foreign language	0	0	13
Record period (attendance, Bible reading, daily notices)	4	4	4

The grade schedule on pages 119-121 illustrates such a plan. It is translated into pupils' and teachers' schedules for core

SCHEDULE FOR NINTH GRADE

	8:45	9	10	11	12	12:40	1:40	2:45
MON.	R	SOC. LIV.		P. A.	L	*SCI.	P. E.	
TUE.	R	SOC. LIV.	SCI.	**MATH.	L 12:40	PRACTICAL ARTS		
WED.	A	PRACTICAL ARTS		L 11:40	MATH.	12:20	SOC. LIV.	
THU.	R	SCI.	HYG.	L	MATH.	SOC. LIV.		
FRI.	R	P. E.	MATH.	P. A.	SCI.	L 1:20	SOC. LIV.	

* Science is alternative to foreign language.
** Arithmetic is alternative to algebra. Science and social living are taught by the same teacher.

teachers as well as for those who carry some specialized classes in ninth year.

There are two principles which must be accepted by a staff before the following types of schedules can be successfully set up. X First, *departmentalization has to be eliminated for some of the subject areas.* Barriers between English, social studies and guid-

SCHEDULE FOR SOCIAL LIVING TEACHER

	8:45	9	10	11	12	12:40	1:40	2:45
MON.	8A4 ·R		8A4	11:20	L	8A4	7A2	
TUE.	R		7A2	L 11:40	8A4	LD 1:20	8A4	
WED	R		8A4	ISOL.	7A2	L	7A2	
THU.	A	/	8A4	11:20	L	8A4	7A2	
FRI.	R		7A2	8A4	12:20	L 1:00	8A4	/

Teacher meets only two classes—8A4 and 7A2.

LD—lunch duty when one of the two classes is also in the cafeteria

Isol.—isolation room is a device used to take care of a cooling-off time needed by pupils who are sent from the room for disciplinary reasons. The assignment does not mean extra work for this teacher since he has no responsibility other than to be in that room at this time. He may use the time, therefore, for clerical work.

/—unassigned time to be used for planning, clerical work, and conferences.

ance, and sometimes science in grades seven and eight, come down first. Teachers of those subjects seem to be more willing to combine them into units of learning that cut across subject matter lines.

In some schools, arithmetic is combined with science. In others, arithmetic is accepted into the unspecialized area and is worked into units along with English and social studies and sometimes science. The idea of unification spreads to other fields of learning also. For example, industrial arts, or shop, gets combined with

SCHEDULE FOR SCIENCE TEACHER

	8:45	9	10	11	11:40	12:40	1:40	2:45
MON.	9B-2 R	9B-2 SCIENCE & SOC. LIV.		L	/		9A-7 SCI.	9A-4 SCI.
TUE.	R	9B-2	9A-4	LD	L		9A-7	9B-2
WED.	R	9B-2		/	L		9B-2	
THU.	R	9B-2		L	/		9A-7	9A-4
FRI.	A	9A-7	9B-2	L		9B-2		9A-4

Three is the maximum number of classes the teacher can have in one day. The record class, social living class, and one of the science classes all consist of the same pupils. This makes it possible for a unit of work to be carried on during all of these periods.

home arts, or cooking and sewing, and they are called practical arts. Boys and girls are then sent to these offerings in unsegregated groups. This gives them the chance to learn together about the working world and family life in both of which they are equally concerned.

As teachers become aware of the importance of unification, the prestige values that have long been attached to some "major" subjects can be dropped. Moreover, recognition that all teachers in the school have the responsibility for teaching reading, spelling, writing, and arithmetic fundamentals tends to develop. Teachers begin to see that these are tools that the children need for getting on with the work in all of the classes. Since they are already responsible for multiple learnings, they are likely to accept these skills as general outcomes for which they are all striving.

X The second principle to be accepted by the staff is that *regimentation of time into blocks that are all the same length is an ineffective device in terms of learning, and that it can be discarded.* X The thought behind the time schedule of the traditional school is that every child must have exactly the same number of minutes of instruction in a subject as every other child gets. A glance at what actually happens many times a day will reveal how impossible it is to accomplish that purpose. For example, Mary, Sally and Jim are all ninth graders bound for their classes in arithmetic. Mary arrives in hers promptly, gets to work at once, and continues to work with maximum concentration and without interruption for the entire period. She therefore gets her *forty-two minutes* of arithmetic. Sally comes into her room late. She stops at the teacher's desk to explain, thereby depriving all the class of some minutes of work. She is distracted, however, and cannot get to work at once. Eventually, Sally gets *twenty-five minutes* of arithmetic. Jim arrives in his room on time, but the teacher is late. When Mr. Smith finally arrives, he is out of sorts and proceeds to "take it out on the class." Jim cannot get to work until the tirade is over, so he has only *fifteen minutes* of arithmetic.

Once the myth of the regimented bell schedule is destroyed, the schedule maker is free to organize the day so as to make maximum use of all of the facilities in the building and to the best interests of the students. When the basic time division is one hour, the requirement of 200 minutes for carnegie unit subjects that are required for college or other certification purposes can be arranged by having those classes meet three or four times a week.

A flexible time schedule can be used effectively to cure one of the most troublesome problems of large schools. When the pupils remain in the building for lunch, and the cafeteria is too small to accommodate all of them at the same time, it is customary to organize lunch periods that are completely separated from each other. With the new arrangement, classes can be fed into the cafeteria at ten minute intervals. By the time the room is well filled, those groups that came first are ready to return to their classrooms. At no time do all the doors in the building open at once to pour a hungry, running, screaming mob of children into the corridors. At no time is the cafeteria so crowded that pupils have to stand while eating their lunch. At no time do long food lines form. Bells are not necessary. The children learn to tell time and to watch the clock just as adults do on their lunch hours. Traffic problems are solved. Hall monitors become unnecessary. Individual and group controls emerge and function in this situation which has so much meaning to the children and to the teachers.

When the principal and his staff have developed an organization that provides for good living in the school, for good human relationships among the faculty members and with the pupils, as well as among the students themselves; when the children get plenty of help as they struggle with problems of living and learning; when there is time enough in classrooms to use many direct learning experiences and to go out into the community to see how life is really lived by adults; then the junior high school of tomorrow is beginning to exist today and the principal is fulfilling his destiny.

Emphasis has been placed on professional leadership, the in-service education of teachers, and school organization because these are the aspects of the principal's work that are vital to the development of a functioning junior high school. There are many other administrative tasks which claim a large share of time and energy.[7] In many schools, these and the counseling and disciplining of students have to be delegated to competent teachers or qualified assistants, before the principal can play the role upon which the program suggested in this chapter depends.

Learning Activities for Members of Pre- and In-Service Teacher Education Classes

THE PRINCIPAL

In addition to reading, try other ways of learning such as:

1. Commissioning committees to interview at least three principals of junior high schools.
2. Attending a school faculty meeting. Document the activities and from that data make a graph showing the time spent on policies, administration, in-service education, other matters. Observe the roles played by members of the group. Identify the type of leadership (authoritarian, laissez-faire, democratic), and describe the reactions of the teachers that seem to you to be the result of the climate generated by the kind of leadership used by the principal.
3. Making a study of the schools represented in the class, with respect to their professional libraries—how they are run, the titles of books, the use made of them.

---

[7] *Current Issues in Secondary School Administration*, Bulletin of the National Association of Secondary School Principals, Vol. 37, No. 192, February, 1953.

4. Devising a plan which your faculty could use for sharing professional reading. Make an annotated bibliography for use in setting up a library in your school.

ORGANIZATIONS

1. Make and evaluate a collection of the schedules used in the schools represented in the class.
2. Interview people who take part in organizing their schools.
3. Make a school, department, or grade schedule.

References

THE PRINCIPAL

BOOKS

Association for Supervision and Curriculum Development, N.E.A., *Leadership for Improvement of Instruction,* 1960 Year Book. Washington, D. C.
Jacobson, Reavis and Logsdon, *Duties of School Principals,* 2nd Ed. Englewood Cliffs, N. J.: Prentice-Hall, Inc., 1951.
Nelson, H. B. (ed.), *In-service Education,* National Society for the Study of Education. 56th Year Book, Part I, 1957.
Wiles, Kimball, *Supervision for Better Schools.* Englewood Cliffs, N. J.: Prentice-Hall, Inc., 1950.
Wisconsin Elementary School Principals Association, *Some Fundamentals of In-service Education.* The Association, 1952.

PERIODICALS

Baker, T. P., "What Is An Effective In-Service Education Program?" *The Bulletin of the National Secondary School Principals Association.* Washington, D. C., March, 1951.
Barnes, Melvin W., "How to Have a Good Faculty Meeting," *NEA Journal,* January, 1953.
Patton, J. L., "The Principal's Responsibility for the Professional Growth of His Faculty," *Educational Administration and Supervision,* May, 1950.
Saunders, Juliet, "Job-Analysis—Junior High School Principals," *The Bulletin of the National Association of Secondary School Principals,* 1959.
"The Secondary School Principal and His Problem," Vol. 35, No. 181,

The Bulletin of the National Association of Secondary School Principals,
November, 1951.
Trump, J. L., "Images of the Future," *The Bulletin of the National
Association of Secondary School Principals,* 1959.

SCHOOL ORGANIZATION

BOOKS

Commission on Secondary Schools, *The Junior High School Program.*
Atlanta, Georgia: The Southern Association of Secondary Schools and
Colleges, 1958.
Educational Policies Commission, *Education for All American Youth.*
Washington, D. C.: The Commission, 1944.
Gruhn and Douglass, *The Modern Junior High School.* New York: The
Ronald Press Co., rev. ed., 1957.
Noar, Gertrude, *Freedom to Live and Learn.* Philadelphia: Franklin Pub-
lishing Co., 1948.

PERIODICALS

Gaumnitz, W. H. (comp.), *Strengths and Weaknesses of the Junior High
School.* U. S. Department of Health, Education and Welfare, Office
of Education, 1955.
Harris, H., "The Core Curriculum," *Social Education,* April, 1950.
Ivok, Leo, "How to Prepare the Schedule for a Secondary School,"
Harvard Workshop Series No. 5. Cambridge: Harvard University,
1944.
"Organizing for Effective Learning," *Educational Leadership,* April, 1960.
Saylor, J. G., "Core Programs in American Secondary Schools," *Edu-
cational Leadership,* April, 1950.

CHAPTER SEVEN

The Teacher's Role

*If the teacher is really a teacher, and not just a master or "authority,"
he should know enough about his pupils, their needs, experiences,
degrees of skill and knowledge, to be able (not to dictate aims and plans)
to share in a discussion regarding what is to be done and be as free to
make suggestions as any one else . . . and in his contributions . . .
will presumably do more to getting something started which will really
secure and increase the development of strictly individual capacities
than will suggestions from uncontrolled haphazard sources.*

John Dewey, *Arts and Education.*
Marion, Pa.: Barnes Foundation
Press, 1947, page 38.

"I'm only a teacher. What can *I* do about it?" This is the question most frequently asked when the urgency of modernizing the junior high school is under discussion. In nearly every school there is at least one person who is anxious to alleviate the frustration felt by so many teachers, and to move forward in the development of a modern school program. Very often these teachers say, "My principal isn't interested," or "My department head lays down the law," or "In our school district we have to follow the old course of study," or "I can get only one book, and the kids are expected to learn it from cover to cover," or "A patriotic society in our town sets up a competitive examination, and if my pupils don't do well I'll get a low rating, and maybe my contract will not be renewed," or "There are people in the faculty who have me too scared to try anything new. They say, 'We don't want any of that around here.'"

It is true that these deterents do exist everywhere. But it is equally true that large numbers of American educators share the American urge to progress, and have the creative drive toward

126

experimentation. Above all, American school people know that if a growing, developing concept of Democracy is to be planted in the minds and hearts of today's youngsters and the generations to come, new and better ways of teaching must be employed.

There are very many things for junior high school teachers to do which will give them satisfaction and move them forward into a program of curriculum change.[1] No one can determine where a teacher should begin without knowing where he is, at the moment, in what directions his interests lie, and from what sources his frustrations come. The teacher himself knows these things, and from among the many alternatives that confront him, he should be able to make a wise choice for himself. The important thing for all concerned to remember is, that *if curriculum change is to occur at all, it must take place in the classroom.*

Elaborate curriculum guides with the most modern content may be written by supervisors and experts with or without the help of teacher committees. New daily schedules may be devised by principals and organizers. All kinds of fine equipment may be purchased by superintendents. Even the size of classes may be reduced to a minimum by sensitive Boards of Education willing to undertake the raising of funds to finance such programs. All these can happen without producing any change in outmoded techniques of teaching. In the classrooms, the sterile "lecture-lesson-assignment-home-study-recitation-test" method may still be continued with its outcomes of memorized factual learnings so soon to be forgotten by a large portion of the student population.

Teachers will change only as they themselves gain new insights, new knowledge, and new experiences. It is essential for all concerned with curriculum development to remember that not too much should be undertaken at one time by one person. The rate of progress will be in proportion to the success experiences each one has. As in every other aspect of life, there is no *one* road to take, nor does any road lead steadily upward. There are bound to be set-backs, discouragements, even retreats. There will be mistakes, but no actual *failures*. If principals, supervisors, parents, pupils, and colleagues all take part in setting up the purposes and in making the plans, and if they all join in the evaluation of

---

[1] See Harold Spears, *The Teacher and Curriculum Planning.* Englewood Cliffs, N. J.: Prentice-Hall, Inc., 1951, *passim.*

whatever has been done, then the word failure can be forgotten and *mistakes will be accepted as learning experiences.* This new attitude in itself will be an important asset for the children to acquire and to carry with them into adulthood. Thus equipped, the individual will be less likely to sink into depression and despair as the eventualities of life take their toll.

To the teachers, then, must be given the responsibility for implementing the process of modernization in their classrooms. What each teacher can do depends upon such factors as personal backgrounds, reading, and interests, all of which contribute to his or her readiness. The direction which a teacher should take depends upon the total situation within which he operates. It is possible, therefore, to give teachers only some suggestions for projects upon which they can embark. The following suggestions have been tuned to the statements many teachers make when the teacher's role in curriculum change is being discussed.

First consider Mr. Blank, who says: "I'm one of the teachers who faces five separate classes every day. I don't know anything about my pupils. I've never done anything except mass teaching. In fact, no one ever seemed to expect me to do anything else. I'd like to, though. How can I begin?"

What can teachers like this do, that will not add an intolerable burden to their already heavy day? There is little likelihood that Mr. Blank has kept abreast of the information which research has uncovered in the field of human growth and development. He will find some fascinating reading waiting for him, but he does not have to start with books. An even better thing for him to do is to begin with the human resources that confront him daily—the children he teaches. He will then soon return to books for help in understanding and interpreting his observations.

Authorities in the field say, "Begin with *child study.* Look at the children in your classes."[2]

What can a teacher see when he *looks at* his pupils? Differences among the children in any junior high school classroom are striking, and, to a teacher who has not really seen individuals before, they may even be somewhat shocking. There are differences in height, weight, and maturity; in color, sex, and facial expression;

---

[2] See Daniel Prescott, *Helping Teachers Understand Children.* Washington, D. C.: American Council on Education, 1945.

in noses, eyes, and teeth; in quality and taste in clothing; and in all the other characteristics of mankind.

Not all the differences to be found will be immediately obvious. Mr. Blank will find many more when he begins to *talk with* his students, forgetting that they are his pupils, and talking with them in a man-to-man fashion. He will uncover a vast range of ideas about fun, religion, and love; about what is right and wrong and why; of aspirations and drives; and of how they feel about school and about him. It is unlikely that the teacher who reaches this point can ever again be satisfied with mass instruction. He will not ever again make the mistake of planning to reach the "average ninth grader" because he will know that there is no such pupil.

Teachers engaged in Child Study soon feel both comfortable and justified when they sit by to watch the children. They lose the pressure and tension which come out of the feeling that they must be forever driving their pupils to learn what is in the course of study. As teachers learn to observe boys and girls, they see that they are quite different in the classroom from what they are when they intermingle freely in corridors and play spaces. Questions will arise about the effect that tensions, anxieties, preoccupations, and distractions have on attention span, concentration, work habits, and level of accomplishment in the daily work. When the configurations of the peer group become clear, new light will be shed on the reasons for the success and failure of some of the students.[3]

Teachers who realize the effect of human relations in the classroom become sensitive to the forces that are at work in the adolescent society. Acceptance by age-mates is of far greater importance to most junior high school children than is the attitude of the teacher. It becomes essential for the teacher to know, if he is to plan adequately, which pupils are the centers of attraction around which small groups cluster. He will want to do something to help the lonely ones, the isolates, and rejectees, knowing that they are often unable to work because of their unpopularity. Those in the fringe area who want so desperately to be "in," will give him concern. The teacher can come to use the talents of those who know how to resolve inter-personal conflicts to the advantage of all. He

[3] See Caroline M. Tryon, *The Adolescent Peer Culture*. National Society for the Study of Education, Chicago: Chicago University Press, 1944.

will also learn what to do with the children who are the trouble makers.

As Mr. Blank talks with his students, questions which cut into other subject areas are bound to arise. If he is really concerned with the growth of his children, he will have to give time to the things they want to know. Some of the required information will not be in the books he has at his command, so he and the pupils will have to search for other sources. Newspapers and pamphlets will come into use. Committees will be needed to set up files, to make and sort clippings, to take care of bulletin board displays. Children are eager to do this kind of work, especially those who have reading difficulties. But reading is involved, and consequently reading skills improve. If the questions raised are really meaningful to them, the students will be glad to search for the facts from other sources. Soon the radio, television, and films will be in use. Children will be going places and interviewing people. The slow learners can do all these things, too, and will be greatly encouraged when they, too, can contribute to the growing fund of knowledge. Mr. Blank's class period will soon provide exciting and challenging experiences for all.

The use of new teaching techniques is not the only result in such classrooms. Not only do these teachers see their pupils as people, but the children, in their turn, see that the teachers are "human too."

The students in classrooms of teachers who are becoming sensitive to their needs soon begin to talk about the problems they meet in the community, about family relationships that baffle or disturb them, about their fears, anxieties, and even their hates. Presently, teachers sense what their pupils are actually getting out of school life. They find that some children are learning to "get there first," others, to be content with the last place; some to struggle; more to conform; a few to bluff; more to be straightforward; some to act; others to sit back and wait; the less gifted to just listen; many to dream while seeming to attend; a few to take part in group work; an occasional one to be a "lone wolf"; a segment to develop skills in the tools of learning and the practice of democracy; the unfortunate ones to fail.

As all these things come to pass, Mr. Blank and his counterparts realize for the first time what the guidance function of the teacher really is. *Teachers who study children, who begin to guide them on the basis of personal knowledge about them, who, in order to meet their needs, use many kinds of teaching techniques and meaningful content questions, are engaged in curriculum development.*

Next, visit with Mrs. Martin who says, "My best efforts fail—sometimes with some of the children, too often with all of them. They just don't like what I give them to do. Maybe they can't learn. What can I do about it?" Perhaps the most immediate need of teachers like this is to search for answers to the question, *HOW DOES LEARNING OCCUR?* When and under what circumstances does it take place? Every teacher must become conscious of the necessity for getting the best possible answers to that question. Although the fact that so many pupils seem to do so little learning in the classroom gives the American teacher his greatest concern, too often he is unwilling to go to books on psychology and philosophy for his anwsers. Of course, that is what he will ultimately have to do, but meanwhile he can find much inside his own classroom that will shed light upon the problem.[4]

Teachers who are concerned about why their pupils do not learn can best begin with the concept of the "direct learning experience." It involves the use of face-to-face contacts with people, places, things and processes. Direct experiences of this kind are productive of learning for all the students, superior as well as retarded.

As soon as a teacher begins to use direct experiences, all sorts of changes follow in the classroom work, as well as in the kinds of home assignments he gives. Moreover, every change that occurs is likely to increase the amount of learning that some of the children accomplish. Because of the nature of these new methods, the teacher will find that he needs more sources of information than he used formerly. He soon discovers that some of them are outside his door and in the community. Waiting there are resource people who can and will come into the school to meet with him and the students. There are the places to which to go for face-to-face conferences with experts. There, too, are the many things that children need to see and handle, and much up-to-date printed matter which they can use to supplement their school books.

---

[4] See Rasey and Menge, *What We Learn from Children.* New York: Harper and Brothers, 1956.

In order to help Mrs. Martin and her colleagues, some specific suggestions for direct experiences follow:

×*The use of people as resources*—all kinds of people—old and young and middle-aged, neighbors, friends and parents, workmen, professionals and white collar workers, principals, counselors and teachers, custodians, janitors and engineers, policemen, firemen, and trash collectors, executives, foremen and sales-people, and dozens of others who are expert in their several ways of living and working. People are usually delighted with an invitation from the school. They love to talk to children and are thrilled if they receive "fan mail" after filling a speaking engagement. These citizens can be interviewed by individuals and committees. They can be called upon to talk, show, demonstrate, and help. Preparation of the children for all of these experiences requires the use of old and new skills in the language arts—listening, speaking, reading, and writing. Pupils on all levels of ability enjoy obtaining up-to-the-minute first-hand information from these "consultants." The use of people in these ways is possible even in traditional classroom work.

Lectures and discussions can be planned, carried on, and listened to both in and out of school. Sometimes pupils should be encouraged and even assigned to attend them along with adults. Learning to take notes, to criticize, and to report on such experiences is especially important for the superior students.

Trips are always highly motivated and exciting learning experiences. They can be taken whether the teacher continues to use a course of study or departs from it in order to do unit teaching. They will take students into such important places as housing projects, the seat of local government, many kinds of museums, factories, the water front, businesses, historical places, social service agencies, hospitals, and dozens of places that make up every American community and reflect every aspect of American life—economic, social, and political. Preparation for trips and re-living them afterwards are rich in opportunities for individuals and groups to develop the social skills, the skills of communication and expression, and the thought skills that are involved in planning, deciding, selecting, and evaluating.

Multiple learnings result from every trip. They extend across subject-matter lines. They afford first rate experiences in human relations education. Pupils and teachers see themselves and each other in new lights. Rapport is built at such times and some of the blocks to learning that are caused by fear, insecurity, and failure begin to disappear.

Work experiences are of vital importance to some pupils. In addition to the actual need for money from which some children suffer, teen-agers have a growing desire to prove to themselves and adults that they are grown-up. Earning money is an adult activity. For some students these needs are so acute that it is necessary to let them work at real jobs for part of the school day. This is especially true for the older boys and girls who have met with much school failure and retardation. The teacher who helps such pupils to solve the problems they meet while on the job renders important service to them and to the community. There are many problems connected with a work-study plan. Building the cooperative relationships between labor and the school, between the school and the parents, between the parents and the child in the school, between the school and the community agencies is a task worthy of the best efforts of the best teachers in the profession. *When they engage in creating work-study programs, teachers are developing curriculum.*

Social action projects are experiences through which the participants learn the ways of democratic action. They include service projects in the school and in the community. Some are aimed at the betterment of life for the in-school group. Others deal with the neighborhood. A few reach out into the large community. Children learn about the problem of social lag through these projects in a way that could never be done by reading. They also learn that democratic processes do work, and thus experience an increase of belief, a sharpening of loyalty, and a determination to work hard to preserve these processes. *Teachers who develop social action projects are on the frontier of curriculum development.*

Constructive, creative, manipulative activities provide children with rich opportunities to react to reality and to relive their learning experiences. They also have important therapeutic values. These are difficult to administer in the traditional classroom, and many teachers hesitate to use them because of their lack of time, materials, and techniques. Their use may have to be delayed until the organization of the school day provides for a period which is longer than the customary one today.

Manipulative activities have to be varied to suit the interests and abilities of the children. Some pupils can draw or paint. Others prefer to model with clay, soap, or wood. Some want to dance; others to make music by singing or playing instruments. Dramatizing, collecting, displaying, exhibiting, building, repairing, operating audio-visual equipment—all have considerable appeal to junior high school boys and girls. For some, the greatest value may lie in learning to do something new.

The regular classroom teacher cannot be expected to teach children how to do art work or construction. For that, they must look to the art and shop teachers. He can, however, recognize the fact that doing creative work, no matter how crude the product may be, releases tension and provides joy to the doer. The responsibility of the classroom teacher is to provide only time and opportunity for the children to express their ideas in these media, realizing that the ideas involved come out of the content he has been teaching.

Maps, charts, graphs, picto-graphs. The collection, study, mounting, filing, displaying, duplication, and interpretation of these are types of "reading" experiences that are especially important today because so much factual material is presented in these forms in newspapers, pamphlets, and magazines. Students need to learn to express their own findings in like manner. They should be encouraged to make a set of charts or graphs as a final report to the class when the material with which they are dealing lends itself to graphic presentation.

Collections and exhibits are activities that are particularly interesting to boys and girls. Moreover interest in making these for school projects may lead to the development of life-long hobbies. Sorting, classifying, and arranging items in a collection, and making appropriate labels and signs for exhibitions are valuable intellectual exercises.

The use of *audio-visual devices,* long a part of good classroom practice, needs to be extended and improved. These experiences are sometimes thought of as vicarious rather than direct because the pupils are spectators rather than actors in the situations. Nevertheless, they are more successful learning experiences for large numbers of children than is the use of the abstract word symbol. Full enjoyment of them, however, depends upon adequate equipment, a good library of films and records, and the teachers' possession of the operational and teaching skills that are required. Among the devices are:

Motion pictures. Films that are appropriate to the unit being studied have to be found, ordered, pre-viewed, presented, and followed up with discussion. Pupils should have a share in all of the responsibilities connected with the use of films and film strips, but the teachers bear the responsibility of training them to do good jobs. Every community presents opportunities for teachers to take their classes to see commercial films that have bearing on classroom work or on problems of human relations. Moreover, pupils can be given assignments to see such films as "homework." It is as important for children to learn to interpret, criticize, and discuss films as it is for them to do these things in connection with the books they read.

Film strips and slides are of great value in the classroom because discussion and interpretation can follow along with the pictures. The teacher can stop the films at any time for further exploration of the ideas in the particular frame.

Radio and television can be used both in the classroom and as home assignments. Regularly scheduled broadcasts are of greater importance in teaching current affairs and social issues than are the programs given by children for the entertainment of children. The responsibility for teaching taste, criticism, and discrimination in selection of programs should be generally accepted by school teachers.

Recordings make it possible to bring into the classroom the very best actors, musicians, and speakers; the most exciting plays, operas, and celebration programs; the most significant speeches, conferences, and discussions. They afford the opportunity of repetition until understanding has been achieved. They can be stopped at any appropriate spot for any purpose the teacher wishes to accomplish.

The emphasis that has been placed upon the use of direct experience does not mean that the use of the word symbol is to be neglected. Books are not to be discarded. There is no implication that reading is not important as a learning device or as an experi-

ence. In fact, among the purposes to be served by the use of many
direct experiences are enlargement of vocabulary and increased
reading readiness.

*Teachers who increase the opportunities for all children to learn,
by introducing many and varied direct learning experiences, are
engaged in curriculum development.*

A third evidence of the desire of teachers to work at curriculum
change is illustrated by Mrs. Smith when she says, "I have always
been sensitive to the pupils in my classes. I know many names,
even though I teach two hundred. I am aware of their many
differences, but I still don't see why my old courses of study and
methods aren't good enough. Why aren't they?"

Traditional courses and methods are not sufficiently oriented
to the concept of *adolescent needs.*[5] This concept, which is frequently referred to in educational literature, is not too well understood by many classroom teachers. They need to know what the
needs are, how to recognize them, and how to satisfy those needs
in the classroom.

Surveys of hundreds of adolescents are available for study. Educational books and periodicals are full of statistics about the interests and wishes of teen-agers. Mrs. Smith can turn to them for
help, but she also will find a vital source of information in her
own classroom. She can even enlist her students in whatever study
she may decide to make. Out of participation will come many important experiences for them.

The following suggestions for ways in which a teacher can get
information about adolescents can be used in any classroom:

Intimate writings are an important source of information. The
boys and girls will respond to the following ideas more readily
than they ordinarily do to the usual "compositions" and "themes."
They can be used as "topic sentences," provocative questions, or
leading ideas. Plenty of discussion is necessary in order to break
down customary reserves. If the teacher enters into the fun of
recalling personal experiences, rapport can be built without difficulty. Children must be given the assurance that whatever they
write will be regarded as confidential by the teacher, if they so

---

[5] See Karl C. Garrison, *Psychology of Adolescence,* 4th ed. Englewood Cliffs,
N. J.: Prentice-Hall, Inc., 1951.

desire. Many pupils, however, write for the audience furnished by the peer group and want to have their papers read to the class. The following list is suggestive:

Whom do I want to sit with? Why?
The kind of boy (girl) I admire is ——
The kind of girl (boy) I'd like to be is ——
One day I was sure the gang looked down upon me
I felt left out that day when ——
I was not invited!
I was really angry that time when ——
Never in my life did I expect to be so happy as that day
If I had my choice, I'd live in ——
My house is all right, but ——
My family is wonderful
If I had my way this is what would happen in my home
Life with my family upsets me because ——
When I have my own home I'll ——
Now that small brother (sister) of mine
My older sister (brother) ——
If I could only have ——
I know I'm disliked because of my ——
There are things about myself that I wish were different
When I grow up I'll ——
I can't get along with fellows (girls) my age
I'm happiest when I'm with the gang
I had a terrific problem
The job I want is ——
If I only had some money
My first date
What I need is ——
If I had three wishes ——
I wish I knew ——
I wish I knew more about ——
Just give me a hundred dollars to spend
That day I was scared out of my wits
I remember when I was very little ——

Questionnaires and interest inventories can be both home-made and commercial. Committees of pupils can assist in preparing and selecting the ones to be used. From such instruments, teachers will discover that among the personal emotional needs of adolescents are the need to belong, the need for security, the need to be recognized, the need for success, the need to be praised, the need to be popular, the need for prestige and status, the need to increase knowledge and understanding, the need for love, the need to have fun, the need for new adventure, the need to have friends, the need to do things, the need for all kinds of skills. Some needs are connected with fears and anxieties. Others are physical and physiological in nature. Many of them are social, and have to do with the individual's relationship with others. Still other needs have to do with values—ethical and spiritual, and a philosophy of life.

Investigation of actual problems that confront teen-agers is another way to get at adolescent needs. When they are identified they can be used as the basis on which to develop learning experiences the outcomes of which include skill in attacking problems and planning activities, the ability to think clearly, the dispelling of fears and anxieties, and creation of social sensitivity and insight. Classroom work on such problems will provide opportunity for the use of the group processes. They call for research and the organization of facts into usable forms. They can be dealt with best by developing experience units around them. The following suggestions are offered for investigation:

Daily Experiences Which Confront Adolescents

Association with age-mates in gangs, cliques, clubs, secret societies.
All that goes into the use of leisure time.
Money and all that goes along with its use by the consumer, the saver, and the investor.
Education.
Minority and class tensions, anxieties, conflicts, fears, differences, similarities, discriminations.
The use and abuse of utilities in the community.
Betterment of life—from the securing of traffic lights, safety, and recreational facilities to enforcement of pure food and other laws.
Housing, tenements, rent control, restrictions, segregation, codes, laws.
City planning, roads, highways.
Transportation of goods and people and the problems of the air-age.
Strikes and labor-management problems—also the getting, holding, and advancement in jobs.
Civil liberties.
Crime and juvenile delinquency.
How, when, and where to get help for those in need—social agencies and social security.
Government and control of people—from the school itself to Washington, D. C.; from student government to politics; from the neighborhood to internationalism.

War, peace, the United Nations—current issues facing Congress, the nation, the world.

This atomic age.

Wastage of human and natural resources.

Weather—from causes and effects, to the purchase of adequate clothing.

Animal life—from pets to the zoo; from home to the wilds of Africa; from their use for food and clothing to direct study of their body and cell structure; from "pure science" to occupational information pointing to careers and jobs.

Plant life—from raising a flower or vegetable to interdependence and "the balance of life"; from seeing the job outlets provided in horticulture and agriculture, to preparation for scientific research.

What is right, true, good, beautiful—moral, ethical, spiritual values and the choice of thought and deed.

Teachers who are basing classroom work on their discovery of the needs of their pupils are engaging in curriculum development.

A fourth complaint, which often makes teachers eager to do something about curriculum change in the classroom, sounds like this: "Nothing in the way of school work interests children nowadays. All they want to do is play or be amused. I can't see myself entertaining them and I simply will not try to compete with the movies and television for their interest."

Herman Horne has this to say about interest: "Interest in education is not ease, it is effortless activity; it is not a classroom vaudeville with the teacher as chief performer, it is engrossing occupation; it is not an amusing entertainment of the pupils; it is not play, it is attractive and compelling work; it is not pursuing the line of least resistance, it is discovering the line of greatest attraction. And the true opposite of interest is not hard work, it is drudgery."[6]

Teachers who are worried about their inability to capture the interests of their pupils need to look into the problem of motivation and to consider what are the *blocks to learning.* Motivation of the pupil to his best effort, or even to participate at all, is a most important problem in the modern classroom. Many teachers feel that here is their most serious difficulty, and are willing to do whatever is necessary to cure the ill. They say, "I can't get on with my job when my classes are cluttered up with kids who just gum

---

[6] Herman Horne, *The Philosophy of Education.* New York: The Macmillan Co., 1927.

up the works; who delight in throwing in a monkey wrench when things are going well; who flatly say 'No, I won't take part'; who persist, in spite of my best efforts, in being just sitters." These are the types of reactions that many teachers classify rather loosely under the heading of "bad conduct" or "discipline problems."

In order to understand this kind of "conduct," a teacher must know more about behavior and its causes. In his efforts to solve these problems he must assemble facts about the individual concerned, getting them from all available sources. There must be investigation of parentage, socio-economic background, family relationships, the person's place in the family group, the out-of-school load he carries, possibly the early childhood weaning and toilet training experiences, the social class and caste attitudes he and his parents have and how those in the school affect him, and conflict which may exist in the value systems of the people with whom he is associated.[7] Some of the obstacles to learning can be found in the child's feelings about education, in the degree of success he experiences, in his knowledge and understanding of the teacher's goals, in whatever incentives he himself may possess, and in the amount of acceptance or rejection from which he suffers in his in-school relationships.

A study of the accumulated facts about a child will reveal the pattern of the blocks to learning which have been built up in him. They frequently cluster around such areas as lack of love and failure to win affectional security at home and in the classrooom; fears and anxieties of all kinds; inadequacies and inequalities (imagined and real) in the essentials of life—money, clothing, and food. Some are caused by actual or imaginary mental and social inferiorities. A sense of belonging may be needed. There may be little in the way of accomplishment and achievement both in and out of school due to lack of opportunity or to need for understanding and knowledge of prerequisites.[8]

The blocks to learning have been carefully studied and analyzed. The effects of teachers' attitudes and actions, the words and gestures they use, the results of the long assignments of reading and

---

[7] Raths and Abrahamson, *Student Status and Social Class*. Bronxville, N. Y.: Modern Education Service, 1950.

[8] See Louis E. Raths, *Application of the Needs Theory to Education*. Bronxville, N. Y.: Modern Education Service, 1949.

memorizing uninteresting materials, have all been noted.[9] *Teachers who actively search for blocks to learning, who learn what to do to prevent and remove them, who develop functional classroom experiences in the light of their findings are engaged in a most fruitful area of curriculum improvement.*

A fifth group of teachers is caught in the gap that always exists between a system of philosophy and its implementation. Knowing why and what to do is often a far cry from knowing how. Among these teachers are Mr. Jones and Mrs. Green who say, "Oh yes. We know all the theory. We really do believe in Dewey and Kilpatrick—always have, in fact! Of course, we want to use modern methods, but our teachers in school and college didn't and we've never seen anyone really teach that way. We don't even know how to begin."

One of the most important differences between the traditional and the modern classrooms lies in the use of *group processes.* The modern teacher knows that the survival of Democracy may depend upon the ability of citizens to participate in group thinking, to plan intelligently, to discuss calmly, to make choices that are good and decisions that are wise, to identify that which needs to be done for the betterment of life, and to carry plans forward until they flower into group action projects. If graduates of the junior high schools are to possess these characteristics, they must have plenty of opportunity for practice in meaningful situations while they are in school.[10]

X In order to make effective use of group processes, a teacher must know what constitutes an effective group. The following conditions are essential.[11]

Opportunities for much interaction among the students and with the teacher. The first step is getting acquainted. The next is to replace the traditional one line of communication, teacher-to-child-to-teacher, with many lines running in many directions.

Belongingness. Mistrust is replaced by the certain knowledge that everyone is respected for his worth to himself and to the group. Everyone is given a chance to contribute and everyone feels wanted.

[9] See Burrell and Raths, *The Do's and Don'ts for the Needs Theory.* Bronxville, N. Y.: Modern Education Service, 1951.

[10] See Lewin and Lippett, "An Experimental Approach to the Study of Autocracy and Democracy," *Sociometry*, 1938.

[11] See Association for Supervision and Curriculum Development, *Group Processes in Supervision.* Washington, D. C.: The Association, 1948.

Identification of common problems, purposes, and goals. As members of a group find their similarities, they become able to identify themselves with the common objectives and see their own gains as they work toward the solution of the common problems.

Acceptance of social control by the members of the group. As this is accomplished, individuals become willing to trust to majority decision and action. Much distasteful disciplinary action by the teacher becomes unnecessary.

The use of consensus rather than voting when decisions affecting the total group are being made. Too often the majority means only one more than half. Groups come to understand that better feeling and more effective work follows, if decisions can be postponed until there has been enough discussion to get agreement. The emergence of group decision without force of pressure is the highest form of democratic action.

As a class becomes a group, the *atmosphere in which it functions undergoes a change.*[12] Where once the atmosphere was punitive, it soon becomes permissive. Hostility changes to friendliness. Competition yields to cooperation. Autocratic command is replaced by democratic agreement.

Important changes in behavior take place. There are significant alterations in emotions as well as in actions. In place of negative attitudes, positive good feelings are in evidence. These good feelings are directed toward the teacher, each other, work, the group, things outside the classroom and the school. Individuals who were formerly pitted against each other, or who tried to dominate each other, begin to work together.

The concept of leadership grows. Instead of one leader who is usually above and apart from the group, the leadership is centered in the group. Every pupil begins to understand and to exercise his respective role, finding that at one time he is leader, and at another time he is follower.

Where formerly there was only one path to be taken, that set up by the teacher, now alternatives can be offered by him and by the students. From among them the teacher and the pupils together choose those roads which seem to them to be good, desirable, and exciting.

The prevalence of conflicts and demands for attention which so frequently accompany an "I-centered" atmosphere is changed. "We-centered" activities are in order and in them each child begins

---

[12] See Association for Supervision and Curriculum Development, *Group Processes in Supervision.* Washington, D. C.: The Association, 1948.

to accept his responsibilities, not only for his own part but also for the whole. Shirking is likely to diminish.

In place of hostile criticisms there is an effort on everyone's part, especially the teacher's, to use plenty of praise, recognition, and reward. The result is less verbal aggressiveness and less seeking favor from the teacher, who is now apt to be treated and accepted in a much more matter-of-fact fashion. Scapegoating disappears as children are released from the necessity of expressing hostility towards both classmates and teacher.

Where once there was indifference on the part of a significant part of the group, *there is likely to be a growing feeling of pride in belonging, of evidence of security in the group, and of resistance to leaving it.* Instead of competition for first place and the highest marks, there is cooperation for excellence of group output. Productivity increases and often reaches a high level. Many sitters cease to be inactive. Instead of finding satisfaction in being rebellious and defiant, they find it in working with their peers on problems of mutual interest and concern.

Teachers who organize committees for the purpose of having children experience effective group work, and who seek ways in which to bind the total membership of the class into a working whole, are engaged in curriculum development.

There is yet a sixth group of teachers whose problems are expressed by Mr. Baker when he says, "I'm tremendously interested in all this talk about learning Democracy through experience in the school. No classroom I have ever been in was really democratic. After all the teacher has to be in control. He is supposed to be the authority and the leader. Should that be changed? I wonder." Mr. Baker can begin his work in curriculum development by learning how to *make a democracy of his classroom.*

Democratization of the classroom begins as soon as the teacher takes a new look at the goals toward which he and his pupils are supposed to be working. Who sets them up? Is it the Board of Education, the principal, the supervisor, or the curriculum committee? Does the individual teacher have anything to do with them, or does he just accept whatever he finds written in the course of study or the curriculum guide? Let the teacher who is in search of democratic methods sit down at once with paper and pencil to record *his* aims for *his* classes for that day and then for the days that are to come. None but he should be entrusted with the final say in such a matter, for no one else knows his children. Goals can hardly be set up by anyone who does not have first-hand knowledge of the present level of development, skill, ability, and maturity of the learners in question. It cannot be done satisfactorily unless there is also full knowledge of the actual equipment, facilities, and supplies that are at the teacher's command.

Acceptance of the goal-setting function, however, is only the first step. The teacher takes the second step when he finds ways of letting the students help with that job, for who is more concerned than they? They must know the teacher's aims for them. They must clarify their own incentives, desires, and objectives. This requires time, it is true, but it also provides most excellent opportunities for thought, for functional experiences in the language arts, and it serves as a powerful motivating force. Furthermore, participation in making a policy is the democratic right of all those who are to be affected by it.

When the pupils participate in determining objectives, they are helping to make important decisions. From this point on, the teacher must try to avoid making any decisions by himself that can possibly be thrown open to the class. This necessitates considerable thought and self-control. Instead of offering one idea, from now on, he is constrained to offer several alternatives. He must also allow for the time that making decisions consumes, and recognize in it the possibility of creating habits of thought and action that will be of lifelong value to his children. One of the important outcomes is realization on the pupils' part that, to make wise decisions, all the possible facts have to be gathered and examined for their relative worth. No one can learn to do critical thinking by reading about it. Actual practice in meaningful situations is essential.

The process of clarifying goals on the basis of individual and group concerns is the first step in *Pupil-teacher Planning*.[13] The next step is not too difficult. The teacher asks his class, "What shall we plan to accomplish today?" Gradually he extends this until it encompasses tomorrow, this week, this report period, this semester.

---

[13] For complete discussion of pupil-teacher planning techniques see Gertrude Noar, *Freedom to Live and Learn*. Philadelphia: Franklin Publishing Co., 1948.

Thus short- and long-term plans are made. As children find themselves free to do so, they will express their interests, concerns, desires to know, and to know more about. The teacher can then say, "You have said what it is that you want to know. Now how shall we get the information we need? Who shall be responsible for doing what?" This does not mean that the time has come for the teacher to discard his course of study. What is called for is a change of attitude toward the course of study. From now on, instead of using it as a directive, the instructor begins to use it as a guide. In fact most modern curriculum bulletins are called "Guide Books." They no longer contain specific directions for the number of lessons to be taught in each of the logically developed sections of subject matter. Many of them are so written that they can easily be used in unit teaching. They indicate in many ways that "covering content" is not to be the determining drive for the teacher as he creates a democratic classroom. They give many suggestions to the teacher concerning the ways in which he can help his pupils to identify their common problems, find out how their individual interests affect the group, get the facts that are needed to answer questions that are raised, develop plans to solve problems, allocate responsibilities so that every one has a share in the work to be done, move into action, and, when the job is done, look at it critically so that the next plans and products are better.

Another extremely important characteristic of the democratic classroom is the way in which marks are determined and grades are recorded on report cards. Most teachers have been brought up to believe that they alone have the right to determine the level of accomplishment and the degree of success gained by their students. The habit of self-evaluation, however, is essential to the mature adult, and if children are to develop it, they must practice it during their growing years. Every individual needs to face himself frequently and squarely, with the questions, "What have I done well, what poorly? Where are my weaknesses? What must I do to acquire the skill I need?" Children readily accept the responsibility for helping to decide what their own marks should be. Participation in evaluation helps to remove animosity and hostility from the classroom. If parents are admitted to the process as well, much fear can also be cleared away. These are blocks to learning in most schools.

ᴿ Evaluation of the group, its actions and products, is as important as evaluation of the individual.ᴿ Children need to practice the habit of looking at their elected leaders in a critical fashion. They also need to judge the quality of their followership. Actual achievement has to be equated in terms of growth if fair play is desired.

Through experience in group work, in planning, in sharing responsibilities, in learning to value each other regardless of differences, in participation in policy making, and in evaluation of self and others, junior high school children learn the meaning of the principles and the practice of democracy. Teachers who are giving their pupils freedom to live that way and to learn those things are engaging in curriculum development.

John Dewey, writing in the Paul Monroe (ed.) *Encyclopedia of Education*, gives general direction and inspiration for creative teaching in the democratic tradition, as follows: "With respect to freedom, then, the task of the educator is three-fold. First, to keep alive plasticity, initiative, capacity to vary; to prevent induration and fixation in fossilized automatic habits. . . . Secondly, to confirm preferences; to build up and strengthen positive and constructive interests in specific directions. Nothing is more fatal practically than the growth of a spirit of indifference, of boredom, or of miscellaneous and easily diverted responsiveness. Thirdly, to make preferences *reasonable;* that is to say to develop in individuals the habit of forecasting the consequences of acting upon a given preferential tendency, of comparing one set of results with another, and by these means enlightening preference as to its own deeper and more abiding nature."[14]

Teachers have a positive role to play in modernizing the junior high school. They must be willing to change their ways of looking at children. They must make themselves masters of the best knowledge that is available about how children grow and develop. They must get a firm grasp upon what is known about the learning processes and be willing to implement this in their day by day classroom work.

---

[14] John Dewey, *Encyclopedia of Education*, Paul Monroe, ed., Vol. 2, pp. 705-706. New York: The Macmillan Co., 1911.

Teachers have a definitive role to play as they modernize the junior high school. Without their determination to make democracy work as a way of life in the school, there will be less hope for its ultimate survival. The coming generations must be equipped with the know-how of the democratic processes as well as with a burning faith in the basic democratic principles. The world will look to them for the practice of a way of life in which the worth and integrity of the individual is recognized and participation in all aspects of democratic social life is common. Many children have their last chance to learn these in the junior high school for they will go no higher on the educational ladder.

Teachers have a critical role to play in modernizing the junior high school. They can move forward courageously and with the determination to make this school serve the needs of its children and of America, or they can, by reason of inertia, reaction, and fear, refuse to change, and thereby decide that this type of school shall gradually pass out of existence.

Learning Activities for Members of Pre- and In-Service Teacher Education Classes

After reading as many references as you can, try the following:

1. Hold a "gripe session."
2. Make daily records of the behaviorisms and talk of an adolescent. Set up an hypothesis for the causes of something that especially disturbs you. Seek the facts either to justify or to negate that.
3. Set up discussion groups or panels of adolescents to explore their interests, needs, attitudes towards teachers, reactions to school work, feelings about adults.
4. Make new plans for your classroom work in which you incorporate some one or more teaching techniques you have not previously used.
5. Observe in a junior high school classroom.

References

BOOKS

Kearney, Nolan, *A Teacher's Professional Guide*. Englewood Cliffs, N. J.: Prentice-Hall, Inc., 1958.

Prescott, *et al.*, *Helping Teachers Understand Children*. Washington,
   D. C.: American Council of Education, 1945.
Sheviahov and Redl, *Discipline for Today's Children*. Washington, D. C.:
   Department of Supervision and Curriculum Development, NEA, 1944.
Spears, H., *The Teacher and Curriculum Planning*. Englewood Cliffs,
   N. J.: Prentice-Hall, Inc., 1951.
Stiles, L. J., ed., *The Teacher's Role in American Society*. New York:
   Harper and Brothers, 1959.
Willard, Abraham, *A Handbook for the New Teacher*. New York: Rine-
   hart and Co., 1960.

PERIODICALS AND PAMPHLETS

National Commission on Teacher Education and Professional Standards,
   The Education of Teachers: Curriculum Programs. Washington,
   D. C., 1959.
Pennsylvania Department of Public Instruction, *Curriculum Improve-
   ment by a Secondary School Faculty*. Harrisburg, Pa., 1950.
Stannard, C., "Prescription for a Good Junior High School Teacher,"
   California Journal of Secondary Education, November, 1946.
Vars, G. F., "Problems of a Beginning Core Teacher," *Educational
   Leadership*, October, 1951.

CHAPTER EIGHT

Community Relations

The democratic school draws upon and contributes to the community. Such a school cannot hope to maintain a successful program if community resources are not available for instructional purposes, or if the community itself is not open to students and teachers as a work-service laboratory. It is therefore essential that administrators, teachers and students alike understand how every interview, excursion and survey, every extended field study, service project and work experience is a venture in public relations—a situation through which they interpret the school and its program to parents and community groups.

Edward G. Olsen, *et al.*, *School and Community*. Englewood Cliffs, N. J.: Prentice-Hall, Inc., 1945, page 335.

The dictionary definition of a community is: (1) a body of people having common organization of interests or living in the same place under the same laws, and (2) society at large; the people in general; the people of a particular region, or the region itself. Schools consider all those descriptions when they talk about their communities, and they must do so, for the communities of the schools across the nation differ so widely.

There are large urban junior high schools whose pupils come from a dozen or more communities or neighborhoods. Some of them are miles apart, and each differs from the other in population make-up. In one sense they all constitute the school's community, for the varying needs of the children and parents have to be met. Parent representatives of all groups should be consulted in policy matters. The immediate neighborhood in which the school is located becomes more intimately associated with it and is apt to be considered the school's community. On the other hand, the entire city is also the community of the school, for from it the school draws resources and into it the students go for first-hand experience.

Consolidated schools which draw their students from many surrounding villages and townships, or which serve an entire county, are like the large urban school with respect to community problems. The several places from which the children come are often very different from each other in social class and occupational interest. Children come in by bus, and often do not feel as if they belong because they cannot take part in so many of the after-school activities. These problems affect community relationships.

When the junior high school is merely a part of a twelve- or a six-year school, it does not face separate community problems. Those schools, however, are often such an important part of community life that the community becomes the curriculum and inter-action is of the highest order.[1] There is often a close attachment between a junior high school and its community, when the region can support a school by itself. Then the school becomes the center of educational and cultural life. Whether or not the community is used by the school for laboratory purposes depends upon the type of curriculum and educational procedures that are in use.

No matter what constitutes the school's community, there are certain common elements in the jobs that the junior high schools have to do in establishing good patterns of interaction. In the first place, going to junior high school may be regarded with apprehension and anxiety by the child and his family. This is particularly true when the parents have had less than seven years of schooling. The happiness and pleasure they experience in the school, when their needs are met there, are a determining element in the attitude of the community toward secondary education. The following episode illustrates the point.

The pupils and teachers in a large urban school were hurrying back to class from an atom bomb drill in the early part of the

---

[1] Floodwood, Minn., was such a school until the attack on modern education caused it to return to traditional education. See National Society for the Study of Education, *Education in Rural Communities*, 21st Year Book, Part II. Chicago: The Society, 1952.

year 1951. Suddenly a small boy, walking beside a teacher to whom he was not known, looked up at her with eyes alight and said, "Teacher, Teacher, I think this is the best school I was ever in!" He felt secure and cared for.

Such spontaneous expressions of appreciation are not uncommon. They are heard frequently among the junior high school students. Early adolescence is a period of enthusiastic search for adventure, and the child who comes to the junior high school from the smaller, elementary building finds many new and exciting experiences there. He increases his list of acquaintances and friends as he immerses himself in the peer society. He finds a new and interesting relationship with adults when they talk to him in a man-to-man fashion. He delights in the development of new skills, both mental and physical, which results from his experiences in the practical arts shop and the gymnasium, and in the classrooms where new areas of information are opened to him. He gets the thrill of emotional satisfaction as he participates in the production of music. His opportunities to do creative art open new avenues of success.

There is probably no more effective agent for the promotion of good public relations than the satisfied, enthusiastic, happy, growing youngster who can go home each day with some evidence of accomplishment, having had a success experience. Unfortunately there are too many pupils coming from junior high school classrooms with little evidence of satisfaction or achievement. There are also too many homes in which parents are entirely uninterested, and in which the children have no opportunity to display their products or express their happiness in their school lives. There are also large numbers of influential citizens and powerful interest groups which have no connection with children in the public schools. These people have to be reached in some other way since all of them are either supporters or potential attackers of public education, and because all of them pay for the schools. *It becomes a necessity, then, for every member of a school staff to accept his responsibility for being an active agent in the interests of public education and an ambassador of goodwill in the community.*

The American public owns the schools and should feel responsible for the construction of buildings, for the provision of materials, facilities, and equipment, for the securing of adequately trained teachers and for the development of curriculum designed to help the children of America to realize their potentialities to become well rounded persons, and to achieve the goal of effective participation in our democratic institutions and way of life.

This does not mean that educators should turn over their own professional responsibilities to the lay citizens. It does not imply that untrained people should be expected or permitted to do the technical work connected with planning and constructing buildings, curriculum research, or classroom instruction. It does mean that *the educational staff, recognizing the rights and duties of the citizenry, are under the obligation of making contacts and arrangements which will facilitate community participation in policy making.* Provision for such cooperative participation and for constant interpretation of the school to the community constitutes a second part of the school's community relations problem.[2] This phase cannot be done successfully unless the *staff members are informed and intelligent about the community or set of neighborhoods from which the students are drawn.*

The principal of a modern school includes community study in his plans for his in-service education program. A series of investigations into the structure of the community and the nature of its population should be undertaken and it will prove to be highly rewarding to the teachers. The data to be gathered will require them to go into the community for direct observation, to pay home visits, and to conduct interviews with parents and other citizens. It will also mean the construction of questionnaires and the study of all available school records. From these activities facts can be mobilized about:

Number and kinds of churches and their location
Number and kinds of schools and their location
Play areas and recreation facilities
Number and location of taverns, tap rooms, and neighborhood "hang-outs"
Kinds and locations of movies and cultural opportunities

---

[2] Many school systems issue pamphlets or leaflets describing various phases of the curriculum. A particularly good example of this is the "How We Teach" series, issued in Seattle, Washington.

Types and locations of residential areas
Businesses and industries
Distribution of racial, religious, and ethnic groups.

Comprehensive community studies of this nature require much time which will be reduced if committees are organized to share the work. Planning committee work and deciding how to report various findings to the total faculty are valuable experiences for teachers. From them, and from the direct learning experiences they have when they make a community survey, teachers learn what community resources are available and gain the courage to use them in their teaching.

Although direct experience is a powerful learning device, books play just as important a part in teacher education as they do in the classroom. Although they may have gathered many facts from people and places, the faculty needs a more complete picture of the structure of American society and of the problems of rural and urban life. They also need the help of experts to interpret the implications of cultural expectations for education. Among the authors to be consulted are Davis, Havighurst, and those who wrote the *Year Book* of 1952 for the Association for Supervision and Curriculum Development.[3]

When a school has studied its community, the staff are better able to handle a third facet of the community relations problem, namely, responsibility for leadership in the community of social action projects designed to better the quality of life. As teachers move out and around in the neighborhood, they cannot avoid getting to know and be known by the people who live and work there. They will inevitably become involved in discussion of community problems. The specific needs of their children which are not being met in the community will become the focus of these discussions. It is reasonable to suppose that around those needs some social action project will be initiated.[4]

Leadership for such community work should come from the

---

[3] See Warner, Havighurst and Loeb, *Who Shall Be Educated.* New York: Harper and Brothers, 1944; Warner, Meeker, Eells, *Social Class in America.* Chicago: Science Research Associates, 1949; ASCD Year Book, *Growing Up In An Anxious Age.* Washington, D. C.: The Association, N.E.A., 1952.

[4] Gucky, Brown, and Corey, "Do Schools Build Better Communities?" *School Executive,* December, 1952.

people. It may well be, however, that the principal, an administrative assistant, a counselor, or a teacher may have to take the initiative. Among the many activities that can begin this way are:

1. The organization and administration of a community council. This will require participation by members of the staff in the capacity of group leaders and ordinary members. They will attend meetings, listen to and discuss reports of committee work, participate in committee enterprises, and carry the results back to the school.

2. Coordination of community services around the specific needs of individual children and their families. This will involve them in initiating action, enlisting the aid of staff specialists, seeking the help of community agencies, conducting and participating in discussions and action outcomes.

3. Organization of teen-age canteens or other needed recreational after-school or evening opportunities. This will require teachers to man the activities and to enlist the aid of volunteers who will require training.

4. Organization of a speakers bureau which will enable staff members to present the school and its program to all kinds of community groups.

5. Organization of an effective P.T.A. which will include in its activities study and discussion of the problems of modern education. This will require leadership and participation of the faculty.[5]

A fourth aspect of the community relations problem is the school's responsibility for giving its students first-hand knowledge of their community. It must become the laboratory in which pupils learn the processes and practices of democratic life. The school accomplishes this by taking children out into the community on many occasions. As they go, they will create around them new bonds of understanding and goodwill for the school.

Going out is not enough. The community must come into the school. Its resources include many people to be talked to and heard from. Some of them are willing to come into the school as

---

[5] The secondary schools in some cities, such as Seattle and Minneapolis, are building effective P.T.S.A. groups. The S represents students who are enrolled in the organization with their parents, and are useful in building up the membership of adults. They also make valuable contribution to thought and action in the groups.

consultants. They bring up-to-the-minute information about life and how it is carried on in community living. Much of what they have to tell is not in print or is in books that are hard for many of the pupils to read.

When adults come into the school to take part in its activities, to meet with children, to witness a performance, they are less likely to make false accusations about the behavior of the students and the quality of instruction. They also become more aware of the necessity for having the best qualified teachers and of paying them adequate salaries. Bond issues meet with little opposition from men and women who have learned at first hand that buildings are antiquated and overcrowded, or that there is too little play space and insufficient equipment. This kind of inter-change between a school and its community helps to marshal all people of goodwill solidly back of public education.

Inevitably the community in its turn reacts upon the school. As teachers have personal experiences with all kinds of people, all social classes, all ethnic backgrounds, all racial and religious minorities, they become better able to understand the children in their classes. It is to be expected that prejudices will be softened if not uprooted. It is to be hoped that people of all groups will become welcome members of the staff. There is no reason for not admitting to the several divisions of the staff—clerical, instructional, administrative, counseling, and custodial—representatives of all minority groups that make up our American population. In the school they will help to interpret the different culture patterns. Such a staff is able to create an example of democracy to which the community can turn for help.

⟨ *The multiple role, then, for the junior high school to play in the community is to introduce the people to secondary education; to provide opportunity for citizens to participate in policy making and curriculum development; to lead community agencies into social action projects that will better the life there; to make sure that the citizens of tomorrow will know about the problems of community living; and to rally support behind public education in America.*

The school of today will find obstacles in its path as it moves forward. Some of them are set up by traditionalists who do not wish to see the schools depart from solely book study. They will have to be convinced of the multiple outcomes of direct learning experiences by documentary evidence gathered in the course of action research projects.

Involvement of teachers in making the community survey will not be accomplished without difficulty. Many who do not live near the school will be unable and/or unwilling to sacrifice the time it requires. Some school districts solve this problem by making community study the content of in-service education courses which carry credit toward degrees and/or salary increments.

Social action projects also cost heavily of time and energy. It may be necessary to make participation in them purely voluntary, or to release key people from part of their classroom work to engage in them. These teachers would, of course, be obligated to keep the faculty informed of their activities and learnings. Objection to teacher participation in such projects may come from citizens who regard this kind of project as "politics." Teachers have the right to engage in political activity, however, and will need to show their ability and tact as community leaders. Meanwhile, all kinds of action projects can be developed inside the school, which will affect the community and help the people to create better living conditions for themselves.

The nature of the population in some communities will present an obstacle when attempts are made to draw the parents into school affairs. Where lower social classes predominate, the lack of proper clothing and of facility in the use of English deter parents from accepting invitations from the school. Some of them are afraid of teachers. Moreover, it is always difficult to get parents of junior high school boys and girls to come to meetings. Adolescents do not want their parents to join the P.T.A. They consider this a hangover from the elementary school and feel that they are "on their own" in school matters. Some of this resistance can be overcome by giving the students themselves a part in every such enterprise. They should help in the planning as well as in the carrying out of the projects.

There are many ways of bringing the community into the school. The traditional ones are the big dramatic productions which the people pay to see. Sports events and field days attract thousands of spectators. Graduation days or closing exercises bring in people who have never before set foot in a public school building. Many modern schools invite parents to special assembly programs at which outstanding students are recognized, installations of student officers are held, and culminating activities of units of work are produced. One example of this kind of program is the reception for parents that seventh graders like to arrange as the culmination of their orientation unit. They introduce their families to the teachers, show them the building, and explain the new ways they have learned of working together.

In almost all schools, the principal calls together the parents of newly admitted pupils. He takes this opportunity to tell the reasons for the junior high school and what he hopes it will do for their children.

In some schools there are regular evening events to which the pupils bring their parents. This gives opportunity for wholesome interaction as they inspect classroom work, talk to each other, to the teacher, and to their children. If demonstration teaching is done at these meetings, much can be done to break down resistance to new methods. In schools where curriculum change is going on, meetings should be devoted to joint parent-teacher-pupil discussion of new policy, content, and methods.

Although the mounting costs of education are due primarily to tremendous increases in school population, to the high prices of materials and labor, and to the necessity for paying teachers adequate salaries, blame will be placed on changes in the curriculum by some people. This is another of the common blocks to be overcome. Groups of citizens may band together in an effort to prevent the school of tomorrow from coming into existence. There are also people who would destroy the kind of education that will produce intelligent consumers and effective citizens. It will take courage to progress in face of their activities. Educational leaders will have to continue to regard personal and professional integrity as of greatest worth.

The doors of today's junior high schools are open for community use. Teen-agers stay after the regular school day is done. Then they troop back in the evening for recreational adventures. Sports, games, plays, dances, music, films, and creative hand work are made available to them. Adult groups, too, assemble there for their adventures. Choral groups, Americanization classes, election polls, discussion groups, vocational training, and recreation are provided. Tomorrow, all the junior high schools of America can become community centers into which the people, young and adult, will enter to learn, and from which they will leave, dedicated to the service of democracy.

Learning Activities for Members of Pre- and In-Service Teacher Education Classes

In addition to reading, set up other learning experiences such as:

1. Arranging for the showing of a film.
2. Arranging for interviews with some of the top community officials.
3. Sitting in on meetings of the Mayor's Committee for Human Rights, the Civil Liberties Council, The F.E.P. Commission or any other such agency.
4. Discussing with school administrators the problems involved in forming and carrying on parent-teacher associations.
5. Making a map of the community showing population distribution—races, ethnic groups, religious concentrations.

References

BOOKS

Berkson, I. B., *The Ideal and the Community*. New York: Harper and Brothers, 1958.
Conant, James B., *The Child, The Parent and The State*. Cambridge, Mass., Harvard University Press, 1960.
Getzels, J. W., *The Acquisition of Values in School and Society*. Chicago: University of Chicago Press, 1958.
Governor's Fact Finding Commission on Education, *Do Citizens and Education Mix?* Hartford, Conn.: The Commission, 1951.
Hamlin, H. M., *Citizens Committees in the Public Schools*. Danville, Ill.: Interstate Printers and Publishers, 1953.
John Dewey Society, *The Teacher's Role in American Society*. New York: Harper and Brothers, 1957.
Lippitt, Ronald, *Training in Community Relations*. New York: Harper and Brothers, 1949.
McCloskey, Gordon, *Education and Public Understanding*. New York: Harper and Brothers, 1959.

PERIODICALS AND PAMPHLETS

Ames, D. A., "Community Occupational Survey as a Public Relations Instrument," *The School Review,* January, 1953.

Hinton, Carmelita, "A School That Attempts to Be a Community," *Progressive Education,* March, 1952.

Kersey, V., "The Evidence In and Out of School," *The School Executive,* May, 1952.

National Association of Secondary-School Principals, "Public Relations for the American High School," *The Bulletin,* September, 1960.

National School Public Relations Association, *It Starts in the Classroom: A Public Relations Handbook for Classroom Teachers.* Washington, D. C.: The Association, 1951.

_____*Pebbles,* Washington, D. C.: The Association, 1960.

PART
THREE

Modern Curriculum
Content and Techniques

CHAPTER NINE

Content in
the Multi-period (Core) Class

The ultimate aim of education is, of course, the self-realization of all persons. But, as we have seen, self-realization is to be achieved through a balanced participation in all the institutions of society. The immediate aim of education is, therefore, to prepare young people for effective participation in those institutions. The institutions of society are the objectives of education. It follows as a corollary that the curriculum must be composed of the intellectual resources used in operating those institutions.

Ross L. Finney, *A Sociological Philosophy of Education.* New York: The Macmillan Co., 1928, page 93.

The curriculum of the junior high school must be based upon goals which are close to the stream of living in today's world. These goals can be stated effectively in terms of the characteristics which the administrators, the teachers, the students, their parents, their future senior high school teachers, and their future employers in the community think the graduates should possess. In many places representatives of all of those groups are called in by school administrators to express their desires and hopes for the children, to help to set up the objectives of the program, and to determine the policies upon which the curriculum makers are to proceed.

The following list of outcomes is stated in terms of the attitudes, appreciations, skills, information and behaviors which can be attained by pupils as they live and learn in a modern junior high school:

1. Wholesome attitudes toward self as a person and as a growing organism.

2. Acceptance of own sex role. This requires knowledge of what it involves and respect for the position of the sex group in society.

3. Adjustment to the opposite sex. This requires knowledge of the social and physiological role played in life. The outcome to be desired at this stage of development is the ability to meet, talk, work, and play together.

4. Physical skills that are useful in games.

5. Muscular coordination and skills that are useful in creative handwork and in physical labor, and respect for workers in those fields.

6. The know-how of working and playing in groups.

7. Skill in sharing in the making of group decisions and in cooperating in carrying them out.

8. The ability to make wise personal choice.

9. Skill in handling the basic mental tools that are needed to live and learn in modern life—reading, writing, talking, listening, and numbers.

10. Significant social and political concepts including those ideologies that threaten democracy.

11. Significant scientific concepts and knowledge of the natural environment.

12. Desirable social attitudes in regard to property, conservation of human and natural resources, politics, race, religion, and social class.

13. Some ability to do reflective and critical thinking.

14. Control over the emotions and some knowledge of the causes.

15. Ability to accept and adjust to disappointment and experiences involving failure, and to use them as learning experiences.

16. Knowledge of own strengths and weaknesses.

17. Ability to make moral judgments.

18. Development of a socially acceptable scale of values and of aesthetic appreciations—the good, the true, the beautiful.

19. Development of the beginnings of a philosophy of life.

Examination of the foregoing statements of purposes leads to agreement on the required content of the curriculum. To educators, content means *subject matter*. Therefore the junior high school must provide learning opportunities in the fields of language arts, social studies, mathematics, science, physical development and health, the practical arts and the fine arts. There is nothing different in that list from what exists at present in the most traditional curriculum that can be found.

Subjects, however, are not enough to accomplish all of the objectives that have been listed. In at least two-thirds of them, *human relations* play a major role. Curriculum revision must take into consideration and provide opportunities for students to learn from experience how to relate themselves to others in ways which promote effective personal and social living in the democratic tradition. Among the requirements are skill in the *group processes.*

About half of the goals listed above refer to *thought processes.* However, departmentalization, dependence on textbook study, and memorization of facts for tests offer few opportunities to achieve thought skills.

If subject matter, human relations, and skills in the group processes and in thinking are to be provided, it becomes clear that for the junior high school of tomorrow and to meet the needs of today, curriculum builders will have to *plan the kind of schedule and teaching-learning experiences which will give the pupils many opportunities to practice the desired skills, to acquire the required information, and to develop the desirable appreciations and attitudes which are needed by the intelligent, effective citizen who is capable of generous, rich, and abundant living.*

Many teachers, administrators, and college professors are of the opinion that the use of schedules which provide for blocks of time within which unit teaching across subject matter lines can be accomplished offers the best single promise of implementing modern educational philosophy and of securing the objectives desired in the junior high school. This type of organization of time, of content, and of methods is generally known as core. Interest in its use is increasing in spite of the fact that in the 1950's the term "core" became a target of abuse by people who sought a scapegoat on which to blame the weaknesses of American education.[1]

Nevertheless, as the building of new junior high schools followed upon the heels of population increase, administrators sought to incorporate some part of the core-concept into their programs. Thus the "double-period" became prevalent. For the most part this means that a teacher meets one group of children for two periods, usually successive, in which he teaches two subject areas. These are most frequently language arts and social studies, occasionally, mathematics and science. The double period is used as a scheduling device to do two things: 1) provide for integration of guidance with teaching in the double periods and 2) reduce the pupil-load for the teachers involved. Administrators and teachers readily admit that

---

[1] Ninety-one per cent of the administrators queried in 1959 by Dale L. Knapp, in a study of curriculum change in Ohio, said that the block-time class resulted in improved educational progress.

with only this first step toward core, attendance improves, behavior problems decrease, teachers and pupils like each other better, and teachers are better able to meet instructional needs. Thus learning is increased.

With help and encouragement, teachers of double-period classes see that the arrangement provides them with time enough to take trips, to see and discuss films, to engage in dramatics, to call in speakers and consultants, and to utilize all the enrichment devices that are impossible in a single period. Moreover teachers also begin to see the interrelationships of the subject areas. When they do so, pupil-teacher planning of units of work and the use of group processes are methods they are often willing to try. Integration of subjects in unit teaching soon transforms a double-period class into the beginning of a core curriculum. When the double period is lengthened to encompass one-third to one-half the day and other subject areas are no longer unrelated, a true core begins to function. Then, when the concepts of unit teaching, group process, and diversified learning activities are spread into such subjects as general science, health education, general mathematics and practical arts, all the outcomes of a good core program or curriculum can be realized.

Unfortunately, in very many school districts, administrators have been unable to remove the following barriers to the development of the core type of organization and instruction:

(1) The teacher turnover each semester or year places too great a burden for in-service education upon the principal and introduces elements of insecurity and instability into the school. (2) Administrators change, and a progressive principal or superintendent is followed by a conservative or reactionary one who prefers traditional course of study requirements and departmentalized schools. (3) When the authorities are unwilling to supply a few essential additions to equipment, materials, and books, teachers become weary of struggling against the odds. (4) Often there are too many resistant and hostile forces within the school system itself: teachers who are unwilling to accept the responsibility for determining curriculum, saying that this is the administrator's job. (5) The antagonistic forces in the system join with community groups who are eager to reduce costs or the civic effectiveness of public education or both. (6) There

are too many unsupervised, indifferent teachers who have chaotic classrooms no matter what the curriculum plan may be, and whose poor work is erroneously ascribed to the new responsibilities they are "forced to meet" for which they are inadequately prepared and with which they receive no help. (7) A renewed powerful demand for a return to subject matter and a so-called "hard education" has reinforced the stand of the traditionalists who have opposed core curriculum from its inception.

It is undoubtedly true that as they move away from traditional content and techniques, difficulties and dangers confront untrained, unsupervised, and inexperienced teachers whose own scholastic backgrounds have been solely in specialized subject-matter fields, and who have depended upon lecture, book-study, recitations, and test techniques. Their classrooms are apt to be characterized by laissez-faire methods when they begin to experiment. Laxity leads to little real accomplishment by the students. Dissatisfaction and insecurity grow rapidly in such soil. However, in increasing numbers of schools, teachers who recognize those dangers and plan conscientiously to avoid them do have the courage to break with tradition even at the risk of going through a period of confusion.

Interest in the development of core curriculum is growing because of the many articles in periodicals which report successful programs and the attainment of the desired outcomes. Some of these reports are of action-research projects.[2] Others come from schools which have developed and are using the plan and techniques.

Several factors contribute heavily to success in the development of a core curriculum: (1) Strong leadership in the democratic tradition. If a director or coordinator of curriculum is not available, then the principal, vice-principal, or supervisor shoulders the task. (2) Acceptance of the philosophy by the total faculty of the school, and gradual incorporation of the techniques into all the classrooms. (3) The emergence of teacher leadership as the result of administrative encouragement. (4) The development of pupil-teacher planning techniques in the determination and administration of classroom activities. (5) A comprehensive professional program of study

---

[2] Hilda Taba and staff, *Reports on Projects Published*, Washington, D. C.: American Council on Education, 1950, 1951, 1952. Final Report—"Intergroup Education in Public Schools," 1953.

groups, teacher planning committees, the use of consultants, and the free exchange of information, opinions, and experiences among the teachers. (6) Coordination of curriculum by someone in authority. (7) Constant, critical evaluation of the program and its outcomes by all who are involved.

One of the important methods schools use to move themselves toward the desired outcomes is enlisting the services of all who are concerned, in the development of content and learning activities. This produces good results. Children identify themselves with the need to learn, and accept responsibilities for doing what is necessary to learn, when *they* set up the goals *they* want to reach. Behavior problems decrease when students are busy finding the answers to questions *they* have raised and are expressing themselves in creative activities. Teachers get more intimately acquainted with their pupils and derive satisfaction from seeing them grow and develop. Teachers begin to realize their own worth when their superior officers recognize their abilities and place trust and confidence in them. They feel less frustrated, and are released for creative teaching when they are no longer held responsible for driving children to accomplish ends that are not within reach, using tools too difficult to manage.[3]

Although the details differ widely from school to school, there are certain common elements in the successful core programs that are in use. The plan which is described and illustrated in Chapter 6 calls for a block of time, exceeding the usual period in length, but including from one-third to all of the day at the seventh grade level. The portion of the day changes somewhat from grade to grade as more opportunities for specialized electives are provided. This time represents the center or heart of the day for the child, because he spends it with the teacher who cares most about him and whom he gets to know best.

The teacher of the core group is responsible for multiple learnings. He must devise teaching-learning situations to meet the needs that his pupils have in common as well as those which are peculiar to the individual, in unspecialized learning areas.

---

[3] Teachers have said that these are the results in schools in Minneapolis, Philadelphia, New York City, Schenectady, Buffalo, Denver, Tulsa, Springfield, Ohio, and other places where modern methods of determining curriculum content are used.

Included among these are the needs for individual and group guidance, for remedial and developmental work in the language arts (English), for increased skills, appreciations, and information about the democratic way of living and governing (social studies), and for increased knowledge and control of the natural environment (science). Among the skills needed by all for effective living and learning are the thought skills—the ability to attack and solve a problem, to plan alone and with others, to think critically, to make wise choice and good decisions, to judge and evaluate. Development of these becomes the responsibility of the core teacher.

Of course the core teacher shares these responsibilities with the other members of the staff. Counselors, when they are provided, and the principal help with guidance problems that go beyond the range of the classroom. Reading should be taught by every teacher in every classroom in so far as it relates to the work that is under way. The other modes of communication: listening, talking, writing, should also receive constant attention in every classroom. If all teachers were to make uniform efforts, leaving technical instruction and practice to the core teacher, pupils would be less likely to think of correct usage and good English as part of the English course to be used only when a mark in English is desired, and more likely to relate them to the necessity for effective communication with other people.

Certainly thought processes are called for in every classroom. There is no reason why pupil-teacher planning, group work, collective thinking, making wise choice, doing critical evaluation should not be required in all parts of the program. Time is a factor, but practical arts and fine arts classes are usually double periods, and so approximate the time of the daily core period, although they usually come less frequently in the weekly schedule.

Creative activity can characterize all phases of the work in the junior high school. It is important in the gymnasium where regimented drills no longer achieve all the desired outcomes. Shop work becomes an exciting adventure to both boys and girls when they see their own ideas translated into metal, wood, clay, or plastics, and when each one plans and makes the thing he wants, not the cookie cutter, broom holder or ash tray that is in

the course of study. The fine arts are not so good as they can and
ought to be when the child does not find in those classrooms the
chance to use all kinds of art media to express his own thoughts
and emotional reactions.

In all areas of the curriculum, as teachers move from the traditional toward the modern, they have problems out of which grow
common needs. They have to: (1) develop content in the classroom with the help of their pupils instead of getting it out of
courses of study; (2) devise many ways of proceeding from one
learning experience to the next, realizing that a logical or chronological basis is not the only or even the best way to determine
sequence; (3) provide many and varied learning experiences, knowing that reading is the most abstract and the most difficult way to
learn for large numbers of children.

When subject-oriented teachers are scheduled to core for two or
three periods a day, they have neither past experience nor printed
guides to fall back on. They are not used to arranging for the variation of activities that must be planned for the long time stretch.
Teachers can adapt the following suggestions to meet their specific
needs.

Decisions about content are made by various persons in many
different ways in the junior high schools across the land. In some
schools the teacher, personally, has no part in deciding it, although
as new curriculum guides are constructed it is becoming customary
to call in teacher representatives. For the most part, the teachers
get the content they are to teach from old and new courses of
study, syllabi, and guides that are distributed by State Departments
of Education and in the larger cities, by local curriculum authorities.
These publications vary all the way from subject-matter outlines
through subject-matter units, to a set of suggested themes or
emphases within which the teacher has a greater or less degree
of freedom to develop experience units.

There are places where the individual school has complete
autonomy in curriculum building, subject only to the permission
and supervision of the administrative authority. In some of these
schools the faculty, working under the direction of the principal
and/or the curriculum coordinator, pre-determine the units to be
studied, evaluating, and, if necessary, changing them from time

to time. In other schools the classroom teacher is given the responsibility for making decisions. He usually does this cooperatively with the children in the class. Where this extreme freedom is granted, the professional study program usually includes discussion of the teacher's responsibility for keeping constantly in mind *a framework of reference within which lie the essential content areas.*

There are two aspects of content to be considered—*scope* and *sequence*. Scope has to do with the areas to be included, the questions to be explored, the problems to be solved, the units to be studied, the "ground to be covered," the facts to be learned, the outcomes to be expected. Obviously that definition of scope which implies that the selection of units of study is to be based on the passing whims and transient interests of the boys and girls is not acceptable. Often what children say when they are asked "what do you want to study?" does not even represent the concerns of a majority of the students. It can be dictated by the pupils who dominate the peer society. It is equally sure that adequate breadth and depth of scope will not be secured when teachers fail to recognize the nature of the roles they must play in the planning process. Finally, it will be impossible to prevent repetition and omission of essential elements if the coordinator or principal fails to keep records of what is going on in the classrooms. These can be made up in such form that they show at a glance the units that are under way in the entire school. They can also be arranged so that they show what every group has studied throughout the three year span.

If, then, the scope of a program is to include that content which is most closely related to the needs of the children in the classroom, its determination will depend upon the following conditions: (1) *finding the real interests and concerns of a group of students;* (2) *identifying student needs in relation to the culture of which they are a part;* (3) *making sure that the teacher plays his appropriate role;* (4) *keeping track of the units of work.*

Teachers who are working with full or even comparative freedom in the choice of content for the core classes need to keep constantly in mind a frame of reference within which are the learning needs common to all American youth, and out of which must come the social and personal learning experiences which all must have if they are to become effective citizens in our society.[4] In some schools or school systems, these are formulated into a set of basic questions or issues. In others, they are stated as the dynamic processes and problems of a civilized society into which children must be inducted as they mature. One such list follows:[5]

1. Conserving life and health
2. Conserving and using natural and man-made resources
3. Producing, distributing, consuming goods and services
4. Transporting goods and services
5. Communicating information, ideas, and feelings
6. Organizing and governing group actions
7. Providing for and participating in recreation
8. Providing for and securing education
9. Satisfying esthetic and spiritual needs.

During a span of three years, teachers can be expected to guide the classroom planning so that units are selected which will increase knowledge and understanding in all of the above areas. Some of them will be interwoven with others and may not require or even lend themselves to separate units. This is true of number nine, and partially true of number five in so far as it applies to the use of language for communication.

The term *sequence* refers to the order in which learning experiences are arranged. This includes a line of development which is supposed to articulate the grade levels, as well as the succession of units to be studied in each semester or year. In this respect also, junior high schools vary all the way from the traditional to the most modern practices. On the extreme right are the schools that use courses of study or syllabi in which the content to be taught is arranged in logical or chronological outlines. In some of the schools operating core curriculum, units are designated for each grade level. They are pre-determined by either a centralized curriculum authority or by the faculty of the school, and arranged presumably on a maturity scale. Other schools include in the guides for teachers, "over-arching" grade themes within which the teacher has freedom to plan with his class those units which are appro-

---

[4] See Educational Policies Commission, *The Education of Free Men in American Democracy*. Washington, D. C.: The Assoc., 1941.

[5] Social Studies Curriculum Guide, *Toward Social Competence*. Philadelphia, Pa.: 1951. Long Beach, Cal., has broken these areas into 16 categories.

priate and important to his pupils. Such planning may be based on some logical connection or the new unit may grow out of immediate and discrete needs. Another variation is that in which the teacher must give part of the term to required units, but is free to develop others with his class according to their needs and interests. Again the sequence is not specifically indicated. On the extreme left are the schools in which there are no specific requirements other than the frame of reference previously described.

In programs of learning that consist of experience units which cut across subject matter lines, and in which pupil-teacher planning is a reality, predetermination of the order or sequence of those units is not likely to be successful. Examination of a common pattern will reveal its fallacy. It is usual to find that on a predicated basis of "interest and maturity," neighborhood and community study is assigned to seventh grade. But it is also allotted to tenth grade! The eighth grades get problems of national import. But these are also assigned to eleventh grade! That leaves the international issues for the ninth grade. And they are also the problems for the twelfth grade! Quite obviously such a sequence is not based upon the maturity levels of the students since it places ninth and twelfth year pupils in the same category. It seems to indicate that in the tenth year, the students are less capable of dealing with national issues than are those in the ninth year.

The following examples indicate the problems which arise when predetermination of units is tried. A seventh year class, after completing an orientation unit during which they become deeply interested in the school government, said, "Now we must learn more about how our country carries on these governmental functions." The teacher was confused and embarrassed when he had to reply, "No, I'm sorry. The study of the national government belongs in the eighth year. You will have to wait until next year for that unit." The children were let down and suspicious because they had been led to believe that they could say what they believed they needed and wanted to study next and have their needs respected. Another example further illustrates the point. An eighth grade group, after studying a unit about our democratic way of life, wanted to compare it with the way other people live in other lands. The teacher had to refuse them because the study of things outside of the United States belonged in the ninth year.

The double-barreled problem of scope and sequence is closely tied up with educators' fears that if teachers and pupils are the responsible agents in planning, there will be serious omissions and wasteful repetitions. Certainly there will be omissions no matter who makes the plans or what the scope may be. This is no less the case when the traditional teacher uses his single prescribed textbook which is designed to follow the course of study. For only the teacher "covers the course of study," and no course can possibly include all that is to be known in the field, and no subject-matter field can provide all the information that is required to answer most of the questions raised about the important problems of our times. When the teacher and his pupils are seriously concerned with their educational tasks, they will make certain that questions, problems, and issues of importance to them are included in the year's work. Moreover, they will do the necessary work in such a way that all of them realize that they do not yet have all the facts and all the answers, but that they have merely touched on matters that must continue throughout life to be the centers of their interest, reading, discussion, and study.

When students have been granted freedom to plan their units of work, they develop the habit of stopping at intervals to consider such questions as: What does education for effective citizenship include? What are the characteristics of the educated person? How far along the way to those goals have we come? In the light of our progress and our needs, what must we study next? Sometimes they use a different approach to the next unit. They try to clarify further their *common* problems, to determine which of them is most pressing, and then proceed to plan for solving that one. These opportunities to practice the skills of critical thinking and to make the stream of their own lives the content of their study are of greater significance in determining sequence than any pre-determined scheme or logical arrangement can possibly be. It is unlikely, moreover, that the expressions of need and interests so derived will have too much to do with grade levels.

Fear of wasteful repetition is rarely justified. Most children are seriously engaged in the business of growing up. They have great curiosity and want to learn ever more about the world in which they live and the society into which they have been born. They are eager to get help in thinking through problems of ethical and spiritual values. They are unwilling to forego pressing forward into these matters in order to dawdle away time doing something they did once before, on a lower grade level. Furthermore, selection of a unit is always done in accordance with a set of criteria the children construct. Repetition is usually used as a reason for eliminating a suggestion.

It is probably true that some children in every group, in order to get out of work, may try to sway opinion in favor of a unit they previously enjoyed. Teachers must not only be forewarned of this possibility but they must also be forearmed. This means that they are responsible for knowing in advance what units their classes have previously studied. They must also accept responsibility for guiding and directing thought during the planning periods. When repetition is suggested, the teacher must say a forthright "No." Of course, he must also state his reasons for making that decision. In such cases most of the children are usually on his side. Those that are not become subjects for interview and counseling procedures.

Lawrence G. Thomas summarized this point of view toward scope and sequence when he said, ". . . truths . . . are learned as the solutions of problems in the lives of the pupils. What these problems are depends upon the present particular circumstance in the lives of the pupils and on the current stage of their development. In this matrix are found the unrealized potentialities from which the problems and goals of the class activities are constructed. Thus a curriculum cannot be more than broadly outlined in advance by the teacher, and will consist largely of an array of resources which the teacher anticipates may be called upon as the current activities of the class lead on to new interests and new problems. The actual details of the curriculum must be constructed cooperatively in the classroom from week to week."[6]

Unless the reader has worked with children in this manner, he may be unable to picture what children are likely to plan as they move through the three years of a junior high school. The following records show what an actual group of students studied during their stay in their school.[7]

---

[6] L. G. Thomas, "The Meaning of Progressive in Progressive Education," *Educational Administration and Supervision,* October, 1946.

[7] Taken from the files of the Gillespie Junior High School, Philadelphia, Pa.

Learning Experiences of a Class Which Met Two Hours Daily From Seventh Through Ninth Year

7A Grade—Fall term:
1. Orientation unit
2. Unit on city—approach: What part did Philadelphia play in the early life of the nation? What is its role today?

7B Grade—Spring term:
1. Unit on Astronomy—approach: What makes the world go round?
2. Unit on Animal Life—approach: If we are dependent on animal life, we must know more about it.
3. Unit on Safety—approach: There have been some accidents in our school recently that should have been avoided. What can we do about it?

8A Grade—Fall term:
1. Unit on Aviation—approach: People say this is the air age. What does that mean in terms of us?
2. Unit on China—approach: Is it true that World War III has already begun in China?
3. Unit on Juvenile Delinquency—approach: When you read the papers it sounds as if all teen-agers are delinquent. What makes children go wrong?

8B Grade—Spring term:
1. Unit on Latin America—approach: What does the "Good Neighbor Policy" mean?
2. Unit on Conservation—approach: People talk about what will happen when oil and coal give out. Could that happen?

9A Grade—Fall term:
1. Unit on Intercultural Tensions—approach: There was a neighborhood fight. Feeling is high. Can anything be done about this sort of thing?
2. Unit on Internationalism—approach: What has the United Nations accomplished for world peace?

9B Grade—Spring term:
1. Unit on Government—approach: We do not know enough about how our government works.
2. Unit on Labor—approach: A strike is going on. How did it get started? How can the workers and management get together?

In addition to the above units of study, the class was involved in certain parallel activities every term. Although these areas did not vary, the specific content in each depended upon the developmental needs of the pupils who, of course, changed as they grew older and as they built backgrounds of accomplishment and skills. Thus the daily two hour period was given over in part, and at intervals through the week, to the following:

Literature—reading and study
Corrective and developmental work in the Language Arts
Corrective, developmental, remedial reading
Creative writing
Discussion of current affairs—reading and talking about the news
Guidance
Celebration of patriotic holidays
Participation in Student Government work and enterprises.

The chart on pages 178-179 shows that the units selected by several class sections in any grade may be quite different, but that in a three year period every group gets a rounded program without duplication.

In charts like the one shown here, the whole story about the units that were studied cannot be told. Only the general area within which the units were developed can be indicated. The actual content is always determined by the approach and the specific needs and interests of the children in the classroom. For example "Intercultural Problems" in one group may be directed to a study of religious differences, whereas in another group it might have to do mostly with racial problems. "Transportation" in an early grade might be concerned with the differences between the present and the past, but in a later grade emphasis would be placed more likely on the effect of present means of travel upon world unity.

Whenever such records are examined, it is important to realize that space forbids recording the actual questions or problems which are the central points around which units develop as pupils state their concerns and decide what they need to know and do in order to answer their questions and solve their problems. In order to answer questions about these, it would be necessary to consult the reports of the units that are kept on file in every school in which this type of curriculum is used. Reports of some of the many units noted on the chart above have therefore been included in the fourth section of this book.

The following tables show the extent and frequency of units that were actually chosen by the pupils in a junior high school during an eight year period. The background framework was the teachers' constant awareness of (1) the necessity for inducting their pupils into society, (2) meeting needs consequent to developmental tasks, (3) making sure that new concepts were formed and old ones wid-

UNITS SELECTED EVERY TERM BY
THROUGH THREE YEARS OF

Section	7A Grade Sept. 1947	7B Grade Feb. 1948	8A Grade Sept. 1948
1	1—Orientation Unit 2—Community History 3—Money	1—February's Great Men 2—The Heavens 3—Animal Life 4—Safety	1—Air Age Is Here 2—Plant Life 3—Juvenile Delinquency
2	1—Orientation 2—History of School Neighborhood 3—Personal Health	1—Famous People 2—Animal Life 3—Conservation	1—Recreation and Leisure Time 2—Intercultural Tensions 3—Money
3	1—Orientation 2—Transportation in the City	1—Astronomy 2—Prehistoric Man 3—Latin America	1—Housing 2—State History 3—Money
4	1—Orientation 2—Ways of Government 3—Astronomy	1—America's Greatest Presidents 2—Can I be President — (self-appraisal and careers)	1—Juvenile Delinquency 2—Intercultural Differences and Similarities
5	1—Orientation 2—Fire Protection 3—Government Protections	1—Transportation 2—The Russian Way of Life	1—United Nations 2—Astronomy 3—Conservation
6	1—Orientation 2—My Community and Me	1—Bird Life 2—School Gardens 3—Transporting Goods	1—Mexico 2—Labor Problems
7	1—Orientation 2—Intercultural Concepts	1—Our City 2—Our State 3—Conservation	1—Animal Life 2—United Nations

From the files of the Gillespie Junior High School, Philadelphia, Pennsylvania, 1950.

ened and deepened, (4) the essential skills that were to be developed and strengthened. The figures indicate the number of times a unit in that particular area was studied by classes during the grade level under which it is included. For example, the 24 after "Other Lands and Peoples" means that in the eight years, 24 seventh grade groups chose such units.

CLASSES WHICH REMAINED TOGETHER
JUNIOR HIGH SCHOOL

8B Grade Feb. 1949	9A Grade Sept. 1949	9B Grade Feb. 1950
1—The "Good Neighbor Policy" 2—Constitution	1—Communism 2—Housing	1—Teen-age Problems 2—Labor 3—Conservation
1—Government Service 2—Housing	1—Labor vs. Management 2—State History 3—United Nations	1—The Russian Threat 2—Our Personal Next Steps
1—Juvenile Delinquency 2—United Nations	1—Atomic Energy 2—Our Government in Action	1—Mental Health 2—Labor Movement in America 3—Conservation
1—Intercultural Unit (continued) 2—Money 3—Conservation	1—One World 2—Atomic Energy 3—State History	1—Labor Unions 2—Recreation and Leisure Time 3—On to Senior High
1—Standard of Living 2—Birds 3—Money	1—Intercultural Problems 2—Mental Health	1—Labor 2—State History 3—Self-Appraisal for Next Steps
1—One World 2—Russia	1—Money and Taxes 2—U. S. Constitution	1—State History 2—Getting Ready for Senior High 3—Conservation
1—China 2—Gardens 3—Money	1—Transportation 2—Government Operation	1—Russia 2—Mental Health

In the modern school, however, formal units of study do not constitute all that is to be accomplished in the block of time devoted to "Core," "General Education," "Common Learnings," "Block," or "Social Living" (whatever term may be used). School and community drives for welfare funds, celebration of holidays, recognition of patriotic events, programs connected with nationally recognized religious festivals, and participation in school administration and control are all carried on there. It is there too, if the allotted block of time is designed for the purpose, that individual and group guidance is done.

These activities are often thought of as "parallel activities" and are considered to be as important as every other part of the program. There is much content in them as well as opportunity to learn the basic skills needed for effective participation in modern life. Unless, however, the learning experiences connected with these observances and projects are carefully structured and planned, there will be omission, repetition, boredom, and waste of time.

The following suggestion is one way to provide for the most frequently observed holidays and social community activities. The individual school must, of course, make its own plan in accordance with the desires of the community, the faculty and the student body.

OTHER ACTIVITIES IN THE MULTI-PERIOD CLASS

Fall Term Holidays and Drives	*Grade Emphasis*
1—Fire prevention	7A—Dramatization and home chores 7B—Spreading information in the neighborhood 8A—City (or local) fire department 8B—Safety first, fire laws 9A—Costs 9B—Chemistry of fire

2—Hallowe'en	All grades—
	  What does fun mean?
	  How to have fun at Hallowe'en

3—Social services: Red Cross, Community Chest, Infantile Paralysis funds, "Save the children" drives for funds and gifts, CARE, Christmas projects, etc.	7A—The kinds of services people need 7B—Survey of services available in the neighborhood 8A—City welfare agencies 8B—Dramatization 9A—Costs 9B—Implications for Democracy

OTHER ACTIVITIES IN THE MULTI-PERIOD CLASS
(Continued)

4—Constitution Day	7A—Colonial governments 7B—Continental Congress—dramatization 8A—The men responsible for the Constitution 8B—The Preamble and the Bill of Rights 9A—The structure of the government 9B—Important sections of the Constitution and amendments
5—Patriotic Holidays: Columbus Day, Armistice Day, Thanksgiving, special days connected with state history	7A—Biography 7B—Historical events 8A—Historical consequences 8B—Implications for Democracy 9A—Dramatizations 9B—Poetry and literature
6—Religious Festivals: Christmas, Hanukkah	All grades—programs, room decorations, dramatizations, poems and stories, parties, songs, dances, etc.

Spring Term Holidays and Drives	*Grade Emphasis*
1—Patriotic Holidays: Lincoln, Washington, Carver, other heroes, Memorial Day, Flag Day, Fourth of July, etc.	7A—Historical events 7B—Dramatization 8A—Biography 8B—War and peace 9A—Implications for Democracy 9B—Historical consequences
2—Religious Festivals: Easter, Passover, etc.	All grades, as for the Fall term
3—International Good Will Day	All grades—discussion of immediate events that are pertinent
4—Clean-up Week	7A—Home chores 7B—Dramatizations 8A—Spreading information in the neighborhood 8B—Governmental agencies, departments 9A—Implications for Democracy 9B—Costs, social action

Some parents and teachers object to activities like the foregoing ones. They call them entertainment or play. Some years ago, Herman Horne recognized their confusion between learning and play when he said, "In the school the place of play is fundamental beside work. . . . Its educational effects in the way of unintended preparation for later living are incalculable.

"But as the school must not work at play, so must it be said that it must not play at work. . . . Nor must children be deceived into working under the guise of play, which confusedly mixes opposite elements in life. Yet the work, as work, may be made so attractive that they will love to do it. Indeed the highest and noblest kind of work has this element of play in it, this element of joy in the activity for its own sake . . . The work itself should be so compelling in interest that it is freely willed, and that the element of drudgery is largely lacking."[8]

The point of view toward scope and sequence of curriculum content that has been presented is in accordance with the philosophy of Dr. L. Thomas Hopkins.[9] According to Dr. Hopkins, continuity, progression, coordination and articulation are effected within the living organism. The individual picks from each experience that he has only that which is meaningful to him. No one can refuse to give him freedom to make that selection for himself, or prevent him from using it in building his own inner articulated organism.

Educational systems are built on the theory that a series of courses or units of increasing difficulty and a set of graduation requirements constitute articulated educational experiences which will produce an articulated person. This might be the result if anyone could be sure that the students who experience the courses or units leading to graduation will accept them and use them to construct their own inner articulations. Only that which is so used functions in building personality and affects the course of life.

It so happens that the individual selects, out of each experience that he has, only that which fits into his real and personal articulation and which therefore has meaning for him. Such must, in the nature of events, be specifically related for each one to his own

---

[8] Herman Horne, *Philosophy of Education.* New York: Macmillan Co., 1927. Quoted by permission.

[9] L. Thomas Hopkins presented this philosophy at Schoolmen's Week, Philadelphia, Pa., April, 1952. A complete statement of this concept can be found in the report of the Life Adjustment Conference held in Washington, D. C., October, 1952, published February, 1953. It can be obtained from the Government Printing Office.

life and to the life that goes on around him. This cannot be determined by curriculum makers who do not know him as an individual, and who may be far removed from the time in which he lives and the place in which he has his being. The logic of their sequence will not necessarily function when the learner makes his selection. It becomes evident, therefore, that both scope and sequence should emerge from the needs, interests, and problems that are of immediate importance to the learner. If they do, the student will have a greater number of possibilities from which to make his selection.

When students participate in the selection of questions to be studied and problems to be solved, curriculum content inevitably comes out of the stream of their living experiences. It is true, of course, that individual differences will be evident, and that the school will have to take them into account. Such differences are among the factors which determine what elements each pupil selects out of each experience for his own inner use. "Responsibility for improvement of the quantity and quality of those selections rests with the learner, not the teacher. The teacher helps him to understand and use the *process* by which he makes and integrates his selections into himself."

Hopkins' philosophy places emphasis on process, which becomes content in so far as the skills of the process have to be learned by practice in meaningful situations. Participation in curriculum planning, such as he proposes, results in continuous "clarification of earlier meaning through present situations," which again involve the pupils in selecting, critical thinking, and evaluation. As students find these processes to be ever more meaningful and useful, they select them more frequently for the purposes of their own inner articulations. "The meaning is what produces the desired behavior, not the old-type repetition" of subject matter content.

Full implementation of this philosophy is still to be achieved. The inability of schools and teachers to move at a rapid pace into ungraded schools, and to do so without predetermined scope and sequences, is not a reason for believing that this may not, should not ultimately be attained, no matter how long the process may take. Progress in the desired direction is being made whenever teachers are permitted to use scope and sequence as tools to accomplish the purposes of education rather than as fences behind which to hide.

References

BOOKS

Alberty, et al., *Utilizing Subject Fields in High School Core Program Development.* Columbus, Ohio: Ohio State University, 1950.
Aldrich, Julian C., *Social Studies for the Junior High School.* Washington, D. C.: National Council for the Social Studies, 1956.
American Education Research Association, N.E.A., *Review of Educational Research: Curriculum Planning and Development,* June, 1960.
Hopkins, L. T., *The Emerging Self.* New York: Harper and Brothers, 1954.
Koos, L. V., *Junior High School Trends.* New York: Harper and Brothers, 1955.
Noar, Gertrude, *Freedom to Live and Learn.* Philadelphia: Franklin Publishing Co., 1948.
Quillen and Hanna, *Education for Social Competence.* New York: McGraw-Hill Book Co., 1952.

PERIODICALS AND PAMPHLETS

Alberty, H. B., "Sound Core Program," *N.E.A. Journal,* Jan., 1956.
"Block-Time Classes and the Core Program in the Junior High School." Federal Office of Education, Washington, D. C., 1958.
"Block-of-time Programs in Junior High Schools and Six-year High Schools in New Jersey." New Jersey State Department of Education, March, 1960.
Board of Education, City of New York, *Developing a Core Curriculum in the Junior High School Program.* 1958.
Commission on Secondary Schools, *The Junior High School Program.* Atlanta, Ga.: Southern Association of Secondary Schools and Colleges, 1958.
Jurjevich, J. C., Jr., "Methods and Results in a Junior High School Core Class," *Educational Leadership,* May, 1957.
Mickelson, J. M., "What Does Research Say About the Effectiveness of the Core Curriculum?" *School Review,* June, 1957.
Noall and Winget, "The Core Curriculum Project," *Bulletin of the National Association of Secondary School Principals,* Jan., 1959.
Oliver, D. W., "The Unit Concept in Social Studies: A Re-Examination," *School Review,* June, 1958.
Schwartz, B., "An Investigation of the Effects of a 7th and 8th Grade Core Program," *Journal of Educational Research,* Dec., 1959.

CHAPTER TEN

The Language Arts Program

There is no research to show that the most promising way to improve one's written or oral expression is through the continued study of formal grammar, yet the secondary school holds to the practice and permits the public to think it a false step to minimize this emphasis.

Harold Spears, *Principles of Teaching*. Englewood Cliffs, N. J.: Prentice-Hall, Inc., 1951, p. 113.

In the junior high school of today and tomorrow, the responsibility for developing skills and for teaching appreciation in the field of the language arts belongs both to the English teacher and to the core, common learnings, or double-period teacher. Because the need for effective use of English is common to all children in America, the school does and must continue to provide a program through which every child will increase his ability to read, write, and spell. The program must include many opportunities to increase understanding and appreciation of the best that has been written in literature, and in poetry. Children must learn to use printed materials as sources of information and to enjoy them in leisure hours.

Although the language arts teacher, whether this be a separate subject or included in the core or double-period class, has the general responsibility for teaching good usage, grammar (for the most part informal), writing (spelling and composition), and reading, all the other teachers in the school should share in the program. Whenever a child in any classroom needs help with English, especially reading and spelling, the teacher concerned should provide it. For example, the arithmetic teacher has to teach the spelling of the mathematical terms he uses and the reading of the problems he assigns.

The language arts program, however, is the place for teaching whatever technical English is necessary to establish understanding and to develop habits of good usage in speech and writing.[1] This means that individual and group needs have to be discovered; formal and informal teaching must be planned; group and individual drills have to be provided.

The language arts program also includes teaching both remedial and developmental reading. This means that the teacher must take time and know how to diagnose reading difficulties; he must devise ways and means of working with individuals and small groups. Slow readers need one kind of instruction, advanced readers another kind. It is in this class that appreciation and understanding of poetry and prose must be broadened and deepened. There must be provision for free reading suited to individual needs; occasional periods spent in listening to good stories read by one who knows how (usually the teacher); opportunities to talk about books in conversation circles as well as in class groups; the chance to discuss the people in the stories, the human relations problems that are involved, and the people who write the books and poems.

When language arts is integrated in units of study in the core class, reading—of books, pamphlets, newspapers, pictures, graphs, maps of all kinds—is probably the most important source of the facts children need to answer their questions and solve their problems. They have to learn to read for information and to organize what they get into forms that are suitable for presentation to their classmates.

Language arts provides opportunities for learning how to speak and write effectively. This can become particularly meaningful in a core program where there is need to use telephone calls and letters to arrange for trips, to brief speakers, and to get information. A meaningful situation occurs when pupils have to introduce speakers, ask them questions, and thank them at the end of a program. Letters written to secure materials, invite and thank speakers and consultants, inform parents about school events, invite people to programs, parties, and demonstrations are real. They have to be delivered, and so become full of meaning and importance.

In English language, arts, and core classes, creative writing is used in connection with units of work, writing plays, skits and radio

---

[1] R. Waldrep, "Core Teaching Has Plenty of Room for Grammar," *The English Journal*, January, 1953.

broadcasts, poems and stories. "Intimate writing," developed around open-end questions, is one of the instruments the teacher uses to help children externalize their problems and to find how he can help them with human relations.

The foregoing paragraphs give the general, over-all picture of the language arts program which, in many schools, must be administered by core teachers who may have had little or no previous experience in teaching English. All of them, however, having qualified for their positions in the junior high school, are able to use good English, have taken many required English courses in college, probably did excellent work in English in the secondary school, and certainly are able to learn and re-learn whatever their pupils need be taught. There are many books devoted to the *how* of English teaching. In addition to those, however, the core teacher needs help in planning his time and work so that language arts is not neglected, for he has many other things to teach. This chapter is designed especially to give that help, but English teachers who work with children in single periods will also find suggestions in it.

Literature and poetry can be taken care of in two ways. Appropriate stories and poems can be found for almost every unit that a class undertakes. The students should go to the library for a browsing period early in the unit to discover these books. If the teachers make records of those that are good, each time a unit is studied the search for them becomes easier. Librarians can also give assistance to both the teachers and the pupils. Verbally gifted pupils can use the more mature books, even those on an adult level, while the slow readers search through magazines and newspaper files.

Reading for Fun

If all the literature work is connected with a unit of study the children will tire of it and miss the chance to learn that reading is fun. All kinds of books other than those pertaining to the unit must be provided on all ability levels. The teacher will find it wise to allocate specific time for this kind of reading every week.[2] In many schools, the period is called "Reading for Fun." In the Ohio State University Laboratory School, the teacher often takes the class to

[2] R. E. Potter. "Reading Unlimited," *The English Journal*, January, 1953.

the living room of the home-making department's apartment, where they sit in the easy chairs and spread out on the floor in the same way that they would when they read for fun at home. Some part of the period is usually spent in talking about the books and their authors. Improvement in taste and selection is one of the desired outcomes.

The teachers of core classes, as well as those who teach English in double periods or in a fully departmentalized school, need a basic plan for periods that are spent on literature. Routine procedures will help the pupils to accomplish their goals, and will enable the teachers to use the period for identification of needs for instruction in reading, good usage, and speech.

A plan that can be used with success divides the long period into three parts. The first and third parts are devoted to talking about the authors and the characters in the books that the pupils are reading. The third part is especially devoted to telling incidents in the books that the children want to share with each other. The goals and outcomes of these experiences are increased interests in books, improved taste in selection, knowledge of how to talk about books, and help with personal problems of human relations that have some similarity to those described in the stories.

The middle and longest part of the period is devoted to silent reading of books that are chosen by the pupils to suit their own interests and abilities. Sometimes the teacher varies this by having all the children read the same book while he, or able readers, read aloud. If there is silent reading going on, the teacher does not withdraw to his desk to mark papers or do clerical work. This is the time when he is busy watching individuals, helping them, discovering their needs. Individual and group teaching and home assignments grow out of all the activities in this period, which should be one of enjoyment for the children.

The plan below shows how the teacher sets the stage, what he does during each part of the period, how he discovers needs, and how he meets those needs by planning further work to be done in school and at home.

Many teachers do not see how home assignments can be made on the basis of individual needs. The following suggestions help to clarify the point with respect to language arts. Some do not understand how to substitute functional for formal teaching of grammar and good usage. The following plans include suggestions for that. Other teachers, especially those who lack experience and those who are changing from traditional to modern methods and content, do not know how to plan for their classroom work. Following is a suggested method.

PLAN FOR READING PERIOD

15 minutes Setting the scene	30 minutes Reading	15 minutes Culmination
Teacher tells about a book—exciting curiosity	Students read books *First requirement:* a classroom library	Individuals read aloud choice parts they have found
or		*or*
Pupils who have read or are reading a book tell about exciting incidents, interesting people	*or* free access to school library	tell exciting events *or*
or	*or* encouragement to bring books from home	describe people *or*
Pupils read from cover of a new book or a review of it in a newspaper or magazine.	*Second requirement:* books on all levels of reading difficulty *Third requirement:* acceptance of the child on his own level teacher's objective: to raise level, broaden choice, improve taste *Fourth requirement:* some device for registering or recording so as to keep track of each child's reading. An individual folder, on the outside of which such records are made, is good.	tell why they do or do not like the book *or* conversation groups can be formed of those who are reading the same book, the same type of book, or different books.

WHAT THE TEACHER DOES DURING THE READING
HOUR AND HOME STUDY ASSIGNMENTS

15 minutes Pre-reading talking	30 minutes Reading	15 minutes Post-reading talking

For a few pupils each week (different ones until they are covered) make note of:
 	
1. *Speech needs:*
  a. defects
  b. enunciation
  c. pronunciation
  d. voice tone and quality
 	
2. *English needs:*
  a. errors in word usage
  b. errors in grammar
  c. incompleteness of sentences
  d. mannerisms: use of "and," "so," "eh," "right," etc.
 	
After the reading period:
1. do corrective teaching to the class if a common need is present
2. make home assignment of drill
 	
At another time:
1. do corrective individual or small group work
2. make individual home assignments on basis of discovered need
	Watch pupils to discover:
	1. lip movements
	2. finger following
	3. eye sweeps
	4. speed of getting to work
	5. page flipping
	6. non-readers
	  Make note of individual needs
	  Work with the individual
	
	or
	
	  Talk to an individual so as to help him make a more suitable choice
	
	or
	
	  Call small group together at rear of room for an
	1. oral reading lesson,
	2. diagnosis of comprehension needs,
	3. drill in word analysis
	
	After the reading period:
	1. make home assignments:
	  set time limits for completion of book
	
	or
	
	2. set up what is to be done for a "report" avoiding old fashioned type — encouraging expression of reaction in art form, dramatics, pantomime, original writing.
		Do any of the things suggested in column I.
		
		or
		
		  Sit with conversation group to lead, stimulate, encourage. Note non-readers and non-participants so as to plan future individual conferences.
		
		Make home assignments
		1. as indicated in Pre-reading column
		
		or
		
		2. Set up groups to prepare for dramatizations, panel discussions, etc., to be given the following week.

Reading Skills

"I have devoted special pains to learn, with some degree of numerical accuracy, how far the reading in our schools is an exercise of the mind in thinking and feeling, and how far it is a barren action of the organs of speech upon the atmosphere. The result is that more than 11/12ths of all the children in the reading classes in our schools do not understand the meaning of the words they read, that they do not master the sense of the reading lessons, and that the ideas and feelings intended by the author to be conveyed to, and excited in, the reader's mind, still rest in the author's intention, never having yet reached the place of their destination," said Horace Mann, Secretary of the Massachusetts Board of Education, in his 1838 report.

This statement made so long ago may give the present-day teacher food for thought when he is inclined to blame the lack of reading ability on modern educational methods. We are well aware of the fact that large numbers of junior high school pupils are not able to read at the so-called seventh, eighth, and ninth grade levels. Some of them read below the fourth grade level. A few cannot read at all. On the other hand, there are many students who read on the senior high and even on college levels. The fact that children with such a wide range of accomplishment in a fundamental skill are all in the junior high school is due to change in promotion or classification policies and practices.

Time was when poor readers were required to repeat grades. They remained with younger children, and most of them became behavior problems. Among the adults in America are large numbers of people who were forced to leave school at a tender age because they could not master the reading skills as rapidly as teachers believed they should. As a result, some of them dislike the public school system and have hatred for teachers. Others of them are determined to see to it that their own children get a better deal in school than they received. During the past decade they have given their support to the educators who have based promotion policies on the research studies that have shown that the best single factor to use in grouping children is chronological age, not reading ability.

For better or worse, many children who cannot read or who

read poorly are now in the junior high school. Teachers who know that, regardless of reading scores, these pupils belong in the school, are seeking ways of reaching and teaching them. Although reading is only one way to learn, it is an exceedingly important tool for effective living. New emphasis is therefore being placed on the development of techniques of teaching reading in the secondary school. This instruction is not limited to the retarded readers. The gifted pupils also need to learn how to increase the speed and effectiveness of their reading skills.

Many books written by experts in this field are available to the serious student and to teachers who are desirous of becoming experts.[3] However, many teachers and administrators have need of a few practical techniques that can be used with little difficulty.

There are some principles upon which the reading program should be based. First: *Continuous growth of all the pupils depends upon the direct teaching of reading skills in every classroom.* This takes sole responsibility away from the English department and enlists the efforts of teachers of foreign language, social studies, science, fine and practical arts and physical education. Teachers of core classes, general education, social living, and common learnings accept it as one of their primary responsibilities.

The implementation of this principle means that every teacher in every classroom has to stop scolding the child who cannot read and begin to teach him. The retarded reader needs help in every subject area to recognize the words that are used, to say them correctly, to spell them, to write them and to get their meaning when he sees them on the printed page. Such help would not only raise the reading level of the child but would also at once increase his chances for success in the subject concerned.

The second principle: *A child will learn to read only when the material placed before him is of such a nature and on such a level that he is able to read it.* This means that in every classroom the use of the same book by all the pupils has to be eliminated. The teacher, in some cases, may have to get along without books for some pupils because none are available that contain the desired content written at the low reading levels that are needed by them. He may have to write some things for these pupils. At the same

---

[3] See books written by Paul Witty, Emmett A. Betts, Guy L. Bond, E. W. Dolch, Dora Smith, and others.

time this also means that the able readers should not be held down to the use of materials that are on the "grade level." The lack of challenge in them can serve to bore and frustrate children who are able to read adult materials. They should be given free access to all the materials that can be secured.

The third principle: *Unless there are many opportunities to succeed, many challenges to increase skill, many reasons for using materials that grow in difficulty, and an abundance of reading materials available in the classroom, the growth for which the school is responsible will not occur.* This again points to the need to change the practice of using one text book, copies of which are given to each child, and of using the same literature book for a whole class to read at the same time. It re-emphasizes the necessity for keeping records of growth and for adjusting instruction and materials in accordance with improvement in skills.

A school meets certain problems as it moves into a reading program. Testing, diagnostic, and reading materials on many levels have to be secured. Time has to be allocated for both remedial and developmental instruction of individuals and groups. A special reading room may be desired in which the materials can be placed and made accessible to all teachers. Policies of marking, reporting progress, and reclassification have to be formulated and clarified. Teachers have to learn how to test, diagnose needs, and do appropriate classroom teaching.[4] Plans have to be made for the use of consultants and specialized services for clinical cases. All of these matters must become the substance of the in-service education program for the faculty.

The organization of a reading program in a junior high school may rest upon the extent to which the teachers believe that the responsibility is theirs. If they feel that expensive and technical testing instruments that are used to measure eye defects are essential, the program may be indefinitely delayed. It may even be impossible for the school to secure and administer standard reading tests. Many teachers say, however, that it makes little difference to them to know that John reads on either the third or fourth grade level. Their problem lies in his inability to read at or near the junior high school level. It doesn't matter to them that, at the close of the

---

[4] C. M. McCullough, "Behind the Reading Score," *Elementary English,* January, 1953.

year, Sue progressed from fourth to fifth grade in reading. She still will be unable to read the tenth grade books that will be given to her in the senior high school at the beginning of the next term.

There are rather simple testing techniques that all teachers can learn to use which will provide the necessary clues about the levels at which instruction of an individual child must begin. For example, the teacher hands one book after another to the child, beginning with the easiest and increasing in difficulty. As the child reads, the teacher listens and observes him closely. There comes a time when the pupil begins to show signs of trouble. This establishes the level of independent reading ability. As the books increase in difficulty, the teacher must give more help. The child begins to squirm and he gets pale or flushed. Probably this is just beyond the instructional level. Then there are signs of real distress. The child becomes angry, or he becomes fearful. He bites his nails, picks at his collar, or tries to escape altogether by asking to leave the room. This is the frustration level. This procedure may seem to be over-simplified, but it works. It gives the teacher enough information on which to begin. The importance of the program does not lie in statistics that are accumulated, but in the help that is given to the students.

The teacher does not have to test every child in the class. Children who cannot get facts from the printed page need help in reading. The very glib readers need to be watched. They may understand very little of what they read. In fact, that type of difficulty is one of the hardest to overcome. Another sign of the need for help is inability to concentrate on a reading assignment. Reading trouble may be the cause of inability to do committee work. Children are often so concerned about it and so reluctant to reveal their troubles to their classmates that they withdraw into silence and become non-participants even in discussions and planning meetings. This behavior is the result of insecurity and failure to establish belongingness and is due to the fear of ridicule from which they have suffered so long and so acutely.

Poor readers cannot write. Sometimes they use very small handwriting or write so lightly that it cannot be read. Often scribbling and illegibility are devices used to avoid detection. They are also hesitant in conversation, mispronounce ordinary words, confuse words and omit word endings. There are also other cover-up techniques. Many can copy words and so they copy from classmates as often as possible. They produce pages of material copied from the board and out of books. They withdraw into silence and may actually hide by sliding down in their desks. In extreme cases they slip to the floor or out of the room if there is danger of being called upon to read aloud. While the class is engaged in writing, some of the non-readers fill up their papers with carefully written connected letters that do not form words at all, or with strings of words that do not make sense.

Most of these children are extremely ashamed of their disabilities. They try to stall by saying, "Oh, I have learned a lot in this school. I do much better now!" When the showdown finally comes, some of them burst into tears, others get sullen and hostile. Some become aggressive and have temper tantrums in which they hurl blame at the teachers. Many retreat into silence and truancy.

There are some signals that the teacher can discover only by observing his pupils. He can do this while they are reading for fun or doing independent research work. Facial expressions and bodily movements reveal needs. Boredom and anxiety are easily recognized. Poor readers soon begin to fidget. Their eyes wander far from the book. Lip movements and finger following are obvious. Some children spend the time flipping pages. Others look for pictures. There are some who will flatly refuse to open the book, and others who soon fall asleep.

Once the teacher has identified his problem children, he can begin a systematic search for causes. This will require time. The help of counselors and psychiatrists will be needed, if they are available, for some cases. Plans should include interviews with the child and his parents, home visits, testing, physical and eye examinations, observation of play and group life, and documentation of personality characteristics. Help will be needed with interpretation of the findings.

Many research studies have been done on the causes of reading difficulties. One reported in *Reading in Modern Education* by Paul Witty gives the following facts:[5]

14 per cent of the poor readers have defective vision
12 per cent are victims of generally poor physical conditions
4 per cent are left-handed

[5] Paul Witty, *Reading in Modern Education*. Boston: D. C. Heath & Co., 1949.

3 per cent have defective hearing which may be generally poor or selectively tuned to certain pitch or quality tones or to certain letters.

With respect to social causes that lie in the home and family backgrounds, Witty reports the following:

82 per cent of the families have little or no interest in reading

44 per cent are indifferent to reading

43 per cent actually dislike books

42 per cent have cases of varying degrees of emotional maladjustment

40 per cent are involved in more or less serious personal conflicts.

Study of the previous educational experiences of the children in the survey revealed that all had had constant school failure and the resulting discouragement. They had not been able to secure recognition and praise either at home or in school. These factors were accompanied by the child's increasing conviction of his own incompetence. Neurotic and even psychotic personality disorders can be expected in such cases, as well as inability to read.

It becomes increasingly obvious that the teacher who meets a class for only one period a day, and who meets many other classes as well each day, cannot be expected to do this kind of study of his pupils each semester or very rapidly. In fact he may not be able to do it at all. This is one of the reasons why the provision for core classes is so necessary.

The teacher who is engaged in developing the reading program will eventually be ready to designate a small group (it should be limited to eight or ten children) with whom he wants to do some special reading work. By then he must be more or less in command of the techniques of teaching the mechanics—word recognition, phonetics, comprehension, and speed.[6] He has to decide when and where the teaching is to be done. Outcomes have been good in schools where the teacher works with his reading group at least twice a week right in the classroom while the rest of the class is busy with research, silent reading, or writing. The children in the reading group cannot do these things successfully, and should be withdrawn from them until increased skill make it possible for them to participate on a fairer basis.

---

[6] See Lee and Lee, *The Child and His Curriculum*, 2nd ed. New York: Appleton-Century-Crofts, 1950.

As he plans for this group, the teacher varies the work from day to day so that the children receive help with word recognition, accuracy, comprehension, finding the answers to questions, reading to remember, reading for pleasure, association of ideas, organization of ideas, speed, and even such special techniques as skimming. As often as possible, the reading material used should have some relation to other things that are going on in the class. For example, the words studied should be those that the children need for the unit that is under way. Having mastered them, books can be scanned to find chapters that can be called to the attention of appropriate committees next day. Magazines and newspapers can be examined for headlines, pictures, and cartoons that committees need. Maps, charts, and graphs can be "read" and clipped for special groups to use. Dramatics can be made up without the use of books and prepared for presentation to the class. Facts learned from experience, radio, and films can be written down as the pupils report them. The children will be able to read them back to the class next day. These success experiences are vital to the children. They will in themselves help them to achieve status among their peers. The emotional tone created helps to remove some of the blocks to learning how to read.

Not all of the time should be spent in doing things to serve the progress of the unit being studied or the discussion of current affairs. Some of it should be devoted to reading for fun; for these children, too, need to know that books can be fun. Sometimes the teacher will want to read to them while they follow in their own books. When the reading level is right, the pupils like to read aloud.

In some schools, where the schedule provides for multiple periods, it is possible to add to the staff one or more teachers specially trained and skilled in teaching reading. It occasionally helps the general morale if those teachers spend half their time in language arts classroom teaching. In some schools, the reading assistants not only teach children but also arrange to work in the language arts classrooms so that the teacher there has the chance to observe, to learn the techniques, and then to try them out under the observation of the reading assistant. As this kind of help is spread throughout the faculty, all of the teachers become able to teach reading to all the children.

The following is designed to assist teachers in administering a reading program.

Directions for Administering a Program for
Reading Instruction

The purpose of the program is two-fold: (1) to increase the reading skills of pupils who read below seventh grade level; (2) to improve the teaching skills of the teachers.

To accomplish the first purpose, it is necessary to select the pupils with care. The reading assistant can help the classroom teacher to administer and interpret the reading tests. Records of scores obtained on reading tests in previous grades, as well as the teacher's more intimate knowledge of the child in question, are of value and should be used in making decisions. The first group to be set up should contain six or eight children. Another six or eight pupils should be designated for later involvement in the program.

Accomplishment of the second purpose, improvement of teaching skills, depends upon the classroom teacher's attention to matters of planning for the periods during which the reading assistant will be in the classroom. It will also depend upon the way in which the teacher plans to use the new skills in the other classes with which he works. Practice and experimentation will consolidate gains and improve techniques. As difficulties are encountered and as problems arise in these adventures, they should be discussed with the reading assistant. If it is desired, the reading assistant can arrange to observe in the classroom and to give the teacher the benefit of constructive criticism.

The plan for the program should permit the reading assistant to spend two hours each week in the classroom with the pupils who are to receive instruction. One of these periods should be the regular weekly hour reserved for "reading for fun." The other hour should be one that is devoted to unit work. The *Do* and *Don't* suggestions on pages 199 and 200 should be helpful in planning classroom work.

When the reading assistant and the classroom teacher have decided that the latter is ready to try out the techniques that are being used to instruct the reading group with which they have been working, the assistant can take this first reading group out of the room for this period each week. This will enable him to do more technical work with them and at the same time free the classroom teacher to continue the regular literature program with the rest of the class. If it is possible to do so, the teacher should, from time to time, organize similar small groups for reading instruction, as he finds the need for it.

There are still many junior high schools in which additional help for teachers cannot be provided, even though the classroom teachers feel that they are unprepared to teach reading. The following suggestions may seem to be over-simplified, but they will provide help where it is needed. These techniques apply to developmental work as well as to remedial work. They can be used with gifted as well as retarded pupils.

Literature Period

DO	DON'T
Arrange a circle of chairs or reserve a table for the reading group.	Don't seat the reading group in fixed desks or in a row of chairs.
Place the reading group as far from the other pupils as possible and near the blackboard.	Don't place the reading group in the center of the room.
In order to get more space in the room at this time, and to give another group of pupils due recognition, send the best readers in the class to the library for the period.	Don't permit a crowded room to spoil the plan.
Make sure that the books to be used are in the room and ready. If necessary, consult the reading assistant ahead of time.	Don't expect the reading assistant to bring books to the room.
Plan work for the rest of the class which will set you free to observe and work with the assistant.	Don't plan so that all or even a significant part of your time must be given to the class.
Good things to include in the class plans are:	Poor things to plan are:
1. permission to pupils to go to the classroom library one at a time, to exchange books.	1. permission for a general exchange of books.
2. a single, previously arranged conversation circle in a far corner with a specific problem and time limit.	2. two or more committee meetings or conversation circles.
3. Silent reading.	3. general conversation in the class.
4. Quiet, orderly work that has purpose and meaning.	4. reading aloud.
5. Written work that is based on the reading that has been done: making reading records, writing reports, writing stories and plays.	5. busy work.
	6. doing lessons for other classes.

Unit Period

DO	*DON'T*
Plan so that you will be free to observe the assistant. It is important to see him begin his work. If necessary, leave him from time to time during the period to help others in the class, but return to the reading group as soon as you can.	Don't give your attention to the class and ignore the reading group.
Put directions for the continuous work of the general class group on the board so that children will not have to interrupt you.	
Arrange furniture to facilitate the work of both the reading group and the rest of the pupils.	Don't give all the tables to other committees. The reading group needs one.
If the room is crowded, send a committee that is capable of working under its own leader to a nearby vacant room, or to the corridor to continue their work, or to hold a committee meeting.	Don't permit overcrowding to spoil the program.
Make sure that the materials with which the reading group is to work are at hand and ready to use. These should be related to the unit that is under way. They can include newspapers, pamphlets, magazines and books that the pupils can read. The books in general use by the class should also be provided for this group.	Don't send out for materials after the reading assistant arrives.
Plan for quiet, orderly but not necessarily inactive class work.	Don't permit general noise and confusion.
Plan for no more than one committee to meet at a time, and that only if there is sufficient leadership and control in it to permit them to work without you.	Don't plan for all committees to be at work if this means that many pupils will be talking at the same time.
Plans can be made for any group that is working on a project to continue with it, if they are far enough removed from the reading group to present no interference.	Don't permit any project which involves much moving around the room, hammering, or other disturbance.

Unit Period (Continued)

DO	DON'T
Plan for individualized work on the unit. If a small committee wishes to meet quietly for a short time, it must be understood that they return to their individual work at the close of their meeting.	Don't have a speaker, radio program, film, committee reports, trip, or other activity from which the reading group would be excluded because they meet at that time.
Individual work to be planned includes: research in books and other printed materials; vocabulary work; spelling; writing up reports; completing records of unit work; making maps, charts, illustrations, etc.	Don't permit children to be idle, to read comics, to do work that other teachers have assigned, and so neglect their unit work.

Methods for Improving Reading

Comprehension:

1. Allow time for the pupil to look over the text so that he can get the ideas, before asking him to read it aloud or before asking him to answer questions about the content.
2. Help pupil to pick out details:
   a. formulate a specific question for him to look for.
   b. refuse to accept an answer to a question if it has been merely copied out of the text.
   c. teach the form of the outline and how to make one.
   d. give practice in jotting ideas down as they occur to the reader. Some children will find only a few ideas in a long paragraph, others will be able to find many. Praise can be given for each idea that is found rather than for the quantity.
   e. require pupils to write captions, summaries, comments for all clippings pasted in scrap books, posted on bulletin boards, or used to illustrate unit records.
3. Adapt the reading to a purpose. This may be:
   a. enjoyment, which would require that pupils be given their preference with respect to the books selected by them. Some would prefer novels, some science, others poetry. Biographies will appeal to hero-worshippers.
   b. skimming, which is done to become familiar with a book, to decide on its relevancy, to "taste" before deciding to read it all. Methods of skimming are:
      (a) look down the middle of the page to catch key words.

(b) read the first and last sentences of each paragraph.

(c) return to re-read when curious about a passage, or when details are desired.

Word Recognition

1. Determine whether or not the word has meaning for the pupil. Some words have no concepts behind them for some or all the children. If this is the case, direct experience should be provided. This can be given if children can see, handle, work with, examine, see pictures, make pictures of the real thing, take trips. (For example, children who did not know the word "wharf," went to see one.)

2. Teach how to break words into syllables.

3. Teach the vowel sounds and the sounds of syllables.

4. Use context clues.

5. Familiarize with deviations; teach structure analysis.

The children at the high end of the scale also need instruction in reading. Their reading skills should be developed to the highest possible degree. The teacher must find time to spend with them, both individually and in small groups. He can explore literature with them and introduce them to the classics. He can broaden their horizons and improve their taste. Gifted pupils need to learn how to browse in the library and on what bases to select books to read. They need practice to increase speed. They should learn how to adapt speed to the purpose in mind and to the type of content.

The students who intend to prepare in senior high school for college entrance need to learn the techniques of note taking, outlining, skimming, and scanning. The teacher should make as much effort to learn about these children as he does for the poor readers. He ought to know about the individual level of accomplishment, and the breadth and depth of reading background. Only then can he avoid asking them to re-read books merely to satisfy rigid course of study requirements. When the class is engaged in free reading, these students can be permitted to go to the library. That will give them special recognition and a feeling of being accepted on an adult level.

Talking

Talking is an important phase of the instruction in language arts. It is an amazing contradiction of objectives when teachers criticize children for their ability to talk. Certainly they need to have every possible opportunity in the classroom to express themselves in words, striving for clarity, conciseness, and correctness. They also have to learn that *what* they have to say is as important as the form in which they express their thoughts. It is a sad commentary on secondary school teaching when pupils insist that a paper deserves a high rating just because the English is correct, even if ideas are lacking.

In many classrooms talking is still considered a sin. There a child is expected to talk only when the teacher asks him a question and all remarks must be addressed to the teacher. The modern teacher takes full account of the children's right to talk. He knows that they like to, and that above all they want to talk to each other.

If all the possible outcomes are to be achieved, the teacher must open many lines of communication. This will help to change the atmosphere. It will become more democratic. As new freedom is extended to the pupils, however, the teacher will have to remain in control of the situation. The children need to learn that freedom is not license, and that there is a difference between chatter and purposeful talking.

Instead of lines of communication that extend only from and to the teacher, there also will be lines that go from pupil to pupil, pupil to class, pupil to small group, and, as they enter the picture, pupil and teacher to visitor, to consultant, to speaker, to person being interviewed.

The list of experiences that involve talking is long. It includes:

1. presentation of facts, findings, directions, directives, suggestions.
2. formulation of questions and problems.
3. answering questions.
4. reading aloud—poetry, prose, textbooks, and literature books.
5. finding solutions to problems.
6. expressing opinions, ideas, beliefs—learning to distinguish one from the other.
7. relating experiences, stories, descriptions—all of which may be real or imaginative, factual or creative.
8. exchanging ideas in conversation—almost a lost art—and in discussion.
9. pooling information in committee meetings and class work.
10. dramatics—radio plays, assembly programs, classroom dramatizations, sociodramatics, psychodramatics.

From those experiences children learn the following:

1. facts—many of which some pupils could not learn by reading.
2. the importance of facts and of ideas.
3. to be accurate in thought and speech.
4. to clarify thought and to put it into words.
5. to challenge statements for authority and proof.
6. words—new ones, meanings, pronunciation, enunciation, correct usage, variation, diction.
7. idiomatic expressions.
8. new concepts and the enlargement of those already in mind.
9. poise and tact.
10. roles to be played in the discussion process.
11. types of discussions and how to be an intelligent and effective participant in discussions.
12. grammar, functional—completing sentences in order to convey thought—the relation of words to each other.
13. style—variety, the use of modifiers, of long and short sentences and the value of simplicity.
14. methods of addressing a person, a group, an audience.
15. the art of listening.
16. the meaning of the fundamental freedoms—the right to speak, and to be heard, and what that means in the classroom.

Talking experiences do not just happen in the modern classroom. They are direct experiences from which all can learn, and they must be as carefully planned as are the other learning situations. Whenever it is possible to do so, the pupils should be admitted to the planning process. If the experiences are to be effective, goals must be set up and provision made for evaluation. Among the kinds of experiences that should be used at various times and for specific purposes are the following:

1. discussions—panel, forums, round tables, symposiums.
2. conversation circles.
3. committee meetings for pooling thoughts and findings and for planning.
4. presentation of reports.
5. addressing the group on a prepared subject—speaker of the day.
6. conducting interviews and being interviewed.
7. role-playing—spontaneous and prepared dramatics.
8. making all kinds of telephone calls.
9. thanking people, introducing people, and using other forms of etiquette.
10. telling stories.
11. audience-reading.
12. questioning speakers and visitors.

It is essential for the teacher to look at every learning experience he sets up in order to determine what outcomes he can expect; how to observe in order to note changes in behavior which indicate that learning has occurred; and how to record the individual's growth. Possible outcomes of talking experiences are:

1. increased attention given by the individual to another who is talking.
2. increased control exercised in the group so as to permit freedom of speech and the right to be heard.
3. increased understanding and use of parliamentary procedures.
4. intelligent listening.
5. associative listening.
6. independence of thought.
7. intellectual honesty.
8. ability to plan.
9. ability to think critically.
10. ability to make wise choices.
11. development of imagination.
12. recognition of need for more information.
13. the habit of challenging statements for authority and truth.
14. keener appreciation.
15. enrichment of life through vicarious experience.
16. evidence of moral and ethical values and a philosophy of life.
17. understanding and practice of democratic principles and processes.
18. increased respect for others, courtesy, open-mindedness.

Creative Writing

Before anyone can write, he must have plenty of time to gather information, ideas, and inspiration. In the classroom this means that the children need as much time as possible to talk, to listen to the teacher, to exchange experiences, to try out various ways of saying things, and to explore many titles and topics about which they have something to say. The teacher has to help them in these preliminaries. The more he does so the better the writing is likely to be.

After the best efforts have been made, however, in all likelihood only a few pupils will be ready to write at once. Others will want to sit and think or dream a while. They will get started slowly. There will be some who will be entirely unable to put a single sentence on paper. It is at this point that the teacher who knows how to help them can do a great deal to gain the confidence of his slow learners and give them the success experience which they need so badly.

The following suggestions were gathered from classroom teachers who, from time to time, varied what they did until they found techniques that work well.

1. Set the tone, the atmosphere for a successful experience for all. Use what other children have written as examples to read. Your own writings are interesting to the children. Samples from the best literature are important.

2. Put many ideas and suggestions on the board so that they can be seen as well as heard, and referred to later.

3. Put suggestive words, phrases, and the words pupils cannot spell on the board.

4. If none of the suggestions click, let the individual have free choice of what to write about.

5. Give clear directions and plenty of time to carry them out. Any scolding at this point will serve to kill creativity.

6. Call together in a circle for further conversation those who cannot begin—use the rear of the room or the corridor so as not to disturb those already at work.

7. Provide an immediate experience about which they can write at once:

a look out of the window,
a walk around the hall
observing the class at work,
a look at one's best friend,
picking up an object from the table,
browsing through some pictures,
listing to the radio, to a newscast, a commerical, part of a story (to try to finish it).

8. Help the small group to do a piece of group writing.

9. Go to an individual, sit beside him (or call him to sit beside you) and write the first sentence for him as he tells you what he wants to say; or write the first one and have him try the next one.

10. Sit with a child and let him talk to you while you write down what he says, or the list of words that he needs. Encourage him.

11. Let those who can do so begin with a drawing.

12. Carry around a package of small papers and as you find children who need words which they cannot spell, write them and hand them to the child. In some cases the first two letters will help the child to use the dictionary.

13. Distribute papers of varying size—large to the gifted, small to the slow.

14. Have each child write a single beginning sentence—exchange papers for the next one and so on.

15. Insist that each child produce something but accept what is done in consideration of the individual's ability.

16. Make sure that the slow children have the chance to read their papers (or hear you read them) to the class. They, too, need an audience.

17. Always permit the slow ones to write about their own experiences.

18. Use concrete illustrative materials to stimulate their ideas.

19. Avoid handing back papers full of "red marks." Instead make comments about the ideas, the improvement, that you like.

20. When you read these papers to the class, do so as if they were properly spelled and punctuated.

21. Allow the gifted children to help their slower classmates, individually, and to act as leaders of their group in conversation and group writing experiences.

22. Provide outlets—help them to polish their writings and send them to the school publication, to parents, to the principal, to the librarian.

23. Post all the work, not just that of the gifted students.

Help is as much needed by the gifted pupils as it is by the less able. In fact it may be of greater importance since they are the ones who may have use for the skill at some future time.

The following ideas were contributed by very successful teachers.

1. Early in the term, with the help of the pupils, compile a list of titles and suggestions. Challenge the gifted children to write about as many of them as possible, setting no due dates but indicating a time limit. Have the writing done outside of the class with provision for personal conferences for help and criticism. The competitive aspect of this plan will appeal to some. Quantity without quality should be refused credit.

2. Gather the gifted writers together for specific instruction from time to time. They need to learn how to use a variety of descriptive words, the values of sentences of different length, and stylistic effects.

3. Refuse a high grade to the student who does not produce at his ability level even though the product may be the best in the class. Confer with him about this so as to avoid misunderstanding and discouragement.

4. Encourage these children and help them to write for publication in the school newspaper and magazine and for the local press. Anything good enough should be sent to other periodicals for consideration.

5. The gifted pupils are the ones who should write the plays and skits to be presented by their committees. They need to learn how to use the ideas of the committee members in doing this, as well as to be original.

6. Special committees of gifted children can be entrusted with the creation of scripts for culminating activities.

7. The work of these pupils should be displayed along with that of others.

8. Use greater care in the marking and correcting of the papers of gifted writers. Add comments of praise as often as possible. Never neglect

the thought content. No matter how good the form and grammar may be, if thought content is lacking, poor, or incorrect, the paper should not be accepted.

9. Assign them someone to leadership groups when group writing is to be done.

10. The gifted need status in the peer group. Too much spotlight on them may serve to destroy their popularity, which in turn will react badly on the quality of their work.

11. Use gifted writers as secretaries of clubs, student organizations, class, and committees.

12. Give to superior writers the task of organizing pooled information into the committee report.

13. Let them assemble the ideas offered by the group into letters of invitation, of thanks to speakers.

14. They should have major responsibility in the formulation of questions to be asked of speakers, consultants, or during interviews.

15. Permit and encourage them to assist less able classmates—correcting their papers, helping them write reports.

16. Ask them to search for free and inexpensive materials needed in the unit work and write letters to get them.

17. They, too, write for an audience, and the class should hear their products and help them with comments and appreciation.

Learning Activities for Members of Pre- and In-Service Teacher Education Classes

Besides reading, do some of the following:

1. Compare the required reading lists in several courses of study with what you know to be the ordinary interests of junior high school children, and with the reading abilities of at least half of them.

2. Have a class discussion on the use and abuse of comics.

3. Write a paper or poem on subjects usually assigned to ninth grade.

4. Have a panel discussion on the teaching of grammar.

5. Observe a junior high school class during a reading period.

6. Try to discover the reading level of a child without the use of a reading test.

7. Write a story, or some facts, or a description, using very simple language but content that would interest an adolescent.

References

LANGUAGE ARTS

BOOKS

Applegate, M., *Helping Children Write.* Evanston, Ill.: Row, Peterson and Co., 1954.

Jewett, A. J., *English Language Arts in American High Schools*. Washington, D. C.: U. S. Office of Education, 1959.
LaBrant, Lou, *We Teach English*. New York: Harcourt, Brace & Co., 1951.
National Council of Teachers of English, *Language Arts for Today's Children*. New York: Appleton-Century-Crofts, 1954.
Palmer, H. E., *The Teaching of Oral English*. London: Longmans, Green and Co., 1959.
Tidyman and Butterfield, *Teaching the Language Arts*, 2nd ed. New York: McGraw-Hill Book Co., 1959.

PERIODICALS AND PAMPHLETS

DeBoer, J., "Implications of Group Dynamics for English," *The English Journal*, May, 1952.
"English Language Arts," *The Bulletin of the National Association of Secondary Principals*, Oct., 1960.
Jewett, Arno, ed., *English for the Academically Talented Student*. Washington, D. C.: National Council of Teachers of English and N.E.A., 1960.
McCarthy, Dorothea, *Factors That Influence Language Growth*. Chicago: National Council of Teachers of English, 1953.
Miller, H. R., "What If They Don't Know Grammar?" *The English Journal*, November, 1951.
Phelps, Waldo, "Integration of Speech Education with English and Social Studies," *The Bulletin of the National Association of Secondary School Principals*, May, 1952.
Tovatt, A. L., "Diagraming: A Sterile Skill," *The English Journal*, February, 1952.
Waldrep, Reef, "Core Teaching Has Plenty of Room for Grammar," *The English Journal*, January, 1953.

READING

BOOKS

Dolch, E. W., *Psychology and Teaching of Reading*. Champaign, Ill.: Garrard Press, 1951.
Gray and Rogers, *Maturity in Reading*. Chicago: University of Chicago Press, 1956.
Hildreth, G. H., *Teaching Reading: a Guide to Basic Principles and Modern Practices*. New York: Henry Holt and Co., 1958.
Veatch, Jeannette, *Individualizing Your Reading Program*. New York: G. P. Putnam's Sons, 1959.
Willson and Schneyer, *Developmental Reading in the Junior High School*. Danville, Ill.: Interstate Press, 1959.
Wood and Barrows, *Reading Skills*. New York: Henry Holt and Co., 1958.

PERIODICALS AND PAMPHLETS

Alberty, H. B., "Core Programs and the Talented," *Educational Leadership*, February, 1959.
Gray, W. S., "Improved Reading Programs," *Education*, May, 1951.
————, "Summary of Reading Investigations, 1949-50," *Journal of Educational Research*, February, 1951.
Metropolitan School Study Council, N. Y., "Five Steps to Reading Success in Science, Social Studies and Mathematics," *Reading Group*, 1954.
New York City Board of Education, *Reading, Grades 7, 8, 9*. 1957-1958.
Strang, Ruth, "Gifted Children Need Help in Reading, Too," *Reading Teacher*, January, 1953.
Traxler and Townsend, *Eight More Years of Research in Reading*. New York: Educational Records Bureau, 21 Audubon Ave., #64, Jan., 1955.

CHAPTER ELEVEN

Other Curriculum Areas

The modern junior high school curriculum provides for individual differences partly by offering some areas in which subject matter is more highly specialized.[1] These are the electives, from among which courses students choose one or two, depending upon the type of organization in the school. In some places, one elective is chosen in the eighth year and two in the ninth. More often, in the seventh and eighth grades, pupils are limited to the choice of the order in which the various kinds of shop, home arts, and fine arts courses are to be taken, with the understanding that eventually every child shall have them all. In most schools, the ninth-year electives are directly connected with that curriculum which the individual child thinks he will take in the senior high school, and it, in turn, is connected with preparation for a remote vocational objective. Thus individual differences in abilities, interests, economic backgrounds, motivations, and aspirations serve as screening devices. The guidance staff —advisers, multi-period teachers and counselors—spend considerable time in and out of class, helping students and their parents to clarify the issues involved and to make wise decisions.

The electives most frequently offered in the junior high schools are a foreign language, usually Latin, French, or Spanish, algebra, general mathematics, and general science. Within the last five years considerable interest has been shown in Russian. Some schools, notably in New York City, offer Hebrew. In efforts to provide more fully for the verbally gifted, a few schools add advanced courses in English—especially Literature and composition. Occasionally geometry is offered. In schools where the vocational possibilities of the fine arts are recognized, instrumental or vocal music, and painting

[1] Excellent discussion of the use of areas of specialization can be found in Alberty, et al., *Utilizing Subject Fields in High School Core Program Development*. College of Education, Ohio State University, 1950.

211

or sculpture may be offered. Those schools which still maintain a traditional curriculum offer so-called majors in shop, home economics, and junior business training which begin in the fourth semester.

If the junior high school is to remain an institution in which exploration, rather than specialization, is a governing principle, the pressures of subject-matter specialists and of groups with vested interests in one or another special discipline will have to be carefully appraised and resisted. It is not to the advantage of most boys and girls between the ages of thirteen and fifteen to be subjected to the constant pressure of subject-minded teachers striving for factual learnings. This is true even for the gifted, if they are to become creative rather than conforming people.

Foreign Language

Ten years ago the study of foreign language was regarded as of doubtful value for all but college-bound students. Now, because of the increasing need for understanding of and close relationships with countries around the world, parents and teachers have come to believe that most children should have some experience with a language other than English.

Some educators think that if children learn even the rudiments of a language, they will understand more about the culture of the people who speak it. To achieve that end, however, the foreign language teacher must make considerable change in content, emphasis, and methods. Instead of beginning with grammar, reading, and translation, pupils and teacher are learning to communicate with each other in the foreign tongue. This, of course, does not require book work. Thus the fear of failure due to the difficulty of reading and translation is replaced by the fun of talking, singing and playing games. It would seem that the changes dictated by the "oral-aural" method make it essential to have qualified teachers who can speak the language with some degree of fluency.

If, however, important objectives lie in promoting good intergroup and international relationships, then the geography, history, politics, art, music, and literature of the people must be added to the study of words and pronunciation, which can be done by teachers who do not have command of the language. For example, social studies teachers can include the study of other cultures in their courses.

What language to offer in the junior high school and how much to require are problems complicated by the demands of the colleges. These vary to such an extent that it becomes essential for counselors to keep constantly abreast of college requirements so that student choice can be guided accordingly.

Who should study a foreign language in the junior high school is still a matter of controversy. Some teachers believe that only children who are successful in English, or those who have high IQ's, can possibly learn a second language. When less able children take these courses they usually fail, especially when the teacher uses traditional methods of teaching.

There are others, however, who agree that it is dangerous to make hasty judgments about verbal ability on the basis of tests in which only English is used and which favor middle and upper social class vocabulary. Children of first and second generation families may have difficulty with English but not be lacking in verbal ability. In fact many of them already speak two languages— Italian, Polish, German or Spanish at home and English on the street and in the school. Ultimately, decision concerning adding courses in foreign language will have to be based on time. If new courses are added, old ones must be dropped, unless the school day is lengthened.

There are some fallacies that still persist in the reasons for teaching foreign languages. For example, some parents and pupils have the idea that knowing Spanish will enable a girl to become a private secretary to an importer or a bank president because they need someone to write and translate correspondence from Latin American countries. That is wishful thinking. Qualification for such positions requires college education plus greater facility than can ordinarily be gained in two years of high school study.

Another somewhat doubtful reason given for the study of foreign language in junior high school is the likelihood that the individual will travel abroad. People who advance this reason seem to forget that one language will not serve the person very far in Europe. Moreover there, as elsewhere in the world, more and more people are speaking English. It is true that learning a different language provides some background of method and of experience in saying and hearing different sounds and of realizing that the concepts may be different even though the words may seem to be similar. However learning a European language is of little use in learning the unrelated Asiatic and African tongues.

How foreign language is to be taught and to whom, rests upon many contingencies rather than on the teacher's assumptions about the student's possible success in and use for that language.

Mastery of words and phrases is essential and can be done only by memorization. However, little children learn words and phrases which have meanings and which they use correctly in sentences long before they can learn to read. In the same way, junior high school pupils can begin with expressions that they can use immediately, both in and out of the classroom. They can learn them by ear much faster than by the use of the printed word symbols. The fun they have serves to motivate and speed the learning process. In the modern classroom, books are not being used at all during the early weeks. Reading, writing and translation are postponed until tongues and ears are accustomed to the new sounds.

People in the community are a resource available to the foreign language teacher. War veterans can be interviewed or brought into the classroom to tell about their experiences. It is important for students to hear at first hand whether or not studying foreign language at school was helpful to them. Parents and other teachers who have travelled abroad enjoy showing their pictures and treasures, and relating their experiences. Members of other professions can be interviewed to get their opinions about the values foreign language study had for them. Refugees in the community can be called upon to help with pronunciation, idiomatic expressions, and descriptions of their cultural backgrounds. Committees can be sent to the bank president, the manager of the importing company, the superintendent of the telephone company, and others, to discuss the relation between school language credits and employment possibilities.

Display materials of all kinds can be obtained from many sources. Foreign embassies have maps, pictures, and posters. Steamship companies and tourist agencies have travel folders, pictures, posters, and menu cards in foreign languages. Letters sent to these sources should be on school stationery, countersigned by the teacher, and must indicate that the material is for class, not individual use.

Recordings of all kinds are available to the foreign language teacher. Some of these are lessons. Songs, speeches, plays, and news broadcasts are equally important and are more interesting to the pupils. Newspapers, journals, magazines, and films are invaluable as teaching aids. Foreign language films shown commercially in urban localities afford the opportunity to take the group on a trip. Cities also may provide the chance to go to the foreign language theatre, to interview foreign stars of the screen and stage and musicians from abroad, to tour the foreign sections of the city, and to visit international institutes. The United Nations and UNESCO have much material awaiting the request of the teacher. Posters and pamphlets in all the languages of the world can be secured.

Foreign language also has a place at all grade levels in those core units that deal with other lands and people. Every time such study is undertaken, the pupils should have the experience of twisting their tongues around the sounds used by the people they are trying to understand. As the unit progresses, the pupils, identifying with their new foreign acquaintances, will find much joy in using new foreign names for each other's American names (such as "Giovanni" for "John") in using the new language to say good-morning and good-bye, in using new words for familiar articles of food and clothing, and in singing new songs. All the adults who know the language can be called upon to assist—other teachers, the foreign language specialists, foreign-born parents and students, from the local colleges and universities, veterans and refugees. If the pupils add correspondence with pen-pals in the foreign land to their activities, it will stimulate some of them to learn to read and write the new language.

Where school systems have access to television broadcasting facilities or even to public address systems, foreign language study is being introduced even without qualified teachers. The Westside Community Schools District 66 of Omaha, Nebraska, reports success with a three-year experiment of that kind. There, a well-qualified Spanish supervisor broadcasts a daily fifteen minute lesson in conversational Spanish from the central office. Teacher and pupils learn from it together, and follow it with a short drill period. The supervisor visits to check progress every two weeks. The same

WHITWORTH COLLEGE LIBRARY
SPOKANE, WASHINGTON

school system offers an eighth-grade class in Spanish, held before the regular day begins.[2]

Very few junior high schools are equipped with foreign language laboratories. Teachers who have access to them are not in agreement regarding their practicality or success. The use of electronic and mechanical devices is, in some places, linked with experiments in staff utilization, such as the teacher team, which is a promising development. The team usually consists of a teacher who can properly be called a "linguistic scientist" to direct the classroom teaching and an assistant to help children use the machines correctly and check on their use of time. Sometimes clerical assistance is also provided.

A junior high school's problem in providing foreign language courses will depend upon what opportunities are provided in the elementary schools as well as in the senior high school that the students will attend.

Science

With the launching of Sputnik by Russia came a sudden awakening of American laymen, political leaders, and scientists to the need for more money, interest, and manpower with which to develop missile and space programs. Ensuing discussions brought into sharp focus the absence of good science teaching and teachers in the junior high schools of the country. The efforts of the National Science Foundation, established in 1950 to advance science education, were soon enhanced by grants from foundations to develop science programs for the gifted, and by including science in the National Education Defense Act, which provides funds for teacher education.

Missiles and satellites are not the only reasons why America needs a citizenry literate in science. Factual information about the world we live in is also closely related to personal and public health. People do need to know something about radiation and fall out, but of equal importance to them is knowledge about fluorine in water, pure foods and drugs, mental illness, population explosion and control, preventive medicine, inoculations against virus and

---

[2] Reported in the *Bulletin of the National Association of Secondary School Principals*. January, 1960.

virulent diseases, drug addiction, and very many other things in their own lives which properly fall under the heading of science.

About 25 years ago, science was included in the week's program for seventh and eighth grades. Courses were designed for two or three periods a week. They followed up nature study taught in the elementary school, and to a considerable extent were involved with seasonal changes and geography. When junior high programs were simplified in an effort to cut down the number of subjects studied under different teachers, these short courses disappeared. A ninth-grade, five period course in general science remained but was usually lost to children high in verbal ability who elected foreign language. This neglect of science in the junior high school was due, in part, to the fact that large numbers of teachers had no college preparation in the subject. Most buildings have at least one fairly well equipped, all purpose science room.

The new emphasis on science has now returned short courses to seventh and eighth grades in many schools, and is making science a required course in the ninth grade. However, where adequate courses are not available and teacher education has not caught up, the instruction in science remains inadequate. To take up the slack, some school systems are using television. The advantages and disadvantages depend upon the ability of the teacher who teaches the television lessons; the addition of visiting authorities and the use of kinescopes or video tape of the wonderful science programs which frequently appear on national networks; the relative number of periods spent in looking at television screens and in classroom follow-up; and possibly upon whether or not television is being used merely to save employment of teachers.[3]

Unfortunately, in many schools science teaching remains as it was before Sputnik for all but gifted students. Ninth-grade classes are held in science laboratories where students do a few experiments, watch teacher demonstrations that are apt to be unsuccessful, examine models and diagrams, make some drawings, record observations that are often formulated by the teacher, write conclusions that are dictated by the teacher, and hand in notebooks upon which their marks are partially based. When activities are so formalized and emphasis is placed on memorization of facts, pupils are apt to

[3] Maurice U. Ames, "Teaching Science by Television," *Clearing House,* September, 1959.

lose their natural curiosities and develop a dislike for the subject.

Something better exists in all grades when unit teaching has been developed. Then, seventh graders are permitted to participate in selecting their units and they ask for study of animal life, weather, earthquakes, and the heavenly bodies. Eighth graders are more likely to choose aviation, machines, electricity, and magnetism. In the ninth grade, atomic energy,[4] heredity, and evolution are important because by then the children are in search of new concepts; they want to know the meaning of life. Such units, although not predetermined, satisfy the criteria of increasing difficulty and appeal to maturity levels.

In modern schools that have a general education or core program, units of work invariably cut into the science areas even though they may have begun in the social studies field. Problems of communication, transportation and conservation, health and home life, and natural and human resources are intimately concerned with both subjects. Today, however, science units are being omitted in core programs because science courses are being added. Some programs look much as they did twenty-five years ago —two periods per week in grade seven, three in grade eight, five in grade nine.

Unfortunately, much science teaching is still done from textbooks alone. Discussions center around pictures and diagrams instead of around actual samples of the things that are being studied. Notes are dictated or copied from the board. Tests are given to measure the number of facts that have been memorized. One month after receiving "A" in such a course, students cannot remember what they studied and do not care to talk about it. Many pupils in traditional science classes are bored, others find the reading matter too difficult. It is still not unusual to hear a science teacher complain that half of his pupils cannot read the books that he is required to teach.

Science teaching will improve many fold when teachers accept the material which nature places at the school doors, and discard the books except for reference work and research. Outside are the grasses, weeds, flowers, leaves, ferns, and trees. There are the birds

---

[4] For help with such a unit, see *Living With the Atom*, a booklet prepared for ninth grade by The Bureau of Secondary Curriculum Development, New York State Department of Education, Albany, N. Y.

and their eggs and the insects. There are the reptiles, toads, frogs, and turtles, and the fish, and small animals. There are the clouds, rain, storms, winds and snow, the stars, planets, and the sun. There are the soils, stones, hills, rivers, and lakes. These are only a few of the things that fascinate children, and even non-readers can learn about them.

The physical science materials are equally easy to get in any school and community. From the homes and home arts department come all the simple machines, the soaps and detergents, the mixtures and solutions, the processes of burning gas and cooking. From the shops come the tools, electrical apparatus, the metals, clay and glass, and the processes of plating and etching. Book study may not be necessary for many, but for those who become deeply interested and who can read, there should be a large variety of reference books and free access to the library.

Science courses for the gifted include all kinds of direct experiences with things, plants and animals, and vicarious experiences with pictures, films, radio, and television. Trips and hikes provide opportunities to study nature at first hand. Visits to museums enable pupils to enlarge the scope of their experience and to get information about the far away in time and space. Many people are interviewed in the field and consultants and speakers are provided by colleges, laboratories, businesses, and professional associations. All of these would also enhance the learnings of less able pupils.

With good teaching and encouragement many students become deeply interested in collecting. Identifying, classifying, mounting and arranging specimens are absorbing occupations which call for intellectual effort. Students will also adventure into experimentation and invention if time, facilities, a little help, and encouragement are provided.

Among the most interesting courses being experimented with is "Earth Science" used in New York City for the high ability classes. There is also a special similar course offered by the Pennsylvania State Department of Education as a substitute for general science. In some schools, biology is being "brought down" from senior high and used in ninth grade. In connection with this development, the Biological Sciences Curriculum Study Organization is developing teacher education programs and is producing text materials.

Science seminars are being used with gifted pupils in an effort to break through subject-matter walls. They also promote the development of projects and the use of films, consultants, and resource persons.

Some school systems are providing science opportunities outside the school day. These include field trips and courses offered before the day begins and after it ends. Local community agencies, laboratories, industries, and universities are providing consultants, materials, and even financial aid to enable teachers to study.

As science programs develop, the junior high school needs to keep in mind that science should be *doing*, not just *looking* at a screen, or *hearing* and *reading* about science. Attention must be given to the objectives of teaching and learning the scientific method and of developing the habit of critical thinking.

Science holds peculiar attraction for the young adolescent caught up in the wonder of life and wanting to know what makes things work. As he looks at modern invention and discovery and the possibilities of the space age, he dreams of the infinite opportunities of the future. All junior high school pupils are like that. All of them need to know about this world in which they live. It is good that the emergencies of the immediate present have taken science in the junior high school out of the category of electives and placed it among the required learnings for all pupils.

Mathematics

In the light of events occurring in the late 1950's, mathematics assumed new importance at all school levels. It became a focus of attention in discussion of the needs and programs for the gifted. Moreover, new concepts of mathematical configurations and computations were being considered. Various organizations began to organize projects and much foundation money was allocated in the form of grants. As the 1960's got under way, it was likely that interest would be sustained in this curriculum area.

One of the significant projects for the junior high school is that developed under a grant from the Carnegie Corporation of New York by the College of Education of the University of Maryland.[5]

---

[5] Reported in *Educational Leadership*, December, 1959.

The Mathematics, Engineering, and Psychology departments, the United States Office of Education, Maryland State Department of Education, Maryland State Teachers Association and public school systems are cooperating. In addition to determining which concepts are fitting at maturity levels, course materials are being prepared and will be made available. These are being finalized after experimental use in school systems.

Among the significant elements in the materials developed by the University of Maryland Project are the elimination of the word algebra and the collection of unifying concepts into a mathematical system. Emphasis is placed on understanding rather than rote learning and manipulative skills.

The University of Illinois has also carried on an extensive project.[6] Their ninth-grade course has been in the testing stage since 1953. One feature of this material is the many exploratory exercises which, when used, build awareness of abstractions.

Careful research, experimental testing, and much teacher education are projected, with all thoughtful mathematicians advocating gradual approach rather than crash programs. Extensive financial assistance for teacher education and new materials are possible under the provisions of the National Educational Defense Act. Workshops are being conducted in the week before school opens, on a weekly basis throughout the year, and in the summer.

The conviction is growing that a year of algebra in ninth grade is insufficient, especially for the college bound. The Commission on Mathematics recommends changes in concept, spirit, the point of view of instruction, and in teaching emphasis.[7]

Much attention has been centered on the kind of mathematics the gifted students should have. Unit teaching, as in the social studies and language arts, is seen to be the better way to organize learning experiences, especially when pupils are given the chance to participate in purposing, planning, and evaluating. In addition, systematic instruction and drill in arithmetic is indicated. It is clear that grade-course barriers should be discarded in connection with math and other subjects. Gifted children can proceed rapidly through

---

[6] *Ibid.*

[7] *A Summary of the Report of the Commission on Mathematics,* prepared by the Commission on Mathematics of the College Entrance Exam Board in New York, 1959.

ordinary text materials and go on to the next and the next more difficult concepts and computations. Enrichment is being made possible through the use of such books as Hogben's *Wonderful World of Mathematics*, New York: Garden City Books, 1955; Brandes' *Math Can Be Fun*, Portland, Maine: J. W. Walch, 1956; and number puzzles.

Practical Arts

Practical arts is a term used to cover the learning activities provided for students in the shops and home arts rooms. Shop courses are still technically called Industrial Arts and cooking and sewing are called Home Arts, Home Living, Family Life and Home Economics. For the most part, shop is still available only to boys while courses revolving around the home are offered only to girls.

The shops found in most schools of fewer than one thousand pupils are general wood or carpentry, general electricity and, sometimes, a general shop or hobby center in which half a dozen kinds of activities can go on at the same time. In these are varying amounts of woodworking benches, machines for cutting and shaping metal, electric outlets, wires and tools, and, possibly, such craft and hobby equipment as may be needed for leather tooling and clay modeling.

In traditional schools, for Home Arts, there are multiple kitchen units in one room, tables and chairs, a triple mirror and electric sewing machines in another room. In newer schools a single room may have in it a group of small kitchens, beautifully set up with cabinets, electrical stoves, and other modern electrical equipment such as toasters, skillets, and dish washers.

Modern sewing rooms differ little from the traditional pattern. Electric machines and irons, fitting stands with mirrors, clothing closets, and banks of drawers in which each girl keeps her materials are the usual equipment.

Many older schools and most new ones provide something that resembles living accommodations. This may be one all-purpose room which serves as a living room in which to learn to entertain, and a dining area appropriately furnished. In it girls learn to serve family meals and, in general, middle class dining room skills and behavior patterns.

Newer large schools frequently provide an entire apartment—living-dining room, bedroom and kitchen. Choice and care of furniture, housekeeping, cleaning, meal planning, food purchasing and storage, and the roles played by father and mother are taught in these apartment areas.

It is not uncommon to find laundries in the large new schools. These contain electric washing machines and dryers, mangles, and several types of pressing irons. Based on the modern idea that parents should share household tasks, both boys and girls learn to use that equipment.

Large modern schools have increased the kinds of shops they offer and have changed the nature of the work done there from acquiring skills to creative production. Although the time lapse before pupils will be gainfully employed is understood, courses offered include the study of basic materials and processes, of job opportunities, and of the kinds of human relations which often determine success in job getting, job holding and advancing. These elements are related to personality needs and development in early adolescence.

In the most fully equipped schools, there is likely to be a general wood shop which includes many kinds of machines. In it, each child works at individual projects determined by his interest and his ability, striving for beauty of design and the satisfaction of creative work rather than for craftsmanship. In a modern general metal shop there are likely to be separate areas devoted to jewelry making, metal plating, casting, and forging, and the shop may also contain large machines for cutting, turning, and shaping. The materials used are mostly tin, copper, and silver. As in all the other shops, children love what they create though it is not likely to be perfect. They pay for the materials if they take their products home.

A general electric shop usually contains samples, working models, and the materials needed to understand and maintain the electrical equipment in an ordinary home. There, some pupils do what is needed to begin to acquire the fundamental skills which will enable them to find part time jobs in electric repair shops and garages. However, many boys get inspiration in these shops which leads them eventually to become electricians, radio and T.V. repairmen, electrical engineers, and radar and electronics experts.

Graphic arts shops are found less frequently in junior high

schools. In them, pupils learn to print, to take, develop and enlarge photographs, and to do silk screen work. All of these may lead to exciting life-long hobbies as well as to jobs.

Ceramics shops are still less common and often these activities are found in the fine arts studios rather than the shops. Equipment includes kilns, drying cabinets, ovens, and pottery wheels. The activities are directed very largely to artistic production with less time spent in considering the allied industries.

Traditional programs often include mechanical drawing which usually means learning to read and make rather simple blueprints, or merely to copy them. However, the most modern schools teach mechanical drawing in connection with the articles the child wants to construct in the shop. Instruction in making more difficult and intricate blueprints and mechanical drawings should be provided for the few pupils who have high ability and who are especially interested in architecture and engineering.

From the time junior high schools began, practical arts courses were called "minors" and were offered in very small packages. In seventh grade and for one semester in eighth grade, girls went to cooking and sewing each for two periods per week. Boys were sent to a shop for two periods and to mechanical drawing for two weekly periods. During the second term of the eighth year, those pupils who were not considered bright enough to study a foreign language and algebra or Junior Business Training, were sent to practical arts for five periods a week—girls to cooking and sewing and boys to shop. These courses were continued in the ninth year and, for many students, became the curriculum tracks on which they rode through senior high school.

Although in the past, children supposedly chose their courses, if the school records of tests and achievements seemed to indicate lower abilities the guidance they received practically forced them into practical arts curricula and into grooves from which they could not escape. The same conditions may still prevail in some schools. Thus the practical arts courses and the children who take them become labeled and stigmatized. Negative attitudes towards them may reach even to the teachers of those courses, placing them on the lowest prestige levels of the hierarchal totem poles. Unfortunately, in too many schools little fact and much unsupported opinion operate when teachers give marks and scores, and little or no attention is paid to the unknown and unknowable potentiality of the children who may be late-bloomers or otherwise emotionally blocked.

A new look at the entire practical arts program is mandatory for the junior high schools of tomorrow. In the first place, segregation by sex is no longer justified. Patterns of home life, and the role played by men and women there and in business and industry have changed. The change has implications for the school.

Although few students go to work from eighth or even ninth grade, the drop-out at the tenth grade level continues to be large. It is not amiss, therefore, for consideration to be given to the possibility of job outlets for boys in home arts fields at the junior high school level. The food industries are owned and operated by men. Food is grown, manufactured, transported, and sold by men. The chefs, bus boys, and waiters in restaurants, hotels and resorts are men. Men frequently buy the food for the family and assist with or even take over the cooking and baking in the home. To exclude boys from the kitchens in school or to permit them only in boys' cooking clubs or in camp cookery courses is a mockery.

A look at the clothing and laundry job outlets reveals many opportunities for boys. Men are fashion experts, clothing designers, factory owners, cutters, supervisors, power machine operators, tailors, and cleaners. They manufacture, buy, and sell textiles, nylons, and all other materials. They own and operate the laundries; manufacture, demonstrate and sell laundry equipment, and very often do the laundry in their homes. Again it becomes obvious that excluding them from the home economics courses is no longer tenable.

The home arts department is the logical place for courses in family relations, baby care and baby sitting. Few families operate with and through a woman alone. So it has become essential for boys and girls to study and work together in these courses. In their so doing may be some hope for the inculcation of attitudes and the development of human relations skills which will reduce the incidence of family breakdown and divorce.

On the other hand, girls and women now find employment in every kind of industry, even on assembly lines.

In the school where combined classes of boys and girls have adequate time for the study and practice of home arts and shops, there are few complaints from pupils or parents on the grounds that home

making causes boys to be sissies or that shop makes girls masculine.
Nor do thinking people place this work in the category of unnecessary frills. Moreover, the teachers express pleasure in teaching the
combined classes and can produce evidence of growth on the part
of both boys and girls.

The therapeutic values of artistic creative handwork in the shops
are, of course, of as great importance as any other possible outcomes. This is true for both girls and boys. Both sexes find keen
enjoyment in making articles of all kinds and in repairing home
equipment. For both boys and girls the avocational, leisure time
possibilities are great. For both groups alike, careers in arts and
crafts may be fostered.

One additional important reason for the elimination of sex segregation in practical arts classes is that there, boys and girls can learn
to talk to each other, to work together, to understand each other's
role in family living. This, coming in early adolescence where one
of the developmental tasks is heterosexual adjustment, is a most
important way of meeting adolescent needs.

Some schools are finding ways of scheduling practical arts classes
which enable pupils to go there for extended periods on successive
days. This lessens loss of interest and of materials, speeds up acquiring of skills, and doubles production. An example of such a schedule
in a core program appears below.

	8:45	9	10	11	12	12:40	1:40 · 2:45
MON.	R	SOC. LIV. (11:20)		L	SOC. LIV.	MATH.	HYG.
TUE.	R	MATH.	ART		SOC. LIV.	L	SOC. LIV.
WED.	R	SOC. LIV.		P.E.	L	MATH.	MUSIC
THU.	R	MATH.	SOC. LIV. (11:20)	L	SOC. LIV.	PRACTICAL ARTS	
FRI.	A	PRACTICAL ARTS		SOC. LIV. (12:20)	L (1:00)	SOC. LIV.	P.E.

Television

A number of forces have combined to make the use of television in schools for regular teaching purposes a growing but still highly controversial educational issue. Educational foundations have placed large grants at the disposal of school systems willing to experiment. Commercial producers of television equipment and telephone companies have contributed and sold their resources and skills to develop programs. National broadcasting networks have produced magnificent science programs, the tapes of which should be (if they are not already) accessible to schools. Universities have developed and broadcast courses for teachers, with credit granted for written examinations. Broadcasting companies have been eager to use in their commercially free time excellent science programs developed by educators. And, of very great importance, teaching by television can be done for hundreds at a time, thus cutting down the necessity for large qualified mathematics, foreign language, and science staffs, the members of which are still hard to get.

One of the earliest closed circuit experiments began in Hagerstown, Maryland, in 1956. In 1958 the Fund for the Advancement of Education reported that 569 public school districts made use of regular television programs. In the September 1959 issue of *Clearing House*, Maurice U. Ames reported visits to ten schools to observe their use of television. An extensive program is underway in Philadelphia, and the list, however long now, will not be accurate tomorrow, for many school systems are developing programs for many reasons.

Television programs differ in their purposes. Some add elements which are not generally available in a school, and call it enrichment. Some substitute the television set for the teacher. In the least satisfactory programs, one or two hundred pupils spend four out of five periods a week seated together in a semi-dark auditorium looking at the screen. In other schools two or three periods out of five, per week, are spent viewing and are supplemented by either three or two periods of classroom work. However, what is done in the classroom varies from drill and book work to student participation in experiments and discussion. Many good teachers assign pupils to viewing and reporting on the excellent out-of-class programs available to the public. There is no limit to the programs that can thus be used by teachers of literature, science, music, creative writing, history, and social problems.

Much can be said both for and against the use of television for in-school teaching. On the positive side, it may and usually does bring the best teachers, sometimes great master teachers, to the service of far larger numbers of children than they could otherwise reach. It also makes it possible for children in distant places to have vicarious visits to museums and laboratories, music halls and theatres, and to far distant lands. There they see and listen to the great men and women in all walks of life. There they have cultural experiences heretofore denied to all but city dwellers and to those who could travel. There is small doubt that children would benefit enormously from in-school opportunities to discuss the human relationships, the problems of living, and the contrasting behavior patterns and background influences they witness night after night in their homes. Little chance to do this yet exists in most schools.

Also on the positive side, those teachers who are selected to do the broadcasts have opportunities for research and for careful planning that inevitably enhance their own work and enable them to demonstrate to the watching teachers the best possible teaching methods.

Some educators claim that watching television lessons promotes attention, self control, the skill of listening and sharpens the memory. The opposite is also claimed by many teachers who are assigned to watch the pupils during the broadcasts. They say that television also adds frustration and consequent aggressive behavior or withdrawal whenever the sound track goes off, or the teacher's voice drops below audibility, or interference erases the picture. What can the classroom teacher do then? How can the lost instruction be replaced? Moreover, some educators fail to sense the fact that a teacher may feel debased when his role becomes largely that of monitor, "orderkeeper," drillmaster, lesson assigner, examiner, and record keeper.

According to the January 31, 1960, issue of *The Washington Post*, the District of Columbia school system renounced the use of television in the regular instruction program. This was done after research which indicated that children cannot learn effectively by watching television in school. It is undoubtedly true that when television comes in, active participation of pupils in planning goes out. It is obvious also that interaction of pupils with the teacher and each other, which increases learning opportunities, is not possible during a television lesson. Much more experimentation, action research, and scientific evaluation will be done before final answers are available. It is likely that television as enrichment will increase. It is equally likely that with improvement of classroom instruction, with all-out efforts of colleges to do a good job of teacher education, and with salary schedules high enough to attract the best minds and personalities to teaching, efforts to replace teachers with television will cease.

The Library

Another area in which new techniques of programming, of using materials, and of instruction are needed, is the library.

Most elementary schools are still without libraries. As a result, junior high school curriculum makers have usually scheduled entering pupils, at the seventh grade level, to attend formal courses in the use of the library. These may be only one or two periods a week for a semester or two. Course content often includes the use of the Dewey Decimal System, card catalogues, reference books, and encyclopedias. All of this bears little relation to the fact that many children are quite unable to read these cards and books. Moreover, in many schools no attempt is made to tie up this kind of instruction with the work actually in progress in the classrooms which the pupils attend. Tests on the course, rather than on the children's ability to use the library, are usually given and marks are recorded for "Library" on report cards.

For too many pupils the program described above serves to deepen their dislike for books and to develop an aversion for the library itself if for no other reason than that in that sacred place of learning strict silence and immobility are enforced. The futility of the program is serious. Just as serious, however, is the fact that the scheduling of classes to the library inevitably closes it to all the other students in the school for the normal uses to which it should be put. To be sure, book circulation goes on both before and after school, but that is no time to expect the many children to come who have other demands on their time. Neither is it an incentive to the indifferent child who easily contrives to reach the building just as the last bell rings and who always forgets to stay at the close of the day.

In many schools where the traditional program of library instruction for beginners is maintained, the librarian is regarded as a regular classroom teacher and her schedule is arranged accordingly. This means that she must bear her share of the burden of proctoring duties outside of the library. Consequently, the library is closed during those periods.

In schools where a modern curriculum is in use, the librarian faces quite a different task and plays a different role in the program and life of the school. There she is never out of the library for other duties. The library door is always open to those who have need to use books there, or to get books and other materials for their classes.

This does not mean that a class group is never given instruction in the use of the library and its contents. Quite the contrary. Whenever a teacher in the course of classroom work finds that more books, materials and references are needed than are available in the room, he calls the library, and if it is free, the class group goes there at once. Then, with a pressing need to be met, the librarian finds receptive minds. She gives the specific instruction that is required at that moment and the children move to the shelves to get the books they want, to search for facts in the reference volumes, and to practice using the card catalogues. Picture files are usually ready for the pupils who have difficulty with reading. Books on the lower reading levels as well as those of more adult nature are pointed out by the librarian as she and the teacher assist the students to find appropriate materials.

Of course, when there is complete freedom to use the library in this way, some particular teachers may never find the time or the reason for going there. The librarian, who is deeply concerned that every child shall have the best possible experience connected with books, becomes aware of the fact that certain classes do not come. She arranges for a conference with those teachers who are a bit remiss and helps them to recognize the advantages of coming to the library and to include it in the plans made with the pupils.

The librarian in the modern junior high school has a definite part to play in the in-service education program of the faculty. The principal, who is responsible for knowing what use is being made of the library, must arrange to devote professional meeting time to discussion of the library facilities, to display and examination of new additions—books, maps, charts, picture files, and periodicals—and to planning to meet the library needs of both pupils and faculty.

Where space permits or when a second room can be added, committee work can go on in the library. There should be nothing to prevent a small group from leaving a classroom to go to that committee room or the research room to consult the files, to use the books on the reserve reference shelves, to work with the fugitive materials, or even to hold committee meetings. Libraries in new buildings have ample provisions for such activities. Assistance from the librarian or her supervision may or may not be needed, depending upon the classroom teacher's judgment, the job to be done, the maturity, experience, and leadership in the particular group concerned.

When the library begins to function as a reference room, teachers will find it most convenient to send individual pupils there to get facts when questions arise that cannot be answered from sources at hand in the classroom. To be sent on such a mission is recognition of the ability of a student to conduct himself as an adult and to serve the group of which he is a part. It is a challenge that can be extended to a high-ability pupil.

The resourceful librarian will find many ways in which the usefulness of the library can be increased. She will begin to group books around the titles that are recurrent in units. Classroom librarians will be permitted to take such packages out of the library for use in the classroom. Clippings and pamphlets, which are often called "fugitive materials" because they are used up and should be replaced frequently, need to be packaged and decentralized for classroom use. In order to keep at hand a supply of fugitive materials, stacks of back issues of magazines can be made available to committees for clipping purposes. Children can work in the library at the job of making collections of pictures, maps, charts, graphs, and cartoons, which also need to be mounted, sorted, and filed for use.

Library clubs are popular with both students and librarians. In them, students learn to issue and receive books, repair damage, replace books on shelves, and prepare new books for cataloguing.

Many librarians received the inspiration for their careers in such activities.

Browsing corners for teachers are important in the modern school library. Copies of all the text and supplementary books should be at hand for teachers to work with. This will save them time and frustration, especially when crowded buildings make it impossible for a teacher to use his own room during unassigned periods. Remedial reading materials and samples of books on all reading levels should be placed on the shelves for teachers to examine at their convenience. Teachers are grateful when they can find professional books that are required for college courses, in their own library. Pleasure reading, the professional journals, and the daily papers make the library an important place for the faculty as well as the students.

It is ridiculous to suppose that a single person can possibly administer a modern junior high school library. There is not enough time in the day for one person to do the physical labor involved, to say nothing of the instruction of so many children. In some schools, therefore, a member of the clerical staff is assigned as library assistant. In other places teachers are given library duty. The best plan is to employ a second librarian.

The same basic principles that govern curriculum change in other areas can be applied to the library. First, *plenty of materials of many kinds, on a wide range of difficulty, should be secured in order to meet a wide diversity of pupil and teacher needs.* Some of this can be obtained without expense if the teachers will part with the treasures stored in their closets. When they are willing to share these with each other, a large quantity of resource materials becomes immediately available to all.[8]

Second, *books, clippings, files, and fugitive materials should be organized under the headings most applicable to units that are frequently studied in the classrooms.* These must be accessible to students in the library and ready for temporary issue to a class that is in need of them.

Third, *cooperative participation by the librarian and the teachers is needed to secure and to circulate new references that are required for unit work as soon as they come in.* The librarian must be con-

---

[8] Ruth Seeger, *Library Resources in Educational Research.* Columbus, Ohio: Ohio State University.

tinuously on the alert for new free and inexpensive materials. A committee of pupils can be trained to write for them. They, the classroom groups, and the teacher library committee can assist in reading, sorting, and classifying these as they come in.

Fourth, *there should be opportunity in the library for productive useful work to be done by those children who have little ability to use the books.* Such jobs can include sorting magazines, clipping and mounting pictures, graphs, and maps, doing important housekeeping chores, mending books, caring for plants, and assisting with bulletin board displays.

An important aspect of the librarian's work is leadership of the teacher committee whose responsibility should be to discuss the relationship of the library to the curriculum, changes that are needed, and ways in which the entire faculty can be drawn into the effective functioning of the library so that it may become the heart and center of learning in the school.

The librarian should not only permit but also encourage teacher groups to come into the library to discuss with her and with each other problems of curriculum content and of how to tie literature and poetry into unit work. She can add greatly to the teachers' feelings of security in their new program if she will help them to find the factual backgrounds they need and the available literature books, and if she will tell them about the books that the children read for fun.

The modern school is blessed when it has a librarian who helps to build fine personal, social, and professional relationships in the faculty group.

Evaluation and Reports

Until testing, marking, and report forms are changed, reorganization of curriculum suffers delay. Classroom teaching, in large measure, depends upon the values emphasized in the tests that the teacher must give. Where tests are produced and administered by some central authority—the curriculum office, the State Department of Education, or even the school principal—the teacher fears that the results will be used in rating him and in renewing his contract. When the tests given are factual, memorizing facts becomes the most important thing for pupils to do.

In the same measure, the development of the entire program depends upon the values that are brought to bear on the principal by the community, the local superintendent, and the state department. Where fear of criticism is the controlling factor and where importance is attached to silence in the halls, participation in contests, and even to the position of window shades, the school is shackled to traditional content and procedures.

Dewey said, in describing a good school, it "is primarily concerned with growth, with a moving and changing process, with *transforming* existing capacities and experiences; what already exists by way of native endowment and past achievements is subordinate to what it may become. Possibilities are more important than what already exists, and knowledge of the latter counts only in its bearing upon possibilities. The place of measurement of achievements as a theory of education is very different in a static educational system from what it is in one which is dynamic, or in which the ongoing process of growing is the important thing."[9]

The modern concept of evaluation in the classroom involves more than testing and marking. Carl Rogers says, "Testing to see if a student meets some criterion held by the teacher is directly contrary to the implications for significant learning. The natural place of evaluation in life is as a ticket of entrance, not as a club over the recalcitrant."

Discussion of the value of learning experiences, of the processes that are used, and of the outcomes can be structured into the daily and weekly work of the class. These are most fruitful when end results are looked at in terms of previously determined goals. For example, after a session spent in planning a unit, the teacher raises such questions as, "Did we do a good job with this plan? Why? Why not? How could we improve upon it?" At the close of a class discussion, the following questions may be put before the class: "Did we accomplish our purpose? Was the leadership satisfactory? How many took part? Could we increase the number next time? How? What shall we guard against next time?" Committee meetings, progress and final reports of group work are scrutinized by questioning: "Did anything interfere with our committee work? Did we pick the right officers? Did we help them to do their work? Did they help us? What made our reports successful?" At the close of a unit the entire

---

[9] John Dewey, "Progressive Education and the Science of Education," *Progressive Education,* July-September, 1928.

class engages in a lengthy evaluation session. At that time they discuss such matters as: "What does this all add up to for us? What did we get out of it? What still needs to be done in the next unit? What do we need to know more about? In the light of our strength and weakness, of what we do and do not know, what must we do next?"

Children will develop the habit of judging the worth of the people with whom they associate, of the processes they use, of their own actions, and of group and individual end products, when their practice of evaluation is continuous, cooperative, and constructive. They will learn to view their present performances and accomplishments in terms of their previous and their best achievements. They will learn to look at group work in terms of their own contributions to it.

It is probable that children so trained will be better able to make wise selection of candidates for public offices. They will also be likely to hold incumbents responsible for doing a good job. They will surely sense the importance of participating constructively in group efforts to improve the quality of democratic life in their communities. They will be more willing and better able to accept the responsibility of holding public office. They will be better equipped to face facts about themselves and more likely to demand more of themselves. These outcomes far outweigh any that can possibly come from an evaluation program that consists of tests and marks.

The outcomes that have been described are those to be sought from the total program. Evaluation of the offerings of a school must engage the serious attention of all who are concerned. The decision to change curriculum usually grows out of some kind of evaluation of the old, whether it be done formally or informally. Unless it has been found wanting, there would be no reason to change it. As new organization, new content, new methods are put into effect, comparisons of them with the old ones are bound to be made. Questions about the learning outcomes and the effect upon discipline will have to be answered.

Of course, modern education must be held to account for its claims of superiority. Research studies have already been done and can be consulted. The most pretentious of them is reported in Volume IV of the Progressive Education Association's Eight-Year Study of Thirty Schools, *Did They Succeed in College?* This investigation gives evidence of the superiority of modern schools in developing the characteristics and skills needed for effective social and democratic living. It also shows that students who had experienced modern preparatory programs did as well in academic work as those whose training had been received in traditional schools.[10]

Research in education has taken on a different look as schools have become interested in Action Research projects. The kind of controlled situations that were formerly required are too difficult to devise. As we become more and more convinced of the uniqueness of each individual, it seems to be impossible to set up studies in which one child is equated with another, one group is set up as a check upon the other, one teacher is measured against another. Attention is now centered upon effecting changes in situations, in children, in teachers, in content, in methods. What is done to create change has to be documented. Behavior of people has to be observed and described. What is said and done has to be written down. All such data have to be analyzed and interpreted.

There is a widespread tendency to compare the teacher who is beginning to use modern methods with the one who is long experienced in traditional techniques. This is hardly fair. Moreover it is easier to hide poor teaching in traditional book work than it is in classrooms in which there is constant activity. Instead of trying to make such comparisons, the *values* of each type of teaching should be clearly determined and compared.

As parents, teachers, and pupils together evaluate the purposes, practices, and outcomes of their schools, they will need to keep in mind the following principles summarized by Wrinkle when he said: "The need for marks as persuasive devices, as pressure instruments, to induce an increased application of student effort is based on an assumption that students do not want to do what the school wants them to do. In a large measure this is not merely an assumption; it is a fact. As a result of objectives unrelated to the needs, interests, and purposes of students, predetermined learning activities, preselected learning materials, and legislated or college-dictated courses of study, teachers have found it necessary to threaten students who, whether by choice or intent, learn slowly, with failure, and to encourage students of superior ability to apply themselves by use of the honor roll and similar devices. Marks may pro-

---

[10] Margaret Willis, "Social Studies and Citizenship Education," *Social Education*, May, 1960.

vide effective temporary substitutes for real interests, meanings, recognition of values, and worthwhile purposes, but they should not be assumed to have permanent carry-over values. When stimulation is removed, the activity is likely to be discontinued."[11] X

Evaluation is a controversial issue. Hot argument is carried on over the use of marks: should there be a three or four point scale? Should letter symbols represent the words for which they stand or be the first four letters of the alphabet? On a deeper level, there is much thoughtful discussion of how to measure growth, the meaning of marks, and their effect upon the children. Teachers are baffled by the problems presented when they try to determine marks in relation to individual ability, the level at which a child begins, and the growth he makes. The use of grade norms, median and raw scores, and so-called average I.Q.'s serves further to confuse the issues.

Consider, for example, the problem the teacher faces when he records marks for a spelling lesson in which he taught ten words and then gave a test to find the extent of learning in the class. Mary Smith is one of the pupils. She is verbally minded and knew all the words before the lesson began. She made a perfect score on the test. She did not grow at all, however, and her success was not due to the effectiveness of the instruction. Should she have a high mark?

Sue Jones is also in the class. She is a lower class child, rather slow, and was not familiar with any of the words at the beginning of the lesson. She learned to spell half of them. Sue grew considerably, and her learning reflects good teaching. However, Sue will get a mark of 50 per cent or "poor," or "F," all of which stand for failure. Such simple illustrations serve to bring teachers face-to-face with the necessity for replacing regimented marking schemes with something more significant to them, to the students, and to the parents.

Various forms of grouping by ability, developed in the latter part of the 1950's, add confusion to the problems of evaluation of a child's work and growth. In some places, top marks, "A," for example, are forbidden to all except those in the highest ability groups. Pupils in the middle groups, no matter how well they do the tasks assigned, cannot get marks above "B." Those in the lower

---

[11] William L. Wrinkle, *Improving Marking and Reporting Practices.* New York: Rinehart and Co., 1947.

groups are pegged at "C." Such a practice must, of necessity, destroy effort and aspiration in the large majority of the pupils in the school.

With the renewed emphasis on college and the great increase in the numbers applying for admission to college has come extremely bitter and injurious competition for marks. This is particularly unfortunate, because there is evidence that too many of those who struggle for and often receive "straight A's" are not interested in learning, or scholarship, or excellence.

Pressure for uniformly high marks in all subject areas, exerted on the high ability groups, often produces unfortunate results. A research study done in 1957 revealed that some very bright children were learning to dislike one or more subjects, and/or the teacher, school, and possibly education itself.[12]

Another highly questionable practice being used in some cities is the use of tutoring groups in which the very best students are enrolled for the purpse of learning how to take tests so as to insure entrance to college or the securing of scholarships. In some cases the parents must pay for this privilege. In all cases, such a practice is obviously one which fosters great inequality of opportunity.

The kinds of rating scales and report forms to be used should be determined cooperatively by all who are concerned. When administrators, parents, teachers, and pupils meet together to clarify their individual and common problems and to set up goals, they will be able to resolve some of the conflicts that cloud these issues. As they determine the methods to be used to evaluate growth in the direction of their goals, the effectiveness of teaching methods, and the outcomes of the total program of the school, some of the confusions will be dispelled. People have to learn to accept the mistakes that children and teachers make and to identify them as learning experiences. When they do so, the insistence on failure for punitive purposes will disappear.

Another aspect of the controversy is concerned with the use of tests and measuring instruments. Questions are raised about the validity of standardized tests and about the use of them for statistical purposes rather than diagnosis of individual needs. The modern teacher is often accused of not using tests at all. This is far from

---

[12] Ernest A. Haggard, "Socialization, Personality and Academic Achievement in Gifted Children," *School Review*, Winter, 1957.

the truth. He uses all the measuring devices that are available and that he and his pupils can construct. He gives frequent short-answer tests to encourage continuous search for information. He uses long objective tests of all types, commercial and home-made, to discover the extent and depth of knowledge the pupils have acquired, and to increase their ability to handle that kind of instrument. Essay tests give the students a chance to organize their thoughts and to show that they can express themselves in good English. Oral quizzes introduce the element of fun in competition.

Information is not the only item about which the modern teacher collects evaluative data. He writes descriptions and documents speech and action in order to have a basis for determining growth

EVALUATION OF PUPIL PROGRESS

Objectives to be Achieved	Techniques to be Used to Measure Growth
Orientation to school. Adjustment to the peer group. Adjustment to teachers. Development of democratic abilities, skills, understanding.	Observe emotional reactions. Check attendance records. Observe the quality of group life, attitudes to children. Use social distance scales. Record complaints about the child and his complaints about teachers. Make anecdotal records of participation in student elections. List offices held, services rendered. Note initiative and interest, frequency and quality of suggestions made. Record the help needed in reaching decisions. Note quality of participation in group discussions, roles played.
Development of thought habits: clarity, resisting undue influence, making decisions, insisting on fact and authority, prompt and intelligent attack on problem, setting up own goals, planning work, adherence to plan, evaluating self and others.	Observe and record actions, speech, comments about others and what others say about the individual under consideration. Use testing devices. Interpret records made by committee leaders. Inspect individual progress graphs.

EVALUATION OF PUPIL PROGRESS

Objectives to be Achieved	*Techniques to be Used To Measure Growth*
Development of work habits: neatness, ability to gather information, thoroughness, ability to follow directions, promptness, accuracy, ability to observe, ability to keep honest, useful records, ability to correct own and others' errors, stick-to-it-iveness, self appraisal.	Evaluate written work. Set up tests. Make anecdotal records. Record promptness to school and classes. Use testing devices. Inspect record book regularly. Record completeness of jobs undertaken. Use inventories.
Establishment of health habits and the correction of defects.	Daily inspection. Confer with medical staff about follow-up of medical examination. Study attendance records. Inspect charts made of rest and nutrition habits.
Development of personal characteristics: self reliance, responsibility, self control, obedience, creativeness and originality, less egocentricity, courtesy, appreciation of work, appreciation of the good, the true, and the beautiful.	Observe them and make anecdotal records. Evaluate creative writings and other artistic forms of expression of learnings. Observe and make notes of instances in which these traits were in evidence.
Development of tool skills: reading, writing, speaking, spelling, listening, looking, living in peace and harmony, using democratic methods and practices.	Use standard and home-made tests —short, long, objective, essay, games, contests. Examine class work for evidence of skills. Have pupils keep personal growth charts. Keep anecdotal records. Observe and record actions.

EVALUATION OF PUPIL PROGRESS

Objectives to be Achieved	*Techniques to be Used to Measure Growth*
Development of standards in reading and appreciation of literature and reading as a leisure time activity.	Have individual records kept of books read. Inspect them for evidence of growth in taste, types of books chosen, remarks made about them.
Knowledge of: current affairs, people and life near at hand and in remote places, how food, shelter, and clothing are provided and affect life, processes of consumption and distribution of goods and services, own abilities and potentialities, human development, hygiene, nutrition, first aid, value and use of museums, use and making of maps, charts and graphs, American history and institutions, American freedom and way of life, American government, how to use leisure time.	Where information is factual, use all kinds of tests. Analyze and interpret tests to discover individual growth. Inspect and evaluate with him the records each child keeps of class work. Record evidences of aspirations. Observe while on trips. Hear reports of week-end and vacation activities. Have records made of leisure time activities and of summer vacations. The diary is a useful device.

in character development, personality adjustment, the skills of citizenship, and the development of thought habits.

Growth in the ability to plan, to think critically, to use good judgment, and to choose wisely can be observed and recorded. To do so, the teacher makes use of controlled, meaningful situations that call for the use of those abilities. The techniques to use in evaluation of any element depend upon the objectives and outcomes that are sought. The preceding tables are full of suggestions.

Many secondary schools have developed original report forms which are helpful to both parents and teachers. These tend to take the emphasis away from subject matter measurement and place it on the development of personality. Some make it more possible for teachers to rate their students in terms of individual growth which has a relation to the individual's ability.

St. Paul, Minnesota
PUPIL'S PROGRESS REPORT
Secondary Schools
19___ – 19___

Credit _____
Credit Withheld _____

Name _____
Subject _____

Teacher _____
Homeroom _____
Period _____

Marking Period	1				2				3				4				Final Mark			
Times absent from class																				
Times tardy to class																				
1. Conduct (Courtesy, respect for teachers, administrators and others, and respect for property. Graded "S" or "N")																				
2. Achievement (In relation to ability Graded "S" or "N")																				
3. Achievement (In relation to others in this class)	4	3	2	1	4	3	2	1	4	3	2	1	4	3	2	1	4	3	2	1

Note: Credit is granted or withheld on the basis of ALL THREE ITEMS above.

EXPLANATION OF GRADING SYMBOLS:

S – Satisfactory.

Item 1
and
Item 2

N– – Needs improvement. This symbol is a danger signal. If your child receives an "N" on Items 1 or 2, you are urged to contact the school.

Item 3

4 – Pupil is in the upper 25% of this class.
3 – Pupil is in the 25% just above the mid-point of this class.
2 – Pupil is in the 25% just below the mid-point of this class.
1 – Pupil is in the lowest 25% of this class.

Inc. – incomplete, work must be made up.

The form on page 242 used in St. Paul, Minnesota, is sent to parents and supplemented by simplified records kept in the school office. Progress reports and letters to parents are used in addition to conferences.

State Departments of Education are taking the lead in many parts of the country. They not only survey the school systems, calling in citizens and professionals to testify, but they also issue manuals to guide the schools in their own evaluative activities. One of the most interesting and valuable of these publications was developed by a state-wide committee in West Virginia. That Bulletin, called "Criteria for Evaluating School Growth," deals with a twelve year program. The principles of evaluation implemented in the bulletin are:

1. Evaluation procedures should be cooperatively developed and applied by the entire school staff.

2. Evaluation should be based on progress rather than on preconceived standards.

3. Evaluation should result in the improvement of the total school program.

4. Evaluation techniques should lead to the identification of the next steps to be taken.

5. Evaluation should be a continuous process in keeping with worth-while objectives planned by the entire staff.

6. Evaluation must be a democratic process. All people affected should be included.

The areas to be evaluated in any school are organization, curriculum, the program in action, use of instructional materials and resources, pupil growth, and community relations. Throughout the directions for evaluation, emphasis is placed on growth. For example, pupil growth is to be judged on the basis of, (1) provisions for continuous progress, (2) continuous appraisal of growth, and (3) growth in social maturity.

References

FOREIGN LANGUAGE

BOOKS

Huebener, T., *How To Teach Foreign Languages Effectively*. New York: New York University Press, 1959.

PERIODICALS AND PAMPHLETS

Alden, D. W., ed., "Materials List for Use by Teachers of Modern Foreign Languages," Foreign Language Program Research Center, 50 Fifth Ave., New York 11, 1959.
"Foreign Language Laboratories in Schools and Colleges," *Bulletin #3*, Washington, D. C.: Government Printing Office, 1959.
Moore, R. S., "On Languages: Are We Battling for Defeat?" *School and Society*, December 19, 1959.
Mueller, T., "New Trends in Modern Foreign Language Teaching," *The Clearing House*, January, 1960.
New York Board of Education, "Modern Languages and Latin," *Curriculum Bulletin #9*, 1959.
Parker, W. R., *The National Interest and Foreign Languages*. U. S. National Commission for UNESCO, New York, 1954.
"The Teaching of Modern Languages and Intercultural Understanding," *Modern Language Journal*, April, 1955.
Wisconsin Cooperative Educational Planning Program, "Modern Languages in a Modern Curriculum," *Bulletin #323*, Madison, Wisconsin, May, 1950.

SCIENCE

BOOKS

Cummings, H. H., ed., *Science and the Social Studies*. National Council for the Social Studies, 27th Year Book, 1957.
National Science Teachers Association, *Science in the Junior High School*. Washington, D. C.: National Education Association, 1959.
National Society for the Study of Education, *Rethinking Science Education*. 59th Year Book, Part 1, 1960.
Richardson, J. S., *Science Teaching in Secondary Schools*. Englewood Cliffs, N. J.: Prentice-Hall, Inc., 1957.

PERIODICALS AND PAMPHLETS

Ames, M. U., "Teaching Science by Television," *Clearing House*, September, 1959.
Grobman, A. B., "Life Sciences in American Schools," *Educational Leadership*, December, 1959.
"How Good Is Soviet Science?" *Fortune Magazine*, February, 1957.
Killian, J. R., Jr., "Education for the Age of Science," *N.E.A. Journal*, February, 1960.
"Laboratory Exercises in the Life Sciences," *Science Teacher*, March, April, May, 1956.
Patterson and Kraus, *Thousands of Science Projects*. Washington, D. C.: Science Clubs of America, 1957.

MATHEMATICS

BOOKS

Council of Teachers of Mathematics, 24th Year Book.
Glennon, V. J., ed., *What Does Research Say About Arithmetic?* rev. ed. Washington, D. C.: Association for Supervision and Curriculum Development, 1958.
Mueller, F. J., *Arithmetic: Its Structure and Concepts.* Englewood Cliffs, N. J.: Prentice-Hall, Inc., 1956.
Spitzer, Herbert F., *Practical Classroom Procedures for Enriching Arithmetic.* St. Louis: Webster Publishing Co., 1956.
Studies in Mathematics Education. Chicago: Scott Foresman & Co., 1959.

PERIODICALS AND PAMPHLETS

Allen, Frank B., "Mathematics Tomorrow." *N.E.A. Journal,* May, 1957.
Board of Education, New York City, *Four Cycles of Mathematics.* 1960.
Garstens, H. L., "Experimental Mathematics in the Junior High School," *N.E.A. Journal,* May, 1959.
Grossnickle, F. E., "Arithmetic for Those Who Excel," *Arithmetic Teacher,* March, 1956.
Jones, R. S., "The Mathematics Teacher's Dilemma," *University of Michigan School of Education Bulletin,* January, 1959.

PRACTICAL ARTS

BOOKS

Groneman & Feirer, *General Shop.* New York: McGraw-Hill Book Co., 1956.
Fleck, Fernandez Monvez, *Exploring Home and Family Living,* Englewood, New Jersey: Prentice-Hall, Inc., 1959.
Hall, Olive A., *Home Economics—Careers and Homemaking,* New York: Wiley & Sons, 1958.
Williamson and Lyle, *Homemaking Education in the High School,* New York: Appleton-Century-Crofts, 1954.

PERIODICALS AND PAMPHLETS

Balin, Robert P., "Encourage Creativity," *Industrial Arts and Vocational Education,* November, 1960.
Bartel, Carl R., "An Aid to Project Planning," *Industrial Arts and Vocational Education,* November, 1960.

Department of Home Economics, National Education Association, *Homemaking for the Young Adolescent*, February, 1956. *The Gifted Student in Homemaking Education*, October, 1958. *The Slow Learner in Homemaking Education*, March, 1959.

Industrial Arts in Education. 1010 Vermont Avenue, Washington 5, D. C.

Industrial Arts for the Middle Grades. State Dept. of Education, Atlanta, Georgia.

Mouser, Robert J., "Mark Those Projects Fairly," *School Shop*, October, 1960.

Projects Department, *Industrial Arts and Vocational Education*.

TELEVISION

Ames, M. U., "Teaching Science by Television," *Clearing House*, September, 1959.

Brunstein, J. J., "Ten Uses for Commercial Television in the English Classroom," *The English Journal*, December, 1958.

Buehring, L. E., "Hagerstown Experiment—After Two Years," *The Nation's Schools*, February, 1959.

Foshay, A. W., Dir., "Interaction in Learning: Implications for T.V." Teachers College Record, Columbia University, February, 1960.

McDonald, A. S., "Television, Books, and School Marks," *Journal of Developmental Reading*, Autumn, 1959.

Stickel, W. E., "Qua Via . . . Video?" *Childhood Education*, December, 1959.

"Teaching by T.V." (Pamphlet) Ford Foundation and the The Fund for the Advancement of Education, May, 1959.

LIBRARY

BOOKS

Hanna and McAllister, *Books, Young People and Reading Guidance*, New York: Harper and Brothers, 1960.

Rossoff, M., *Library in High School Teaching*. New York: H. W. Wilson Co., 1955.

Stewart, Hiller and Alberty, *Improving Reading in the Junior High School: A Librarian and a Core Teacher Work Together*. New York: Appleton-Century-Crofts, 1957.

Tooze, Ruth, *Your Children Want to Read: A Guide for Teachers and Parents*. Englewood Cliffs, N. J.: Prentice-Hall, Inc., 1957.

PERIODICALS

American Association of School Librarians, *Standards for School Library Programs*. 1960.

"The Effective Secondary-School Library," *Bulletin of the National Association of Secondary School Principals*, November, 1959.

EVALUATION

BOOKS

Baron and Bernard, *Evaluation Techniques for Classroom Teachers*. New York: McGraw-Hill Book Co., 1958.
Wrightstone, Justman, Robbins, *Evaluation in Modern Education*. New York: American Book Co., 1956.

State Departments of Instruction:
Connecticut: *Assessment Guide for Use in the Junior High School*.
Oklahoma: *Manual of Evaluation of the Junior High School*.
Utah: *Junior High School Evaluative Criteria*.

PERIODICALS AND PAMPHLETS

Hershey, John, *Intelligence, Choice and Consent*. New York: Woodrow Wilson Foundation, 1959.
Keller, I. A., "An Evaluation of the Dual Grading System," *The Bulletin of the National Association of Secondary School Principals*, November, 1955.
NEA Special Features: "What Is Effective Evaluation?" November, 1959, and "Reporting," December, 1959.
Robinson, H. M., ed., *Evaluation of Reading*. Conference on Reading, University of Chicago, 1958.
Research Division, National Education Association, *School Marks and Foundations*.
Wilson, C. H., "Our Report Cards Are Failing," *N.E.A. Journal*, September, 1959.

CHAPTER TWELVE

Techniques of Instruction

The child cannot get power of judgment excepting as he is continually exercised in forming and testing judgments. He must have an opportunity to select for himself, and to attempt to put his selections into execution, that he may submit them to the final test, that of action. Only thus can he learn to discriminate that which promises success from that which promises failure; only thus can he form the habit of relating his purposes and notions to the conditions that determine their value. Does the school . . . afford at present sufficient opportunity for this sort of experimentation? Except so far as emphasis of the school work is upon intelligent doing, upon active investigation, it does not furnish the conditions necessary for the exercise of judgment which is an integral factor in good character.

> John Dewey, *Moral Principles in Education.* New York: Houghton Mifflin Co., 1909, page 53.

How often administrators and teachers exclaim with impatience, "But good teachers have always done that!" when they discuss the use of new teaching techniques. If they are concerned with the *art of teaching*, they may be right because that depends so much upon the personality and the undefinables through which a teacher relates himself to his students. But when the *science of teaching* is in question, there can be no denial that there are new methods which teachers, however good they may seem to be, do not usually use. Some of these techniques are born of new knowledge about human growth and development. Others have been devised because of the necessity for giving children those experiences through which they can learn to behave in accordance with the fundamental principles of democracy.

Departure from the lecture-book-assignment-home-study-recitation-test methods of teaching subject matter began long ago. Many teachers who came into the junior high school from elementary schools where they used many direct learning experiences and much variation of activity were not satisfied with the dependence on textbook study which characterized the departmentalized replica of the senior high school in which they found themselves. Some of them, therefore, introduced the less formalized procedures and various direct experiences in spite of the restrictions and limitations of subject matter. Because it was evident that children were happier and more successful in many such classrooms, supervisors and principals became eager to spread the use of the methods to other classrooms.

For some years conferences and periodicals and books were full of plans for "individualization" and "socialization." "Supervised study" and "group study" were introduced in order to get children to do more work for themselves. "Dalton" schools sprang up and "contracts" were popular with their "minimum and maximum assignments," and there were the Morrison techniques. All of these were good because they moved teachers closer to the needs of individual children. They threw light on how to meet differences in rates of learning, levels of accomplishment, and abilities. They helped teachers to see that the individual is also part of the group and has to learn to function in it. They placed the responsibility for learning on the pupil and emphasized the fact that the school, not the home, is the place for the teaching and learning of school work.

Educators began to evaluate the quality of American citizenship and to wonder what role the school was playing in that picture.[1] Research showed that the ability to verbalize does not necessarily accompany the ability to act. Many people pay only lip service to the ideals they voice. Teachers became conscious of the fact that although people learn from experience, opportunities to experience democracy in the school were almost non-existent. The autocratic school system interposed barriers to the practice of democracy. The teachers had been trained to be dictatorial in their classrooms and subservient to the dictates of administrators.

A great wave of democracy set in. Community-wide policy-making councils were created. Teachers were appointed to curriculum revision committees. In schools faculty councils were elected to

---

[1] L. B. Kinney, "Developing Problem-Solving Skills in Adolescents," *The High School Journal,* January, 1952.

work with the principals on matters of teacher welfare and school policy. Schools were given some degree of autonomy and were told to make the school program fit the needs of the community. They were instructed to *democratize* their classrooms. To accomplish this, teachers had to learn to use new methods.

All of the necessary changes have been accomplished in some places. Many other places have made some changes. Although the junior high school of tomorrow exists in some measure in almost every district, there are today a large number of schools in which practically no change has occurred in classroom teaching. Change is slow because it is difficult for teachers to use methods they have never personally experienced. Help is reaching them in the form of articles and books in which the techniques are described.[2] Observation of teachers who use modern methods gives security and courage, especially if the observers have the chance to talk with the pupils and teacher in the demonstration class. The greatest help comes when teachers in college courses and in-service education programs carried on in their own schools actually experience new ways of learning.

Books describing and illustrating modern methods are available.[3] There are, however, some recurrent questions still to be answered. This chapter, therefore, will be devoted to the questions teachers raise as they change from traditional to modern methods. They ask:

"When a teacher begins to use new teaching techniques, does he have to toss the books out of the window and throw away his course of study?"

The question implies that the pupils in a modern school are not expected to use books and that reading is not taught. Neither of these implications is true. The modern teacher no longer uses *one* book, a copy of which is supplied to every child who must carry it back and forth every day. He does not expect the students to memorize the facts that are in a single book, nor does he assign pages to be studied at night. He does not feel compelled to begin

---

[2] Robert H. Beck, "Schools Can Foster Democratic Values," *Educational Leadership*, May, 1951.

[3] Gertrude Noar, *Freedom to Live and Learn*. Philadelphia: Franklin Publishing Co., 1948; Faunce and Bossing, *Developing a Core Curriculum*, rev. ed. Englewood Cliffs, N. J.: Prentice-Hall, Inc., 1958; H. H. Giles, *Pupil-Teacher Planning*. New York: Harper and Brothers, 1941.

at the first page and continue through a specific book, hoping to reach the end by the close of the semester.

The change in the use of books is due to several reasons. First, a number of children in every classroom cannot read at the grade level. Still more of them do not learn readily from books even though they can read. Second, material that the pupils need is not yet in the books that they have. It was not known when many of the textbooks that are now on the classroom shelves were written. Some of the material has not been put into any school books as yet, although the information is available in printed form if the right sources are tapped. Third, children must be taught that no one author is complete or infallible, and the teacher must guard against the possibility of allowing any one writer to dominate their thoughts.

Instead of ordering one and the same book for every member of the class, the modern teacher orders many titles in groups of six, or twelve, and has many single copies of other titles. All the teachers in the school do their planning and ordering together and share the books they buy. School funds are used to get more books and others come from community sources. The result is not a reduction in the use and number of books, but rather is it an enriched program of reading many books.

Books alone are not enough for the modern classroom. Pamphlets, magazines, and newspapers are essentials. These are often ordered through regular channels; or, funds are raised to buy them. Many teachers and parents are glad to share their subscription copies with the children.

Guides for teachers have replaced courses of study, but they still need to be examined in terms of directives, content, suggested techniques, and applicability to the location of the particular school and to its pupils. Some syllabi still in use were written long ago and need revision. Even so, the teacher may find in them a wealth of background materials that he still needs. In some of the courses written in the early 1930's, the content was organized into subject matter units just as it is in some of the new ones. They contain important suggestions for learning activities that teachers do not yet carry out. Certainly they should not be cast aside. Most modern curriculum guides are intended to help the teacher to democratize the classroom and are full of helps of all kinds. There should be no precipitate throwing away of guides of any kind. The teacher has only to change his attitude toward them and to use them in a different way.

Teachers always ask the question:

"When does pupil-teacher planning begin and how is it carried on?"

Many teachers have always permitted their pupils to plan some things. Whenever the teacher presents alternatives to children, planning is going on. When the pupils ask, "May we have dramatics on Friday?" they are engaged in planning. When the teacher says, "How much time will you need to complete this job?" she is admitting them into the planning process.

Teachers in the modern schools recognize these opportunities as they arise and make efforts to extend them into ever more meaningful areas. Gradually they relinquish what they have heretofore regarded as their "rights"—to make all the decisions about what is to be studied and when, about who is to be responsible and for what. As participation of the students in planning increases, it has to become somewhat more formalized. A simple guide line then becomes useful for the teachers and their students. It consists merely of the words which when answered, lead into a plan. They are: WHAT, WHY, and WHY NOT; WHERE; WHEN; WHO IS TO DO WHAT; and HOW. There is nothing sacred about the order.

As pupil-teacher planning for units of work, or for any part of a unit, proceeds, the teacher guides it by asking the questions through which he and his pupils identify their goals:

Why do you want to engage in this activity?
Why are you concerned about this problem?
Why do you need (or want) this now?
What do you hope to accomplish?

From the WHY, discussion goes on with the WHAT. This sets up the framework for content, for fact finding or research. The teacher asks:

What must you find out to satisfy your desire?
What do you need to know to answer that question?
What shall we plan to do in order to solve our problem?
What materials do we need?

The next step may be HOW:

How are you going to get that information?

How can you get the books you need?

How are you going to record and organize the facts when you have them?

How can you reach people who know?

How can you question the experts?

How can you secure speakers?

Then comes the WHEN. It sets up time limits and may lead to some delimitation of the unit. The teacher asks:

When will you do this reading?

When will that art work get done?

When can the trip be taken?

When shall the speaker be called in?

When can the film be obtained?

The WHERE has to be settled. The teacher asks:

Where will you go for books, magazines, pictures, films, and other resources you need?

Where will you hold the committee meeting?

Where will the mural be painted?

Where shall we give our program?

But planning can rarely be completed in one period. It goes on continuously as one part of the unit is finished and as new needs arise. At every stage, planning must also be done in relation to the discovery of strengths and weaknesses. Evaluations of successes and failures are guide lines. Evidence of progress and growth needs to be sought and recorded.

The questions noted above are merely samples of those that the teacher uses as he plays his role. He is responsible for guiding the process; for making sure that facts are secured; for showing new possibilities to the students; for delaying decision until there has been sufficient exploration and thought; for helping pupils to see their mistakes; for arranging time; for bringing in those elements that he feels are important. The teacher who turns the leadership of planning sessions over to a child is abdicating his responsibility and is asking for trouble.[4]

---

[4] Miel, ed., *Cooperative Procedures in Learning.* New York: Teachers College, Columbia University, 1952 is the most complete reference on teacher-pupil planning.

The next question to be answered is:

"How do we plan an experience unit?"

The teacher who uses modern instructional techniques often finds that his problem is largely one of adequate pre-planning. This does not mean that he develops a rigid time schedule, writes out the questions he intends to ask, and sets up a "presentation" in the way that used to be required in college. In place of rigidity and regimentation, the modern teacher has to develop flexibility and to devise many alternatives aimed at providing for individual differences. Instead of setting forth lessons to be learned, he sets up desirable learning situations. Generalized objectives are replaced by pupil concerns and pupil goals. Evaluation discussions and devices are indicated throughout the plan instead of a comprehensive test to determine factual learning, given at the end.

Different kinds of plans are needed at various stages in unit teaching. One of the most important of these is the overall survey the teacher needs to make before the actual planning takes place in the classroom. It is at this point that the teacher can best use a resource unit. From it he gets a general overview for his own background of information. He reviews the suggested content in terms of the approach his class is making and adapts it to the maturity level of his group. He considers the list of possible activities and of reference books in the light of the facilities and equipment in his school and classroom, the available resources in his community, and other factors that bear upon his specific situation. Only when he has made such a survey can the teacher guide his class in making wise decisions as they move forward in the planning process. Without it, classroom planning may become chaotic.

The following plan, for a unit that deals specifically with *fish*, shows what happens as a teacher inserts direct learning experiences into a traditional subject matter unit. It also shows how a teacher includes possible alternatives from which pupils will make their final choice. This is a pre-planning survey, not a teaching plan.

BEFORE—*(Traditional)*	AFTER—*(Modern)*
Objectives	
teacher—To cover the topic described in the General	To make children aware of the relation of fish to themselves.

Science syllabus.

To create a desire to learn more of the natural world.
To set up experiences which would give children a chance to work and play together.
To use group processes.
To offer challenges to bright pupils.
To help non-readers to contribute to group work and find other ways of learning and of expressing themselves.
To increase children's interest in and enjoyment of school.

pupils—To do the lessons assigned by the teacher. To get good marks.

To develop good human relations in the class.
To improve their skills and abilities.
To have fun.
To learn facts.
To begin a new hobby.

Content
1. Characteristics of fish.
2. Classification.
3. Structure.
4. Uses to mankind.

Same for 1, 2, 3.
Add—use of fish symbol in art and religion; use of democratic processes; social skills, thought skills.

Activities
1. Put week's assignment on board.
2. Make large diagram of fish on board.
3. Present the topic and label the diagram.
4. Show some pictures of fish.

1. Provide for research as many books on fish as can be obtained (motivation—permit browsing—allocate to bright pupils).
2. Secure and display around room colored pictures of fish (motivation).
3. Secure and show films on tropical fish, deep sea diving, fishing industry.
4. Secure large biological model of fish.
5. Arrange for demonstration dissection of either raw or cooked fish.
6. Contact Home Economics Department and arrange for fish luncheon (teach etiquette).
7. Investigate possibility of trip to an aquarium or hatchery (teach techniques of planning—teach proper conduct in public vehicles).
8. Secure paper, paints, crayons, and art teacher as consultant for art work.

BEFORE—(*Traditional*)   AFTER—(*Modern*)
(*Continued*)   (*Continued*)

9. Investigate possibility of Saturday hike where fishing can be done (good human relations—leisure time activities—planning—responsibility).
10. Arrange with local sports store for demonstration of fishing tackle, bait, flies, etc. (teach good sportsmanship, leisure time activities).
11. Consider possibility of having someone teach interested group to make artificial flies (letter of invitation and thanks).
12. Get clay, soap, tools for carving and modeling (permit some of this while research is being done by readers).
13. Suggest and assist pupils to secure, furnish, care for an aquarium (teach principle of balance in life—good activity for non-readers).
14. Find a tropical fish enthusiast and arrange for talk on and display of tropical fish (teach reproduction).
15. Stimulate interest of brighter pupils in making scientific investigation, developing booklets, developing reference lists, hunting up classification, accumulating clipping files, sending for free and inexpensive materials.
16. Don't forget keeping of records of all kinds by everyone.

Evaluation
1. Give, mark, return tests.
2. Re-teach facts not known.
3. Give another test to those who failed.

1. Arrange for tests of facts learned.
2. Have discussion of strengths and weaknesses of planning:
   Committee work,
   Committee leaders,
   Behavior on trips,
   Learning experiences,
   Development of interests, skills, abilities.

Note:

How many of the activities included in this pre-planning survey could be undertaken by a class, would be determined by all the surrounding circumstances.

One of the obstacles to be overcome in a modern classroom is the scarcity of materials. Teachers immediately ask the question:

"Should availability and kind of materials needed affect the selection of a unit?"

In the interval which occurs between making many suggestions for the next unit and choosing one, the teacher and a committee of pupils should investigate the materials that are available in the school and the possible sources that exist outside the school. Their report to the class must be one of the factors used to determine final choice. If there seems to be enough with which to begin, but it is limited in both quantity and quality, that might determine the length of time to be spent on the unit and would limit the plans that are made. Difficulty of materials is indicative, to some degree, of difficulty of content. That would help to delimit the scope of the unit.

If material is lacking, the teacher can handle the problem in either of two ways. He can defer the unit and have the children select another, or he can proceed with types of experiences that are independent of reading matter while the pupils and he bend their efforts to securing printed materials. These experiences would include trips, interviews, speakers, films, strips, and recordings. The children could also write materials from the facts they would be gathering. There would be no limit to the ways in which they could continue to express their reactions and learnings. The clarification of ideas could begin at once with the teaching of terms, words, phrases. Doing this would also aid the children to read the material as soon as it became available. Newspapers and magazines could be explored and a clipping file begun. As questions to be answered and jobs to be done arose, small committees could be organized and commissioned with the specific tasks.

Much of the material needed in many units cannot be secured at once or through ordinary school channels. Resourceful teachers have found other places ready and willing to give and lend things to them. The question teachers ask is:

"From which community sources can materials be secured?"

The following things are being done in some cities. Teachers take the initiative by going to the agencies and asking them to develop

plans according to their facilities which will meet the needs of the
local teachers. In most places the agencies listed are glad to be of
help in the ways outlined below.

Public libraries:

   1. Issue small collections of books to the schoolteacher for a period of
2 weeks renewable once or twice thereafter.
   2. Librarian will usually be willing to work at the collection of books
around all problems submitted to her by the school.

World Affairs Council or similar agency dealing in the problems of inter-
     nationalism, United Nations, etc.:

   1. Give or lend materials dealing with all the other nations, UNESCO,
U.N., peace, democracy, government.
   2. Give advice on where to get materials.

Inter-group agencies—Anti-Defamation League of B'nai B'rith; National
     Conference of Christians and Jews, Fellowship commissions;
     Mayor's and governor's committies against discrimination.

   1. Give, rent for handling charges, or lend books, pamphlets, posters,
films, film strips, recordings dealing with problems of inter-cultural education, human relations, democracy, delinquency.
   2. Help children and teachers to find materials.

Red Cross:

   1. Gives and lends films, kits of articles, books, recordings, models,
pictures, flags, scripts, etc., dealing with other lands and peoples.
   2. Provides speakers and consultants.

Museums—historical, art, commercial, science:

   1. Arrange field trips.
   2. Lend resources.
   3. Send out speakers.
   4. Plan lessons and demonstrations to take place in the museum.
   5. Send exhibits to the school on a free or rental basis.
   6. Show and lend films.
   7. Arrange for lectures in the museum.

Government agencies and offices:

   1. Give materials—pamphlets, reports.
   2. Send speakers.
   3. Arrange trips and interviews.

Industries and Labor organizations:

   1. Arrange trips.
   2. Give materials.
   3. Send speakers.

Organized agencies are not the only sources of materials needed in the modern classroom. Nature provides an almost endless supply. Both the teacher and the students, with little effort, can keep a science corner filled with leaves, twigs, flowers, stones, birds' eggs, nests, samples of woods, samples of soils, insects and a host of other things that are fascinating to children. This material will be the source of many questions that can be developed into experience units of the greatest importance and interest.

The homes of the students are also a source of materials. From them can be secured the simple machines—levers, pulleys, and wheels. They will supply samples of textiles, consumer goods of all kinds, historical and cultural treasures, and coins. The teacher and pupils who wish to do so can work for long periods without the use of textbooks.

Administration of committee work, which is a requisite in a modern classroom, may be exceedingly difficult for a teacher who has himself experienced nothing but mass instruction, class work, and recitation. Answers to his questions about such techniques must come from the experiences of those who have pioneered in the development of the methods.[5] These answers, however, are not final, nor can any one set up a single pattern for committee work and say that it will work better than all others. The creative teacher uses many kinds of procedures for selecting and directing children's learning activities. He experiments to find those groupings which are best in each special situation that arises. No one can tell a teacher exactly what to do because no one but he is sufficiently aware of all the factors in his classroom to be accounted for. In the last analysis, only the teacher can decide what is the best way to set up committee work in his classroom.[6]

The following questions are those which arise in every locality when teachers have their first experiences with group work.

[5] See Faunce and Bossing, *Developing the Core Curriculum*, rev. ed. Englewood Cliffs, N. J.: Prentice-Hall, Inc., 1958; Rose Schneideman, *Democratic Education in Practice*. New York: Harper and Brothers, 1945.

[6] H. A. Thelen, "Classroom Grouping of Students," *School Review*, Spring, 1959.

"How many committees should be organized?"

The teacher should make every effort to avoid developing a pattern. The number of committees should depend upon many factors. Among these are the specific number of jobs to be done, the complexity of the content, the quantity of available materials with which to work, the number of potential pupil leaders and their skill, the talents and abilities of the various members of the class, and the need for a variety of special tasks which have to be delegated to special committees as the unit unfolds.

"What is the best size for a committee?"

There can be no answer to this question. The teacher must avoid setting up any abitrary number of students for all committees. It must be varied to suit the nature of the job to be done. Two or three children may be enough for one kind of job while seven or eight may be needed for another. One section of the content may require more research than others, and should therefore have more pupils assigned to it. Occasionally, too many children want to work on one aspect of the unit and are too disappointed when their requests are not granted. In that case it is entirely feasible to set up two committees to cover the same area. The rivalry between them might be productive.

"Where can committees meet and when?"

If only one committee is to meet, while the rest of the class is doing individual work, a corner of the room could probably be used. If the teacher wants all the children to work in their respective committees at the same time, the room may not be large enough, and the noise may be too disturbing. A committee can, at any time, take their chairs out into the corridor. If they are required to work there in such a way that no one objects, and if they are required to report their accomplishments to the teacher and/or the class, the adventure is successful. Teachers can make use of near-by empty rooms for special committee meetings. Again, pupil leadership has to be made responsible and the teacher himself must occasionally slip in to see that all is going well. If the library is free, it can be used, especially for a committee that needs to use books. Some new buildings have committee rooms.

Committee meetings can also be part of the home or after-school assignments. Then they can be held at home or in the classroom after dismissal. They can also be scheduled for lunch time if the children wish and if the lunch period is long enough. Before school is also a good time for meetings.

"On what basis should committees be organized?"

When a need arises that can be met best by having a small group of pupils specially delegated to a related task, a committee should be formed and commissioned. Among these is the need for getting information whether it be from books or other printed materials or from places or people. Shared labor requires committees. The need which children have to work together, revealed by a study of sociometric patterns, may be a basis on which committees should be organized. Specific individual abilities in art, dramatics, reading, and construction may result in organizing groups to accomplish specific purposes. Occasionally the positions in which children are seated may be used for speedy organization of conversation or discussion groups.

Pupils sometimes suggest that leaders be picked and that they in turn should pick their "teams." There are many dangers in this process, especially for the unpopular children. Wise teachers will help the children to see what may happen and to avoid the use of this method. Sometimes small groups should be organized around common needs. These may be needs for some special skills—reading, methods of research, language usage. Occasionally the basis may be related to size, maturity, amount of physical energy—all depending upon the purposes to be served.

Other ways of deciding upon membership in committees, all of which may be appropriate at some time, are appointment by the teacher, selection by a steering committee of students, and volunteering. Most frequently, committees are organized on the basis of personal interests expressed by the children in various ways. Raising hands is not too good because it enables pupils to choose just because they see where their friends will be. A better way is to have two or three choices written on slips of paper. At times the pupils should write short papers telling why they wish to work on some specific area of the content. The teacher can make very wise decisions from careful reading of those statements.

It is not out of the way for both the teacher and the class to make suggestions as to where certain members of the class will do their best work or make their best contribution. One interesting plan is to make signs indicating the committee content or purpose, put them up in various places, and have the pupils who wish to work on that problem assemble around each of the signs. An excellent experience is to have a general class discussion concerning the several parts of the whole job, followed by cooperative planning which includes the make-up of the several committees that are needed. When planning sub-group work, teachers ask:

"Should all committees meet at the same time?"

In the beginning it is wise to plan so that only one committee is meeting at any time. While they do so, the other pupils in the class should be engaged in individual activities that do not require them to communicate with each other. If this is done, the teacher is free to meet with each committee in turn, to help it to get started, to pool findings or to plan reports. Moreover this plan prevents confusion and noise.

The following chart shows what each committee does as the work proceeds from day to day.[7] This sequence of activities, if displayed on a large chart, will help every child to know "what comes next," and committee chairman to plan.

Gradually the teacher learns to observe his class as it works in committees, and so finds where there is strength which he can use or weakness which requires his help. When children have developed the abilities required to work without constant teacher help, observation of them as well as the requests made by chairmen are the bases on which the teacher plans which committees he himself will work with every period. If the committee chairman presides, the teacher is there to help with planning, finding materials, organizing answers, developing summaries, securing participation, and making it possible for all to do their best by constantly encouraging and praising them for the quality of their work. Teachers who, themselves, have not worked on committees ask:

---

[7] Gertrude Noar, *Freedom to Live and Learn*. Philadelphia, Pa.: Franklin Publishing Company, 1948.

PLAN FOR COMMITTEE WORK

Sequence of Activity	Committees			
	1	2	3	4
1	All committees meet to elect officers and distribute materials			
2	Every child works as an individual in the general area assigned to his own committee or at essentials for which all are to be held responsible. This is preparation for the first planning meeting			
3	Meets with teacher to plan content, allocate jobs, develop progress report	Teacher gives directions for individual work to continue		
4	Gives report to class; notes suggestions	Listens to the report of Committee No. 1 makes records raises questions makes suggestions		
5	Teacher gives directions for work as individuals	Meets with teacher for first planning	Teacher gives directions for work as individuals	
6	Listens to and records report of Committee No. 2	Makes first progress report	Listens to and records report of Committee No. 2	
7	Meets to pool information, plan activities, develop progress report (teacher help may be needed)	Teacher gives directions for work as individuals	Meets with teacher for first planning	Teacher gives directions for work as individuals

PLAN FOR COMMITTEE WORK (Continued)

Sequence of Activity	Committees			
	1	2	3	4
8	Gives second progress report	Listens to and records progress report of Committee No. 1		
9	Listens to and records report of Committee No. 3		Gives first progress report	Listens to and records report of Committee No. 3
10	Teacher directs work as individuals	Meets to pool and plan and develop report. Teacher help may be needed	Teacher directs work as individuals	Meets with teacher for first planning
11	Hears and records first progress report of Committee No. 4			Gives progress report
12	Listens to and records report	Gives second progress report	Listens to and records progress report of Committee No. 2	
13	Meets to pool, etc.	Works as individuals	Meets to pool, etc.	Works as individuals

And So On ....

"How does a committee plan for its work?"

The teacher must do some pre-planning in every area of the total job. He then can assist each committee to make its plan. No group of children can be expected to do an adequate planning job without the help of the teacher. As the pupils become more experienced, the teacher will not need to give them so much help.

Some teachers have the entire class explore every aspect of the unit in order to give ideas to the committees. They raise questions which the committee uses as a basis for its planning. One of the pitfalls when pupils plan for research is the tendency to split a question or problem into a number of simpler ones and to assign only one such fragment to each member of the committee. The teachers must make sure that the committee realizes that each of its members must work on the whole problem, exploring different sources for the facts. They then have to learn how to pool their findings, to organize them, and to plan a report on them for the class.

At the outset, the teacher will need to check each group to make sure that they decide what work is to be done and by whom, and that time requirements have not been forgotten. The class assists each committee with planning when, as progress reports are given, they raise questions, make suggestions, and give directives for further work to be done. However, children do not all respond well and cause teachers to ask:

"What can be done about a pupil who refuses to participate?"

This happens most frequently in connection with reading. The teacher has to be ready for the probability. He must give it his best thought when he is doing his over-all pre-planning as well as when he gets ready for each day's work. One way to deal with such a child is to have some relatively easy books ready to hand out, saying, "This has exactly the information you need and I will help you to find it." A gifted pupil can be sent to him to give him help and encouragement as only children know how to do. The committee librarian can be asked to work with him. Sometimes he should be given a task that his committee needs to have done but which does not involve reading. The teacher may have to suggest this to the pupil leader before the committee meeting begins. A sub-group may be organized quickly to plan a related activity—taking a trip, getting equipment ready for the showing of a film, securing the recorder and records, searching for appropriate radio and television programs. In this way, several recalcitrant pupils can be grouped together and enlivened.

The teacher will have to make special efforts to see to it that these non-participants have some kind of success experiences every day. They require daily praise and encouragement. Care must be taken to make sure that they are not asked to do what is impossible for them to accomplish, even though others in the class can be expected to be successful in those same tasks.

It is important for the teacher to accept the fact that these children will not do home assignments. If the fight on that score is removed, the children will be more likely to attend regularly and will be drawn into committee work more easily. One interesting way to meet this problem is to organize these pupils into a service corps and let all other regular groups have the privilege of requisitioning their services for specific tasks that need to be done. For example, a member of the service squad could be sent to the library to get a reference book that committee A needs at once. Another might be asked by committee B to help with getting paints ready. A third could be asked by committee C to cut some clippings from newspapers.

The teacher has a special responsibility for almost daily checking of the unit-record books of non-participating students. He can always find enough that is not up to date in them to require a child who is unwilling to work with a group to attend to his own record keeping. The causes of non-participation need to be explored with the help of counselors and parents. Very often withdrawal has been caused by too many experiences with failure in school. Sometimes individuals who have had no previous experience with group work do not understand the reasons for it and the benefits to be obtained. The teacher constantly has to interpret to the class the meaning of the processes they are using.

It is not always the below-average child who refuses to take part in committee work. Sometimes it is the one who has been used to getting to the top on his own merits and efforts, who has been trained to be highly competitive. One thing that helps these pupils who are usually verbally gifted to learn to share their abilities with others, is to use them as resource persons and put them "on call" to help others. Those who are gifted in art, dramatics, organization, construction, and music should be given similar status.

The term "research" should be used for the mobilization of facts from all sources instead of being limited to book work. This helps to dignify every kind of job, to recognize every kind of ability, and to make real the principle of the worth and integrity of every individual. All of these things help to draw in the habitual nonparticipant. But not all groups of children work well, and the teacher who finds this to be so, asks:

"What can be done, when a committee fails to function?"

Children are not born with ability to do group work. They have to learn it. Failure can be prevented as well as cured. One way to do the former is to arrange for demonstration of committee meetings of various kinds—choosing of officers, planning meetings, pooling of findings, organization of materials, and so on.[8] As soon as committee meetings begin, the teacher must observe them and move at once to the one which displays the greatest weakness. He assists them to make better plans, to control the members, to handle materials, to get the meaning out of their findings, to use experts among themselves or in the class, to raise questions to take back to the class. He observes the way the chosen leaders carry out their tasks and, if necessary, later on, gives them further training. Occasionally, he must help the group to see the mistakes they made in selection of their leaders. If a child who does not know how to act as leader can be given the chance to sit with another committee as observer, he soon learns what to do for his own group.

When a committee has trouble, the teacher must sit with it to discuss strengths and weaknesses. Self evaluation and evaluation of each other are important bases upon which to plan for improvement. The last step to be taken, if all other methods are unsuccessful, is to break up the group, assign its members to other groups, and arrange for its job to be undertaken by the committee which first completes its work. If this has to be done, it is advisable for the teacher to make every effort to salvage some part of the committee's work, however small, so that the discouragement is not too great. The entire class should also be given the benefit of the experience in group discussion.

Unless plans for reporting are made, classes do not make steady progress. Teachers ask:

"How many reports should a committee make and when?"

There are two types of reports for groups to make. The progress

---

[8] The Judy Co., Minneapolis, Minn., in cooperation with the Communication Center of the University of Minnesota, has developed an excellent device for teaching how to do committee work.

report is an interim report made for several purposes—to assist the committee, to assure the teacher and the group that work is going on, to keep the class informed and to keep the unit constantly moving forward. No specific number of progress reports can be set up. They should be given as often as the committee, the class, and the teacher desire. If frequent reports are given, they create a tone, an atmosphere in which work and accomplishment are evident. Teacher assistance is usually needed in the preparation of them, especially at the beginning of a unit, and when pupils are less able to work by themselves.

Efforts should be made to prevent crystallization of these reports into any set form. Good forms to be encouraged include: (1) Reporting on process: This is how we worked. These are the problems we met. There are the plans we made. These are the questions we raised. This is what we did. This is the help we need. (2) Reporting factual information as far as it has been obtained. (3) Combining facts and process. (4) Giving evidence of the fulfillment of responsibilities delegated by the class. Teachers also want to know:

"Who should give the reports and what should be in them?"

Reporting progress can be a challenge for a gifted pupil. It is the kind of challenge he should receive, since it provides for the development of leadership abilities. Frequently the task of reporting belongs to the chairman of the group, but only if he speaks sufficiently well. Sometimes the report can consist of organized minutes of meetings from which details and irrelevant matter have been eliminated. In this case, the secretary can give it. A panel can be selected from among the members to discuss a question before the class. One able child can be commissioned to write the material on the board as it is presented, and then time should be allotted for the class to take this down in their record books.[9] In an early report, a committee should teach the class the words they need to know, including meaning and spelling. Less verbal members of a group can pass illustrative materials around the room and do other jobs that facilitate the reporting process. These include exhibiting collections, preparing bulletin board displays, and making posters to be used in final reports.

---

[9] See Gertrude Noar, *Freedom to Live and Learn.* Philadelphia: Franklin Publishing Co., 1948.

Some kinds of reports annoy or bore a class and should be avoided. For example, children should not be permitted to read lengthy reports. Material that has been copied out of books should not be presented. It should be written in the child's own words, or read directly from the book if that is desirable. Members of a committee should rarely be permitted to give individual answers to small questions which the committee has not woven together into a meaningful whole. When a spokesman has finished a report, other members of the committee should be permitted to add anything which they feel is important. Always, the members of the class should be permitted to ask questions about the material presented and to raise other questions to which they want answers.

Final reports should be given only if there is need for them. Some committees can cover their work better in terms of progress reports. The final one should differ in form and contain summaries, meanings, evaluations. The important factor here is the crystallization of learnings that have occurred, the binding of parts into a unit, the clinching of accomplishments around the goals that were set up.

Types of activities that make good final reports include: (1) dramatizations—skits, broadcasts, sociodramatics, role-playing; (2) discussions—round table, panel, symposiums; (3) presentation of original and collected illustrative materials—illustrations, posters, maps, charts, pictures, murals; (4) exhibitions—collections of books, records, historical treasures, dioramas, constructions made during the unit; (5) quizzes and questionnaires that bring out the new knowledges, attitudes, ideas, beliefs that the children have acquired. Committee work requires that teachers re-think their roles. They ask:

"What does the teacher do in connection with committee reports?"

The teacher works with children at all times and in every way. His role in the preparation and giving of reports is varied. It includes:

—Writing down significant facts on the board while the report is being given.

—Taking notes, and making sure that pupils who are able to are also doing so, in order to help with a summary later and to make sure that significant items are not omitted.

—Preparing and issuing mimeographed materials if it is important to provide reading material that can be secured in no other way.

—Teaching terms, words, phrases that convey concepts that the entire class should have but that are too difficult for pupil leaders or reporters to clarify.

—Either during or after the report, by questioning the committee, pulling out essential facts that may have been slighted or omitted.

—Allowing time for and encouraging the pupils in the class to raise questions.

—Allowing time for the class to make records when the report is over and assisting them in doing so.

—Leading the discussion of the total class group to make sure that ideas are clarified and that essential meanings and concepts are being established.

At this time the teacher makes use of such questions as:

What does all this add up to?
What do we now know, think, feel that we did not before?
How has this changed our attitudes, actions, beliefs?
Have we accomplished our objectives?
What steps have we taken towards becoming better educated citizens?
How does this fit into the total pattern of what we have to learn?

Throughout the answers given to the questions teachers ask runs the thread of *help*. The teacher's role as *helper* is clearly drawn. At no time should the children be expected to proceed entirely on their own. While committee work is in progress, the teacher must be on his feet, active in the service of his pupils. At the same time children must be set free to help each other. Cooperation in securing the best possible results, in making up the finest possible report, in making an excellent contribution to the class, is the desirable keynote for all groups. Competition for the best group work is wholesome.

> "Where active work is going on . . . helping others, instead of being a form of charity which impoverishes the recipient, is simply an aid in setting free the powers and furthering the impulse of the one helped. A spirit of free communication, of interchange of ideas, suggestions, results, both successes and failures of previous experiences, becomes the dominating note."[10]

---

[10] John Dewey, *The School and Society*. Chicago: University of Chicago Press, 1900, page 29.

Another question that gives teachers great concern is:

"How can we get children to carry their value judgments into action?"

Understanding of values, making value judgments, and identification of relative values in real life situations are outcomes that are sought in all phases of the curriculum. In few classrooms, however, do the pupils have the chance to derive them from real life experiences. However, when a discussion begins with something that has actually occurred in the school, the teacher can try to have every child identify himself with the situation and accept the problem to be solved, as his own. The pupil has to recognize that the matter touches his life at the moment and is likely to affect him in the future. It is difficult to bring this identification about for some pupils, but when it is accomplished it serves as a powerful motivating force for serious thought about values and consequences.

The following illustration shows how a teacher used questions to guide discussion in such a way that identification was achieved. Whispering campaigns, rumors, and name calling were the causes of growing tensions in the school. The teacher encouraged the pupils to describe their experiences as fully as possible. Then he said, "Does this kind of thing occur among adults?" There were many stories related to prove that it is a common experience. The terms "libel" and "slander" were used and learned. Then the teacher said, "Are these considered wrong and dangerous enough for people to want to control them by law?" The students knew this was true and gave some examples of lawsuits with which they were familiar.

Questions were raised by the teacher and the pupils about how the laws were made and how the courts were conducted. The children wanted to know how laws are initiated, passed, and put into effect and whether or not the people can stop a law from being passed. They were eager to find out how a law can be enforced. Their plans included investigation of the use of judge, lawyer, and jury, of what kinds of people these officials usually are, and of the training they need for their work. A trip to court was suggested, and a committee was commissioned to plan it. While on the trip the students talked to important people and found out how court decisions are reached, recorded, and used to help others to make future decisions.

During the discussions that took place, as reports of findings were made to the class, the teacher used the following questions to lead the students to think about their own lives as future adults: "What kind of person do you like to live next door to?" "What kind of person will you look for as a life partner?" "What kind of people do you want as teachers of your children to help you to bring them up?"

Then he brought them back to the classroom situation out of which the unit grew. He asked, "What kind of person must you be to get the kinds of people you want as neighbors, friends, and partners? What must you do now in order to become that kind of person?" At this point, with skillful direction, the children began to consider plans for developing a campaign that would spread out over the entire school to eliminate rumor and name calling.

Whenever teachers can, they must require their students to face the gap that exists between their words and deeds, their thoughts and actions. The following questions will help them to do so: "This is what you say; this is what you do; how do you account for the difference between them?" "How can you close the gap between thought and action?" "If this is what you believe, how do you account for this contrary action?" "Which are you going to change, your belief or your action?" "How can you bring that change about?"

Both teachers and parents always ask:

"Should children be expected to do any schoolwork at home?" What kinds of homework can we give?"[11]

In and around every modern school there is bound to be controversy over the question of homework. Teachers who, under the pressures of covering courses of study, used to give long home assignments find it difficult to get along without them. In fact, the demand for homework returned along with pressure for "hard education." That practice, however, pays no attention to the changes that have occurred in home living. It also fails to take into account the unfairness to children and the conflicts that develop because some parents do the homework for their children, others with their children, while some give no help at all. There is always the ques-

---

[11] See Avram Goldstein, "Does Homework Help? A Review of Research," *Elementary School Journal,* January, 1960.

tion of who learns when father does the arithmetic for Johnny. It is no secret that the conscientious child often has to pass his work around for others to copy.

The policy of no homework no longer meets with parental approval. They want their offspring to spend part of their leisure time learning school lessons. Some of them feel that home assignments enable them to keep track of what goes on in the school and absence of assignments is frustrating to them.

In schools where curriculum change is under way, it is important for the parents to be called in for interpretation and planning. Homework is one of the things that should be discussed at those sessions. If parents do not respond to such invitations, articles can be written for the school publications, and bulletins and letters can be sent to the homes. The school policy concerning homework can be made clear to individual parents who come in to see the principal, counselor, or teachers. If these measures are taken there will be fewer occasions on which parents will ask, "Doesn't my child ever have any lessons to do at home?"

The following suggestions for home assignments are logical outcomes and accompaniments of the kind of in-school experiences that children have in modern schools:

1. Every child can be expected to read his literature book every night. The amount to be done should be adjusted to the individual's capacity and may be expected to vary each night because of peculiar conditions in the life of the child. The pupils should be encouraged to read as much and as long as they can and to keep track of time and quantity with a view toward increasing both.

2. Every child can be expected to read the newspaper every night. In case some are not able to buy them or the family does not provide them, the papers that have been used in school during the day should be given to them. Some children will be able to read only the headlines. Others will include important news articles. A few can be assigned editorial reading. Some can be asked to make clipping files for the class. These can be files of sports news, cartoons, comics, news articles, pictures, and stories.

3. There can be specific assignments in specialized areas for most students. What these are will depend upon the structure of the curriculum. They may take many forms in additions to book study. Parents and children expect to have drill exercises in arith-

metic and spelling words as a regular part of the work to be done at home.

4. Out-of-school work (homework) in any subject area can include looking for and mounting appropriate illustrative pictures, graphs, charts, maps. Facts and opinions can be gathered by talking to people, going to see places and things, listening to the radio, watching television, as well as from books.

5. Shop, home arts, music, and art teachers can also assign homework. This can be the finishing of something begun in school, collecting materials for the next day's work, practice of the skills learned in class, making things at home that are needed or wanted by the child or the family. This may require the school to provide or lend tools and art or shop materials on the same basis that books are provided.

6. Pupils should be expected to do some work at home that is connected with the unit that is under way. This always includes the writing of the unit record book. Records to be entered include word lists; facts that are being accumulated; descriptions and reactions to films, broadcasts, speeches, trips; conclusions that are drawn; decisions that are made; plans that are in process.

7. Creative writing begun at school can be finished at home. Papers that have been marked or criticized by the teacher can be rewritten at home (if rewriting is thought to be profitable).

8. Drill work in English or foreign language can be assigned for homework if it is done on the basis of individual need.

9. In the ninth year, when pupils are studying foreign language and algebra on an elective basis, longer and more difficult assignments in those subjects can be given if they are kept within reason. The total time that junior high school pupils should spend in *study* at home should probably not exceed an hour.

Much emphasis is being placed, in both educational and social circles, on the use of the group process. The first question that is raised in this connection is:

"How can 'groupness' be created and what are its characteristics?"

The teacher's day is happier and his work is easier when the class ceases to be a collection of individuals and becomes a functioning group. Sometimes this seems to occur spontaneously. More often it is the result of consciously directed effort. There are tools which the teacher uses and specifics for which he works.

The first steps are taken when the class faces a problem that concerns all of them. As they proceed to solve it, they find out how a group works when it attacks a problem and moves toward its solution. They also learn that a group, working together, can do some things more easily and with better outcomes than any one of its members can do alone.

The processes used to create a group and move it forward are those which give opportunity for the following:

Interaction—pupil with pupil, with group, with teacher.

Establishing relationships.

Collective thinking—pooling thoughts and findings and organizing them for use.

Discussing—of new facts, ideas, beliefs, attitudes, values, experiences; in which prejudices are exposed, moods are changed, understandings are created, conflicts are harmonized, integration is accomplished, new and more useful ideas are discovered.

Planning—identification of a problem, clarifying purposes, setting up goals, considering procedures, making decisions.

Dividing labor—getting all to participate and contribute, using special abilities, delegating responsibilities.

Recording—experiences, thoughts, findings, proposals, decisions, actions.

Reporting—progress, findings, and actions.

Evaluating—individuals, processes, changes, actions.

Group actions proceed at several levels. They reflect the degree of change from autocratic to democratic action which is taking place in the class. The teacher has to be able to identify them and deal with them in accordance with the effects they may have upon the children and the learning process. The following are characteristics of the various stages of development in the use of group processes:

Hatred, suspicion, desire for revenge.

Divisions—of individuals from each other and/or from the group.

Exaltation of individuals.

The use of "selling for a price."

Domination of the "elite" while the many carry out their dictates.

Exploitation by the "powerful."

The discovery of the highest degree of self realization by everyone—even the least.

Compromise, exploitation, bargaining, domination, competition, and cooperation—all will be tried at various times and the teacher has to be on the alert so that he can help the students to distinguish one from the other and to judge their relative values.

As the teacher becomes experienced in the use of group work, he will learn about the many roles that people play as they work together. In time, he may be able to help his pupils to recognize their customary roles and to try new ones in order to help the group to accomplish its purposes. The following descriptions of the roles people play have been taken from *The Dynamics of Group Discussion* by D. M. Hall.

Roles Played in Discussion Groups[12]

Autocratic Group Roles

1. *Aggressor*—the person who threatens or attacks the status of others, who disapproves the acts, feelings, or values of others. He controls by fear.

2. *Blocker*—the negativistic person who opposes beyond reason or attempts to block any action the group desires to take. He attempts to set group members against each other.

3. *Recognition-seeker*—the person who attempts to direct attention toward himself by boasting or claiming long experience or great accomplishments. He answers, repeats, or relays statements of others. He maintains social barriers and class distinctions. He remains aloof and expects special considerations.

4. *Dodger*—the person who displays his lack of involvement in the group process by horseplay, cynicism, or lack of interest. He refuses to do his part and attempts to get others to do the work.

5. *Dominator*—the person who attempts to show authority or superior judgment or who tries to manipulate certain members by flattery, threats, or conditional promises. He makes awards in his own rights and seeks control of the property of the group, and demands that requests flow through his hands.

6. *Help-seeker*—the person who plays for sympathy.

7. *Special-interest pleader*—the person who pleads for some special

---

[12] D. M. Hall, *The Dynamics of Group Discussion.* Danville, Illinois: The Interstate Printers & Publishers, 1950, pages 13-15. Reprinted by special permission.

interest, often offering to "let you get yours later if you let me get mine now."

8. *Blamer*—the person who blames others for his difficulties and short-comings, and always excuses himself.

Democratic Group Roles

1. *Initiator*—the person who suggests new activities, new ideas, and new problems. He understands the value-attitudes and needs of the group and is able to outline objectives based upon them. Accepting the role of "change-agent," he realizes that changes are easiest when the cultural atmosphere changes. He knows that changes in atmosphere are most easily accomplished by a change in the type of leadership. He knows, too, that hand in hand with the creation of the new must go the destruction of the old, for only in that way is it possible to liberate the forces of the new pattern.

2. *Orientor*—the person who seeks to have the group define its goals, outline its activities, and determine the direction its discussion is taking with respect to its goals. He verifies the facts and actions and interprets the experiences of others. He may even call the group to return to the subject at hand.

3. *Facilitator*—the person who keeps communication channels open by asking for a restatement, a definition of terms, or a summary. He sets out to determine the abilities and experiences of each member, and he sees that everyone in the group knows about these particular skills. He realizes that mere introductions seldom furnish enough information. He knows that a permissive atmosphere encourages participation and hinders filibustering. He asks that action proceed promptly.

4. *Encourager*—the person who stimulates others to greater activity by giving them approval, encouragement, and recognition for the part they play. He often invites individuals to participate and offers to help those who are slow.

5. *Harmonizer*—the person who, realizing that progress is based on differences, makes a rational attempt to have all sides considered. He is sympathetic and considerate and minimizes or relieves tension by declaring that differences are desirable and that we must integrate them. His attitude is permissive, and he often reduces conflict by pointed and humorous anecdotes. He attempts in various ways to hold the group together.

6. *Summarizer*—the person who pulls the ideas together in order to show their relationships and who suggests how they might work out in practice.

7. *Fact-seeker*—the person who seeks facts, opinions, and examples in order to clarify the thinking and evaluate the conclusions already drawn.

8. *Fact-giver*—the person who contributes from his beliefs or experiences, cites an authority, or offers a generalization.

9. *Compromiser*—the person who, operating within a conflict, offers

to give ground, admit his errors, or yield his status in order that action may proceed. If, however, the yielding is due to fear or is an attempt to seek a special favor, it becomes an individualistic and debasing role.

10. *Expeditor*—the person who arranges the facilities, distributes the materials, and performs services that promote the comfort and efficiency of the group.

11. *Spokesman*—the person who speaks the general opinion of the group in defending it against outside pressures and opponents and in promoting its progress.

12. *Status role*—the person whose value-attitudes, abilities, or accomplishments are respected both within and without the group and who thus gives status to the group.

13. *Recorder*—the person who records the official action of the group and reports this action to its members and to outside groups.

14. *Evaluator*—the person who compares or contrasts facts and seeks to determine the progress made in order to reward the group more objectively. He sets standards to achieve and seeks out and urges the application of superior methods and procedures. Whenever he makes awards he does so in the name of the group.

15. *Analyzer*—the person who keeps records of the processes going on within the group in order to determine the rate of integration or disintegration.

A question frequently asked by teachers is:

"How can the quality of discussion be improved?"

Discussion is such an important part of classroom work that its techniques should be studied by every teacher. Progress in securing the unity of mind that is essential for peaceful settlement of a dispute, whether it be between individuals or nations, is dependent upon the ability of people to lead and to participate in discussion. Classroom discussions are more often question-answer exercises than exchange of thought for the purpose of gaining enlightenment or of moving toward action.

If students are to learn discussion skills, they must have opportunity to practice them in meaningful situations. This cannot be done until the teachers have greater proficiency in these skills than many of them now possess.

When teachers criticize student discussions, they are apt to say, "The children are too glib. They use words with little regard for meaning. They indulge in fantasy and wishes rather than realities. They offer rumor, opinions, and superstitions as if they were facts. They fail to challenge statements and to call for authority and source. They do not change faulty points of view in spite of presentation of contrary evidence." It requires maturity and experience to do all of those things, yet few adults exhibit those characteristics in their discussions. Traditional methods of teaching did not give that kind of facility to secondary school or even college graduates. Junior high school pupils have plenty of time to learn how to carry on effective discussions, if their teachers will help them.

The purposes of discussion are to reveal the need for information, to supply facts, to clarify thought, to throw new light into dark places, to teach the use of the scientific method of inquiry, to open minds, to give experience in reserving judgment, to help the participants to make a wise choice of ideas, to develop the ability to use language effectively, and finally to move toward the solution of problems by taking appropriate action.

There are many kinds of discussions. The teacher and pupils in each instance must cooperatively decide on the one which will best meet their needs. The general group discussion, the panel, the symposium, the forum, the round table, the debate are all familiar and need no description here. During the course of a semester all of them should be used (with reservations about the debate).

Some of the basic techniques of leadership are the same. The first and most important is *adequate preparation*. It is essential that the topic, the question, or the problem be determined sufficiently far ahead to enable both the leader and the group to give it considerable thought, to do some reading about it, and to converse with others. This will enable all of them to bring to the discussion some information, facts, illustrations, names of authorities, and sources, as well as a partially developed point of view.

Few discussion experiences will be successful unless those who are taking part can *face each other*. It is not satisfactory to talk to the backs of people's heads. If formal classroom seating in rows is maintained, the students will inevitably address all of their remarks to the teacher who stands or sits at the front of the room. He in turn will feel called upon to answer or comment on each of them in the old one-way line of communication. One indication of an increase in the democracy of the classroom is the freedom of the pupils to talk to each other during discussions, and the ability of the teacher to withhold comments during such interchanges.

The teacher who wants to be sure that the discussion will move forward and will include the elements that he has intended to be covered, will do well to *write down several key questions*. They should represent the various phases of the issue to be explored. If he then arranges to have these clearly in view, and even on separate pieces of paper, as the discussion proceeds he can jot down what is said in connection with each of them. This will enable him to summarize at a moment, if the need arises. A lull may come which the leader fills by saying "Up to this point you have said . . ." Or there may be some confusion which threatens to prevent progress. He glances at his notes and says, "I believe you already stated . . . Now do you wish to change your mind?" Disagreement may begin, and he tries to effect a compromise by saying, "According to my record here, you both agree that . . . Let us begin again from that point." He may use the next of his key questions when he senses that the group has pursued the first one long enough. In order to lead forward he says, "Let us move on to a consideration of another aspect of the problem." He might vary that with, "We need to explore further. How would you answer this question?"

If possible, the teacher or a competent recorder should *write on the blackboard the main contributions* of facts and ideas offered by the participants. This gives a sense of importance to them as well as to the individuals who contribute them. If he can organize them into an outline form as he goes, relationships are shown and better thinking results. At the close of the meeting such an outline helps the participants to follow the summary which is given by the leader. It is useful if the teacher wants the children to make a notebook record of the facts. From it the group also can pick out what needs to be further explored. They can shape the question for the next discussion. They can use it quite effectively to evaluate their work in terms of the purposes they wished to achieve.

It is obvious that the teacher will be unable to function well unless *he knows the personnel* in his group. He needs to be sure of the "experts" upon whose factual material he can rely. He will want to keep his eye on the timid and shy so as to seize every opportunity to draw them in. A facial expression or a bodily movement may be the only hint revealing a child's readiness and desire to say something, but when the leader is sensitive and sees them, he can throw a question or ask for an expression of opinion, saying: "Do you agree with that point of view?" or "Would you like to add something to what has just been said?" These children must also be praised for their contributions, no matter how small they may be. The teacher can do this with a word, a smile, an encouraging nod. It will help them to move out of their customary roles of non-participants into activity.

There are other individuals in every group who play less pleasant roles. The teacher must know who they are and plan his strategy accordingly. Among these are the show-off, the destroyer, the time waster. At times, he needs to keep the ball out of their hands, to know how to temper the bombshell that may be thrown, to control laughter without shutting off good will, and to get the ball back from a child who is running away with it. The teacher must learn to do all of this with adroitness and tact, and without a display of anger or personal dislike.

While he is leading a discussion, the teacher must *remember that the speed and level of thought are not equal* for all the pupils. This may be the reason for him to feel that it is necessary to repeat everything that is said, but if he does so, boredom and inattention increase and much time is wasted. Moreover, the discussion begins to resemble a recitation period. (In recitation periods, repetition of answers by the teacher is poor technique.) The more often that the ball is passed from one child to another, the more successful the discussion will be. The leader has to control the flow of remarks with gestures, nods, or by calling the next speaker by name.

It is not necessary, however, for the teacher to abandon the use of words of praise after a student has made a good contribution. It will not interrupt the flow of thought; rather, it will stimulate others to take part in the discussion. Many teachers get into the habit of saying "all right" to everyone. This is tiresome and irritating. There are many other words and phrases that can be used: fine; good; excellent; that is a splendid statement; we will gladly accept that; a good beginning; push that further; that's clear thinking; try again, we will help you; we do not get that, but we do want to know what you are thinking; illustrate that point.

It is hard, at times, for the teacher to keep those children who think quickly and talk easily from monopolizing the discussion. He may occasionally find it necessary to pass over them in order to slacken the pace or to give everyone a chance to be heard. One of the measures of success in a discussion is the proportion of the mem-

bers of the group that take part. Restraint of the able students will
be compensated for if the more difficult tasks are thrown their way
and they receive praise for the quality of their responses. For example, such a child can be called upon to summarize or review, to
pose a new question, to lead off into another phase, to prepare a
statement to begin the entire discussion, or to pull the whole thing
together at the end. These experiences will help gifted children to
become discussion leaders.

Every leader has trouble with members of the group who talk ir-
relevantly or too long or who drag the discussion off on a tangent.
The leader is often loath to interfere for fear that doing so will appear to be a rebuke which will prevent further participation by the
person involved. After the group becomes experienced, its members
will themselves find ways of disciplining such children. For example, they begin to squirm when a child holds the floor too long.
They say, "That's off the subject; let's get back." Sometimes they
use even harsher ways of reproving the offenders and they also begin off-side conversation which may cause the discussion to deteriorate.

If one of the objectives of discussion is to teach the pupils that
in our democracy people have the right to say what they think, the
teacher must *accept whatever is said without showing displeasure,
anger, surprise or shock.* Unless he can do so, the children will not
lose their insecurities and will continue to be afraid to express themselves. Many classroom discussions fail because the students do not
have faith and confidence in the teacher. Fear of ridicule, sarcasm
and reprisal must be destroyed. This is accomplished in planning
sessions by accepting everything that is offered, at least temporarily.
At a later time in the discussion, attention can be recalled to anything that is unworthy or that should be discarded. By then the
class will no longer remember from whom it came, and no one will
feel rejected or ashamed because his contribution was rejected.

The teacher who wishes to develop skill in leading and participating in discussion, will do well to have his class study those phrases,
words, and statements that are useful in distinguishing between
fact and rumor, opinion and belief, an accepted generalization and
a personal point of view. Among these are: "In my opinion," "To
my mind," "I believe," "It seems to me," "In my reading I found,"
"Some people say," "The fact has been established," "Rumor has it,"

"My father thinks," "The expert suggested," "Public opinion polls reveal that," "The book says," "It may not be true," and so on. The difference between arguing and argument must also be established.

The pupils' concept of freedom can be broadened if the teacher will refer to it in connection with certain problems that arise in every discussion period. It takes some time before the children can act so as to insure to all freedom to speak, to be heard, to listen, to differ without prejudice, to be secure and unafraid. Eventually, fear of the teacher, of the peer group, of criticism, of ridicule, of reprisal, of inadequacy will all vanish. If all the children are received equally and with understanding, are given praise as well as help, there is a real chance that all will develop greater respect for themselves and for the worth and integrity of each other. These are worthy outcomes of discussion experiences.

It is essential at the outset of a discussion for the class and teacher to *set up goals and purposes*. Then, after the discussion is over, time must be taken to *have the group evaluate their performance and their accomplishments in terms of those objectives*. Determination of strength and weakness will pave the way toward improvement.

Until the junior high school teacher himself learns the role of discussion leader, he will not be able to teach it to his pupils. No child should be required to act as leader without assistance from and preparation by the teacher. When a pupil is ready to assume this position, the group must be prepared for it and made ready to cooperate with him. Although under these conditions the teacher becomes one of the group, he must remain alert to the roles that members of the group play so that he can counteract influences that seem to be getting in the way of effective discussion. If the pupil leader is allowed to fail, the chances are that other children will be afraid to accept responsibility for leadership on subsequent occasions.

Many curriculum authorities emphasize the use of resource units. Teachers ask:

"Do we have to write resource units? It takes too long. Where can we get the time?"

Where schools have been engaged in administering traditional programs of departmentalized studies, teachers are often unable to secure more than a minimum number of books. They usually have a basic text which follows the course of study and which children are expected to learn from cover to cover. One or two additional titles may be available for supplementary use. Under these conditions, teachers feel unwilling to change content and methods. Lack of appropriate reading materials makes them feel insecure.

Where there is sufficient and adequate leadership, teachers gain the courage both to search for and to write curriculum materials suited to their needs. In most cases the materials they want for reference and that they create take the form of resource units. This raises the question of their competency to write background materials that reflect several subject areas, when they are subject-matter specialists.

The answer to that question must take into consideration the nature of the problems that are usually studied in junior high school classes. In the first place, because pupils have a part in deciding what they shall study, the centers of interest around which the units are developed usually come from the stream of life. It is not unreasonable to suppose that secondary school teachers are, or can become, conversant with the vital issues that confront the world today.

In the second place, the maturity and mental ability levels of the students preclude the possibility of their delving very deeply into most of the questions they raise. The important objectives of unit teaching are to stimulate curiosity; to open doors to problems and lines of inquiry; to meet needs of knowing more about society, self, and the natural environment; to develop initiative; to establish ways of working alone and with others; to build the habits and skills of critical thinking; to establish methods of research; and to assist in development of good human relations. The background of factual material with which the unit is concerned is of such a nature that every teacher can learn it. In fact, if he asks his pupils to learn it, most certainly it should not be too difficult for him.[13] However, it will be more difficult for the teacher to learn the necessary teaching skills.

In the third place, no one any longer expects a teacher to be a walking encyclopedia even in his special areas of preparation. Knowledge has accumulated so rapidly that no one is master of all

---

[13] See Faunce and Bossing, *Developing the Core Curriculum.* Englewood Cliffs, N. J.: Prentice-Hall, Inc., 1951.

the facts in a field of learning. Because of this, the teacher has changed his attitude toward himself and his job. When children ask questions, he is not ashamed to say, "I do not know the answers, but let's find them together." He knows that the pupils have respect for that kind of answer and for the teacher who gives it. They are glad to know that he is willing to walk along the way with them.

The need for reference materials and resource units has stimulated their development all over the country. Some are written in summer workshops. Educational associations have employed experts from various fields to cooperate in the production of units which have been printed and sold.[14] The Federal Office of Education has prepared some which are available without cost, or at a small charge. Many school systems have departments of curriculum in which experts and/or teacher committees prepare resource materials.[15] These are often issued as "Guides to Instruction" and can be purchased by teachers outside the system. Some individual schools are willing to exchange resource units which are usually in mimeographed form.[16] Books on secondary education contain examples of units that have been written in many schools or constructed by the authors.

Examination and extensive use of resource materials and units reveal certain weaknesses: After a relatively short time, the details of content are no longer up to date. New knowledge, new inventions, new social problems develop with great speed. Too often the suggested activities are heavily academic, and fail to take into account the large numbers of poor readers and the many other ways to learn besides reading. The lists of references for both students and teachers soon contain obsolete titles and bear little relation to the books that are ordinarily available to junior high schools. These deficiencies are frustrating to the teacher. Moreover, he finds the unit bulky and has difficulty in selecting from it those things which are applicable to his specific needs. Finally, the inexperienced teacher and the one who knows little about unit teaching attempt to use the resource unit as if it were a syllabus or course of study to be

---

14 The National Association of Secondary School Principals, *Problems in American Life*. N.E.A., Washington, D. C.

15 Arlington, Va., and Philadelphia, Pa., are examples.

16 Such an interchange was conducted under the direction of members of the Department of Education at Columbia University, 1950-51.

covered, and sometimes give it to the students as notes to be copied.

The teachers' needs for an organized body of content, for many suggestions about activities that "will work," for information about the resources in the immediate community, for titles of books that are available and usable by the students in the school, have to be met by organized effort on their part. They must constitute themselves a curriculum committee to meet at regular intervals to pool their experiences and share their knowledge. Furthermore, they must see to it that the products of their labors receive recognition, are duplicated for use in the school, are reviewed at least once a year, and are revised as experience with them dictates.

If this work is to be done well, teachers must keep the following kinds of records of what happens as they work with children:

The questions children ask.

The anxieties and concerns children express.

The content leads that are required to answer questions and solve problems that are recurrent in the classrooms.

The books that can be obtained in the school, the public library, and from other sources in the community.

The kinds of materials that are suited to teacher use, to the use of verbally gifted students, to slow learners.

Activities that are successful.

Good trips to take.

Names and telephone numbers of key people to contact.

Names and addresses of people who are willing to come as speakers and consultants, or who will be available for interviews.

Outcomes that have been good.

Evaluation devices and instruments.

As soon as it becomes evident that a particular unit is of more than passing interest to pupils, or that there is need for study of a particular problem, or that a local, national or world-wide issue demands attention, the resource unit committee of teachers should be called together to pool their experiences, their findings, and their best thought. The materials they gather can be quickly organized into outlines into which the products of additional research can be inserted, and the whole can be made immediately available to the teachers in the school. When such a framework is constructed, its makers do not regard it as a complete or finished product. Everyone who uses it feels free to change, delete, or add to any part of it. No one makes the mistake of trying to use it as a plan for teaching, but all are grateful to have at hand a maximum amount of resource suggestions from which they can select what is best suited to the needs, interests, and abilities of their several classes.

Several such outlines are in Part IV of this book.

Teachers become alarmed over the magnitude of some descriptions of units. They ask:

"What is a social action project? Does every unit have to include one? Are there other ways to end a unit?"

A social action project is a group activity planned to better life in some way. It may be directed at conditions in the classroom. Examples of this are projects to decorate the room, to secure movable furniture from the board of education, to raise money to buy a piece of audio-visual equipment. It can involve the entire school population, like a drive to improve inter-group actions, or plans to reorganize the student government, or bettering the conditions in the cafeteria and securing lunch-time recreational facilities. A larger project would spread into the neighborhood as, for instance, a clean-up or fire prevention campaign, or securing a traffic light at a busy intersection. A really huge project could involve the entire community. For example, in Floodwood, Minnesota, the school pupils convinced the town that they should have their own milk pasteurization plant. In Philadelphia, Pennsylvania, all the schools were involved in the year long project that helped the citizens to win a new city charter.

The need for improving some element in the real life situation of the students may be the initial interest out of which a unit of study develops. In that case, an action project cannot be avoided. When an important issue that pupils want to know about is the center of interest of a unit, at some point in it a student or the teacher raises the questions, "Are there others who ought to know about this too? Who are they? Should we tell them what we have learned? How? When? Where?" This leads to a culminating activity that is full of the elements of social action.

Some units can best be concluded by gathering all the new materials that were secured, the maps, charts, and pictures that were mounted, the illustrations that were painted, and the factual materials that the students found and organized in written form, for presentation to the school. An assembly program developed around the presentation will involve other classes. Presentation to the librarian alone would not require a surrounding program. Some units can be closed with dramatic presentations. This may be an assembly program for the school alone, or parents may be invited, depending upon the nature of the unit and the kind of program.

Sometimes social action is projected when the pupils set up the criteria against which they intend to measure proposals for units from among which they are to make a choice. They invariably include in the list, "Can we *do* something about it?" and choose the one which presents the best possibility for action.

Social action can be part of many units, but it is unreasonable to expect that every unit will end in something spectacular. Some units should just be pulled together quickly, if they peter out, and end with serious evaluation discussion. A subject-matter unit is less likely to end in action than an experience unit. A large project is a difficult and time consuming enterprise. However, if junior high school pupils have the opportunity to engage in one of them at some time during the three year span, they will remember it as one of the high lights of their school lives.

Many schools have used social action projects in connection with extra-curricular activities or clubs. Notable among these were the Fellowship Clubs in Philadelphia, and the Youth Builders which began in New York City and spread to many states.[17] Suggestions for action projects are included in Part IV of this book.

Learning Activities for Members of Pre- and In-Service Teacher Education Classes

In addition to reading, try learning from such activities as:

1. Taking any important social issue or problem with which the junior high school children should become acquainted, and listing the subject areas into which they would have to go to get answers and solutions to the questions and problems they would raise in discussing it.

2. Making a plan for a subject you are required to teach; converting it

---

[17] Sabra Holbrook, *Children Object*. New York: Viking Press, 1943.

into an experience unit; starring the places at which you give pupils opportunities for making choices.

3. Showing the film strip, *A Core Curriculum Class in Action,* Wayne University, College of Education, Detroit, Michigan, 1948.

4. Using your college class as if it were a group of junior high school students and trying out the following techniques:

Identifying a common problem to be used as the center of interest for developing a unit.

Setting up criteria on which to base choice of a unit.

Setting up individual and group goals.

Planning content and activities.

Organizing committees.

Holding a committee meeting to pool experiences, to plan a progress report.

Deciding on a culminating activity.

References

GENERAL

BOOKS

Association for Supervision and Curriculum Development, *Leadership for Improving Instruction.* Washington, D. C.: The Association, 1960.

Educational Policies Commission, *Education for All American Youth.* Washington, D. C.: The Commission, 1944.

Faunce and Bossing, *Developing the Core Curriculum,* rev. ed. Englewood Cliffs, N. J.: Prentice-Hall Inc., 1958.

Featherstone, W. B., *A Functional Curriculum for Youth.* New York: American Book Co., 1950.

Hopkins, L. T., *The Emerging Self.* New York: Harper and Brothers, 1954.

Johnson and Michael, *Principles of Teaching.* Boston: Allyn and Bacon, 1959.

Nelson, H. B. (ed.), *The Dynamics of Instructional Groups.* The National Society for the Study of Education, 59th Year Book, Part II, 1960.

Noar, Gertrude, *Freedom to Live and Learn.* Philadelphia: Franklin Publishing Co., 1948.

Parrish and Waskin, *Teacher-Pupil Planning.* New York: Harper and Brothers, 1958.

Stratmeyer, et al., *Developing a Curriculum for Modern Living,* rev. ed. New York: Teachers College, Columbia University, 1957.

Zapf, Rosalind M., *Democratic Process in the Secondary Classroom.* Englewood Cliffs, N. J.: Prentice-Hall, Inc., 1959.

PERIODICALS AND PAMPHLETS

Fry, Bryan and Rigney, *Teaching Machines: An Annotated Bibliography*. Report #28. Los Angeles: Department of Psychology, University of Southern California, 1959.

Furman, D. W., "Teacher-Pupil Planning with Slow Learners," *Social Education*, October, 1954.

Mott, Kenneth, "Language Arts–Social Studies Fusions," *The Bulletin of the National Association of Secondary School Principals*, March, 1960.

Musselman, et al., "Improving the High School Program Through Unit Teaching," *Bulletin of the Bureau of School Services*, College of Education, University of Kentucky, June, 1952.

Otto, H. J., "Grouping Pupils for Maximum Achievement," *The School Review*, Winter, 1959.

Strang, R. M., "Guided Study and Homework: What Research Says to the Teacher," #8, American Educational Research Association, N.E.A., July, 1955.

Wrightstone, J. W., "What Research Says About Class Organization for Instruction," *N.E.A. Journal*, April, 1957.

DISCUSSION TECHNIQUES

BOOKS

Chase, Stuart, *Roads to Agreement*. New York: Harper and Brothers, 1951.

Gully, H. E., *Discussion, Conference and Group Process*. New York: Henry Holt and Co., 1960.

Hall, D. N., *The Dynamics of Group Discussion*. Danville, Ill.: Interstate Printers and Publishers, 1950.

PERIODICALS AND PAMPHLETS

Anderson, R. C., "Learning in Discussions," *Harvard Educational Review*, Summer, 1959.

Farley and Overton, "Does Class Discussion Improve Understanding?" *The School Review*, October, 1951.

Keltner, J. W., "Trends in Discussion Research," *Adult Education Bulletin*, February, 1949.

Schrieber and Staff, "It Pays to Talk It Over," *Community Relations Service*, 165 East 56th Street, New York 22, N. Y.

Thelen, H. A., "Group Dynamics for the Classroom Teacher," *Educational Trend, Educator's Washington Dispatch*, 1949.

RESOURCE UNITS

BOOKS

Snow Hill, Maryland. *Resource Bulletins*. Worcester Co. Board of Education, 1952.
Wiles, Kimball, *Teaching for Better Schools*. Englewood Cliffs, N. J.: Prentice-Hall, Inc., 1960.

PAMPHLETS

Anti-Defamation League of B'nai B'rith, *Prejudice and Discrimination, and Human Rights*. 515 Madison Ave., New York 22, N. Y.
National Association of Secondary School Principals, *Consumer Education Series*. Washington, D. C.
National Association of Secondary School Principals and National Council for the Social Studies, *Problems in American Life*. Washington, D. C.
Reynard, H., *University School Resource Units*. Columbus, Ohio: Ohio State University, n.d.

AUDIO-VISUAL AIDS

BIBLIOGRAPHIES

Educator's Guide to Free Films. Educational Progress Service, Randolph, Wisconsin, 1952.
Film Catalogues. Anti-Defamation League of B'nai B'rith, 515 Madison Avenue, New York 22, N. Y.
Films, Inc. Rental Libraries: Wilmette, Illinois; Portland, Oregon; Birmingham, Michigan; Los Angeles, California; Boston, Massachusetts; Dallas, Texas; Atlanta, Georgia.
Free Film Index:—Films from Industry. Modern Talking Picture Service, 45 Rockefeller Plaza, New York 20, New York.
Instructional Films. New York: United World Films, Inc., 1445 Park Ave., New York, N. Y.; *Text-Films—1953 Listing*. McGraw-Hill Book Co., 330 W. 42nd St., New York 36, N. Y.
Sources of Visual Aids for Schools. Washington, D. C.: Supt. of Documents, Government Printing Office.
The American Heritage in Films. Chicago: The American Library Association.

CHAPTER THIRTEEN

Classroom Management

Classroom management plays a vital role in modern education. More difficult problems are present in the room in which children learn by doing than in the one in which book work, writing, and recitation predominate. Although specific routines cannot be taught to students in teacher education classes because schools have so many different ways of doing things, there are some devices and procedures with which the prospective teacher can be equipped. The unpleasant experiences of substitutes and new appointees who have not learned some of these methods often cause them to withdraw from the profession. On the other hand, mature and experienced teachers who change their classrooms into places in which children have freedom to talk to each other, to move around, and to carry on all kinds of activities also need to review methods of classroom management. The fear of being unable to solve these problems often causes a mature teacher to retreat from first attempts to use new methods to the security of the traditional techniques.

There are some simple devices and routines that work well, no matter who the teacher is or how long he has been teaching. It always helps a teacher to control the situation when he has carefully thought through and planned these matters. As he does so, he can foresee, if he has imagination, what pranks the boys and girls might try, and can forestall them. Junior high school children like to make the teacher the butt of their pranks if they sense his fear of them. This is illustrated by the little girl who, finding a new teacher in the room, said to her, "Some teachers are scarey and some aren't. You look scarey and we're gonna scare you good!"

Routines for entering and leaving the room are important controls.

It is advisable for the teacher every day and each new period in the day, to meet his class at the door of the room. If he forms the habit of walking to the door when the bell rings and of dismissing his class from that position, he can prevent them from making a hasty and noisy exit. He can, at the same time and from the same spot, supervise the corridor and greet the pupils who are coming in for the next class. Then the child who planned to stumble in for the amusement of the class cannot do so. The girl who comes shouting down the hall must quiet down as she passes the teacher. A friendly hand can be placed for a moment on the shoulder of the child whose face seems distorted with fear or anxiety. A smile may change the attitude of the boy who is scowling or who is in a rage because of the scolding someone administered.

Of course, there will be youngsters who do not respond to such friendly overtures. The attention they are seeking from their classmates may be of such great importance to them that they do not care how it is secured so long as they get it. These pupils quickly reveal themselves. The teacher at the doorway can ask such a child to stand there beside him until the class has assembled. The chances are that he will quiet down. A personal friendly word of concern said in a soft voice, or a direction for him to get out some materials that the class will need, or a chance to write something on the blackboard will do wonders to cure his ills and meet his needs.

The practice of lining children up against the wall in the corridor, waiting until all have arrived, and then requesting them to tiptoe into the room should be abandoned in the junior high school wherever it may still exist. The new teacher ought not to use this device unless it is required in the school. In that event, he should demonstrate as soon as he can that the pupils do not need such methods of control. When a class has to do this, the traffic is blocked. The teacher is apt to become frantic in his efforts to police the long line to enforce silence. The level of personal responsibility is debased. A hostile pupil leader can easily give a signal for stamping or tripping as the class files into the room. The period begins with scolding and punishment. This kind of experience can serve to block learning for many children.

Occasionally, inexperienced or insecure teachers set up unsatisfactory routines for dismissal. These have the flavor of the elementary school and the pupils do not like them. It seems ridiculous to make junior high school students "sit in order" to get them ready for dismissal. It is of doubtful value to make them stand a row at a time, face the rear of the room, and then march out by the side aisle. The procedure used by adults is the one that should be practiced. People get up and walk quietly forward when they leave a room. Crowding, pushing, and shoving have to be avoided. The teacher does have to establish some routine. Unless he prepares his group for dismissal by saying, "The class is dismissed" or "Good afternoon, boys and girls" or simply, "You may go now," and insists that they wait until he does so, they are apt to jump up and rush out with no respect for the courtesies that are required.

The wise teacher will not permit himself to be surrounded by some eager pupils while the class is either entering or leaving the room. If he does so, his vision is cut off, his attention is distracted, latecomers slip in without his notice, all sorts of pranks get under way. If a routine time and procedure for personal conversation with the teacher are set up, the children will soon learn to observe it.

A good device for getting students to come into the room promptly and to settle down quickly is to have a ten-minute job written on the board for them to do at once. While they are at work on it, stragglers can be attended to individually and without amusing the class. Then the teacher can give his full attention to checking attendance, glancing at his plans for the day, opening supply closets, and will have things under complete control. Class work then begins without confusion and the teacher is relaxed, instead of tense with hurry and apprehension.

Routines prevent noise and disorder.

There are times during class periods when general restlessness and noisiness seem to arise and grow spontaneously. This is so in the traditional classroom as well as in the modern one. Many factors conspire to produce this condition. The teacher who finds himself in the middle of such a situation must think quickly. Has the group been inactive too long? Are too many pupils being kept at tasks that are too difficult? Is there evidence of fatigue or boredom? Is the teacher's voice too loud or raucous? Has he been talking at or to the children too long?

No matter what the cause, immediate action is necessary. Then, when he knows more about the causes, the teacher can take them into account as he plans for future experiences. In all events, the work under way should stop when noise gets the upper hand. Relief exercises may be called for. Leadership of them can be delegated to a pupil and rotated from time to time. The physical education teachers are usually glad to prepare the children for the activity as well as for leadership of it. Maybe only a "break," to stand up and stretch, to move around the room, to open the windows, to talk to each other, will be needed.

When the physical needs have been taken care of, in all probability the learning activity should be changed. If the class was having a discussion, silent reading might follow. Reading could be followed by discussion or writing. Class work might lead to individual activities or committee work. Collection and distribution of supplies may be provided for at this time. If the teacher was talking, he should stop. Few adolescents can listen for more than fifteen or twenty minutes. If the pupils were deeply interested in what they had been doing, they would appreciate having the chance to help to make the decision as to whether or not they should continue or postpone further activity.

Disorder frequently arises while the teacher is talking. If this occurs the cause may lie in the pitch and/or volume of his voice. He must learn to listen to himself, to stop talking and not to continue until silence has been established. Then a conversational tone, free from anger or annoyance, with attention given to pitch and quality, will help to soothe the nerves of the listeners. The inexperienced teacher has to learn to hear noise. He must learn to deal with it in ways other than the raising of his own voice in an effort to get above it. Screaming and yelling are resented by children and cause anger and hostility. If they are resorted to by the frustrated teacher who has become aggressive, the pupils react in kind. Junior high school boys and girls love to confuse the teacher by talking to themselves out loud, by reading aloud, and by making all kinds of noises, if they find that it produces a violent reaction. They also indulge in these when they think that the teacher either does not hear or does not care. In a remarkably short time the noise spreads throughout the room and it becomes impossible to locate the guilty ones. At that point the distracted teacher may resort to a mass punishment, usually detention, which is rarely successful.

In many classrooms the pupils and teachers, after discussing the problem, plan for the use of signals to get attention or restore silence. This helps a great deal when small groups are at work all over the room. One signal that has been very successfully used is flashing the lights. Another is the tapping of a small bell. Sometimes the raising of a hand, while the fingers of the other hand are put to the mouth, serves to remind everyone to lower the voices.

Routines should be followed when giving directions.

One of the errors most frequently made by inexperienced teachers is connected with the giving of directions. They forget that memory spans are short. They pay no attention to the fact that children must be listening closely. They often begin without telling the class to stop other things. The procedure to be followed is clear. First the class must be told to stop everything else. The teacher must wait until they do so. It takes time to return from a day dream, or to stop writing a sentence that is in one's mind, or to finish the page that is so interesting, or to put on paper the color that is already on the brush. Only when everyone is listening can new directions be given with a reasonable expectation that they will be carried out.

The next step is to separate the several things to be done and to give only one direction at a time. While time is elapsing for the carrying out of that one, the teacher should write it on the board, if not all of it at least key words, phrases, pages, and so on. This will enable the pupils with the shortest memory spans, or those who were not giving complete attention, to get the direction without troubling others. Instead of standing at the front of the room, it is advisable for the teacher to circulate among the children to give help where it is needed. This kind of routine takes into account individual learning rates, memory spans, abilities, maturity. When they are not used as the basis for planning, pupils become bewildered and confused. Some will have to turn around, or reach across the aisle to get help from classmates. The overly dependent ones will leave their places and go to the teacher for assistance. Others will call out for help. Some will give up and retreat to idleness or find mischief to do. A few will become discouraged, frustrated, hostile. If there are many who need help, the teacher can press the rapid learners into service, letting them go to the desks of children whose hands are raised. They will be glad to get the chance to move around instead of sitting idle while waiting for the rest to catch up.

There are routines for handling individual offenders.

In every classroom there are boys and girls who become centers of disturbance. As soon as such a child begins to attract unfavorable attention, the alert teacher must find something for him to do. He may be able to send him on an errand, or ask him to distribute or collect materials. There may be a closet shelf that he can put in order, or books to be obtained from the library. Frequently the child who "acts up" is reverting to behavior that is characteristic of a younger age level. He should not be given attention at that level, but as soon as possible some opportunity should be made for praising him for a performance that is appropriate to his own age level. In this way he will learn that growing up brings not only responsibilities but also the reward and encouragement that he craves.

No child should be subjected to a severe scolding in front of his classmates. This serves to center attention on him in exactly the way he wishes. At the same time it may do harm to a sensitive child who is not really guilty of the wrongdoing. Sometimes the one who is punished is the victim of another who has terrified him into silence. When a disturbance occurs, the wise teacher goes quietly to the child in question, puts a hand gently on his shoulder, stoops down to whisper an admonition in his ear, and usually gets the response he is after.

On the other hand, there are times when a pupil should be sent from the room without delay and without many words. In this case it helps if the teacher has a written slip ready on which he has placed what he wants the child to do, where he is to go. If it is possible to do so, the teacher must have a word with the child at the door so that he knows why he has been dismissed. Too often these children reach the principal's office without knowing why they were sent. Too often they carry with them a deep sense of injustice because they cannot understand why they alone have been selected for punishment when others in the room were guilty of the same actions. If one child is singled out of a group when more are involved, resentment, defiance, hostility, and scapegoating may result.

Many young teachers use detention as punishment but get into difficulty with it. They must take the time to find out what the school policy is, whether or not there will be transportation difficulty for the children detained, and what are the after-school responsibilities of the pupils. When a detention is ordered, the teacher cannot accept an excuse from the child who fails to keep the appointment. The very next day there must be a conference about the matter. The detention, whether long or short, must not be a time when the child sits "in order" at his desk while the teacher marks papers or does clerical work. Neither should the child be required to do a clean-up job in the room. Unless this after-school meeting is for the purpose of clarifying a situation, of coming to an understanding, of setting up a plan, or of establishing rapport and confidence, it is worthless.

Routines are needed for distributing supplies and doing housekeeping tasks.

Until controls have been established, it is well for the teacher to limit the number of things that are going on in the room at any one time. For example, distribution of paper should be completed before books are passed out. Later, when those who are responsible know exactly what to do and can be depended upon, several children can operate at the same time without causing too much confusion. Short cuts can be worked out. For example instead of circulating around the room in order to give a book to each child, the distributor can place a pile of them on the first chair or desk in each row and ask the children to pass them back or across as the case might be. Those who distribute things should also be expected to account for the complete number when they are collected again.

A time should be set at which housekeeping jobs begin. These tasks include picking up paper from the floor, replacing furniture that has been moved, adjusting window shades, and cleaning boards. A classroom chairman can be entrusted with the task of reminding a busy teacher when the time arrives.

Substitutes and new teachers need to be fortified with well-thought-out plans. They must be sure that all the materials they need are on hand. Without fear or hesitation they must assume command of the situation. The boys and girls are very ready to say to newcomers, "That's not how Mrs. Blank does it," or "We don't do it that way here." A chorus may sing out, "We'll get the books for you" as a group of pupils rise from their seats and make for the door. If the first evidence of this kind of behavior is met with a firm rejoinder, "But I am your teacher now. We will do this my way for the time being," the children are likely to respond to directions as they are given. Persistent objectors should be required to return at the close of the day for conference.

Much classroom tension and conflict rise out of the failure of some children to bring their supplies—paper, notebooks, textbooks, pencils, other tools and materials. Clever and resourceful teachers work out devices which take the fight out of the situations which arise. For example, a boy who habitually loses his pencil can be required to have two, one of which he places in a special spot to which he can go for it and to which he returns it at the close of the period. In classes where forgetting is widespread, the boys can make a peg board on which a set of pencils is placed. Responsibility for keeping them sharp and ready for use, for replacing those which are used up, and for collecting them at the close of the period, can be delegated to the worst offender.

If loose leaf notebooks have a way of becoming dirty, disorderly hodge-podges of papers, individual inexpensive manila folders can be filed in the classroom and always be made accessible to the owners. Records of classroom work, rough and finished copies of written papers, and marked test papers can be kept in them. Teacher, child, and parent get much satisfaction from examining the contents of these folders. They are invaluable when marking time is at hand.

Routines are necessary for keeping track of printed materials.

Classroom librarians are indispensible in the modern classroom. The teacher alone cannot keep track of books and fugitive materials when the children have free access to the reference shelves, and frequent change of reading books is encouraged. Book receipt forms must be made up to suit the needs of the group. A single one will do if there is space on the back for the titles of books that are taken out during the semester. Three-by-five cards can be used and kept in a file, or even a ruled notebook will do. The important thing is that there is a plan, that the pupils help to develop it, that duties connected with it are delegated to reliable children, and that the teacher checks occasionally to make sure that all is going well.

If group work is going on, each committee must be held accountable for the material used by its members. One of the most reliable pupils of each group should be made its librarian. This is the only way that materials can be kept intact. Even then, and in the most methodically run classrooms, losses will occur. The wise teacher will make sure that the class librarians do not bear the brunt of his ire over losses. The members of the group and he will have to discuss the matter, attempt to locate the missing items, and make plans for possible replacement. Even replacement may be inadvisable. It may lead to trouble because children do not always have or cannot raise the funds, or because of the personal relations involved when guilty people refuse to confess. Care must be taken that such occurrences do not serve to discourage children from reading or from taking books home for work. The only time there is no loss is when books and materials remain safely on the shelves, unused.

When a text book is required, it is useless to suppose that every child will carry that book back and forth every day. The books will be left at home, or in the lockers, on the busses, and at the play field. The daily struggle over books is a reason why some children get to hate school, and others escape from the wrath of the teacher by cutting the period. Instead of beginning the period by recording "black marks" or demerits for pupils without their books, or listing their names for detention, or sending them out of the room, the problem can be solved by having extra copies on hand and ready for immediate distribution and use. Certainly the teacher will not leave the matter there. In conference with the guilty ones, and in the presence of counselors and possibly parents, he will make every effort to build up a sense of responsibility in these students. The fault may lie in the pupil's inability to identify with the work that is under way. When school study makes no sense to the child, all efforts to force him to bring his book to class every day may fail.

A "permissive" climate is important.

Many people are confused about the kind of climate which does and should pervade the junior high school of today and tomorrow. Certainly it needs to be purposeful and it will be if the children participate in determining their goals and procedures. Certainly it must be orderly and quiet. This goes along with purpose and does not negate the necessity for permissiveness. The meaning of the word permissive is not always clear. Permissiveness in school has to do with giving children the right to be creative, to be different, to think, to explore. It supersedes regimentation, uniformity, silence, and emphasis on unthinking obedience, rote learning, and regimented drills. Teachers need always to refrain from telling children what to think, what to say, and what are the "right" answers. The entire school needs to be pervaded with an atmosphere of success. Teachers and children need to be "on the same side," striving together to discover the uniqueness of each child and to bring to flower the best in him.

Learning Activities for Members of Pre- and In-Service Teacher Education Classes

In addition to reading:

1. Exchange experiences with other members of the group.
2. Try some of the routines suggested in this chapter.
3. Observe in a junior high school.
4. Show and discuss the film "Maintaining Classroom Discipline," Mc-Graw-Hill.

References

Brown, E. G., *Managing the Classroom.* New York: Ronald Press Co., 1952.

Burton, W. H. "Basic Principles in Good Teaching-Learning Situations." *Phi Delta Kappan,* March, 1958.

Eye and Lane. *The New Teacher Comes to School.* New York: Harper and Brothers, 1956.

New York City Board of Education, "A Check List for New Teachers," N. Y., 1952.

Wey, Herbert, "Why Do Beginning Teachers Fail?" *The Bulletin of the National Association of Secondary School Principals,* October, 1951.

CHAPTER FOURTEEN

Discipline

Among the meanings which Webster's "New World Dictionary" gives to the word discipline are: *Training* that develops self control, character, or orderliness and efficiency; and, *treatment* that corrects or punishes. These are also the meanings implied when the classroom teacher and other school personnel talk about discipline. Children who lack self-control and orderliness, as well as those who are popularly called "difficult pupils," constitute serious problems in the junior high school. Moreover, the teacher's inability to use effective, established methods of punishment and control, and to invent new ones is often considered by his superior officers to be his greatest weakness.

Junior high school administrators and teachers know that some of the behavior problems with which they struggle are inherent in the very nature of the physical and emotional changes through which their pupils are passing. Others are caused by conflicts between the children and school personnel. These tend to disappear when the content of the curriculum is made more meaningful, when the teaching techniques become more democratic and effective, and when the structure of the school day is changed to permit a long period with one teacher. That arrangement allows for the development of warmer personal relationships with faculty and peers. There are also deep seated disorders which give teachers great concern and their causes need to be uncovered. When behaviorisms are seen to be clues to causes, progress toward finding cures can be made.[1]

It is axiomatic to say that all behavior is caused. Causes of each specific manifestation must be sought in the totality of the indi-

---

[1] William C. Kvaraceus, "Delinquent Behavior," *Culture and the Individual*, Washington, D. C.: The National Education Association, 1959.

vidual's life. Thus some of them are found in the *home* when it is unsatisfactory because it is physically substandard, or too small for privacy, or too over-materialized in its emphasis on the preservation of the things in it, or when the child finds that it compares unfavorably with the standards and ideals which the school, the movies, television, and the advertisers set before him.

Parents become causes of behavior problems when they are too dominating, too autocratic, or exert too much pressure; when they are too uninformed about and inconsistent in the use of disciplinary measures; when they are in conflict over "old world" and "new world" standards; when there is discord between them; when they are separated or divorced.

The *self* becomes a cause of behavior trouble when it is physically impaired, lacking in strength or complete development and when the individual has not been helped to adjust to the deficiency. Deficient mental abilities and emotional controls are contributing factors to bad behavior. Limited social opportunities and experiences caused by poverty or parental indifference may be part of the picture.

Society is responsible for bad behavior patterns when it presents conditions which cause conflicts in value systems that the child cannot resolve. These, for example, may come about because of the child's inability to fulfill the desires created in him by modern advertising. Other contributing factors are to be found, for some children, in the differences between the social class mores of the group in which the child has his origin and being, and those of the middle class to which the teacher belongs. Many conflicts arise out of interpersonal and inter-group relationships.

The *school* itself causes misbehavior when there is no one in it who knows and cares about the individual child; no one to whom he can go to talk about important things; no one who is willing to accept him no matter what he does; too many who reject him. Much cause for bad behavior lies in the school's failure to find the child's level of accomplishment and rate of learning or failure to provide success, praise, recognition, rewards, fun and adventure. Many misdemeanors are committed by the child who is not regarded by his teachers and classmates as being personally worthy and is not treated with respect regardless of his ethnic origin, race, religion or social class.

Adolescent boys and girls, by the very nature of their developmental tasks, inevitably exhibit behaviors for which teachers feel called upon to reprove or scold them or to inflict more serious punishments. The necessity the child experiences to free himself from adult control, one of the tasks to be accomplished as he matures, bumps against the teacher's belief in *his* right and responsibility to direct children, to order them about, and to assign them daily tasks without consulting their wishes. Conflict, acted out in sullenness, insolence, profanity, obscenity, disobedience and violent forms of aggression, often results. It does little good for the teacher to attempt merely to curb or cure the symptoms. He will reduce the incidence of rebellion when, in the classroom, students are permitted to participate in expressing their desires, clarifying their purposes, planning their learning activities, accepting responsibilities, and evaluating themselves, their groupmates and their productions. Doing these places the child in a more grown-up role. Moreover, the teacher who understands the frustrations which surround the adolescent's need to grow up, though he may feel anger at bad behavior, doesn't have to act angry. Instead he may use the situation to initiate person-to-person and group discussion of the phenomenon of emancipation and how to achieve it peacefully.

A second set of bad behaviors which plague the junior high school teacher arise out of another developmental task—namely, understanding and accepting the sex of self and adjusting to the opposite sex. The surrounding difficulties may lead to unseemly giggling, to acting up and whistling in order to get attention, to the use of sex language, sex drawings on walls and in text books, sex stories, and sex play and experimentation. Teachers often become terrified and infuriated by sex behavior, forgetting entirely that the junior high school years are a period of emotional turmoil connected with sex urges, fears, and activity. Punishment may serve to repress and suppress the behavior in one or another classroom but it may also cause outbreaks in corridors, lavatories, cafeterias and play areas.

Sex behaviorisms which give teachers great concern are:
—too obvious interest in the opposite sex—"boy (or girl) craziness,"
—hysterical and continuous giggling,
—"wolf-whistling,"
—overt behavior used to attract attention of the other sex—vulgar

sitting position, hip wiggling, wearing overly tight jeans, low
neck dresses, too short skirts,
—use of symbols of grown-upness—excessive use of cosmetics, adult
clothes, hair arrangements,
—curiosity evidenced by touching, pushing one child into a crowd
of others, lifting skirts,
—reading pulp magazines and lurid tales of love and crime,
—going steady,
—experimentation: masturbation, necking, petting,
—unwholesome activities such as writing obscene notes, writing on
walls and in textbooks, making sex drawings, telling sex stories,
bringing pornographic pictures and printed matter to school,
circulating "swap" books filled with personal boy-girl relationships,
—illegitimacy,
—venereal disease,
—perversions.

The children in all schools have the right to be together at lunch
time, in play areas, and in classrooms. These are all places in which
the school can provide opportunity for them to experience normal
associations and to get from wise adults whatever direction and
guidance they need.

Probably no part of the junior high school curriculum can offer
greater opportunity for instruction and guidance in inter-personal
relations than the practical arts program, if the practice of segregation by sex in these classes is ended. Both sexes are equally in need
of creative industrial arts experiences, of practical experiences in
home making, of help with personal grooming and etiquette, of
guidance in family relations and baby care, and of consumer education, all of which can be incorporated into the practical arts
program. While they make useful articles in the shops and good
things to eat in the kitchens, boys and girls learn to help each other,
to talk together, to plan and work together effectively, to understand and appreciate each other's role in the family and the working
world.

If junior high schools are to cope with the problems their pupils
present, they can no longer afford to delay inaugurating a program
of sex hygiene. Parents and other members of the community will

have to be called in to assist in the development of the necessary policy, if traditional opposition is to be overcome. As curriculum is developed it will become obvious that some of the instruction must be done on an individual basis when the need for it arises. Some of the content can be offered in mixed class while other aspects should be saved for classes segregated according to sex. Part of the information required can be included in science and social studies or core units, for example, various aspects of mental hygiene and human relations. Adolescents need and want instruction and learning experiences which will increase their understanding of and adjustment to problems of inter-personal conflict, of emotionally caused illness, and of mental illness. When anxiety is allayed by information, unwholesome behaviorisms are decreased.

Whispering, talking, and communicating with classmates by gestures, facial expressions, and writing notes are a cluster of behaviors which bother teachers. They are readily given up when pupils are permitted to work together in pairs or small groups during part of the period for purposes of planning, pooling information, and evaluating. Discussions in which many lines of communication are permitted, rather than recitation in which one child at a time talks to the teacher, also help to eliminate the side remarks in which some children are prone to indulge. In classrooms where pupils can at times communicate with each other, they usually are quite willing and able to be silent and self controlled when it is necessary.

Silence is essential when pupils are working individually with books or writing. No teacher should fail to accept his responsibility or to exercise his authority to secure it. He and the students together must establish the ground rules which are needed to secure for each the right to be heard (only one person talks at a time), the right to hear, the right to conditions which enable every one to work effectively.

Some teachers attempt to punish children who talk in class by assigning them ridiculous tasks such as writing "I will not talk" five hundred times. Others assign compositions on such subjects as "Work" or "Silence" or "Consideration for Others." Rarely can the guilty parties do such writing and there is no evidence that such punishments are effective. The most noticeable result of assigning compositions is hatred for writing.

Disobedience with respect to the learning tasks set up in class and for homework is another source of frustration, anger, and worry for the teacher. Children forget to bring their books, pencils, and other essential materials and equipment. The most commonly used punishment is requiring the child to sit idle while the class proceeds and then to come after school to make up the work. Before administering such penalties, the teacher needs to discover whether or not the child has and can bring the books or other essentials. In states where books are not free, some families cannot afford them, or can buy only one set which has to be rotated among siblings. Very often, a child whose parents cannot buy such equipment as sewing material hides the fact behind a facade of impudence or indifference.

Books are easily lost, destroyed, and forgotten by children who cannot read them. The frustrated child reacts badly to the teacher who provides only one single text and who assigns homework in it, regardless of his reading disabilities. Discipline problems of this kind are best solved by having duplicate books at hand (on a wide range of reading levels), a box of pencils, and plenty of paper and by making these accessible, without comment, for those who need them. When children who have no difficulties exhibit unsatisfactory attitudes regarding books, supplies, and work, then, before setting up penalties, conferences should be initiated with parents and guidance personnel.

Many serious behaviorisms are caused by anger. Among these are desecration of property, vandalism, fighting, persecution of smaller children and of minority group members. The school needs to examine its program to determine what makes children angry. The following principles of behavior and the implications for the teacher and curriculum maker need to be considered.

Every individual behaves in response to his feelings about himself. At times he acts as he sees himself to be. At other times he acts as he would like himself to be. For example, when a child or youth has been unsuccessful in school, has been rejected by his peers or his teachers, has suffered from being treated as the underdog at home, he probably sees himself to be a "bad actor." As such, he will probably not hesitate to desecrate or destroy property or to attack other people. On the other hand, the child who is badly treated and who fails in school often leads a fantasy life in which he sees himself as the big shot, the leader to whom others look for direction. In his fantasy life he demonstrates his strength and power by beating up and destroying someone. When an occasion arises, this child may act out his daydream. His target, of course, is likely to be one he feels is of lesser worth, one whom, he has heard, society also looks down on.

Some people are highly suggestible. This means that the story of one act of violence and/or vandalism, spread across the newspapers and television screen replete with pictures and other details, gives to the suggestible person an idea which he then proceeds to act out. The target he selects is likely to be determined by what he has heard about people or by an attitude already present in his mind developed out of what he has heard at home.

Feelings of guilt need to be alleviated. A scapegoat provides for this release. Some children and youth are ridden with guilt feelings over such things as their own sex activities and feelings, their school failures, their defiance of parents and teachers, and their many socially unacceptable acts. When feelings of guilt and shame mount up, the child is apt to commit an overt infraction of some kind, in a manner that leads to early detection and rapid confession.

Children often lack recognition. Some children are not recognized within the family structure. They are always on the receiving end of directions, controls and punishments. They are not permitted to express ideas or opinions and have no part in decision making. Unfortunately, in many classrooms, these same children are likely to suffer further from lack of recognition. When this occurs, a child may have an insatiable need for recognition, and constantly search for it. Under such circumstances, he may believe that imitation of an anti-social act which he has seen on television or in the press will at least make his family and peers recognize him as someone to be taken into account.

A chronically high level of anxiety which the individual cannot reduce, channel or control, may cause seemingly impulsive behavior. Then, for example, when passing by a building or home which may represent to him people he has heard his adults blame for their own anxieties, with brief premeditation or on the impulse he may seize a stone and throw it at a glass window. All children indulge in both impulsive and planned aggression but as they grow up they receive guidance in how to express their aggressions in non-harmful ways. For example, among the experiences adults help them to have are games in which they fight against the other side or, as spectators, yell at the umpire. However, where antiminority group attitudes exist in the home, children get little help in controlling their aggressive feelings. Instead, they may even be encouraged to believe that expression of aggression against minorities will be rewarded.

Some persons are blocked in their emotional development and remain at the infantile level. At the age of two or three it is normal for children to destroy things. Ordinarily, as they mature they give up destruction and enjoy putting things together. However, should a child be blocked in developing emotional maturity, he may continue to be destructive.

Constant failure, suppression, repression and rejection by peers and by adults in school or at home create anger and hostility. The individual so treated often cannot vent his anger and hatred on those who cause it. Instead, he may attack property—especially the kind valued by adults, such as books, school buildings, churches, synagogues and tombstones.

Some successful and otherwise controlled children, especially in adolescence, may act in terms of a group will. The peer group exerts strong influence upon its members. To be in a gang and, even more, to be its leader is deeply desired by many adolescents. Once a boy achieves such a position, he may be pushed into behavior he knows to be wrong for fear of losing his status. Under such circumstances, a "good kid" can act like a "sick kid" and thereby consolidate his position of strength in the group.

Teachers, especially the inexperienced, often want to use corporal punishment. When a teacher hits an adolescent in front of the class, he runs the risk of retaliation. Moreover, this is so great a denial of the child's need to be treated as a grown-up, that it is likely to result in hatred. Many pupils who watch such an occurrence experience fear, confusion, shame, and disgust. There may also be a kind of illicit excitement among them. The "ripple effect"[2] on children not personally involved in the altercation may seriously undermine the teacher's relationship with the entire group. Punitive personali-

---

[2] Kounin and Gump, "The Ripple Effect in Discipline," *The Elementary School Journal*, December, 1958.

ties are created by constant punishment. Teachers who constantly want to punish their pupils may need to examine their motivations.

Stealing is not uncommon among early adolescents. Teachers need to guard against recording incidents on permanent records which may label a child as a thief. Before taking action in any one case, the causes of the behavior must be investigated. Among the causes are neurotic striving for possessions and a need to be reassured against previously experienced destitution. Children take things when their own possessions are far below standard or there is a great discrepancy between desires and possibilities of fulfillment.

A child may steal in order to gain entry to a group which would otherwise exclude him and because of rejection by the "in-group" in the classroom. Many children who steal have had little or no habit training at home or have no private property rights among a group of siblings who do not have enough of anything to go around. Such a child is used to taking from the common stock whatever he needs, and sees nothing wrong about it.

Occasionally a child takes something from a person, classmate, or teacher, whom he likes but from whom he can get no attention. This may make him want to own something belonging to that person. Temporary severe disturbance in a child's life may cause anxiety which leads to impulsive stealing.

A child who has an uncontrollable desire for self adornment and who steals to fulfill it may be suffering acutely from inferiority feelings. Another may have to prove to himself and his peers that he isn't a sissy and that he isn't afraid. Some children have defective social judgment. A typical answer from such a child is "I didn't ask to be born." Some are frustrated by unfair and unequal competition in school and at home. A few get to believe that everything and everybody are wrong and that the only way to exist is to "beat the game." These youngsters are apt to be hard, bitter, and threatening when discovered in wrongdoing.

Often a child suffers guilt feelings around his sex urges and experiences, his personal failures and rebellion. If these pile up anxiety, then punishment is sought to get relief. Such a child may steal in a way that leads quickly to detection, confession, and punishment.

A whole group of disturbing actions may be called aggression. Fighting back, whether it be physical or verbal or emotional, is the child's easiest way out when he is overwhelmed by feelings of help-lessness against too great odds. The odds are stacked against many children in whose families parents are too superior, too over-pro-tective, or too indifferent. They are also piled high in schools where, for many children, little or no attention is paid to individual differ-ences, to adolescent needs, and to the implications of social class.

Shame and guilt accompany the defeats such children suffer. These, reinforced by frustration, are most likely to result in anger. The child's most wholesome outlet for these emotions is indulgence in some degree of aggression. However, it is only when fighting tends to become an unreasoning and unreasonable constant reac-tion to whatever happens that it can be called abnormal.

In general the aggressors are easily identified. These children constantly wrangle with their classmates, fight at "the drop of the hat," indulge in crossness and temper storms, use sarcasm, have fun and feel proud when they openly evade school regulations, destroy school property, resist and scorn authority, show hatred and hos-tility, enjoy a display of disobedience, take delight in being uncoop-erative, and at times have the kinds of explosions in which they use obscene and profane language and behavior. Sometimes they plan and carry out somewhat dramatic expressions of retaliation just to show adults and their peers that they too have power to hurt. In extreme cases the individual alone or with his gang may go on the rampage in veritable orgies of destruction.

It is not possible to say categorically that certain behaviorisms are specifically due to any one factor. Among the possible causes are constant classroom failure and inability to get recognition: noth-ing the child does is good enough to suit parents or teachers. Re-tardation, overageness, precocious physical development may cause aggression or withdrawal. Rage over an inability to win in conflicts with parents or siblings is often acted out in the classroom. Faulty and inconsistent disciplining at home causes a child to be confused. If the methods he uses to escape punishment at home do not work in school, a child may feel betrayed and unfairly treated. Undue pressures to conform to conventions, religion, parental demands, or peer group code cause aggressive outbursts. Sometimes adolescents suffer from conflicts between self and society which produce the feeling of being "injured by the world." There is aggravation from the constant appeal made by newspapers, pulp magazines, and advertisements to the child's love of the sensational and bizarre, to his need for adventure and fun, and to his unlimited capacity for pleasure.

Among the causes of bad behavior which can and must be removed are the things teachers say and do because they lack information about adolescents and about human needs. They make facetious wisecracks, emphasize and exaggerate a child's mistakes, make fun of a child with witty and clever remarks at his expense, bring pressure to bear on lower class children to make them use middle class language, speech, dress, manners, belittle children who are slow or distracted, tell children they are "too dumb to bother with," reject children, and put them out of the room.

Some children react with violence because of feelings of inferiority and inadequacy. These have many causes among which are: inability to reach parents' standard of achievement; being less acceptable to parents than a living or dead sibling; rejection by schoolmates; having insufficient money to meet demands of school and/or participate in peer group activities; being different from others because of race, religion, social class, ethnic origin, low mentality or physical ability. Family discord may cause a child to be ashamed and to react aggressively towards teachers and more fortunate agemates.

In his report "Delinquent Behavior: Culture and the Individual," published in 1959 by NEA, William C. Kvaraceus says, "pouring all students into a single academic mold causes many pre-delinquents to suffer frustration, failure and conflict, which, in turn, beget aggression that frequently eventuates in patterns of norm-violating behavior." The school concerned about "bad behavior" must finally come to the questions of what are we doing to the children? what are we failing to do? what do we do too much of, what too little? The teacher must ask himself what can *I* stop doing and begin to do, come tomorrow morning?

References

BOOKS

Bandura and Walters, *Adolescent Aggression.* New York: Ronald Press, 1959.

Combs, Arthur W. and Donald Snygg, *Individual Behavior*, rev. ed. New York: Harper and Bros., 1959.
Hymes, James, *Behavior and Misbehavior*. New York: Henry Holt, 1955.
Jersild, Arthur T., *In Search of Self*. New York: Bureau of Publications, Teachers College, Columbia University, 1952.

PERIODICALS AND PAMPHLETS

Combs, Arthur W., "Seeing is Behaving." *Educational Leadership*, October, 1958.
Kounin, J. S. and P. V. Gump, "Ripple Effect in Discipline," *Elementary School Journal*, December, 1958.
Kvaraceus, William Clement, "Behavioral Deviate in the Culture of the Secondary School." (In Syracuse University School of Education: *Frontiers of Secondary Education*, III.)
———"Meeting the Serious Behavioral Problems in Junior High Schools," *Bulletin 43*, National Association of Secondary School Principals, April, 1959.
Sheviakov, George and Redl, Fritz, *Discipline for Today's Children and Youth*. Washington, D. C.: National Education Association, 1956.
"The Educational Program: Adolescence," *Review of Educational Research*, 1959.

BIBLIOGRAPHIES

"Discipline in the Public Schools," *Bulletin 35*, NEA Research Division, December, 1957.
"Discipline," *National Education Association Journal*, September, 1958.
"Selected References in Discipline," *California Journal of Elementary Education*, August, 1958.

CHAPTER FIFTEEN

Meeting the Needs
of the Slow and the Gifted Pupils

The whole question of predestination of individuals, of classes, races or nations, whether this predestination is divine, biological or cultural, is closely tied up with one's belief about human nature. The problem of the I.Q. is, therefore, one of the more crucial problems of our culture. Are individuals, classes or people destined to live within the limits prescribed by their genes, or are their futures dependent upon cultural factors over which they may have some measure of control themselves? If the latter, to what extent can they control these factors individually or collectively? What difference would it make if men not only could exercise some control over the conditions that shape their future, but likewise realized that fact?

George E. Axtelle, "Significance of the Inquiry into the Nature and Constancy of the I.Q.," *Educational Method*, November, 1939, Vol. 19, p. 99.

One of the criticisms of mass education is its failure to provide adequately for superior people. Very often the complaints that are voiced imply that the presence in the secondary school of many pupils with little ability to do academic work makes it impossible to give sufficient time to the able students. Much blame is placed on the policy and practice of keeping children with their age mates in spite of their inability to reach standards of achievement that used to be required for promotion to the high schools.

There are people, both in and out of the school system, who see a remedy for the neglect of gifted pupils in a return to promotion on the basis of fixed examinations in the fundamentals—the 3 R's. They even suggest that those pupils who cannot pass such tests should remain, as they used to do, sitting with the little ones until the appropriate birthday releases them for loafing on the street corners or for such odd jobs as they may find. They believe that the secondary school teachers would then once more be able to devote themselves to the "cream of the crop."

Teachers and parents who make such suggestions labor under the belief that if the promotion practices of twenty-five years ago were re-established, the junior high school teachers would devote themselves to the preparation of their students for college as they used to do and all would be well. Unfortunately, even if that did come to pass, little more would be done for many gifted pupils than was then done. The fact is that the verbally superior students in many schools always did receive a great deal of attention and encouragement. Then, as now, they were often segregated into special "honors" groups where they were drilled and tutored for college entrance examinations. However, today as then, a large portion are still untouched—those whose gifts are in abilities not discovered by "I.Q." tests and whose talents are not cultivated when emphasis remains fixed on getting high marks for learning what the books say. The question still to be answered is what are the gifted getting in their special classes that will best equip them for productive lives in our society.

A new point of view and a new attack on the problem is called for. The first steps in that direction are to identify the superior children and then to clarify their needs. Who are they—regardless of race, creed, or social class? What are their personality needs—regardless of plans for higher education or for the types of jobs they may get?[1] What will society require of them? What kinds of experiences will promote their mental health and social adjustment and will further the possibility of their leading abundant and generous lives?

In the past, large numbers of gifted students have gone unrecognized. Allison Davis says, "A nation begins to die at the brains when it fails to recognize and develop the intelligence of its masses." Many of the children who in school rank as prodigies and geniuses fail as adults to capitalize on their unique abilities. Some crack up

---

[1] See "Dealing with Fear and Tension," *Service Bulletin No. 24*, Association for Childhood Education International, Washington, D. C.: The Association, 1952.

WHITWORTH COLLEGE LIBRARY
SPOKANE, WASHINGTON

when confronted with realistic living. Many are unable to create good human relationships and so meet tragedy in their own personal lives. Others cannot stay within the bounds of law and order. Too few seem to be willing to accept the responsibility of playing major roles in civic and political life.

It could be that *faulty education* is at least partly responsible for the people with superior ability who occupy beds in mental hospitals, cells in prisons, chairs in divorce courts; and for those who hold minor jobs at which they earn no more than a bare living; and for those who look with scorn upon the opportunity to hold government posts.

If education of the gifted student is to be improved, teachers must first find those students. It is too easy to say that the gifted are the ones with high I.Q.'s. That is almost meaningless in the light of modern knowledge about mental complexity and abilities and how to measure them. In the average school, the I.Q. is measured by a verbal test. It gives little more than a verbal ability score, which may or may not be an indication of the real intelligence quotient. Even so it has little validity for many pupils. Allison Davis, in research done at the University of Chicago, demonstrated that most of the tests of mental ability in current use are slanted in favor of the upper social classes with respect to the experiences and the vocabulary used in them. The results, therefore, do not reveal intelligence that exists in children of the lower classes.

Undoubtedly many gifted children do have a high degree of verbal ability, which is an important asset that cannot be overlooked by the school. Therefore, no grade limitations should be placed on the literature books that are given to them. Although they should have constant encouragement to read and write as much as they can, quantity must not be the only basis on which their assignments are made and on which their production is judged. Quality of thought is probably more important.[2]

Some pupils are blessed with the ability to write. This may not mean writing correctly or according to a teacher's instruction or desires. Teachers who emphasize form and correctness forget that a manuscript may be perfect in those respects but not saleable if it lacks truth and beauty and originality. Given those three, the weak-

---

[2] See National Council of Teachers of English and the NEA, *English for the Academically Talented Student*, 1960.

nesses of poor form and incorrect grammar and spelling will not usually prevent a publisher from buying it.

When a teacher hands a specially selected book to a gifted student with a personal word of recommendation, he establishes a bond with him that may motivate that child to do much more reading on a more adult level. The library door should be open to the gifted students at all times. Occasionally, when the class is doing routine work, superior students can be permitted to go there for individual free reading and research.

If gifted children are to realize their potentialities for doing creative work, they must receive consideration commensurate with their talents. Whenever a unit provides opportunity for the writing of original plays, stories, or poems, those jobs should go to the gifted children if they are also creative. They can also serve as the leaders of committees commissioned to do creative writing. Working with them should be some less able children who have ideas and suggestions to contribute, but who cannot do the writing. There are other difficult writing jobs which require the kind of mental complexity usually possessed by superior pupils. These include taking notes during speeches and interviews, writing minutes of meetings, recording and summarizing discussions.

It is important to remember that an "enriched" experience does not mean *more of the same thing*—more books, more compositions, longer vocabulary lists, more spelling words, more exercises. So often the children who need outdoor exercise and rest are burdened with these extra tasks in the mistaken idea that this spells enriched courses for the gifted. Instead, really richer, more meaningful experiences must be devised which will stretch their powers, give free rein to their imagination, broaden their horizons, increase their skills, enlarge their sensitivities, and deepen their sensibilities. It is equally important for these students to learn to share with others, to work well in groups, to serve and help those in need, and to become democratic leaders.

The verbally gifted are not necessarily superior *people*, nor are their talents most frequently sought for in our society. There are many lines of human endeavor in which different kinds of ability are needed. The school must discover children who are superior in other ways and help them, too, to develop their gifts to the highest possible degree.

Obviously there are the fields of music and art. Who can say that a magnificent painting means less to civilization than a great book? Who can estimate the relative values of songs and symphonies in contrast to poems and dramas? We cannot continue to reject children who might have the ability to compose and paint.

Mike, like many who cannot read, was always in trouble in the classroom. The best thing his teacher seemed able to do for him was to send him out to sit in the corridor. One day a teacher in a room nearby, seeing Mike in the corridor and needing help, put a paint brush into his hand and said, "Here, boy, get busy with this backdrop. Just paint big tree trunks and branches." When she returned half an hour later, she gasped at what the boy had created. Neither she nor any one else in the school had known that Mike was an artist. Yet one and all had discarded and rejected him as "too dumb to bother with." The recognition he received that day and the status he secured in the following months as his ability was used and developed, changed Mike's behavior pattern completely and helped him toward the place that he now holds among promising contemporary artists.

There is considerable conflict in the minds of teachers, parents and pupils regarding the value of creativity.[3] In a study undertaken by Getzels and Jackson at Chicago University, it was found that neither teachers nor parents value creativity in the home or the classroom. They also say that the top twenty per cent of high I.Q.'s, misses seventy per cent of the high-creativity pupils.

Never in history has there been a greater need for those with gifted hands—the inventors, the builders, the electricians, those who love machinery, the metal workers, and those who create in ceramics and plastics. All who can construct with skill, insight, and vision are in demand. For the most part, the children who are gifted in these respects go quite unnoticed. Few schools provide sufficient time and equipment for this kind of work. In most schools, shop work and art work are "minor" subjects. Shop is for boys only and for most of them it is limited to the seventh and eighth grades. It is still too often regarded as the "dumping ground" for non-readers. Rarely are girls admitted to shop work although the job

---

[3] Taylor, C. W. "The Identification of Creative Scientific Talent," Report of 1959 Research Conference. Salt Lake City: University of Utah Press, 1959.

opportunities are unlimited, and their abilities are great. Moreover most shop courses are limited to the use of a few industrial tools, machinery, and materials, products to be made are regimented, and creative individuality is not encouraged. If talented pupils, both boys and girls, are to develop their creative abilities, the practical arts opportunities will have to be changed and increased.

What of those students who are gifted with social sensitivity, who seem born with the knowledge of how to deal with other human beings, who have unusual capacity for sympathy and understanding, who seem destined to heal and cure, who know how to command loyalty and devotion? Modern society has great need for leaders of mankind. They are wanted in labor unions, in civic and social organizations, in religion, and, above all, in politics.

There was Alfreda, who could not do arithmetic and had little use for books. Her big eyes were restless and her smile infectious. The teacher failed to see that she sent a signal round the room the day when her best friend, not a well-qualified candidate, was elected to the class chairmanship. Not until much later, when other things began to happen, did a weeping member of the "out-group" confess that "Alfreda was the class boss." When a junior high school girl can achieve that kind of status in the peer group, it is time to place her among the "gifted" and to make sure that she gets the guidance which will make a leader of her in the cause of goodwill and the good life.

There never was a greater need for people with the gift of administration. This is not necessarily coupled with verbal ability. Many boy gang leaders are able to organize and administer remarkably well. If their superior abilities are recognized, developed, and put to use in the school, they will have less need for the mischievous gang activities that often plague a community. The traffic squads, the lunch room officers, and the gardeners can well be placed under their leadership.

Many adolescent children exhibit great business ability. For the most part, the teachers rarely glimpse this because its only outlet is in after-school work. These students could be entrusted with the business end of the school publications, with the promotion and sale of tickets for the school shows, with running the credit union and with carrying on the school supplies store.

It would be a fine thing if pupils who have the ability to teach were discovered, encouraged, and developed. They ought to be the teachers' assistants, helping them to check papers, sitting with the less able classmates to give them individual help, leading reading groups, conducting drill exercises, and helping the committee chairmen and librarians.

What then are the needs of the superior students? They need to discover themselves; to have rich experiences that are meaningful to them; to have the opportunity to develop their special gifts; to have rich exploratory experiences; to be reminded constantly that they must devote their talents to others and to society.

What is the teachers' responsibility in the education of superior pupils? They must first discover them—all of them. Then they must provide experiences especially designed to use and develop their abilities. They must keep constantly in mind the fact that these children need rounded, integrated personalities; that they need help so that they may become adjusted to life and capable of generous living with all kinds of people.

What will society want of them?—Social sensitivity, the ability to meet competition, the willingness and the know-how of cooperation, leadership, devotion to the democratic ideals, and dedication to the goal of one world at peace.

How can these demands be met? The junior high school must give them enough time, with at least one teacher, for him to discover their personality needs and their latent potentialities. In the school, emphasis should be placed on inter-personal and inter-group relationships, and opportunities must be arranged for experiences in which good relationships can be practiced. In other words, these students require training in the skills of relating themselves warmly and positively to other people.

[Across the country, school systems have rushed into plans for grouping by ability.[4] Often an arbitrary line is drawn at an "I.Q." of 120. Those above are separated from their classmates, if their school marks are also high, to be subjected to high pressure in all subject areas. Ernest A. Haggard, writing in *School Review*, Winter, 1957, in an article entitled "Socialization, Personality and Academic Achievement," says that highly undesirable effects are likely to re-

---

[4] "Ability Grouping," *Research Bulletin* N.E.A., June, 1958.

sult from such experiences. For example, he states that there often is "over-intellectualization to the exclusion of other interests and activities." His study reveals that children in these classes become disdainful of adults and hostile towards their peers. Competition is for marks and to maintain a position of superiority rather than for learning and for excellence. There is an increasingly high level of anxiety and a decline in free, creative thinking.

The use of I.Q.'s and records of school achievement often fails to discover high ability pupils who are under-achievers. They are children who seem to be struggling with basic personal and social problems, and they can be helped by special attention.[5]

Reports indicate that about three per cent of those with low I.Q.'s have made honors in college, while one out of four who enter, drops out by the end of the first year. One fifth of those who drop out were in the top twenty per cent of their high school classes.[6] In a follow-up study of gifted pupils, thirty-five years later, Terman and Oden report that thirty per cent of those who entered college failed to graduate. In addition to giving attention to such discrepancies, it is important to note that in our society, the second echelon of people who have good but not first-rate ability are also important. They may not get into positions of command, but they are needed to fill important posts in social, political, and economic life.

In the modern classroom, without homogenious grouping, gifted children can be given major roles to play whenever mental acuity and complexity are required. These occasions exist when the group, or any part of it, is engaged in planning, making decisions, identifying and clarifying common problems and concerns, developing concepts, formulating conclusions and generalizations, recording, reporting and evaluating. Among the roles to be played by superior children are leading discussions, recording proceedings, analyzing data, observing processes, and giving leadership to others who are engaged in artistic creation of a kind to which their talents also lend themselves. All the many abilities of these children need to have free play in a permissive atmosphere, in which freedom to create is a reality.

The gifted children need counseling and guidance. They also

---

[5] Reported by Dr. Wm. Getzels of Chicago University at the Wisconsin Conference on Human Relations Education, Milwaukee, October, 1959.
[6] U. S. Office of Education, *Retention and Withdrawal of College Students.*

ought to be challenged and their abilities stretched so that they perform at their best—not every minute of every day (for that would destroy any adolescent) but in general. They must know that their teachers feel goodwill toward them and have faith in their ability, no matter what their backgrounds may be. In the school there should be plenty of opportunity for them to practice critical thinking, to make wise choices, and to use good judgment in situations that make sense and are important to them.

Finally the very special problem which is presented by the rare genius needs to be explored. The school must consider the danger ahead when that kind of child is advanced in grade placement until he becomes socially out of step, for this frequently makes him unhappy and emotionally maladjusted. Like all other children, he needs to remain with his age mates. In order to meet his mental needs, however, the teacher can remove all grade barriers and restrictions from the materials he uses and the educational tasks that are given him to do. All doors have to be kept open for the genius; in fact the teacher needs to find new fields for him to explore. This kind of child is especially in need of being encouraged, challenged, stretched, and guarded against early specialization. All sides of his personality need development. Every emphasis should be placed upon making him a generous, contributing, outgoing person who is able to live happily with his less gifted associates.

The Slow Learners

The other, much larger group of atypical children for whom educational practices require improvement are those who are noticeably lacking in "gifts." They too have a place in the world, and the school is obligated to help them to find it. "Nothing can be more clear," writes Finney,[7] "than that the humbler economic functions are destined not only to remain, but to claim large percentages of the population. . . . Somebody must remain in them; and for an honest democracy it does not so much matter who; the real question is, what will be their opportunity for a satisfying life in them. The central problem . . . is whether the men with the hoe,

---

[7] Ross L. Finney, *A Sociological Philosophy of Education.* New York: Macmillan Co., 1928, page 282.

the pick, and the shovel are to be brutalized or humanized. If the former, then the hope of democracy—not to say Christianity—is a delusion and a dream; but if the latter, it will come through in education that enables them to utilize the sciences, the fine arts, and the new humanities as copiously and effectively as does any other class of society."

Until sputnik created new fears and with them, new demands for creative people in the fields of mathematics and science, there was more discussion of the problem presented by the "slow learner," "retarded," "non-academic," "underprivileged" pupils than of their more able classmates. Unfortunately, most of the questions raised indicate that many of the junior high school teachers are quite out of patience with and even frustrated by the presence of these youngsters in the school. The children, their parents, their elementary school teachers, and the community are blamed for their failure to progress with sufficient speed to meet the arbitrary demands for accomplishment presented by courses of study, textbooks, and examinations.

In many schools where subject-matter divisions are still rigid, teachers believe they cannot stop "covering the course of study" in order to teach children the reading, writing, spelling, and the arithmetic skills without which they cannot do the daily assignments. Teachers who consider themselves academic specialists want one of two things to happen: (1) that children who are not up to "grade level" (whatever that may be) be "left down" and "made to repeat" (as if this would result in greater accomplishment); (2) that such children be excluded from *their* classes, herded together, and given to some other teacher who is "willing to entertain them."

If all the children in the groups under consideration were really mentally deficient, that is with bona fide intelligence quotients below 70, there might be justification in placing them in segregated special classes where normal progress in learning the skills required for ordinary living is not expected. In the junior high school there are, however, large numbers of children who are not really deficient but who, for one reason or another, have not learned enough about reading, writing, spelling and arithmetic to use the text books, to write the compositions and to do the problems that are on the so-called normal or grade level of accomplishment. In many instances these requirements or standards were devised long ago and by people who were not familiar with the actual emotional, physical, and mental needs of today's children living in very diversified communities.

There is no doubt that among the "slow learners" are pupils who are intelligent but whose learning has been blocked. It is unforgivable for the public school to condemn these children, to exclude them from the regular classrooms, to brand them as unteachable, to limit their associations by segregating them, and to forget that their life needs will extend beyond the three R's. Instead of doing so, every effort must be made to find the causes of their troubles and, if at all possible, to prevent and cure them.

In large cities the lowest group of children are placed in special classes. An attempt is made to avoid stigmatizing them by using such letters to designate their classes as X, Y, Z. However the children are sensitive to differences in treatment and often suffer keenly. For example, in one school, the door of the room used by such a class had no glass in it as did the other classroom doors. When those children had a chance to tell what was hurting them, they mentioned the door and asked that glass be inserted. In cities using a track system, these pupils constitute the third or fourth track, whichever is the lowest. This, virtually, is segregation.

There are many pupils whose difficulties are hard to locate and even more difficult to cure. When they are segregated they suffer severe damage to their self-respect, faith in parents and teachers is often shattered, their belief in democracy is apt to be shaken if not destroyed, they become less fit for effective participation in home life, work and community affairs, and they usually stay away from after-school activities.

In every school system there are many children who do have serious mental limitations. Some are born that way, others are damaged by disease or accident. They are below the normal range of intelligence and cannot be classified in the same way as other pupils. Schools deal with this problem in various ways. In some cities they are in special schools. In other places "special classes," which have various names, are organized for them in the junior high school building. In still other communities, where the compulsory age limit is low, they are soon excused from attendance. By far the most acceptable practice is found in schools that have a core type curriculum. There, these children take their places in the core class along with all the rest. In the specialized areas like foreign language and algebra, they do not qualify, along with many "average" pupils, and so are not hurt when they are not permitted to elect those subjects.

In the block or core classes, both the content and the methods used are of such a nature that the needs of the underprivileged pupils can more nearly be met. They have, in common with their classmates, all the needs that grow out of the basic human drives and the adolescent developmental tasks. The teacher must see them in the light of those common needs. He must also try to project himself into their possible adulthood needs so that the task of preparing them for the lives they will lead becomes clearer to him.

No matter how slow these boys and girls may be, in ten years they will be citizens entitled to and making use of the vote. Some will seek and even be elected to minor political offices. A few may get into higher public positions. The school must therefore accept the responsibility of teaching them about elections and the duties of elected officers in our democracy. Teachers will not be able to do that from books. One effective means to use is the student elections in the school. Another direct experience is a trip to the polls on election day. There the children will be able to talk to the voters as well as the election officials. Visits should be made to registration offices and political party headquarters.

Some of these students will have leadership potentialities. They should be allowed to accept nominations and gain positions of leadership so that they may experience what holding office means in terms of the demands of constituents as well as in terms of the enjoyment of privilege. They are rarely denied, however, if they have some athletic ability. In fact, with *it*, some get college scholarships.

Ten years will see many of the retarded pupils living in their own family groups. They will marry and have children. Junior high school is the last chance they will have for any directed learning about citizenship, community and human relations. The teacher must therefore include problems of inter-personal relations in the classroom work. He can do so by bringing in films, recordings, and speakers. The discussions that follow will help to clarify thought for all the students on such absorbing problems as choice of life partner, marriage, divorce, child care, foster children, early growth and

training, living within an income, moral and spiritual values, problems of relationship with older and younger siblings, sharing income and responsibilities, concepts of cultural and racial differences
and dozens of other matters that are of immediate concern, as well
as preparation for the future. Again it is necessary to emphasize
the fact that these pupils will not be able to learn about such problems from books.

A third thing that all of the poor readers will do is earn a living.
What can they expect in the way of employment and what can the
school do to get them ready for it? In ten years they will be in the
army, the navy, the marines, and on merchant ships. They will be
maids, housemen, and chauffeurs; bell boys, janitors, doormen, bus-
boys, porters, waiters, and waitresses. The factories will take them,
and they will be on the assembly lines. Work is waiting for them on
the docks, in hangars and garages. They will be the helpers of
plumbers, carpenters, and trainmen. They are needed as street
cleaners and in sanitation squads, as sales girls, stock boys, and
packers and in the hundreds of unskilled and semi-skilled jobs
without which our complex urban and rural life could not continue.

There are no specific hand skills which the "intellectual have-
nots" should acquire in school. Their prospective employers say,
"We will train them on the job in from two to six weeks." There are
plenty of social skills, however, without which they will be unable
to hold a job and which the junior high school can help them to
attain. Again, these cannot be learned from books or by just talking
about them. Experience and practice in meaningful situations are
essential. The teacher must devise opportunities for pupils to learn
how to follow directions, how to work with others, how to be of
service in a group, how to listen and contribute to discussion, how
to behave when parliamentary procedures are being used, how to
accept responsibility, how to respond to leadership, how to seek
the assistance of qualified experts, how to respect authority, how
to be prompt and regular, how to plan and attack a job, and how
to be persistent and industrious. Out of many success experiences
will come a sense of personal worth and dignity.

In despair many teachers ask, "What can these pupils do in the
classrooms of a junior high school?" The following jobs have to be
done in the modern school. All children like to do them, but as
often as possible those in which the entire group does not take part,

but which must be done by just a few, should be allocated to the slow learners. From them can come the outcomes for which the school is responsible.

Audio-visual equipment has to be secured and operated.

Materials and books have to be distributed, collected and accounted for.

Housekeeping duties must be carried on and plants cared for.

News items, pictures, charts, maps, and graphs have to be found in newspapers and magazines, and clipped, mounted, and arranged in files, scrapbooks, and on bulletin boards.

Bulletin boards have to be kept in order.

There are radio programs to be heard and talked about.

There are films to see and discuss.

There are units of learning and many activities to be planned.

Trips and excursions have to be planned and taken.

Telephone calls are required when arranging for trips, speakers, and interviews.

There are roles to be played in both prepared and spontaneous dramatic presentations.

Messenger service is needed and there are errands to be run.

Illustrations, posters, and friezes have to be painted.

Class supply closets have to be kept in order.

The class library has to be arranged and kept in order.

Interviews with adults in the home, school, and community are needed.

The class needs hosts and hostesses to take care of visitors.

Newspapers have to be distributed, circulated to other classes, and sold at the end of the week for waste paper.

Classroom equipment, materials and books need repair from time to time.

Finally there is the problem of leisure time, which will present real difficulty in the lives of these non-readers if they do not get help before they leave school. Work in the practical arts shops and in fine arts will be of considerable value to them. Most of them will be as awkward and slow there, as in other areas of instruction, and simpler jobs with more individual help may be needed. Emphasis must at all times be placed on creative and original work rather than the development of great skill.

The therapeutic values of shop work are high for both boys and girls. Both sexes should also have full opportunity to work in the home arts department, where so much can be done to help them to become socially comfortable. There are also many job outlets for both sexes.

Of course, they should participate in all the physical education activities. Occasionally one of the boys will become an athletic "hero." In the gymnasium many of them experience full social equality and gain status because physical prowess has high prestige value.

Every effort is needed to have these pupils participate fully in all the school's social events. Unless they are encouraged to do so, many of them who feel rejected and unwanted will miss these opportunities to be prepared for leisure time activities.

In some schools the segregated classes for the mentally underprivileged are called life adjustment or social living or general education or common learnings. Unfortunately, the stigma that is usually attached to the class becomes associated with the name and tends to discredit the core curriculum in which the core class is called by one or the other of the same names. People become accustomed to thinking that a class called by one of these names is for only the lower ability pupils.

It is true that experimental work in unit teaching, which is characteristic of core curriculum, has often begun with the low ability groups in the school. Teachers are less fearful of making mistakes with them. Pressures attendant on preparation for senior high school can be relaxed. Some administrators are willing to let teachers "meet the needs" if doing so will help to keep these difficult pupils out of the office. Frequently the principal keeps the enrollment low enough to enable the teacher to make a thorough study of the members of the group.

Knowledge about the children is of great importance. Emotional reactions, performance levels, behaviorisms, economic and social backgrounds, and cultural expectations have curriculum implications. The most effective way of gathering these data is to have all the teachers who meet the group share in the program of observation, testing, and investigation, then pool their findings in frequent round table discussions. Consultant help with interpretation may be required. Time should be devoted to finding what each child can do.

Some general characteristics and trends are known. Chronological ages run from twelve to seventeen. The range of mental age is from nine to twelve. The verbal ability scores, determined by mental ability or I.Q. tests, go from 60 to 100. Research done by Allison Davis[8] on the relation of these tests to social class indicates that the school should be cautious in the use of these scores. Occasionally what seems to be a feeble-minded child gets into the junior high school because of socially acceptable behavior. In most schools a small number of pupils who have potential intelligence but who seem unable to meet standard requirements are found in these classes. However, records of psychological tests show that, in general, the pupils who are classified as slow learners have short memory spans, limited reverse memory spans, and hazy or dull imagery.

Although there are as many different personalities as there are children, a certain core of common traits can be described. They are restless and unable to sit still, except for the few who are completely withdrawn. They grow rapidly during the junior high school years and are apt to be unable to understand and endure their normal physical strains, stresses, and tensions. They are adolescent and are becoming increasingly aware of their own physical bodies. They lack both the ability and the desire to place their attention on things outside themselves. They have to move around and cannot be silent for forty minutes. Provision must be made for the "manipulative fringe."

With physical maturity comes absorption in sex. Mentioned previously is the usual interest in dirty stories, obscene language, making drawings on walls and in books, and distributing pornographic matter. The girls, who are usually more mature, torment the boys. They in turn slap the girls, pull their hair, bump into them, and write notes to them. The teacher must be on the alert to prevent unpleasant experiences. He must know what to ignore and how to handle an emergency. A large part of the trouble can be eliminated by providing adequate and appropriate sex instruction.

These boys and girls are often nervous and impatient. The result of unsuccessful struggles with fractions may be an uncontrollable jerk of the arm which sends the paper flying across the room much to the consternation of child and teacher. The pupils are aware of

---

[8] Allison Davis, *Social-Class Influence upon Learning.* Cambridge: Harvard University Press, 1948.

their own inadequacy. This results in typical defense reactions and occasional attacks on the environment. It is evident in surliness, impudence, quarreling, destruction of property, fighting with other children, and hostility toward the teacher.

Much failure through their past years, plus continual scolding at home and in school, create great discouragement in these pupils. Some of them recognize their own inferiority and compensate for it by swaggering or bullying. Others try to do what is asked, but give up easily. A large portion lack the courage to face tasks far beyond their ability, and they escape into illness or truancy.

These children, like all human beings, have a positive need and an unconscious craving for success. The urge to put himself across, to excel in some way, drives many a dull boy to tramp into the room, to come in late, to swagger up to the teacher with a foolish question, to call out an answer, to reply to a reprimand with a volley of impudence, to engage in a fist fight in the classroom, to run in front of an oncoming auto, or to jump a fast moving truck. "Smart guy" and "tough baby" are typical poses. To combat these behaviorisms the teacher must provide many success experiences, distribute praise and rewards liberally, and encourage and encourage and encourage. These children need to develop concepts of self which have "I can" rather than "I can't" in them.[9]

Many of these pupils lead very interesting lives on the streets during the day as well as at night. They can get themselves around town by walking, riding bicycles, and by stealing rides on public conveyances. They get to nearby towns and pleasure resorts by hitch-hiking and by hopping freight cars. It is impossible for the teacher to compete with this outside life sufficiently to eliminate truancy. He can, however, capitalize on it by letting the children talk about their experiences and by giving them help with the problems they meet. He must also remember that these out-of-school experiences are of adult nature and that his treatment of the children must be on a "man-to-man" basis. Many of them, in the large cities, caught by the craving for recognition, security, and power, become trapped in gang life.

Among these boys and girls are some who do not have adequate ideas of property rights. They help themselves freely to whatever

---

[9] Rasey and Menge, *What We Learn from Children*. New York: Harper and Brothers, 1956.

is available. They pilfer in the stores. They pick up food from grocery store displays. At home they take what they want from the pockets of parents and older siblings and relatives. The personal belongings of their classmates are tempting.

Children are often like this because they cannot formulate adequate concepts of truth and honesty, and in face of that, old fashioned talks about character education are quite useless. They can usually say, rather glibly, what is right and wrong and can often tell why, but the gap between what they say and what they do is appalling. They frequently believe that they are not guilty of stealing unless they are caught in the act. One of them cannot inform on others, no matter what the circumstances may be, without being called a "rat." Intimidation spreads a sinister fear throughout the group. The teacher has to let the children talk and, if they can, write about these problems over and over again. Every effort has to be made to create a climate of opinion in the classroom, with respect to such behavior. If wrongdoers can be made to feel uncomfortable and unpopular, changes in attitudes that will lead to changes in actions may be accomplished. Role playing is effective in developing insight that is necessary to effect these changes.[10]

A large proportion of the homes from which retarded children come have been broken in some way. In some cases one parent is dead, in others, one has deserted. Separation of parents sometimes means placement with strangers. Divorce affects children unfavorably. Even in the best of times, in many families both parents are employed and children are on their own most of the time. A considerable number of the parents of these underprivileged pupils are unemployable because of physical and mental illness, deformity, and inadequacy. Some are always on relief, and lacking normal drives and ambitions, prefer the inadequate incomes provided by government or agencies to strenuous labor. Many of these children, for long years, have been accustomed to the visit of the social service worker. Some have been on the streets begging since early childhood. Their families move frequently and that places an adjustment burden on the children that is too heavy for them to bear. They have no roots, and develop strong feelings of rejection.

On the other hand the children may come from homes in which

[10] See George and Fannie Shaftel, *Role Playing the Problem Story*. New York: National Conference of Christians and Jews, 1952.

both parents have been employed for years. Often, these children have been left to their own resources for meals as well as for recreation. The only supervision they get is the yelling and scolding of tired mothers who must do all the drudgery of their own homes after a hard day of outside work.

Incessant quarreling between and with parents has a disastrous effect upon many of these children. Sometimes it is due to conflicting values and standards in first generation families, and when it becomes acute, adolescents are apt to escape by running away. Children also run away from parental cruelty, and when they are unwanted by their parents. Children from homes in which bad relationships predominate are particularly insecure. Such homes occur at all socio-economic levels. In them, children become nervous to the point of neurosis and, occasionally, psychosis. They are inevitably anti-social, without respect for authority, and without habits of obedience. Such conditions, experiences and attitudes whip up anxiety which the child cannot handle. Anxiety in turn not only blocks learning but also causes impulsive behaviors.

The effect of such home conditions on the classrooms is enormous. The children come to school hungry, and that makes them unable to work and to conform. They are irritable and revengeful. It may be that the girls have done hard housework before coming to school. They have to wash and dress the younger children, to run errands, and to gather whatever lunches they are to take along to school. The rush to get there on time often creates an emotional and nervous condition with which the teacher must cope. If the pupil is late, he is apt to be scolded and punished, and because he feels that is undeserved since the lateness is not his fault, he lets loose a torrent of impudence and defiance. He cannot tell the true story to his teacher because it would reflect upon the parent to whom he is loyal. The consequent worry and anxiety produce tension which must result in an outburst. The teacher becomes the parent substitute and receives the full brunt of the child's resentment. Disobedience often is the result of lack of respect for parents. Untruthfulness can be the reaction to cruel punishment. Lack of respect for authority arises from continuous association with drunken relatives, with loud scolding mothers, and with unfaithful, quarreling parents. Boys and girls who come from such homes are preoccupied with distracting experiences. It is true that they do not hear when spoken to and cannot pay attention.

The educational have-nots, when they are also social and economic have-nots, are frequently unable to meet the demands for money to pay the text-book fees, to buy school publications, to join the students association and the athletic clubs, to buy tickets for the school show, to pay for materials needed in the clubs, to join the class party and go to the dance, to provide materials for the sewing class and an apron for cooking, and to contribute to social service drives. They are unhappy when they have to compare their inadequate clothing with that worn by more fortunate classmates. Boys resent having to wear overalls if the peer group is well groomed. Sweaters are often kept on so as to hide torn shirts. Girls who have to do their own laundry may not always be able to wear clean dresses. When classroom discussions emphasize middle class social standards of dress and living which these children know they cannot attain, feelings of inferiority and resentment are engendered and behavior difficulties result.

School records show that nearly all of the retarded pupils perform below grade levels, even when they repeat courses. Their scores on mathematics tests are below grade norms and may even be lower than their ability quotients would warrant. Most of them never receive passing marks in arithmetic on their report cards. Although they are in the junior high school, they cannot do much more than second or third grade work, and many will not get beyond fifth grade competency in dealing with numbers.

Arithmetic has always been required in most schools, and parents object if it is omitted as a special subject for the slow students. Nevertheless, the school must modify its demands and the work for them, or face the dangers of constant frustration it brings to both students and teachers. In some places, therefore, full length periods of mathematics are replaced by short drills in fundamentals which are given during the core or common learnings period. In these exercises the child is encouraged to decrease the time he uses and increase his accuracy. In addition to this drill, appropriate arithmetic problems are done in shop and home arts classes where the pupils measure and count as they cut materials, follow recipes, and plan to earn and spend money. All their problems must be simple because they cannot handle more than one step at a time. Moreover, teachers have to teach them to read their arithmetic books. Concrete devices and illustrative materials have to be used as long as necessary to establish meaning. Only then can number symbols and formulas be tried. Excellent arithmetic or number devices are available and should be used to establish meaning behind the use of number symbols in the processes of addition, subtraction, multiplication, division, and fractions.[11]

School records also show that underprivileged children meet with constant failure in English. Their vocabularies are small. They read mechanically, if at all, on the third to fifth grade levels. Comprehension may be still lower. Spelling is usually below the reading level, and is exceedingly careless. It shows the effect of slovenly speech habits and of having little understanding of sounds. "And" is always "an," "the" is "th," and letters are often disconnected. They usually use capital letters and periods but sprinkle them around without discrimination. Those who do write sentences cannot be expected to use paragraphs. Most of these pupils will never be able to write English better than fifth graders do. They cannot be expected to write themes and compositions. Their best writing is done in response to open-end questions.

It is a waste of time to try to teach these children to spell the words that are in the graded spellers. However, they are interested in learning words that they need to use from day to day. Such words find their most useful application in letters that the children can deliver or send to real people.

Good usage cannot be learned by written drills or by formal grammar lessons. However, oral drills that have elements of fun in them are helpful.

The books that are given to slow readers for pleasure reading must be on their level of independent reading. They ought to have adult content and be written in simple English with words that rarely exceed two or three syllables, and sentences that are simple and direct. Such books are hard to find. When they are given textbooks above their reading levels, they are being doomed to constant experience of failure. Failure destroys everyone.

Classroom work in English must be varied. It is not wise to devote a full period to only reading or writing. Fifteen- or twenty-

---

[11] The Judy Co., Minneapolis, Minn., produces these devices.

minute activities should be set up. Moreover, each day's work must be a unit so that little carry-over is required. The teacher must realize that the children will not necessarily know tomorrow what he has carefully taught them today.

English, generally speaking, is of concern to the non-academic pupils. They are eager to learn to read, not because of reading *per se*, but because they want to be successful in an important school activity. They work hard and quietly during periods devoted to the language arts when the teacher sets up routines for them and adapts his instruction to their levels of ability.

If the group is on a somewhat higher level of ability or is more mature, language arts experiences need to be varied from day to day. Routines are not so necessary. Each kind of activity can be longer and the number in any period can be reduced as children learn to concentrate for longer spans. If they have books that they can read, individual attention can be given to small groups during a half hour spent with books. It should always be followed by discussion of the stories that are of interest to the class. Attention to problems of human relations in the stories will help pupils to think through their own difficulties as they identify with one or another of the characters.

Even slow-learning children need to learn what is going on in the world around them. One of the most successful ways of teaching current affairs is through the use of newspapers, radio, and television.

All groups of retarded children can well spend a period several times a week on current events. Social studies of the traditional variety are beyond their ability and bore them. Their records are full of failures in civics, history, and geography. This is inevitable because they cannot read the textbooks, they cannot formulate concepts of distance in time or space, and their primary interests and problems are in the here and now. Things that are remote from their experience, distant goals, and abstract ideals are impossible for them to understand. Yet they will learn if the teacher makes use of many direct experiences planned around problems that are of immediate concern to them. Pupil-teacher planning must be on a somewhat primitive level, and committee work that requires research in books and highly developed pupil leadership will not succeed. Finished reports and complex culminating activities cannot be expected.

To be slow-learning does not mean that an individual is less able than others to enjoy emotional experience. Moreover, such children are not separated from others in their homes or leisure time activities, nor will they live in segregated groups as adults. It is essential, therefore, that they be placed in heterogeneous groups for all learning experiences that involve appreciation and creative activity in art, music, the dance, work with materials, and dramatics. They do not differ in the ability to love the rhythm of poetry, the beauty of words, and the imagery of description when the frustration of grappling with the abstractions of grammar, the analysis of good usage, and the dullness of obscure meanings are removed.

Knowing what to do and how to do it, so that the mentally underprivileged children in all the junior high schools will grow and develop, is one of the most difficult of the challenges that face the school. It requires the creation of a school climate and learning experiences that will give non-readers the chance to grow toward normal adulthood. It involves the development of methods and course content which will enable the pupils to learn at first hand what democracy means. This may mean re-examination of policies and practices of segregation, for through them children suffer loss of self respect and equality of status.

Dr. Ross L. Finney said, ". . . to select the duller children . . . segregate them from the brighter half, and deprive them of imitative participation in the study of the arts, the sciences, and the new humanities, is a formula for creating a caste stratified society. And the more scientifically accurate the selection the more deadly the results."[12]

Learning Activities for Members of A Pre- or In-Service Teacher Education Class

Besides reading do some of the following:

1. Analyze an intelligence test to determine whether or not it is fair. Try to change some of the questions so that they reflect the words and experiences that are common to both lower and upper class children.

---

[12] Ross L. Finney, *A Sociological Philosophy of Education.* New York: Macmillan, 1928, page 409.

2. Write plans for a learning experience in such a way that both verbal and non-verbal children will learn.

3. Discuss learning experiences such as a trip, an interview, a speaker, making a chart, doing an illustration, role playing, holding a discussion.

4. Visit a group of superior students, and a low ability group. Talk with some of them about their feelings to the group, to lower ability groups, to themselves.

5. Interview a psychiatrist, a parent, a business executive, or a social worker on the subject of ability grouping and its effects on personality.

References

BOOKS

Abraham, W., *Common Sense About Gifted Children.* New York: Harper and Brothers, 1958.

Ginzberg, Eli, *The Negro Potential.* New York: Columbia University Press, 1956.

National Society of the Study of Education, *Education for the Gifted.* 57th Year Book, Part II, 1958.

PERIODICALS

Abramson, D. A., "Effectiveness of Grouping for Students of High Ability," *Educational Research Bulletin,* October, 1959.

Bettelheim, Bruno, "Segregation New Style," *The School Review,* Autumn, 1958.

Bish, C. E., "Teaching the Upper 15%," *Clearing House,* May, 1959.

Boyer, L. E., "Provisions for the Slow Learner," *Mathematics Teacher,* April, 1959.

Dunn, L. M., "The Slow Learner," *N.E.A. Journal,* October, 1959.

Kvaraceus and Dolphin, "Selected References from the Literature on Exceptional Children," *The Elementary School Journal,* April, 1958.

Liddle, G. P., "An Experimental Program for Slow Learning Adolescents," *Educational Leadership,* December, 1959.

Mann, M., "What Does Ability Grouping Do to the Self-Concept?" *Childhood Education,* April, 1960.

Mingoia, E., "Improving the Reading of Academically Untalented Students," *The English Journal,* February, 1960.

Passow and Goldberg, "Study of Underachieving Gifted," *Educational Leadership,* November, 1958.

"The Academically Talented," *School and Society,* April 12, 1959.

PART
FOUR

Resource Materials for the
Teacher

CHAPTER SIXTEEN

Glossary of Terms

The terms that are used in connection with curriculum development are rarely clearly defined and used consistently throughout the country. Some of them have different meanings yet are used interchangeably. It remains for each group of people to decide on which term they prefer and to apply it to their own program. The following statements illustrate this confusion but, in the main, develop the concepts involved.

The Junior High School. This is the *intermediate school* which is designed to carry the pupil over from the content and techniques that are typical of the elementary school to those which characterize the senior high school. For this reason, in many instances, it does not have a unified program. The seventh and eighth grades resemble the elementary school and the ninth grade is like the senior high school. As junior high schools modernize their curriculums they ought to move in the direction of a program suited to their specific needs.

The school usually includes grades seven, eight, and nine. This varies, however, in accordance with population trends and the belief that only in the senior high school can students be properly prepared to do senior high school work. In some places only grades seven and eight are included. In a few places where emphasis is placed on "terminal" education for the less gifted pupils, the grades may run up to tenth. There is a trend at present to retain seventh graders in the elementary school because of their lack of maturity. In many six-year secondary schools, grades seven, eight, and nine are called the Junior High School, are taught by a separate staff, and have graduation exercises at the end of the ninth year, even though the children continue to attend the same school for the tenth year.

In many school districts and in cities in which there are not a sufficient number of real junior high schools to take care of all the children, seventh and eighth grades are retained in the elementary school buildings. In some of these the classes are scheduled to upper floors or separate wings, have a departmentalized program and some activities, and are called the Junior High School.

Curriculum *is the sum total of all the experiences that are provided by the school for its students.* After-school activities and even home assignments are properly considered part of the curriculum.

Curriculum Development or Change is the process that goes on at all times throughout the public schools. It takes place in the classroom whenever the teacher moves away from inadequate practices and content in the direction of meeting the needs of today's children as they live in today's world. Much of this change is stimulated by modern curriculum guides furnished to the teachers by curriculum departments of the state or local district.

The process of curriculum development takes place outside of the classroom in meetings of study groups and committees called into being for the purpose. Conferences, institutes, conventions, and workshops attended by citizens, teachers, administrators, and professors of education are frequently involved in the development of policies and practices of modern education.

Curriculum change is concerned with the structure of the school day, the content of all the parts of the program, techniques, materials, buildings, teacher competencies, and professional education.

Core Curriculum or Program is frequently used interchangeably with the terms *Common Learnings, Social Living,* and *General Education.* There is a common basic philosophy involved when they are applied to the junior high school. In general they all are used to refer to *the kind of school organization in which the students spend a block of time every day with one teacher.* The time exceeds the regular period. In some schools it is nearly all of the day, in others it is half of the day and in still others it is about one third of the day. The Core teacher is responsible in most cases for the record keeping and guidance of the pupils in the class. He is also responsible for those learnings which children have in common.

Core Content is also the content that is usually included in classes which are called Common Learnings or General Education or Social Living. The most acceptable outline of these common needs includes:

Personal problems and adjustments (individual guidance).
Problems of inter-personal and inter-group nature (human relations and group guidance).
General information about the natural environment (science).
The information, understanding, appreciations, and skills required for *effective citizenship in our democracy,* also the study of current social issues and current affairs (social studies).
The use and development of the language arts (English).
Participation in school affairs and government and in celebrations (sometimes called "parallel activities").
In some schools the Core includes mathematics and health education. The facilities of the building, the competencies of the teachers, and the

desires of the community are factors which enter into the determination of what is to be included in the Core.

Units of Learning are sometimes called *teaching units* or *units of work.* They are of two different kinds depending upon the approach and emphasis and the character of the learning activities. The more traditional type which is often used in departmentalized subjects is called the "subject matter unit." The more modern type which is more apt to be cooperatively chosen and planned in the classroom and in which the emphasis is on pupil needs and growth, is called "the experience unit." The unit of learning replaces the traditional logical outline of content which was characteristic of the course of study.

The unit is planned around a question or a problem which is often called the "Center of Interest." Once this has been determined, content can be developed in answer to the question "What do we need to know to answer that question, or solve that problem?" The answers to the next question, "How shall we proceed to get the information we need?" set up the learning activities. The methods used to mobilize information and express the learnings that are accomplished include research, discussions, trips, interviews, speakers, construction, group work, collection, exhibition, art work, music, dancing, films, radio, television, recordings, dramatics, experiments, creative writing, reporting, games, parties, programs, keeping records, testing and evaluating, and others that are devised by creative teachers and pupils.

Resource Unit *is a reference book for teachers.* It consists of material that is as comprehensive and complete as possible and that has been drawn from all the pertinent areas of subject matter. It is organized around a central idea or theme or title or problem or topic. In the best resource units there are sections dealing with pupils' concerns, goals to be set up, outcomes to be achieved, information enough to provide the teacher with background and facts for the pupils, references to be consulted by teachers as well as those which the children might be expected to use, a survey of all kinds of possible activities, and suggestions for tests, inventories, and other evaluation devices. All of the material is in maximum amounts and is unrelated to the specific needs of any particular group of children. For these reasons it cannot be given to children to use nor can the teacher use it as his teaching plan.

Unit Teaching includes the use of subject matter units in traditional classrooms as well as the planning of experience units in the modern school. It usually *refers to the kind of classroom work in which emphasis is placed on meeting the needs of the (individual) children through the provision of many and varied learning activities which cut across subject matter lines.* Pupils have the opportunity to experience integrated learning and to practice the necessary skills in situations that are meaningful to them.

Pupil-Teacher planning *is a teaching technique that enables both the students and the teacher to raise questions and problems around which teaching-learning situations are to be developed.* Decisions are made, preferably by consensus, as to which question or problem is of immediate significance. The necessary content is developed and appropriate learning activities are planned. Responsibilities are allocated and sub-groups or committees are formed. *This technique provides ample opportunity for the practice of planning, critical thought, cooperative enterprise, pooling information and thinking in discussions, the exercise of wise choice and sound judgment, and constant evaluation.*

Common Learnings is the name often given to the Core class or its content. The term is used to designate *the unspecialized knowledge and understandings which are required in common by all citizens in our democratic society to enable them to live together effectively, regardless of origins, goals, and individual differences.* It is usually associated with unit teaching in long blocks of time rather than with a set of required departmentalized subjects. In some schools this type of curriculum is offered only to pupils of low ability. This has served to bring the term into disrepute there and elsewhere.

General Education *is the term most frequently used to designate the subjects which are required of all students.* These used to be called the "constants." When the term first came into use it meant the same thing that is now meant by Common Learnings, Social Living, or Core. In some schools this is the name given to the curriculum which has no specific objectives in view and is usually elected by students with lower abilities.

Life Adjustment Education has been popularized by the fact that it was developed by a committee who related it directly to the needs of youth. For the most part it is *used in reference to the more practical parts of the curriculum and to plans for cooperative work and study developed for older adolescents.* Included in the recommendations of the committee who developed it are plans for a core class in which common learning units are programmed.

Social Living is another name used in some schools to indicate the core class. It is important to realize that in such a program *the word "social" becomes associated with organized life in a civilized society rather than with parties and entertainment.*

The Needs Theory and Approach involves the teacher in *study of the child, of his growth and development, of emotional needs, of the effects of failure to meet needs, of diagnosis and removal of blocks to learning, of appropriate content and techniques.* Among the important factors in this are human relations, the use of rewards and punishments, the implications of social class for the teacher, understanding the role of cultural expectations in learning, identification of values.

Developmental Tasks *are the jobs that the individual must accomplish as he grows and develops.* They vary according to the stage of maturity. In early adolescence (the junior high school years), stated in the briefest form, they are:

Emancipation from adults.

Making heterosexual adjustments.

Understanding and finding a role in the social culture.

Deciding upon an occupational goal and developing the necessary understandings, appreciations, and skills to get, hold, and advance in a job (vocational competency).

Social Needs *include knowledge about and understanding of problems connected with the dynamic processes of life in a civilized community:*

Group life in all of its ramifications.

Democratic government and way of life.

The environment—control over nature (science).

Building a basis for international peace.

Inter-personal relationships.

Sociometrics *includes understanding of, measuring, diagnosing, and making graphic representations of inter-personal relations in a group of people.* The group of age mates is called the peer group. Among the instruments that have been devised to reveal the facts about these relationships are social distance scales, interviews, the open question, and the "Wishing Well." The sociogram is the graphic representation of the forces that operate in the group.

Human Relations Education *includes both content and techniques for the study of inter-personal and inter-group relations*—those which make for harmony and the good life as well as those which cause tension and conflict. This is not another subject to be added to the curriculum but rather an approach and techniques that pervade every part of it. Increased sensitivity to children and their needs is essential to accomplish the objectives. Basic changes are required in order to arrange for children to be with at least one teacher long enough to be known to him as a person. Classroom activities that permit children to be with each other long enough to know each other and to interact as they work and play together, must be devised.

Inter-group of Intercultural Education is the term that was used before Human Relations became popular. It has, however, a more limited meaning and is reserved for the *content and activities that have to do with inter-group relations. The concepts of human similarities, the value of differences, and cultural pluralism are basic to the work.* In schools, emphasis is placed on direct experiences which give children the chance to live, work, and play together regardless of differences in religious, racial, and ethnic backgrounds. Through such experiences it is expected that children will develop the tools and the skills that are needed to resolve human conflicts and alleviate tensions.

Evaluation is a broad concept that includes more than the traditional testing programs and the calculation of marks to be placed on report cards. It is now thought of as a *program involving the pupils in self evaluation experiences as well as the use of all kinds of measuring and recording devices.* In the regular daily and weekly work of the classroom, short and long, essay and objective tests and quizzes are devised and administered in order to measure progress, judge growth, determine weakness, and plan remedial and developmental teaching-learning experiences. Frequent discussions of small and large groups are devoted to evaluation of the individuals and the group, of progress, of process, of products, and of leadership and followership activities. Charts and graphs of accomplishments are kept by the pupils and the teacher. Anecdotal records of what individual children say and do and of the reactions of others to them are kept by the teacher and used as the basis for determining growth in the less tangible areas of thought skills, human relations, appreciations, and attitudes.

The evaluation program of a school also includes *research into the effectiveness of the total program in accomplishing the goals that the faculty, pupils, and community set up.* In order to achieve the outcomes for which they are intended, the evaluation activities must be continuous, cooperative and constructive.

CHAPTER SEVENTEEN

Resource Unit Outlines

Outline for Resource Unit on Juvenile Delinquency

Pupils are Concerned:

1. With keeping out of trouble.
2. About getting along at home with parents, brothers and sisters, aunts and uncles, and grandparents.
3. About what to do with leisure time.
4. About the indifference and/or hostility of neighbors, parents, society in general, and potential delinquents.
5. About people they know who are criminal.
6. About money—how to earn it and how to spend it.
7. About family life.
8. About the effects of heredity.
9. About the choice of friends and how to keep out of "bad company."
10. With self-knowledge—their own feelings of guilt and hatred.
11. With what is right and wrong—with spiritual values, judgments, morals, ethics, and relative values.
12. With the conflict between their desires and the possibility of fulfilling them.

Possible Outcomes:

It is important for children to understand the necessity for finding out the causes which drive some people to do things of which others disapprove. They also need to know how folkways and group mores come to be and how they differ in the various classes in our society. They may be able to understand social mobility and its implications for them and for American life.

Pupil Goals:

1. To learn facts.
2. To do something at once that will help them to keep out of trouble.
3. To change their own and other people's wrong attitudes by spreading information.
4. To help some child in need.

Content:

This can be developed only after the group has formed a central question and defined its specific goals. The elements to be included will easily be identified as the pupils answer the question, "What do we need to find out in order to answer our question (or to solve our problems) and to accomplish our goals?"

In general, the following content outline will contain what is likely to arise. No group should attempt to do all that is here.

1. Cause of delinquency—contributing factors:
   a. Lack of affectional and/or economic security—rejection, broken homes, unemployment.
   b. Money.
   c. Housing.
   d. Heredity—mental illness.
   e. Conflict between adolescents and adults.
   f. Lack of satisfactory leisure time facilities and activities.
   g. Effect of movies, radio, television, comics, pulp magazines, modern advertising.
   h. Inadequate schools and inability of schools to meet individual needs.
   i. Influence of older criminals and delinquents.
   j. Need for adventure.
2. Problems of group life—attitudes and actions that grow out of class and caste differences, discrimination, customs, needs, desires, way of life.
3. Various standards and patterns of rights and wrongs—religious, moral, ethical.
4. Measures taken by society to prevent delinquency—education, laws, police departments, systems of justice, courts, probation, parole, penalties, community facilities, youth organizations—clubs, leagues, sports, teams.
5. Social agencies that can be called upon for help.
6. Penal institutions—location, organization, activities, costs, treatments.
7. Costs of destruction of life and property and of the processes of justice and treatment—who pays and how.

Activities:

Only those should be used by a teacher which in some way further the accomplishment of the goals set up by his particular group.
1. Call in speakers and consultants and send committees out to interview: laymen, lawyers, judges, magistrates, members of crime prevention associations, Chief of Police, policeman, member of department of public safety, probation officer, school counselor, school disciplinarian, social service agencies, leaders of youth groups and of recreational agencies and organizations, ministers.

2. Make surveys. This is an important activity. It brings out the facts. Large graphs, charts, picto-graphs can be made of the findings. These can be used in a culminating activity and presented to the school for the use of other classes.
3. Preparation for speakers and interviews includes:
    a. Telephoning—deciding what to say, how to begin, voice control, writing out the questions and directions that may be needed, practicing.
    b. Deciding what is to be included, making up adequate questions to be asked, deciding what records are to be kept.
    c. Selecting, commissioning, organizing the committees.
    d. Practicing the roles to be played.
    e. Writing thank you notes and "fan mail."
    f. Follow-up discussions.
    g. Dramatizing the experiences for the benefit of others.
4. Presentation of factual information gained through research activities:
    a. Round table and panel discussions.
    b. Dramatics.
    c. Pictures, maps, graphs.
    d. Vocabulary tests and factual quizzes.
5. Committee meetings—planning of content, activities, reports, pooling findings.
6. Trips:
    a. To juvenile and other courts.
    b. To recreation centers and boys' clubs.
    c. To local police stations and magistrate courts.
    d. To seat of local government.
    e. To local house of detention or correction.
7. Gathering materials—books, newspapers, pamphlets, recordings, films, film strips, lists of resource people and places; sorting, classifying, filing materials for pupil and teacher use.
8. Literature reading and discussion—analysis of detective stories, human relations in books, analysis of comics, biographies.
9. Examination of individual programs of leisure time activities.
10. Beginning hobbies and trying out new cultural experiences.
11. Developing and carrying out plans to make unused neighborhood recreational resources usable by helping to man them, getting parents to serve as volunteers, making needed toys and games in the shops, repairing broken equipment, clearing a vacant lot for play space, making up bulletins for distribution to the children and parents of the community *re* what is available and what is needed.
12. Providing a tool lending "library" and kits for children who need them. Art materials and equipment can be handled in the same way.
13. Making and carrying out plans to give security and recognition to isolates.
14. Planning and organizing parents' meetings to discuss such matters as hours for children to be home at night, dating, parties, movies, allowances, smoking, summertime activities.

15. Organizing volunteer committees to serve in local child-caring agencies, hospitals, settlement houses.

Evaluation:

This must be included in the daily and weekly plans as well as in whatever culminating activities are used. Methods include:
1. Factual quizzes—written and oral.
2. Questionnaires—social distance scales, attitude inventories, interest survey.
3. Discussions of strength and weakness of the unit, of the processes used, of the group and individual accomplishments, of planning, judgment, actions.
4. Making up of individual rating cards and growth charts in respect to facts learned, vocabulary, increase in social sensitivity, social skills, thought skills.

Note—The following questions can be used to stimulate and direct evaluation discussions:

1. What does the unit "add up to"?
2. Did we accomplish our individual and group goals—if not why not?
3. Was this a good unit? What made it so satisfying?
4. What did we do well? What was poorly done?
5. What did you as an individual contribute to the group?
6. Was group work successful?
7. Were leaders well chosen? How do you know? Were they successful?
8. Were you a satisfactory follower or leader?
9. What were the mistakes we made? Can we avoid them in the future?
10. What do we need to know more about?
11. In the light of our needs what do we do next?

Action Activities:

1. Clean up a vacant lot and make it into a tot-lot.
2. Organize a ball game league.
3. Create a social service club for the neighborhood.
4. Get some new week-end activities under way. This may require organizing tool lending libraries, lending musical instruments, providing home art supplies, forming hiking clubs and getting adults to sponsor them, teaching new party games, making simple refreshments for parties.
5. Help each child to begin a new hobby.
6. Make a survey and publish the information so that everyone will know what agencies are available in the neighborhood from which help can be obtained.
7. Find part time jobs for those who need them, volunteer work for those who do not need money returns or are too young to work.

8. Do something to help a member of the class who needs it.
9. Write letters to former classmates who may have been placed in corrective institutions.

Outline for Resource Unit on Democracy

Concerns of children that were evidenced by their questions as they identified themselves with the problem:
1. Do we have democracy in this country?
2. What is our obligation in regard to the preservation of democracy?
3. What are our responsibilities? Our parents' responsibilities?
4. What are our rights and privileges?
5. Can we keep democracy? What threatens it? (There is real anxiety here.)
6. How does democracy work?
7. What are the ways of life and government in other lands?
8. How did we get democracy? How is it that other people didn't get it?
9. Why are we told one thing in school, only to find that it isn't like that in the community? Is anything wrong with democracy? Can it be improved?
10. Can we spread democracy all over the world? Should we?
11. Suppose we lose democracy? What then?
12. Are people born equal? What is meant by equal?

Goals:

Only those should be included in any teaching unit that are realizable by the specific group that is undertaking the work. Among those usually identified by pupils are:
1. To get understanding and appreciation.
2. To increase knowledge, to get facts and information.
3. To become a more democratic person and group.
4. To *do* something to:
   a. Lesson prejudice.
   b. Spread information about democracy to others, even to other lands.
   c. Influence others.
   d. Get action through democratic processes in order to make life better.

Content:

The specific content material to be included must be determined in the classroom in accordance with the concerns expressed by the children and with the goals they set up. As soon as a central question or problem has been defined, the question "What do we need to know to answer that question (or solve that problem)?" can be asked. It then serves as the guide line in the development of content. The factual material needed will be found in the following suggestions:

1. Meaning of terms and concepts:
   Freedom, four freedoms, free enterprise, liberty, democracy, socialism, communism, collectivism, capitalism, totalitarianism, monarchy, autocracy, republic, politics, political party, structure of society, social class, discrimination, prejudice, equality.
2. Important documents—Declaration of Independence, Bill of Rights, Constitution, Magna Carta, pacts, treaties, Gettysburg Address, Washington's Address, Emancipation Proclamation, Monroe Doctrine.
3. History—the story of the United States, historical facts of other lands that have a relationship to the problem.
4. Struggles of mankind for liberty—wars, great movements.
5. Democratic processes—voting, compromise, consensus, lobby, referendum, congressional investigation.
6. Democratic practices in the school, the community, the state, the nation.
7. How ideas are spread and opinions are formed—propaganda, the press, radio, television, films, conversation, conference, debate, discussions, lectures, books.
8. Structure and functions of government.
9. Weaknesses in our present way of life.
10. Strength of our present way of life, why we like it. Our rights, privileges, responsibilities.
11. Contrasts with other ways of life and government.
12. Existing threats—what is being done about them. What each of us must do to preserve and improve democracy.

Activities:

The teacher must survey his own situation before planning with his class. Activities must be within the range of ability, and accord with the facilities at his command. Most of what can be done will be found in the following list:

1. Make plans and carry them out.
2. Read for research and pleasure—books, both text and literature; newspapers, magazines, pamphlets.
3. Write—reports, reviews, scripts, stories, letters, experiences, poems, plans, radio programs, quizzes, tests.
4. Listen to radio programs, television programs, recordings, lectures, discussions, panels.
5. Conduct and participate in discussions—class, group, committee, symposiums, panels, round tables.
6. Invite speakers, prepare for them—questions, phone calls, letters of invitation and thanks.
7. Secure and show and see films—analyze them, pre-view them, criticize

them, discuss, write about them, write sequences for them, photograph a prepared sequence.
8. Collect pictures and clippings—file for reference, post for bulletin board displays.
9. Keep records of: facts learned; what the individual read and thought about it; people who were consulted, what they said and what the individual thought about it; radio programs heard, what was said and what was thought about it; places visited and what was seen there; films seen and what they were about; questions raised and the answers found; plans made and how they were carried out; evaluations.
10. Action projects—anything that can be done to better life in the school. If possible a neighborhood or community social action project should be tried.
11. Send individuals and/or committees to interview people in the community—politicians, government officials, citizens. Prepare for these carefully and for the reports of them.
12. Trips to places of historical significance and to political or governmental agencies; to libraries to see documents; to museums—both historical and art; to centers of government—local, state, national; to courts; to polling places at elections.
13. Dramatizations—stage plays, socio-dramas, psycho-dramas; write, produce, act in them.
14. Illustrations—collect pictures; produce murals; do individual work in paint, clay, and other art media.

Evaluation:

Throughout the unit there is the necessity of remembering that complete answers to most of the questions cannot be found, and that the maturity level of the students will condition the extent of information to be required and the depth of understanding that can be expected. Evaluation must be continuous, cooperative, and constructive. It should always be based upon the objectives set up. The following techniques can be used effectively:
1. Write and give short and long tests on the factual material in the unit. These can be varied so as to include essay type, objective, written, oral.
2. Discuss strengths and weaknesses of pupil leaders, group actions and processes, individual and group controls, individual and group products.
3. Arrange for personal and teacher evaluation of self-products, growth.
4. Keep anecdotal records which describe behavior so that growth and change in attitudes, habits, appreciations, judgment, choice, etc., can be measured.

Outline for Resource Unit on Government

Pupil Concerns:

1. Lack of knowledge about:
   a. The Constitution, the local government, politics, election procedures, costs.
   b. The separation of government from the people.
   c. Who is the government.
   d. What should government do.
   e. Difference between what the law says and the way it is carried out.
   f. Relation between government and labor—the problem of strikes.
   g. How the government functions in international affairs.
   h. Social action—how to get things done—better street lighting, garbage collection, etc.
   i. Why the schools can't get more money.
   j. Who determines real estate values.
2. Methods that can be used to get pupils to recognize their needs; arouse their interests; to learn through direct experience; to impart information to others:
   a. Housing—walk in the neighborhood; visit a housing project; see a building development; send a committee to a local housing authority; get a speaker to tell about the laws governing rooming houses; visit a slum area and a re-development project.
   b. The high cost of living—visit a large market or store; send a committee to the tax office; fill out various types of income tax forms; get speaker to talk about rent control; keep records of household expenditures for a week; get information from school office concerning requisitions for several past years.
   c. Government services for protection of citizens—visit local police station and nearby fire house; send committees to visit and interview chief of police, sheriff, fire marshal; call in probation officer as speaker; visit local sanitation department, purification of water department, weather bureau; make surveys on trash and garbage collection days.
   d. Politics—arrange for interviews of ward leaders, committeemen, representatives to state and national legislatures; visit local party headquarters; learn to operate voting machines; visit polling places on election days; listen to campaign speeches in person, on radio and recordings; dramatize political conventions; review and if necessary revise school government constitution, organization, practices.
   e. Government organization—visit local, state, national seats of government; send committees to sit in at meetings of local departments, committees, commissions, hearings; participate in programs for "I Am An American Day" and other patriotic com-

munity celebrations; secure government officials as speakers; see
films put out by FBI; visit government buildings—post office, mint,
federal court.

Activities:

These are especially designed for gathering information and securing
understandings.
1. Collect and display pictures, charts, maps, graphs which may arouse
   curiosity, raise questions, supply information.
2. Make and display charts, illustrations, models, maps, graphs.
3. Test—construct, administer, mark, interpret both pre-tests and after
   tests to determine the pre-study levels and the extent of accomplishment and growth in information, attitudes, appreciations.
4. Browse through illustrated materials dealing with government, community planning, civil liberties, housing.
5. Secure and see films.
6. Secure and listen to recordings.
7. Discuss news articles appearing in the daily press; also editorials.
   Get the facts needed in connection with current affairs from all kinds
   of sources—books for those who can read, people and pictures for
   those who cannot read.
8. Re-live experiences in dramatic form.
9. Express ideas, emotions, learnings in art form.

Content:

What pupils need to know will depend upon the approach they select,
the major problems defined as the center of interest, the questions formulated by the group, and the goals they set up. Most of what they want
to know and can understand is included in the following suggestions:
1. Names of high officials currently in office.
2. Examination of and familiarity with the Constitution of the United
   States.
3. The structure of the federal, state, and local governments.
4. The Bill of Rights.
5. What an amendment to the Constitution is and how it is made.
6. Examination of local and state charters.
7. Government departments, organizations and services and how they
   reach into the individual's life.
8. Costs of government, who pays and how.
9. Government employees—the civil service system.
10. Types of taxes levied, budgets, methods of collection, departments
    and local tax offices.
11. Social security.
12. Governmental social and health services.
13. How the public school system came to be and how it is supported.
14. The school code.

15. How to secure action through governmental processes.
16. Lobbies and pressure groups—how they operate and why.
17. Law enforcement.
18. Social lag.
19. Weaknesses of our government and what is being done to correct them.
20. The strength of our form of government.
21. Relation between politics and government.

Outline for Resource Unit on Russia

Pupil Concerns:

1. Fears—of war, of Russians (a "fierce, conquering people"), of differences, of communism.
2. Adventure and romance.
3. Name calling and witch hunting.
4. Propaganda.
5. Atomic war.
6. Control of space.

Goals Pupils Usually Set Up:

1. To get information.
2. To help to allay their own fears and those of other people.
3. To be able to join adult conversations.
4. To understand our own as well as other forms of society.
5. To increase enthusiasm for and loyalty to the United States and Democracy.
6. To be on guard against subversive influences.

Approaches That Can Be Used:

1. How do the Russian people live, so far as we know, and why do they live that way?
2. What has been tried to improve relations with Russia?
3. What is American policy with respect to Russia?
4. Of what importance is Russia to the world, to the U.S.A., to us?
5. What is the hold that Russia has on the peace and security of the world? How does that affect us?
6. How does the Russian way of life compare with ours?
7. How can we combat communism in the United States?
8. Must the United States and Russia be friends? Can they be? Under what circumstances?
9. What was Russia's part in World War II?
10. What was Russia's role in Korea?
11. What is the meaning of "balance of power"?

12. What is Sputnik? Of what importance was it to America?
13. What is the present state of affairs between Russia and the U.S.A. with respect to control of nuclear weapons?
14. What is "cold war"?

Content:

1. History—the Tsars, the Russian Revolution.
2. Russia's role in World Wars I and II.
3. Russia's "Five Year Plans."
4. Communism in contrast to Capitalism.
5. Russia's way of life.
6. Russia's actions in the United Nations.
7. Russian leaders.
8. The possibility that Russia can become the greatest nation.
9. Population and resources.
10. The role of propaganda in and out of the U.S.S.R.
11. What can be done to prevent war with Russia?
12. Russia's plan for world domination.
13. Tito, Stalin, Khrushchev.
14. China and Russia.
15. Korea and Russia.
16. Russia in Germany.
17. Russia and atomic energy.
18. India and Russia.
19. Russia, the United States and space.

Activities:

1. Reading for facts—books, magazines, newspapers, pamphlets.
2. Radio programs.
3. Speakers obtained from U.N. Councils, universities, refugee groups, international institutions, veterans.
4. Conducting a classroom—Russian style.
5. Films, film strips, slides.
6. Dramatizations—preparation for them, production, writing.
7. Attending adult meetings, lectures, conferences, study groups.
8. Going to a Russian restaurant, art museums, commercial museums.
9. Listening to some Russian music.
10. Learning some Russian words and expressions.
11. Reading some stories and poems written by Russian authors.
12. Writing letters for information, materials, invitations to speakers, thank you notes.
13. Keeping records of the unit:
    a. What I heard and what I thought about it—speakers, radio.
    b. What I saw—places, things, films, pictures.
    c. What I read—books, poetry, news items, editorials, pamphlets, propaganda.

   d. New words and terms I learned.
   e. Questions that were raised and their answers.
   f. Charts, maps, graphs.
14. Making, collecting, filing maps and charts.
15. Doing art work using Russian art motifs, murals, illustrations.
16. Making bulletin board displays.
17. Making a "Five Day Plan" and find out the effect of such a device on you.
18. Committee work.
19. Sending for new materials, sort, and classify them for class use and for the library.
20. Learning some folk dances.
21. Conducting a trial—Russian style; American style.

Culminating Activities:

1. Tell others what was learned by writing letters, organizing a speaker's bureau, presenting materials gathered.
2. Plan and give an assembly program for the school, for a parents' meeting.
3. Have a final discussion meeting to sum up what was done and what it all meant to the pupils.
4. Have an exhibit of art work, souvenirs, written work, bulletin board displays, posters, graphs.

Evaluation:

Quiz, attitude tests, information tests, discussion of strengths and weaknesses of the unit, of the group work, of individual accomplishment, of leaders. Evaluation discussions should not be left for the last but should occur at intervals throughout the unit.

Outline for Resource Unit on Propaganda

Pupil Concerns:

1. What is true and how can I find out?
2. What is right?
3. What is wholesome?
4. How can I better myself?
5. How can I recognize propaganda?
6. How are ideas spread?
7. Does the law protect us?

Goals and Objectives:

1. To learn to distinguish between right and wrong in what is seen and heard and read.

2. To learn to choose wisely.
3. To learn to think critically.
4. To learn to talk effectively.
5. To develop critical attitudes towards the newspapers, films, radio, television, magazines, comics.
6. To learn to "read" advertisements.
7. To learn the devices of propaganda and how to use them.
8. To develop the habit of scrutinizing one's own speech and writing.

Content:

1. Meaning of Clyde R. Miller's, "an attempt to influence the thoughts, feelings, and actions of a person or group with reference to some predetermined end. That end may be good or bad."
2. General concept—intentional propagation or promotion.
3. Unfavorable aspects—anything the purposes of which are to hoodwink, lie, suppress truth, conceal, distort, exert pressures.
4. Favorable aspects—anything the purposes of which are to accept ideas in the interests of one's self or one's group, to convince about goodness such as the value of the individual or society. It replaces violence and censorship as methods of bringing about change. It replaces boycott, bribery, passive resistance.
5. Techniques—symbols such as words, word substitutes—graphs, pictographs, slogans, catchwords, songs, pictures, art, comics, cartoons, whispers, lobbies, pressures, emotional appeals.
6. Techniques—name calling, glittering generalities, testimonials, card stacking, getting on the band wagon.
7. Means—all the avenues of information are used for persuasion: suggestion, radio, speakers, comics, exhibits, spectacles, the press, person to person, rumors, pictures, parades, phone calling, telegrams, films, cartoons, graphs, songs.
8. Who uses propaganda techniques and devices:
   government agencies, politicians, teachers, distributors of goods and of ideas, any one with a cause.
9. How to detect propaganda—its characteristics:
   veiled promotion, direct promotion, half truth, whole truth, trickery, proof, appeal to reason, emotional appeal, symbols, logical appeal, reward promises, stereotypes, join the band wagon, use of big names, use of class values and social approval, promises, partial truth, confusion, distortion, appeals to such desires as: to get rich, to get married, to be loved, to be well, vanity, sex, fear, hatred, pride, antagonisms, class conflicts, caste differences, mob psychology.
10. Fields of use:
   to spread news, ideologies, ideas, sell goods used by governments, salesmen, politicians, political parties, educators, hate mongers, advertisers.

Activities:

1. Read, analyze, discuss, outline speeches made for and against any project, sales talks, advertising, slogans, songs.
2. Draw posters for and against a project, comics, cartoons, graphs, pictographs.
3. Look at and interpret pictures, graphs, maps, statistics.
4. Put on a campaign using propaganda techniques—an election in the school, a sale, a class activity, a drive.
5. Try a whispering game.
6. Use a "Rumor Clinic" device.
7. Write a sales talk, a radio plug, a song, a slogan, some speeches for and against.
8. Conduct a poll of opinion.
9. Make collections of songs, slogans, pictures, comics, graphs, pictographs in which the techniques and devices are clearly shown.

Evaluation:

1. Administer tests, before and after the unit, designed to show the pupils' ability to recognize techniques and devices.
2. Devise some experiences to use before and after which will show the pupils' ability to withstand pressures that are propagandistic.
3. Keep records that will show growth in the use of the ability to challenge statements that are made and to require facts for proof.
4. Look for increased use of argument rather than arguing.
5. Conduct discussions at intervals about strengths and weaknesses and values of the unit, of the individual's work, of the group processes and accomplishments.

Outline for Resource Unit on Human Relations

Approach: Almost any day in every junior high school classroom, there is some occurrence or the reflection of something that has happened outside of the school that can be used as the reason for beginning a discussion of Human Relations. No justification for it is needed. Every thinking person is aware of the fact that, to survive at all, man must learn those skills and attitudes which are the basis of good inter-group and inter-personal relations. Without them man cannot hope for the good life.

The approach to the specific unit in any class will be determined by the immediate necessity which calls it into being. The depth of exploration and the activities undertaken will depend upon the degree of maturity of the pupils. The content will differ widely as it is selected to fit the problem to be solved, the question to be answered, and the goals the children set up for themselves.

The following outline includes materials that will be appropriate for units dealing with inter-personal problems, inter-racial tensions, inter-faith understanding. The problem of internationalism would be a logical next step but has not been included, since it would constitute another resource unit in itself.

Pupils Express Their Concerns, anxieties, and problems in the following ways:

1. My parents don't understand me any more.
2. Will the gang jump me on the way home today?
3. Why don't the kids around here want to play with me? Don't they like me?
4. I'm afraid to go out at night in my neighborhood.
5. I can't get along with my teachers.
6. I'm afraid to go into that store; they won't wait on me or they may even put me out.
7. What's the use; I will never be able to get into medical college.
8. There's no use working hard; I'll never get the kind of job I want.
9. The white (colored, Christian, Jewish, Italian, etc.) kids get all the breaks around here.
10. You can't ever say what you think.

Inter-personal and Inter-group Differences which often seem to cause conflicts:

Color (race), religion, ethnic origin, social class, money, kind of clothing, manners and habits, language and speech, name calling even in fun, what is regarded as fun, degree of emancipation from adults, fundamental values, degree of maturity.

Actions and Reactions of Teachers and Children which call for close observation as factors which contribute to poor human relations:

1. Who gets most of the rewards (upper social class children)?
2. Who gets punished most frequently (lower social class children)?
3. Who gets chosen and who gets left out?
4. Who are usually selected as leaders by the teacher; by the pupils?
5. Which students make up the "in-group," which the "out-group"?
6. Who are the isolates; the fringers?
7. Who cooperates; who competes?
8. Who takes; who shares?
9. Who cries; who laughs?
10. Who dominates; who leads; who follows?
11. Who argues; who settles arguments?
12. Who creates conflicts; who resolves them?

Teacher Objectives:

1. To condition children to the world in which they live and to help them to make adjustments.
2. To give children insight into human motives and actions and to make them more socially sensitive.
3. To implement the democratic principle—"the worth and integrity of every human being"—to accept every child at his face value regardless of what makes him different.
4. To reduce his own emphasis and use of class differences as a basis for judging people.
5. To discover superior abilities in children regardless of class differences. To develop those children who have superior abilities and to make them known to other interested groups or individuals.
6. To provide for widespread participation in many diverse activities.

Objectives Shared by Pupils and Teacher:

1. To understand each other better.
2. To live and work together more happily and more successfully.
3. To learn that by sharing work more can be accomplished and can be done faster.
4. To improve in the skills of learning—reading, writing, listening, talking.
5. To learn more about the principles and practices, the meaning and processes of Democracy.
6. To learn about the ways in which other people worship God.
7. To understand adults and live more happily at home.
8. To make new friends.

Content:

1. Information about:
   a. The major races of the world.
   b. In what ways all people are alike.
   c. The major religions of the world.
   d. Religious similarities and differences.
   e. The ethnic groups that may be present in the school population and those that are in the current news.
   f. Contributions to civilization made by individuals and minority groups—to social progress, to science, art, literature, music, the dance, the theatre, education.
   g. Participation of minority groups in American wars.
2. Study and discussion of differences that matter in a person's life:
   a. Having insufficient money, not enough food.
   b. Being without a decent place to live.
   c. Not having a place to play.
   d. Lacking equal opportunities for education, work, recreation.
   e. Having a different system of values.

3. Study and discussion of differences that ought not to matter: facial features, kind of clothes, size, family income, neighborhood one lives in, kind of work one does so long as one does a good job and it is honest, color, religion, nationality, where one was born, who one's parents were or are.

[*The point of this is to get across the belief that a person is worthy in his own right and should be accepted for his own value.*]

Activities:

Socio- and psycho-dramatics[1]—acting out in several different ways, with several different outcomes any of the following situations and events or others that may be more pertinent:
1. What does or could happen when a substitute teacher comes.
2. A scene at home when permission to stay out later at night has to be requested of Father.
3. Trying to make friends with a child whose color or religion is different from yours.
4. Being on the street with the gang and having no place to play.
5. How a fight begins—slapping back and forth, name calling, whispering, borrowing money, bullying.
6. Being hungry and having no way to get dinner.
7. Wanting some new clothes for the party tomorrow and having no money.
8. A scene at home when Mother objects to your friends.
9. A scene at home when your allowance is all spent and you want some money.

Trips:

These should be arranged by pupil committees under the direction and guidance of the teacher:
1. To the churches of the major religions.
2. To the art museum to see religious pictures and pictures dealing with social problems.
3. To community organizations which deal with human relations—community councils, inter-faith councils, Human Relations Councils, Fellowship Houses, Fellowship Commissions.
4. To inter-faith and/or inter-racial meetings, and ceremonies.
5. Attending each other's Sunday school classes.
6. To settlement houses—especially those of other ethnic groups.
7. In large urban cities, to the districts in which ethnic groups live.

Speakers can be obtained from:

1. National Conference of Christian and Jews.
2. Anti-Defamation League of B'nai B'rith.

---

[1] See Helen Hall Jennings, *Sociometry in Group Relations.* Washington, D. C.: American Council on Education, revised edition, 1959.

3. Community Relations Councils.
4. National Association for the Advancement of Colored People.
5. Citizens in the community.
6. Parents.
7. Youth organizations.
8. Organizations devoted to mental health.
9. School counselors, principals, home visitors.
10. Social service agencies devoted to family relations.

Interviews can be arranged by individuals and/or committees with:

parents, neighbors, store keepers, heads of boys clubs, scout leaders, police and fire officials, trash collectors, mailmen, professionals, school officials, social service workers. The questions to be used, the methods of reporting back, and the evaluation of these experiences are all important activities.

Writing to Be Done:

1. Letters of invitation and of thanks to people who were involved as speakers, in interviews, or in making trips possible and successful.
2. Questions to be used at interviews, given to speakers, or used at the close of speakers' presentations.
3. Requests for materials.
4. Information quizzes—both questions and answers.
5. Stories, skits, poems, songs, slogans, editorials, anecdotes.
6. Intimate writings[2]—the open-end question to relieve emotions and describe personal experiences.

Reading:[3]

Story books, biographies, text books, poetry, history, plays, newspapers, magazines, pamphlets, science books, comics.

The human relations incidents and values in all of those which are fictional writings need to be analyzed. Causes, effects of human behavior can be learned from books if the pupils involved can read them. The important thing to do with comics and pulp magazines is to try to get the children to find out what the characters stand for as people, their value systems, and what is the meaning of their actions toward other people.

Music:

1. Learn folk songs of the several racial, religious, and ethnic groups under study.

---

[2] See Taba, et al., *Diagnosing Human Relations Needs.* Washington, D. C.: American Council on Education, 1951.

[3] See Taba, et al., *Reading Ladders for Human Relations.* Washington, D. C.: American Council on Education, 1947.

2. Learn some of the inter-group religious music—hymns and anthems.
3. Go to hear some of the important musicians, if they are available.
4. Listen to recordings of the music of the great masters of different groups.
5. Compose some music as individuals or as a group.

Posters:

1. Make up ideas for posters and paint them.
2. Use posters as the jump-off for discussions of the human relations situations they depict.
3. Place posters for display in the neighborhood stores.
4. Have a poster exhibition and contest.

Radio, Television, Recordings:

1. Set up committees with the responsibility of watching for appropriate programs.
2. Assign listening to programs for home work and plan to hear reports on them.
3. Secure recordings, play them as the lead into discussions of the problems they portray.
4. Make recordings of pupils' work: original plays, poems, speeches; evaluation of experiences, committee reports, discussions, etc.
5. Develop assembly programs which include the presentations of recordings made by the class, to the school for use of other classes.

Films:

1. Secure and show films on human relations problems. These can be secured from local offices of the Anti-Defamation League of B'nai B'rith, New York University, Ohio State University, and other Human Relations Centers.
2. Take the class to see appropriate commercial films currently being shown in the community.
3. Assign film viewing as homework. Teach film appreciation, criticism, and how to discuss the problems portrayed in them.

Evaluation:

1. Use social status and social distance scales to measure before and after reactions.
2. Make anecdotal records of what children say and do from which changes in superstitions, stereotypes, prejudices, conflicts, anxieties, self hatreds, hostilities can be determined.
3. Have group and class discussions of the value of the experiences the class has had.

Art:

1. Illustrations, murals, costumes, religious motifs.
2. Interpretation and appreciation of the great pictures of the world dealing with human relations.
3. Designs for back drops for plays and programs.
4. Designs for holiday wrappings, cards, and decorations.

Cooking:

1. Learn to make dishes that are characteristic of the various ethnic and culture groups.
2. Go together to have a meal in some of the specialized restaurants.

Dance:

1. Learn the folk dances of the various culture groups under consideration.
2. If possible go to see an interpretive dancer or see a film.

Action Projects:

1. Collect and exhibit articles of interest from various cultures.
2. Plan and carry out the plans for assembly programs combining the products of many of the learning activities mentioned here.
3. Develop speakers to carry the information and creative products to other classes, to other schools, to community organizations.
4. Interchange visits with a school of very different population.
5. Plan inter-group parties, hikes, camp week-ends.
6. Investigate discriminatory practices in recreation and in restaurants in the community and try to do something to better the relations and practices.
7. Determine the status of Fair Employment Practices in the community and of possible pending legislation, and plan whatever it is possible to do, to further such developments.

Approaches and Outcomes of Other Popular Units

Mental Health:

Approach:

"Many people we know are disturbed—some are really ill. What can we do to make sure that we stay well?"

Action outcomes:

1. Have each child break an undesirable habit.
2. Have each child form a new good habit.
3. Plan and carry out some way of getting some of the important learnings in the unit to parents—an assembly program, a speaker at an evening meeting, a film.
4. Have children examine and where necessary change their patterns of rest, exercise, eating, play.
5. Meet with pupils and their parents, if out-of-school loads are too heavy.
6. Have individual conferences which will give children a chance to unburden themselves of fears, anxieties, worries, guilt.
7. Older adolescents might undertake a service program in a local occupational therapy clinic.

Conservation:

Approach:

"How are the people of the world to be fed in face of increasing populations and diminishing topsoils?"

Action activities:

1. Collect available printed materials. Write a report using facts learned in the unit. Send them to a farmer in a backward area.
2. Collect money, earn some, too, and buy "Care Packages" for a school in China, a depleted European area, or a deprived American Indian group.
3. Organize and carry on a "Save Food" campaign in the school cafeteria or in the neighborhood.
4. Raise a vegetable garden.

Community:

Approach:

"Housing needs are acute. The neighborhood isn't desirable; we want to move and can't. What can we do to better the conditions?"

Action activities:

1. Organize and carry on a clean-up campaign in one street. If successful, spread it to other streets and the other classes in the school.
2. Set up a beautification project on the school grounds and/or in the neighborhood.
3. Find out about and join the American Friends Society Work-Camp movement.
4. Organize a cooperative squad to do a reconstruction job on a needy house in the neighborhood.

What New Pupils Need to Know (The Order Has No Significance)	Suggested Learning Experiences	Desired Outcomes	Outcomes Achieved (To Be Noted As They Appear)
Lavatories: Location Cleanliness Conservation of supplies Rules	Go to these rooms to see them and be able to find them on each floor Plan for self and group controls Discuss and learn rules	Health habits Care of property Control	
Lockers: Location Combination locks Where to put belongings How to avoid crowding Route to use at dismissal	Visit locker office Practice use of locks Go to lockers and put away clothes—practice all cautions Practice use of stairs and fire towers Practice getting clothes and putting them on outside of lockers Practice ways of avoiding overcrowding Discuss cleanliness	Freedom from fear Skill Speed Honesty Courtesy Safety	
Schedules (rosters) Areas of learning Time allotments	Make several copies Have one copy posted in the room	Freedom from fear Self confidence Promptness	

OUTLINE FOR ORIENTATION RESOURCE UNIT*

What New Pupils Need to Know (The Order Has No Significance)	Suggested Learning Experiences	Desired Outcomes	Outcomes Achieved (To Be Noted As They Appear)
How to get to school and home: Routes Money—car tickets Clothing needs for weather Safety hazards Conduct and behavior problems	Draw street and route maps Walk around to see safety hazards Inspect gardens of school and homes Interview car and bus conductors Have member of S.A. transportation committee in as speaker Learn about credit union visit office take out memberships elect representatives Make plans for sale of car and bus tickets Discuss clothing needs Learn about banking, elect bankers, begin accounts	Safety habits Self control Group control Promptness Freedom from fear Self confidence Self reliance Thrift Foresight Ability to plan Respect for property	

* Starred units were loaned to the Pennsylvania State Department of Education and appear in the Course of Study in the Social Studies, 1951.

What New Pupils Need to Know (The Order Has No Significance)	Suggested Learning Experiences	Desired Outcomes	Outcomes Achieved (To Be Noted As They Appear)
Lunch (cont'd) Time Menus—selection Disposal of dishes and waste	Send child to get menu each day Practice taking back dishes Practice getting ready for lunch Practice telling time Plan routes to be used and practice conduct on stairs and fire towers Practice proper table manners Discuss emergency borrowing and lending—credit union Elect officers and organize clean-up squads Walk over routes to be used to get to fountain, play areas, lavatories Call on sponsor of L. R. committee, S. A. chairman or S. A. sponsor Write letters to above	Cleanliness Health habits Promptness Safety Skills Better use of money Citizenship	

What New Pupils Need to Know (The Order Has No Significance)	Suggested Learning Experiences	Desired Outcomes	Outcomes Achieved (To Be Noted As They Appear)
Schedules (cont'd) Where to go and when Where to get information Where and when to find teacher	Discuss next day's schedule before leaving Make floor plans Take trips around building each day to locate next day's new rooms Learn to tell time Visit office to see school file of pupil and teacher rosters Assign helpers to those in need Select secretary to keep records for absentees Learn teacher's schedule of unassigned time Learn what to do, where, and when to go before School Calculate weekly time allotments	Understanding of program	
Lunch: Location of cafeteria Rules—traffic, cleanliness, safety	Go to cafeteria to practice all that is needed Visit change booth and practice orderly line, care of money	Freedom from fear Honesty Judgment Health	

What New Pupils Need to Know (The Order Has No Significance)	Suggested Learning Experiences	Desired Outcomes	Outcomes Achieved (To Be Noted As They Appear)
Isolation room: Location Forms to be used Consequences	Read and practice filling out forms to be used Visit the room Read and fill out a form Discuss behavior problems Discuss cooperation marks	Self control Judgment Freedom from fear	
Play spaces: Location Facilities Rules Time	Visit roof Go over the route to be used Organize for group control Assign time for use Discuss safety Discuss behavior	Freedom from fear Safety Courtesy Self and group control Responsibility Promptness	
Administration: Location of main office; or principal Names Relation to the pupil	Visit offices Be introduced to secretaries Learn location of roll books and phones Practice procedures for late arrival and early dismissal Write absence note form in note book.	Freedom from fear Security Social skills Understanding of school and its program	

What New Pupils Need to Know (The Order Has No Significance)	Suggested Learning Experiences	Desired Outcomes	Outcomes Achieved (To Be Noted As They Appear)
Assembly: Location Time Conducting the way Audience behavior Seats to be used Care of property Rules	Go to auditorium Find and occupy seats Discuss behavior Practice response to light signal Show what to do for special assembly seats Practice leaving Discuss care of property	Self and group control Enjoyment	
Library: Use of room for reading and research and How to take out books Catalogues and files Location of books and magazines	Go to the library to see Arrange for instruction by librarian Take out reading cards Select and take out books Go to library to practice Write letter to librarian	Skills Improved tastes Increased reading Care of property	
Infirmary: Location Excuses to go Times	Visit Send committee to interview nurse Call in doctor as speaker Review own defects and plan for correction	Correction of health and safety	

What New Pupils Need to Know (The Order Has No Significance)	Suggested Learning Experiences	Desired Outcomes	Outcomes Achieved (To Be Noted As They Appear)
Home Assignments (cont'd) Research connected with unit Lessons assigned in Math., Hygiene, and other classes Art work connected with committee work Construction, illustration, collection, etc., connected with unit Listening to radio program Seeing relevant films Interviewing parents and others Going places to get information Writing letters Corrective exercises in language arts Getting materials ready for home arts Practicing cooking and laundry skills Practicing home cleaning and decoration skills Planning	Organize bulletin board committee Organize class room library and issue books		

What New Pupils Need to Know (The Order Has No Significance)	Suggested Learning Experiences	Desired Outcomes	Outcomes Achieved (To Be Noted As They Appear)
Administration (cont'd)	Get and record telephone numbers Practice what to say and do and where to go when on messenger service		
Counseling: Location of office Names of counselors Problems handled How to get appointment	Visit office Interview or call in as speaker Read and fill out forms Take home interview blank to be completed Write letter	Security Freedom from fear Guidance for each as needed	
Home assignments Daily reading of literature book Newspaper—depending on reading ability New words Completion of daily records Completion of creative writings	Make list in note books Write letters to parents Plan for daily check up Allocate responsibilities Plan for and keep class book for use by absentees Secure and organize individual record folders Plan for newspapers	Work habits Daily preparation Understanding of program Parental understanding and cooperation Skills in language arts	

What New Pupils Need to Know (The Order Has No Significance)	Suggested Learning Experiences	Desired Outcomes	Outcomes Achieved (To Be Noted As They Appear)
School government (*cont'd*)	Elect officers after using correct nomination procedures Discuss qualifications, duties, responsibilities of leadership and followership Send officers to meetings Arrange for posting of meeting notices Hear reports of meetings Conduct class meetings Learn and practice parliamentary procedures Learn and sing the school song Visit the school store Visit the lost and found office Write letters about school to a friend—mail them Write new school songs, poems, slogans Write election speeches and other campaign materials Evaluation discussions	Ability to talk to a group Ability to converse Habits of self-evaluation	

What New Pupils Need to Know (The Order Has No Significance)	Suggested Learning Experiences	Desired Outcomes	Outcomes Achieved (To Be Noted As They Appear)
Classroom arrangements and routines Way—entering and leaving Use of materials and equipment Use of movable furniture Decoration Ventilation, lighting	Set up supply closet Allocate duties and responsibilities for collection and distribution Select housekeepers Arrange furniture Arrange for emergency borrowing of supplies Seating Plan before school activities Plan for use of room during lunch periods Set up rules and regulations regarding lateness to class	Orderly room Good habits Self direction Controls Good conduct and work in absence of teacher Conservation of supplies and materials Care of property Comfort Attractive room Promptness Maximum use Group loyalty Skills	
School government: Why; how Officers Election procedures Way of social action Parliamentary procedure	Visit S. A. office (301A) Read constitution in "Red Book" Interview, call in as speakers, write letters to sponsor of S. A., sponsor of governmental committees, student chairmen—members of executive committee, student president and vice president	Understanding of and use of democratic processes and practices and principles Orderly methods School spirit Loyalty Poise Self and group controls Self reliance and direction Increased skill in language arts	

CHAPTER EIGHTEEN

Reports of Classroom Work

Taxation—7A Unit Report

Center of interest: What do the taxes we pay buy for us?

Pupil Concerns:

1. Most families do not have enough money.
2. Anxiety over what is said and what is in the newspapers about the wasting and stealing of public money.
3. Fear about not being able to earn money.

Pupil Goals:

1. To acquaint ourselves with ways government raises money in our country.
2. To become better informed citizens as to how our tax money is spent and how it should be spent.
3. To awaken interest in the tax problems of our city and nation.
4. To tell our parents about taxes so they will feel better.

Content Outline:

1. What the national government needs money for.
2. What the city government needs money for.
3. Kinds of taxes and their good and bad points:
   a. Income.
   b. Sales.
   c. On businesses.
   d. Real estate.
   e. School.
4. Levying and collecting taxes.
5. Services we buy with taxes.
6. Tax reforms.

Activities:

1. Films seen and discussed:
   Property Taxation Advancing Civil Service, Defending the Cities' Health, Federal Taxation.

2. Survey of all activities members of the class participated in for which they had to pay taxes. (Movies, sodas, skating, etc.) Chart made of this.
3. Making of charts and graphs to show survey facts.
4. Poster displays of different types of tax papers and forms for water tax, real estate, amusement, income, property.
5. Newspaper reading and clipping and filing of articles and editorials dealing with taxes.
6. Art work—illustrations of services.
7. Writing letters for materials needed.
8. Panel discussion on whether we get enough for our tax money.

Money Is Important—Grade 7A

Problem: How can we use our money wisely?

Pupil Concerns:

1. Having too little money and too many calls upon it.
2. How to make allowances go farther.
3. How to earn extra money.
4. Getting good value for the money spent.
5. Knowing what such terms as "inflation" and "high cost of living" mean.
6. What taxes are spent for.

Pupil Goals:

1. To get information about money.
2. To learn to spend wisely and to stay within a budget.
3. To find out if any part time jobs are available.
4. To have committees do accurate research in order to answer questions.
5. To improve reading, writing and spelling skills.
6. To do better group planning.
7. To pick good leaders to do important jobs.

Content Outline: Things to find out about:

1. How our money system developed.
2. The big jobs that money does for us.
3. Where and how money is made today.
4. How various banking transactions are done.
5. Inflation: how it begins—possible solutions.
6. How to do wise and economical shopping in our own neighborhood.
7. Taxes: who pays them; for what purposes.

8. Teen-age summer jobs: kinds; value to student; methods of obtaining; pay; hours; laws.

Activities:

1. Research activity:
   use of books, pamphlets, newspapers, magazines.
2. Committee work:
   planning; assigning of jobs to individual members; pooling information; presentation of progress reports to class; planning and giving final reports.
3. Keeping of accurate unit record books containing:
   a. Information.
   b. Activities.
   c. Vocabulary lists.
   d. Elementary business transactions; withdrawal and deposit slips, checks, bills, receipts, savings account forms.
4. Keeping of weekly budgets:
   emphasis on purposes for which spending was done; systematic recording, and advantages of budgeting.
5. Survey of neighborhood to determine the most reasonably priced food store.
6. Beginning coin and bill collection—U. S. and foreign money.
7. Round table discussion: Subject—Summertime Job Problems.
8. Radio quiz program conducted by committee with quizmaster, prizes, speakers; Subject—Our Taxes.
9. Dramatizations to portray the development of money:
   "From Barter to Money," written and produced by a committee.
10. Bulletin Board Project: Committee collected, arranged, displayed foreign coins and bills, U. S. coins and bills, posters, pictures, art work, slogans.
11. Vocabulary building:
    a. New words learned.
    b. Test made up and administered by group.
    c. Spelling bee conducted by committee.
12. "Money In the News": Special bulletin board devoted to money in current affairs. The following areas were included. Clippings were changed weekly and interpreted to the class:
    a. Marshall Plan.
    b. Aid for Greece, China.
    c. Inflation—high cost of living.
    d. Tax bills in Congress.
13. Creative Writing:
    a. Thank you letters for imaginary gift of money received telling how the money was spent.
    b. Why save money?

    c. Life in the barter system.
    d. Ways to earn money this summer.
14. Campaign staged to boost number of weekly bankers in school bank; resulted in increase of 50%.
15. Trips:
    a. To a neighborhood bank to observe:
       (1) Banking transactions.
       (2) What goes on behind the counters.
       (3) The safe deposit vault.
       (4) The bookkeeping division.
    b. To the Mint:
       (1) Conducted tour.
       (2) To get questions answered.

7B Report on Mexican Unit

Question Raised: How can we better understand our Mexican neighbors?

We Were Concerned About Such Things As:

1. Do Mexicans live as we do?
2. How do they feel about the people in the United States?
3. Is their form of government democratic?
4. Can we be friends with the Mexicans?

We Stated Our Goals:

1. We wanted to gain in understanding people who are different.
2. We wanted to get information about the Mexican people and their country.
3. We hoped to gain in appreciation of the art, music, and folklore of the Mexican people who seem so romantic.
4. We needed to improve our ability to do research.
5. We needed to continue to improve our reading, writing, thinking and talking skills.
6. We hoped to have "100% cooperation."

Content Outline: Things we wanted to learn about Mexico:

1. Its government.
2. Its history.
3. Our relationship to Mexico.
4. The living conditions in Mexico today.
5. The way the people earn a living.
6. The daily life of the people:

    a. The food they eat.
    b. The clothes they wear.
    c. The churches they attend.
7. The cultural life of the people:
    a. Art.
    b. Music.
    c. Dances.
    d. Customs and folkways.
8. Something about the language.

Activities: What we did to accomplish our purposes:

1. We searched for information by making visits to home and school libraries; by writing letters for books, pamphlets, magazines, circulars, bulletins.
2. We did committee work: meeting to make plans; delegating responsibility to members; pooling information; reporting to class on progress; planning final report; planning our culminating activity.
3. We began correspondence with boys and girls of our ages in Mexican schools (Names and addresses obtained from Mexican Consul).
4. We saw such films as:
    a. *Children of Mexico.*
    b. *Land of Mexico.*
    c. *Arts and Crafts in Mexico.*
    d. *Mexico Builds a Democracy.*
    e. *People in Mexico.*
5. We listened to recordings of Mexican music (both ancient and modern).
6. We learned to speak some Mexican words, phrases, and expressions.
7. We dressed up in Mexican clothing (obtained from Intercultural Kit of the Red Cross).
8. We did some Mexican dances in small groups.
9. We read some Mexican stories; poems; fables; puzzles.
10. We added to our vocabularies by learning to speak and spell new words.
11. We visited another classroom to put on a short program and play records in order to teach friends about Mexico.
12. We did art work—making some Mexican pottery and illustrations of Mexican homes, costumes, occupations, and the market place.
13. We had a bulletin board project composed of pictures, charts, graphs, art work, Mexican flag, wood carvings.
14. We made maps and charts to establish geographical concepts.
15. We dramatized customs, dances.
16. We took a trip to the museum to see an exhibit on the Aztecs of Mexico.
17. We kept Unit notebooks recording our most important information and activities.

Culminating Activity:

"Fiesta of 7B2"—dramatic presentation into which was woven the contribution of each group in the class.

Travel Is Part of Life—8A Class Report

Approach:

Many people spend much time in public conveyances every day. Such transportation costs a lot of money. Vacations involve travel. Almost everything we need and use has to be transported. We ought to do a unit on this now. Let us call it "Transportation on Land, Sea, and Air."

Pupil Concerns:

1. If there is a strike, how will he get to school?
2. Most of our allowances go for car and bus fares, and we don't like it.
3. Many jobs have to do with transportation; maybe they will be able to get some, later on.
4. Many people in the armed services are in transportation work.

Pupil Goals:

To get a better understanding of the present transportation situation in our own city.
To learn more about the kinds of defense services we need.
To get a background of information about the development of transportation and its effect on our country.
To learn to look at both sides of every controversial issue before drawing conclusions (this related itself to a strike).

Content Outline:

1. The facts about the local transportation dispute.
2. The Railroad—past, present, future—its relation to development of the country.
3. Development of automobiles.
4. Development and problems of sea power.
5. Development and problems of aviation.

Activities:

1. Planning, committee work, pooling information, organization, progress reporting.

2. Mural was done by a committee, portraying the development of travel on land, sea, and in the air.
3. Chart showing growth of railroads during the past 75 years.
4. Posters—Red Letter dates in American History.
5. Construction of wooden and cardboard models of trains, automobiles, airplanes, boats.
6. Dramatization by Committee: "Development of Sea Power."
7. Speakers: Two classmates who came from Southampton, England, recently, spoke on, "Our Trip to America on the SS. *Queen Elizabeth*." A teacher who was a pilot during the war discussed his work and experiences.
8. Trip to Franklin Institute to see Transportation Exhibit.
9. Trip to airport.
10. Quiz prepared and conducted by "Sea Committee."
11. Collection and display of pictures on "Transportation, Land, Sea and Air."
12. Writing for materials.
    Reading, sorting, filing them.
13. Interviews: "What is your work like?": trolley motormen, railroad engineer, air pilot, bus driver, parents, neighbors, relatives.
14. Discussion led by committee: "What can we as students do to better relations with local transportation company?"
15. Map Study—tracing a shipment of coffee from Brazil, tin from South Dakota, bananas from Honduras, rubber from East Indies.
16. Films: *The Airplane Changes Our World, The Bus Driver, Air Transportation, The Passenger Train, Traffic, A Boat Ride, This Shrinking World.*
17. Safety survey: After standing ten minutes at a busy intersection and watching traffic, counting the cars that pass during that period, and noting the approximate speed of travel, answers were written to the following questions:
    Do the drivers try to avoid traffic jams? What devices do the police use to control traffic? To what extent are safety rules observed by drivers and pedestrians? What suggestions can we formulate?
18. Preparation of a chart of the average city family's dollar, and what proportion of it is spent on transportation?
19. Spelling, comprising lists of words dealing with transportation.
20. Creative Writing:
    Poetry, stories, personal experiences, evaluation letters.
21. Discussion of controversy between Navy and Air Force leaders. Troubles of unification of the three services, "The billion dollar blunder, B-36."
22. Television programs dealing with Navy—Aviation controversy were seen and reported to class: "Meet the Press," "Court of Current Issues," "Television Newsreel," "Newsweek Reviews the News."
23. Preparation by each pupil of a 6-page folder on transportation including:

Title page, content outline and summary of committees, new words and meanings, my mistakes and corrections, our activities, and books read in connection with the unit.
24. Bulletin Board displays.
25. Stories on transportation:
Just For Fun—Smith and Hazeltine.
When Automobiles Were New—Emily Kimbrough.
Forgotten Highways of Transportation—Sept. '49, Stanley Gaines, Dept. Int. Affairs, Vol. 17.
26. Dramatization by Committee on Sea Transportation: "Story of Magellan's Voyage."

Culminating Activity:

Exhibit in classroom of models, posters, charts, murals, illustrations, folders, record books.

The Study of a Unit on War to Ease Fear— Grade 8A*

Question: Will there be another World War?

Pupil Concerns: Fears about:

1. Atomic bombing and other new weapons.
2. Will we have to fight Russia?
3. Will our country go bankrupt helping Europe?

Pupil Goals:

1. To develop the skill of reading newspapers, listening to radio and detecting propaganda.
2. To develop appreciation and understanding of the concept of one world and of the United States' part in world affairs.
3. To find out what causes wars.
4. To learn about agencies working for peace and why the support of everyone (even children) is needed if these agencies are to be successful.

Content Outline:

1. What were the causes of World Wars I and II?
2. Do these conditions exist today?

---

* This unit was loaned to the Pennsylvania State Department of Education and appears in the Course of Study in the Social Sciences, 1951.

3. The cost of war—in lives, money.
4. What organizations are working for peace?
5. What is the United States doing to maintain world peace?
6. What needs to be done by *all* countries to achieve a peaceful world?
7. Unsolved problems (foreign policy).

Activities:

1. Making maps of Europe and Asia to show:
   a. Underdeveloped countries.
   b. Countries with democratic government.
   c. Dictatorships.
   d. Airplane distances.
2. Making charts showing costs of war in relation to cost of education, recreation, housing.
3. Slides of U. N.
4. Films: "Human Rights Commission," "Visit to the United Nations," "Atomic Control."
5. Creative Writing—feelings about war; descriptions told by veterans.
6. Talks by teacher and principal both of whom had been to U. N. seminars.
7. Making a tape recording of a discussion, "Will There be Another World War?"
8. Committee Research: Recording facts gathered in record books.

Culminating Activity:

Tape recording of findings and conclusions.

8B Class Report—Unit in the Area of Superstitions

One day Mary asked, breathlessly, "Is it true that if you bury an onion your warts will go away?" Dozens of similar questions began popping all over the room. Soon the class was involved in planning a unit they decided to call

IS IT TRUE?

Pupil Concerns:

1. Fears about the unknown.
2. Worries about dreams.
3. Interests in magic.
4. Desires to know the future.
5. Evasion of the truth.

6. Attempts to escape consequences.
7. Efforts to avoid responsibilities.

Objectives and Goals Set Up:

1. To be better informed about the world we live in.
2. To be more comfortable—without so much fear and worry.
3. To learn how to get the facts about any question.
4. To develop the habit of asking for the authority or source of information.
5. To learn how to think, to read, to talk.
6. To help relatives and friends to know the truth.

Activities Done:

1. Reading, writing, talking, committee work.
2. Acting out some things.
3. Doing some science experiments.
4. Doing things forbidden by some superstitions and observing the results.
5. Interviewing people who know—calling in consultants.
6. Keeping a record of events to prove the effect of chance and coincidence.
7. Surveying the student body for commonly held superstitions.
8. A program in assembly aimed to explode the most common superstitions.

Related Content: (determined by the superstitions needing serious study)

1. The sky—constellations—Astronomy vs. Astrology.
2. Pre-natal care and nutrition.
3. Heredity.
4. Mental health—fear, anxiety, worry, suggestibility, hypnotism.
5. Causes and cures of diseases.

Evaluation:

1. Recording of changes in actions.
2. Test on factual information.
3. Discussion of values of the unit.

*Teen-Agers Need Personal Help—Grade 8B** *

Question Raised: What should teen-agers know about etiquette?

---

* This unit was loaned to the Pennsylvania State Department of Education and appears in the Course of Study in the Social Sciences, 1951.

Pupil Concerns:

To be more at ease; to be popular; to be more acceptable to adults.

Pupil Goals:

1. To improve our manners for social and economic reasons.
2. To be able to be at ease with others.
3. To appreciate the meaning and value of etiquette.
4. To improve our skill in conversation and discussion.
5. To improve our reading and writing ability.
6. To improve our spelling.

Content Outline:

1. Eating:
   a. In private homes—simple and elaborate entertaining; how to seat guests.
   b. In restaurants—being seated; what to choose; how to treat the waiter; tipping.
   c. Difficult foods—eating peas; corn.
   d. Silverware—when to use what.
2. Dating:
   a. When.
   b. Dress.
   c. Behavior.
   d. Where to go.
3. Introductions—formal, informal; shaking hands.
4. Behavior in public places:
   a. Theatres—who goes down the aisle first, eating, talking.
   b. Stores—how to treat sales people.
   c. Transportation—how to behave; giving up a seat.
   d. Hotels—signing a register; tipping; who carries luggage; noise in halls and rooms; room service.
   e. Beach—cleanliness, courtesy, clothing, decency.
   f. Street-noise; voices; language; gangs; teasing; private property rights.
   g. School-dress, behavior toward other sex, toward adults, lunch room rights, privileges, responsibilities.
5. Dances and parties—invitations, dress, presents, games, entertainment, food.
6. Week-end visits—taking a gift, fitting in with plans, how not to be a nuisance.
7. The social letter.
8. The business letter.
9. Applying for a job—appearance, voice, language, respect, filling out an application, courtesy.

10. Conversation:
   a. Things to talk about and how—movies, books, people, school, home, human relations, current affairs.
   b. Voice.
   c. Telephone—respect for others, voice, what to say when answering, when calling.

Activities:

1. Research.
2. Dramatics (nearly all committee reports were dramatic in form).
3. Panel discussion.
4. Classroom bulletin board.
5. Spelling and vocabulary list.
6. Spelling test made up and given by a committee.
7. Letters to parents describing unit, asking permisison for our culminating activity and their opinions about the unit. Received written replies from many.
8. Collected humorous rhymes and poems.
9. Attended school fashion show.
10. Attended a matinee performance of "Anthony and Cleopatra" with Katherine Cornell in the leading role.
11. Attended a "teen-age" fashion show at a large department store.
12. Secured and showed films.
13. Made record books.
14. Made illustrations, posters, and cartoons.
15. Telephoned many restaurants concerning our luncheon party.

Culminating Activity:

1. Had lunch at Crystal Tea Room, in the center of the city.
2. Wrote up experiences, impressions, and reactions for the school newspaper.

Books Used by Pupils:

Manners for Moderns—Black
Behave Yourself—Allen
This Way, Please—Boykin
Smarter and Smoother—Dalp
Manners, Now and Then—Arsdale
Courtesy—Dunlap
Gentlemen Aren't Sissies—Jonathan
Profits from Courtesy—Hopkins
Cues For You—Ryan
Your Manners Are Showing—Betz
Etiquette—Post

Manners in Business—MacGibbon
Manners for Millions—Hadida
Manners—Hathaway
Men Too Wear Clothes—Slate
The Young Hostess—Pierce
Personality Pointers—Edwards
It's More Fun When You Know the Rules—Pierce
Good Manners for Boys—Barkour
The Courtesy Book—Dunlea
Everyday Manners—Taylor
Personality Plus—Daly
Charm and Personality—Mead

Intergroup Education—8B Class Report

Approach:

The most important part of life is getting along with other people, in spite of and even because of the fact they are different.

Pupil Concerns:

1. Am I prejudiced?
2. What are my prejudices?
3. How and where did I get them?
4. What can I do about them?
5. Why don't people get along with each other?

Pupil Goals:

1. To understand one's own self.
2. To achieve better understanding of other people: how they act and why; their religious customs.
3. To develop open-mindedness which would help one to get along better.
4. To know something more about race.

Content Outline:

1. Define the terms race, religion, nationality, social class, minority.
2. Similarities and differences that distinguish: the religions in the group, the three races in the school.
3. The nature and origin of some of the prejudices which we have. The dangers and difficulties they get us into.
4. Organizations at work in the community for better cooperation of all peoples.

Activities:

1. Trips to: Fellowship Commission, to motion picture theatre to see *Lost Boundaries.*
2. Films seen in school: *Races of Mankind, Whoever You Are.*
3. Film strips seen in school: *One People, Navaho Indians, All About Us.*
4. Projects: Survey of religions and nationalities represented in the group.
5. Literature reading.
6. Keeping record book of facts gathered by various committees of activities, of speakers, of films, of radio programs and recordings.
7. Creative writing: stories, a skit for assembly, letters, poems.
8. Committee work: gathering information from reference books, newspapers, magazine articles, interviews.
9. Radio programs and recordings.
10. Little dramatizations.

Culminating Activity:

1. Preparation of Sweetheart Boxes for school children of Austria.
2. Letters were enclosed.

Underdeveloped Lands Are Important—9A Unit Report

Approach:

India is a country in the first stages of a struggle for freedom. We need to know about its people's customs, social, political and economic problems, and the possibility for helping them to get a democratic way of life.

Pupil Concerns:

Excitement and enthusiasm over the new student in the class who came from India; a desire to learn firsthand about his country; concern also about Gandhi's death, and its effect on India.

Pupil Goals:

1. To learn about the country from which David (the new boy) came.
2. To understand Gandhi's influence.
3. To learn more about the threats to peace.

Content Outline:

1. Geography of India.
2. People and their customs:

  a. How some Indians make a living.
  b. Games.
  c. Typical Indian towns.
3. India's races and religions.
4. India's problems (social, political, economic).
5. Epics and legends of India.
6. India's great leaders: Gandhi, Nehru, others.
7. India of Tomorrow.

Activities:

1. Radio—Listening to commentators and trying to decide what each one believes.
2. Hearing stories from early Indian literature.
3. Collection of pictures, magazines and news articles, and books from libraries.
4. Bulletin board display.
5. Scrapbooks and experience records.
6. Exhibition of Indian souvenirs.
7. Making and displaying posters.
8. Listening to speakers:
   a. One whose parents recently came from India.
   b. A student from the university.
9. Dramatization of the customs of India which differ from our own.
10. Drawing of maps of India.
11. Learning some Hindustan words and sentences taught by David.
12. Film—*India*.
13. Report on movie *Sabu, the Elephant Boy*.
14. Acceptance of gift to the class made by parent from India.
15. Writing letters of thanks for gift and speeches.
16. Research work.
17. Committee planning, pooling, and reporting.
18. Quiz.

Culminating Activity:

Sharing findings in form of assembly program, "World Mindedness," in which each committee participated.

Unit in the Area of Housing—9A Report

Pupils Were Concerned About:

1. Relationship between housing and well-being.
2. Improving their own living conditions.
3. Why there always is a slum area in every city.

4. Paying too much rent.
5. Constant worry each six months over rent control.
6. The lack of repair in the houses they live in.
7. Wanting to move and not being able to do so.

Objectives:

1. To understand the present housing problems.
2. To understand housing as a fundamental human need.
3. To get information concerning requirements for good housing, laws, housing authority.
4. To learn how to improve one's own living conditions.

Content Outline:

1. Study of history and development of housing.
2. The various types of homes man uses and why.
3. Standards for decent living.
4. How housing affects: health, crime, family living.
5. Housing commission and how to use it.
6. Responsibility of the property owner (the landlord); of the tenant.
7. The government and housing: FHA, Low Rent Housing Projects, legislation (Wagner-Ellender-Taft Bill), discrimination, Veterans Administration Loans.
8. A look at our own community to see what can be done to make it better.

Activities:

1. Committee report on housing through the ages.
2. Report describing Week-End Work-Camp of the American Friends' Committee.
3. Making of models, graphs, plans.
4. Speaker—a neighborhood real estate agent.
5. Study of the President's proposal in his State of the Union address.
6. Reports on Jacob Riis' and Jane Addams' contributions to decent living.
7. Use of picture file from Free Library.
8. Attendance at hearings concerning sub-standard housing held in local magistrate's court.
9. Making charts of individual's own neighborhood.
10. Creative writing—"Where I would prefer to live." "What I would like to do to my house." "We wanted to move, but they refused to let us in."
11. Making scrapbooks.
12. A group letter to a congressman asking him to support measures for good housing.

13. Visit to housing projects.
14. Study of Yardville, U. S. A. project.
15. Films on housing.

Culminating Activity:

1. Presentation of play.
2. Reports on what individuals did in their own homes to make an improvement.

Labor Unit Report—Grade 9B

Question: How do labor unions affect me?

Pupil Concerns:

1. How does labor affect me as a citizen and a potential union member?
2. What are unions?
3. Why do we have strikes?
4. Must I belong to a union before I can get a job?
5. How can I be a good union member?

Pupil Goals:

1. To increase knowledge of labor unions—history, purposes, objectives.
2. To develop an understanding of how labor unions affect the individual as a worker and a citizen.
3. To examine reasons for conflict between labor and management.
4. To learn to act in a manner which will be to one's own best interests in and out of labor unions.

Content Outline:

1. History of the Labor Movement in America—beginnings, purposes, objectives.
2. Areas of union activity today.
3. Labor vocabulary—strike, lockout, collective bargaining, mediation, shop steward, local, sit-down, picket line.
4. Benefits unions give the workers.
5. Important national unions—growth, differences, important personalities in them today.
6. Important local unions:
   a. Who can join—how, when, where?
   b. Comparison of dues, figures.
   c. How is a labor organization run?
   d. Who runs a union?

    e. The individual's responsibility.
    f. How to participate effectively.
7. How organized labor affects the country—prices, politics, employment, standards of living, democracy, peace.

Activities:

1. Bulletin board displays in room and corridors.
2. Panel discussions—committee reports.
3. Speakers from unions—CIO, AF of L.
4. Chart on union organization made and interpreted.
5. Public opinion poll of union members and non-union members among parents, friends, neighbors—to get at how people feel about unions and to find out what they do not know about them.
6. Individual record book of unit including clippings and cartoons.
7. Letters to CIO, AF of L, NAM.
8. Evaluation of the benefits of such a unit in a general discussion and a quiz program.

Culminating Activity: resulted from facts revealed by opinion poll: Preparation of list of terms and their meanings which was mimeographed and distributed by the pupils to their parents and friends.

Does Every Family Have its Share of Mental Illness?—Grade 9B*

Area—Mental Health

Pupils Were Concerned About:

1. Their relatives who have had breakdowns.
2. How to get along better with people, both adults and peers.
3. What causes hate, love, fear, guilt, and anger.
4. Understanding self.
5. Keeping well.

Pupil Goals:

1. To lose their superstitions and terror about mental health.
2. To live better and healthier lives.
3. To do something to help someone who needs it.
4. To improve talking, reading, writing, and listening skills.

---

* This unit was loaned to the Pennsylvania State Department of Education and appears in the Course of Study in the Social Sciences, 1951.

Content Outline:

1. Definition of mental health.
2. Superstitions about mentally sick people.
3. The emotions—what they are, how to control, how to use.
4. Kinds and causes of mental sickness—the nervous breakdown, insanity.
5. The treatment and prevention of mental illness—what the individual can do for himself, what role the family plays, hospitals, clinics, the psychiatrist.

Activities:

1. Films:
   a. *Feeling of Hostility*
   b. *Feeling of Rejection*
   c. *Shy Guy*
2. Speaker: Dr. Vincent Mahoney, Pennsylvania Bureau of Health Welfare.
3. Writing:
   a. Personal experiences dealing with emotions and desires.
   b. One act playlets involving mental health problems.
4. Class Surveys: Kinds of people and students disliked, liked, rejected, feared, loved. Charts made of reasons and then findings were studied by the group.
5. Reading: books, newspapers, pamphlets.
6. Psycho- and socio-dramatics (role playing) dealing with human relations problems.
7. Records kept of unit work.
8. Culminating activity consisted of a long discussion in which the unit was evaluated and the pupils tried to find answers to the question "What has all this *meant* to me and to us?"

Report of Unit on Sports

Class—Maladjusted boys in an ungraded class.

Pupil Concerns:

1. How does a fellow get to be a "big shot" in sports?
2. What can a fellow do to "get in trim" so he has a chance to get on a team next term?
3. Can a fellow earn any money in sports even if he doesn't get to the top?
4. Can we spend some time now learning how to play?

Objectives Set Up:

1. To learn to play a new game.
2. To improve in playing a game already known.
3. To be able to take criticism better.
4. To get some information about the "heroes."
5. To read better.
6. To work together better.

Activities Planned and Carried Out:

1. Reading—newspaper accounts of sports events, the lives of some of the big people, some stories, sports comics.
2. All went together to see some games—golf, track, big league baseball.
3. All relived those games as umpire, coach, broadcaster, captain.
4. Some made some large pictures—individual, mural by committee.
5. All practiced skills needed in favorite sports—got help from gym.
6. Many learned new games and sports—formed mutual help pairs.
7. Most broke a habit bad for health—smoking, eating, too little rest.
8. Most made a new health habit like drinking milk daily, bathing, posture, correcting flat feet.
9. Committees interviewed a "hero," a newspaper reporter, a broadcaster, an umpire, a coach.
10. Saw films—big league games, some with slow motion, health pictures.
11. Wrote letters of invitation, thank you, requests for tickets.
12. Planned, practiced, and made necessary phone calls.

Evaluation Activities:

1. Kept personal habit charts.
2. Kept records which show better relations, better work, better health.
3. Discussed what was good and what was poor about the unit.
4. Discussed work of committee chairmen and quality of group products.

Index

C